THE DANGEROUS
BOOK FOR BOYS

Other books by Conn & Hal Iggulden:

The Pocket Dangerous Book for Boys: Things to Do
The Pocket Dangerous Book for Boys: Things to Know
The Dangerous Book for Boys Yearbook

Other books by Conn Iggulden:

The Emperor Series

The Gates of Rome
The Death of Kings
The Field of Swords
The Gods of War

Blackwater

The Conqueror Series

Wolf of the Plains
Lords of the Bow
Bones of the Hills

Conn Iggulden & Hal Iggulden

Foreword by Roy MacGregor

The DANGEROUS Book for Boys

 CANADIAN EDITION

Collins

To all of those people who said "You *have* to include...,"
until we had to avoid telling anyone else about the
book for fear of the extra chapters. Particular thanks
to Bernard Cornwell, whose advice helped us through
a difficult time, and Paul D'Urso, a good father
and a good friend.

The Dangerous Book for Boys, Canadian Edition
© Conn Iggulden and Hal Iggulden 2006, 2008.
Foreword © 2008 by Roy MacGregor. All rights reserved.

Published by Collins, an imprint of HarperCollins Publishers Ltd. Published by arrangement with
HarperCollins Publishers (UK) Ltd.

First Canadian edition

Note to parents: This book contains a number of activities that may be dangerous if not done exactly as directed or that
may be inappropriate for young children. All of these activities should be carried out under adult supervision only. The
authors and publishers expressly disclaim liability for any injury or damages that result from engaging in the activities
contained in this book.

HarperCollins books may be purchased for educational, business, or sales promotional
use through our Special Markets Department.

HarperCollins Publishers Ltd
2 Bloor Street East, 20th Floor
Toronto, Ontario, Canada
M4W 1A8

www.harpercollins.ca

Library and Archives Canada Cataloguing in Publication

Iggulden, Conn
The dangerous book for boys / Conn and Hal Iggulden. — 1st Canadian ed.

ISBN 978-1-55468-259-1

1. Handbooks, vade-mecums, etc.—Juvenile literature. 2. Amusements—Juvenile
literature. 3. Recreation—Juvenile literature. 4. Boys—Miscellanea—Juvenile
literature. I. Iggulden, Hal II. Title.

AG106.I44 2008   j031.02   C2008-901897-4

9 8 7 6 5 4 3 2 1

Printed and bound in the United States

Don't worry about genius and don't worry about not being clever. Trust rather to hard work, perseverance, and determination. The best motto for a long march is "Don't grumble. Plug on."

You hold your future in your own hands. Never waver in this belief. Don't swagger. The boy who swaggers – like the man who swaggers – has little else that he can do. He is a cheap-Jack crying his own paltry wares. It is the empty tin that rattles most. Be honest. Be loyal. Be kind. Remember that the hardest thing to acquire is the faculty of being unselfish. As a quality it is one of the finest attributes of manliness.

Love the sea, the ringing beach and the open downs.

Keep clean, body and mind.

—Sir Frederick Treves, Bart, KCVO, CB, Sergeant in Ordinary to HM the King, Surgeon in Ordinary to HRH Prince of Wales, written at 6 Wimpole Street, Cavendish Sqare, London, on 2 September 1903, on the occasion of the twenty-fifth anniversary of the *Boy's Own Paper*

CONTENTS

FOREWORD

WHEN I WAS A BOY – and there are those who will say, without much argument from me, that the boy never did grow up – I used to dream of one day coming into possession of a genuine *Junior Woodchuck Guidebook*.

We lived comic books in those days. It was not uncommon to answer the door and find a kid from down the street standing in front of an entire wagon filled with ragged copies he had come to trade: *Superman, Green Lantern, Tarzan, Batman, Little Huey, Woody Woodpecker, Donald Duck, Archie, Betty and Veronica, Casper the Friendly Ghost* and *Wendy the Good Little Witch*. We loved them all, but loved even more those magnificent Classics Illustrated comics that, later in life, would allow so many of us to fake that we had actually read such wonderful works as *Kidnapped, Robinson Crusoe, Moby Dick, Ivanhoe* and *Uncle Tom's Cabin*.

But nothing delighted me more than a comic with Huey, Dewey and Louie, and a quick dip into the marvels and magic of the *Junior Woodchuck Guidebook*. Huey, Dewey and Louie were Donald Duck's nephews – Uncle Scrooge's grand-nephews – and their secret Woodchuck manual was as entrancing to me as Scrooge McDuck's coin-filled mint, where he sometimes would be pictured in an old-fashioned bathing suit, happily *diving* into a massive pool of his own riches.

The *Guidebook* fit easily into the nephews' backpacks and contained such boy-scout essentials as how to make a campfire without matches – but it also held answers to the world's greatest mysteries. The book had been put together, comic readers were told, by the Guardians of the Lost Library of Alexandria and contained all the known knowledge of the entire world – in a book half the size of a brick! It had been found by an explorer and handed on to his son, who then founded the Junior Woodchucks and made sure every good Woodchuck had a copy to turn to in times of need.

And did Huey, Dewey and Louie ever need it! They used the amazing book to find the Lost City of Atlantis. They used it to open the jaws of a fierce dragon. They used it to make rockets and flying carpets, and to save themselves from dangerous traps. They even used it once to translate the ancient cave writings of a long-lost civilization. *The Junior Woodchuck Guidebook* never lied; it never failed them.

Such a book had natural appeal to a kid who spent so much of his time deep in the Canadian woods, with only an older brother and sister, a younger brother and a revolving screen door of cousins to play with. When school let out, the family moved each summer to three cabins and a log house on a rocky point in Ontario's vast Algonquin Park. No running water, no electricity, nothing but water and rocks and bush and being left largely to our own devices. Comics were our television, our movie theatre, our trips to faraway places.

How I wish we had owned a copy of *The Dangerous Book for Boys* – though sister Ann would have demanded equal time for *The Daring Book for Girls*. We made do, however, with what we had, and what we had was a playground that stretched forever into the dark woods, a lake that ran – if one chose to strike out by canoe with enough supplies – to the Madawaska River, which emptied into the Ottawa River, which emptied into the St. Lawrence River, which emptied into the Gulf of St. Lawrence and the Atlantic Ocean and, in theory anyway, was wide open to paddling all the way to India and Egypt and Tasmania.

It was a Huckleberry Finn type of existence. We made our own bows and arrows, and actually hunted small animals, fortunately missing most of the time. We had cliffs to climb, caves to explore and secret meadows to lie in. We built rafts and sailed them. We constructed endless little "villages" along the shore that were peopled by pollywogs, toads, frogs, dragonflies – whatever happened to be in hatch or around at the moment.

We played a game that would fit wonderfully in *The Dangerous Book for Boys*. We called it "Roots & Rocks," and we played it from the time we could walk. The rules were as simple as life itself back then: you could step only on roots or rocks; miss a step and you were "dead." We ran Roots & Rocks races up to the two-storey log house on the high point; Roots & Rocks down to the kitchen cabin; Roots & Rocks all the way out along the cliffs to the highway; Roots & Rocks to the icehouse, to the spring, to the outhouse.

Because the point was pure Precambrian Shield, the tree roots ran like outside veins over much of the granite, and where there weren't roots to clamber along, there was almost always a convenient stone to allow you passage to the next roots. It was as if those roots and rocks held, at the same time, both a magnetic field to catch our bare feet and a spring to throw us to the next safe landing . . . and the next . . . and the next.

To a passing canoeist, we must have looked like a wilderness camp for children having to learn to walk all over again; to us, we were always one step away from death and, it seems looking back now, we've never been quite so alive since. They were, after all, our roots.

We also had a grandfather who served as Chief Ranger for the sprawling park and was, in a way, a walking, talking *Junior Woodchuck Guidebook*. Tom McCormick was a giant of a man but as gentle as a puppy to young children. He did not have a job but a calling and worked every hour of every day as a ranger – his uniform the only clothes any of us lucky enough to be his grandchildren ever recall seeing him in. He was an amateur scientist – in his button-down Lands & Forests shirts, he actually carried about small cardboard tubes into which he would regularly drop such findings as spruce budworms and cicadas, and conscientiously send them off to a laboratory in Toronto where they would be examined for size and health and threat to the forest, the forest that he felt was his duty to protect. He was a botanist, a biologist and, above all, an environmentalist – decades before the word had come into fashion.

To simply "hang" with him was an adventure in itself. You never knew what a new day would bring. There were always white-tailed deer around – our grandmother fed and put out salt licks for them – and sometimes they would get in trouble. He might be called to free a fawn that had caught its back leg trying to leap through thick brush. He was sometimes called to the campground dump to deal with black bears that were becoming too "friendly" with campers. The campers gathered each evening to feed cream soda to the cubs through the thick fencing that was supposed to keep bears and humans apart.

One of the ranger's tasks – surely self-assigned – was to keep the small park museum supplied with wildlife for display during the summer and then safely release it in the fall. One morning we awoke to the slam of a screen door and our grandfather calling for ropes and a burlap sack, only to find once we'd rubbed the sleep out of our eyes that he had spotted a huge snapping turtle sunning itself on the big rock near where we swam.

It could have been a chapter in *The Dangerous Book for Boys*. The Chief Ranger gathered up the ropes, put two burlap sacks together and then took a long rake out of the shed and went quietly down to the water, sneaking up on the huge, sleeping snapper. It was as big a turtle as we had ever seen, the shell alone like a truck hubcap.

The ranger slipped up behind the prehistoric creature so silently that the snapper – which usually bolted back into the water at the first sight or sound of any movement – never even noticed him until the rake was under its belly and a quick pry had flipped it onto its back, where it wiggled helplessly and tried to use its long and powerful neck to roll over.

The ranger used the rake to hold the turtle flat, pressing down on its belly. He then had each of us bring a coil of rope and, one by one, he looped a rope around each thick, long-nailed leg of the snapping turtle. The ropes in place, he had the four rope-bearers move to the points of the compass, so that the turtle could be held while he readied the doubled-up burlap sack. To take the lunging neck and snapping beak out of play, he turned the rake and let the turtle bite into it, the chomp almost breaking the rake handle in two.

Taking the ropes from the handlers, he bundled them up and in one motion picked up the huge turtle and dropped it into the sack. He then threw the squirming sack over his back and headed out the long path through the woods to the parking area, where he placed the angry turtle in the trunk and we all headed off, cheering, for the little museum. There, he carefully untied the ropes and gently dumped the turtle out the sack in the little outside pond where, for the rest of the summer, the giant snapper from Lake of Two Rivers was the biggest tourist attraction in the park.

He took us on strenuous day-long treks back to old camboose winter lumbering camps and long-abandoned timber chutes. He pointed out the wildflowers and the various types of trees – *ever try to pick out a bird's-eye maple by sight alone?* – and he taught us how to blaze a trail so that no matter which way you headed into the woods, you would never get lost.

Sadly, I forget most of what he tried to pass on to us. My siblings and cousins have the same regrets. If we had only had the sense to write it all down, we might have preserved it. We might also have had a bestselling book called *The Adventurous Book for Boys (and Girls)*.

The *Dangerous* side of that imaginary book, however, would have come from our father. The Chief Ranger was Duncan MacGregor's father-in-law and, in some ways, the only thing they had in common was a determination to live their entire lives in the Canadian wild. While one, the old ranger, was totally organized (a man who would record the temperature, the cloud structure and every single thing he did each day in a small journal), the other, our father, took each day as it came. He was a logger, a man who began in the bush camps and eventually worked his way up to become a timber grader with the McRae Lumber Company.

Dunc had lost his father when he was only four years old. He himself had been a wanderer, a kid who could spend the entire day just exploring the banks of the Bonnechere River where he, his many brothers and sisters, and his widowed mother lived. He was obsessed with fishing and hunting and simply being in the bush. And he had no sense of time.

This, of course, often infuriated our mother. But as we have all agreed over time, while it might have been tough to be married to him, it was a joy to be his child. He just let whatever was going to happen happen. In the days before seatbelts and strict highway laws, he was happy to load the back of the mill truck with children and take them flying and screaming down a dirt road, great thick, brown dust clouds rising behind as he fishtailed around corners and pretended he had forgotten how to steer. He thought a child should know how to shoot a gun. He himself loved to hunt and loved to tell the tale of the night he had spent high in a tree after stepping over a log and having landed squarely on a sleeping bear cub. The nearby mother bear decided this was not appreciated.

But more than anything else, my father loved fishing. He taught us to collect bait – setting traps to catch the small creek chub the lake trout loved, searching under rocks for crayfish the bass craved, catching leeches and frogs and even grasshoppers, depending on what he thought might bring a bite. He fly-fished and fished by casting, but most of all, he loved the trout of the deep water, teaching all of us how to troll and wait for the bite that, because of the copper line he favoured, felt less like a tug than a car crash, the rod nearly ripping from your hands.

If you wanted to take the boat out by yourself, that was fine by him. By age six we could all start and handle the little Evinrude outboard that he kept on the wooden rowboat. If you wanted to take out a canoe, however, you had to have the Chief Ranger's permission and someone to watch over you. Our father's recklessness could be allowed to go only so far.

No one ever spoke of "structured time" back then. I had no idea that one day I would become a parent with a more complicated schedule on the fridge door than most cabinet ministers had during parliamentary session. Of course, back then, when I was a kid, we had no fridge.

But something happened between the carefree play of long days and years that stretched from Lake of Two Rivers to an Ottawa suburb. We have lived a quarter century on the edge of a very different kind of "park" that holds three baseball diamonds, two soccer fields, a hockey rink in the winter and various play structures that tell a fascinating story on their own. The play structures that were there when we first moved to the suburbs – as in long slides and spinning platforms – were deemed too dangerous and were replaced by a "safer" structure that, in time, was also deemed too dangerous and was replaced with a structure so "safe" that today, when the wind is right, you can hear from clear across the field small children yawning.

There will be no yawning here, though, not from those who will spend hours and days and weekends scouring Conn and Hal Iggulden's magnificent, brilliant, sensational book *The Dangerous Book for Boys*.

Any book with the intelligence and foresight to place the Swiss Army knife as number one on a list of items in an "Essential Kit" is, in my eyes, a bestseller and a must-read. I once had a dream in which I had a Swiss Army knife so cleverly constructed that it not only held a compass, a toothpick, scissors, a hole punch and several knife blades, but if you knew what button to push, out would swing a canoe, an ice auger, a B.B. gun and even a live *dog* to play with.

You cannot, in my humble opinion, have too much imagination. Your imagination, on the other hand, cannot have too much suggestion – and this is where the real value of this remarkable book emerges. Simply dip in at random and you will see for yourself instructions on making a go-kart, on juggling, on teaching your old dog new tricks, on how to do coin tricks, even careful instructions for boys on how to deal with girls – "It is important to listen." It's also important, boys of all ages should note, to "avoid being vulgar. Excitable bouts of wind-breaking will not endear you to a girl, just to pick one example." And any book that can slip in three separate grammar lessons in the midst of high adventure and play will earn the gratitude of anyone who has ever fallen in love with the written word.

But there is so much more here. Paper airplanes, and bows and arrows. How to build a tree house. Or, in Canada, how to build a snow house. In fact, this is also, in a most welcome way, the *Dangerous Book for Canadian Boys* – with sections that include canoeing instructions and the rules of lacrosse, animal track identification and how to build an igloo. There is also information here on how to build a country: see "Vimy Ridge."

Dunc MacGregor, the Dangerous Father, would have mightily approved of the "Seven Poems Every Boy Should Know." He himself could recite, when so moved, every single stanza of Robert Service's poems "The Cremation of Sam McGee" and "The Shooting of Dan McGrew." He knew, perfectly, Hugh Antoine d'Arcy's "The Face on the Barroom Floor," and one spring evening in Cooperstown, New York, home of the Baseball Hall of Fame, he stood down by the water in the twilight, leaned on his cane and recited every line of Ernest Lawrence Thayer's "Casey at the Bat." He was almost eighty years old at the time.

This magnificent book – which comes complete *without* batteries and requires no accompanying CD or DVD – would have suited him just fine. And, as his son, I can say it suits me even better.

It is, after all, as close to the *Junior Woodchuck Guidebook* as anyone not named Huey, Dewey or Louie will ever come.

—Roy MacGregor

I DIDN'T HAVE THIS BOOK
WHEN I WAS A BOY

IN THIS AGE OF video games and cell phones, there must still be a place for knots, tree-houses and stories of incredible courage. The one thing that we always say about childhood is that we seemed to have more time back then. This book will help you recapture those Sunday afternoons and long summers – because they're still long if you know how to look at them.

Boyhood is all about curiosity, and men and boys can enjoy stories of Scott in the Antarctic and Joe Simpson in *Touching the Void* as much as they can enjoy raiding a shed for the bits to make an electromagnet, or grow a crystal, build a go-kart and learn how to find north in the dark. You'll find famous battles in these pages, insects and dinosaurs – as well as essential Shakespeare quotes, how to cut flint heads for a bow and arrow and instructions on making the best paper airplane in the world.

How do latitude and longitude work? How do you make secret ink, or send the cipher that Julius Caesar used with his generals? You'll find the answers inside. This book was written by two men who would have given away the cat to get this book when they were young. It wasn't a particularly nice cat. Why did we write it now? Because these things are important still and we wished we knew them better. There are few things as satisfying as tying a decent bowline knot when someone needs a loop, or simply knowing what happened at Waterloo and the Somme. The tales must be told and retold, or the memories slowly die.

The stories of courage can be read as simple adventures – or perhaps as inspiration, examples of extraordinary acts by ordinary people. Since writing them, it's been a great deal harder to hop about and curse when one of us stubs a toe. If you read Douglas Bader's chapter, you'll see why. They're not just great stories, they're part of a culture, a part we really don't want to see vanish.

Is it old-fashioned? Well that depends. Men and boys today are the same as they always were, and interested in the same things. They may conquer different worlds when they grow up, but they'll still want these stories for themselves and for their sons. We hope in years to come that this will be a book to dig out of the attic and give to a couple of kids staring at a pile of wood and wondering what to do with it.

When you're a man, you realize that everything changes, but when you're a boy, you know different. The camp you make today will be there forever. You want to learn coin tricks and how to play poker because you never know when the skills will come in handy. You want to be self-sufficient and find your way by the stars. Perhaps for those who come after us, you want to reach them. Well, why not? Why *not*?

Conn Iggulden and Hal Iggulden

ESSENTIAL KIT

—— ✶ ——

IT ISN'T THAT EASY these days to get hold of old tobacco tins – but they are just the right size for this sort of collection. One of the authors once took a white mouse into school, though considering what happened when he sat on it, that is not to be recommended. We think pockets are for cramming full of useful things.

1. Swiss Army knife.
Still the best small penknife. It can be carried in luggage on planes, though not in hand luggage. It is worth saving up for a high-end model, with as many blades and attachments as you can get. That said, there are good ones to be had for thirty dollars. They are useful for jobs requiring a screwdriver, removing splinters and opening bottles of beer and wine, though this may not be a prime consideration at this time.

Leather holders can also be purchased and the best ones come with a few extras, like compass, matches, a pencil, paper and BAND-AIDs.

2. Compass.
These are satisfying to own. Small ones can be bought from any camping or outdoor shop and they last forever. You really should know where north is, wherever you are.

3. Handkerchief.
There are many uses for a piece of cloth, from preventing smoke inhalation or helping with a nosebleed, to offering one to a girl when she cries. Big ones can even be made into slings. They're worth having.

4. Box of matches.
It goes without saying that you must be responsible. Matches kept in a dry tin or inside a plastic bag can be very useful on a cold night when you are forced to sleep in a field. Dipping the tips in wax makes them waterproof. Scrape the wax off with a fingernail when you want to light them.

5. A taw.
Your favourite big marble.

6. Needle and thread.
Again, there are a number of useful things you can do with these, from sewing up a wound on an unconscious dog to repairing a torn shirt. Make sure the thread is strong and then it can be used for fishing.

7. Pencil and paper.
If you see a crime and want to write down a licence plate number or a description of the car, you are going to need one. Alternatively, it works for shopping lists or practically anything.

8. Small flashlight.
There are small and light ones available for keyrings. If you are ever in darkness and trying to read a map, a flashlight of any kind will be useful.

9. Magnifying glass.
For general interest. Can also be used to start a fire.

10. BAND-AIDs.
Just one or two, or better still, a piece from a cloth plaster roll that can be cut with penknife scissors. They probably won't be used, but you never know.

11. Fish-hooks.
If you have strong thread and a tiny hook, you only need a stick and a worm to have some chance of catching something. Put the hook tip into a piece of cork, or you'll snag yourself on it.

THE GREATEST PAPER AIRPLANE
IN THE WORLD

IN THE 1950S, a secondary school headmaster found a boy throwing paper planes from a high window. The headmaster was considering punishments when he noticed a plane was still in the air, flying across the playground below. The boy escaped a detention, but he did have to pass on the design to the schoolmaster – who passed it on to his own children. You will find more complicated designs. You may be sold the idea that the best planes require scissors and lessons in origami. This is nonsense.

  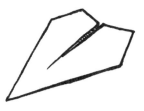

The plane on the right – the Harrier – is simple, fast and can be made from a sheet of 8 1/2 x 11. It is the best long-distance glider you'll ever see – and with a tweak or two, the best stunt plane. It has even won competitions. One was to clear the entire road from a hotel balcony next to Windsor Castle on New Year's Eve. Four other planes hit the tarmac – this one sailed clear across. The one on the left – the Bulldog Dart – is a simple dart, a warm-up plane, if you like. It's a competent glider.

THE BULLDOG DART

1. Fold a sheet of 8 1/2 x 11 lengthwise to get a centre line.
2. Fold two corners into the centre line, as in the picture.
3. Turn the paper over and fold those corners in half, as shown.
4. Fold the pointy nose back on itself to form the snub nose. You might try folding the nose underneath, but both ways work well.
5. Fold the whole plane lengthways, as shown.
6. Finally, fold the wings in half to complete the Bulldog Dart.

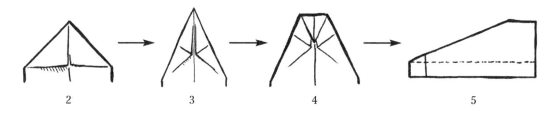

Good – now you know a design that really works. You may have noticed the insect-like plane in the middle of the first picture. It does have complicated 'floats' and inverse folds. However, it just doesn't fly very well and neither do most of the overcomplicated designs. We think that matters. Yes, it looks like a locust, but if it nose-dives, what exactly is the point?

Here, then, is the gold standard. It flies.

THE HARRIER

1. Fold in half lengthwise to find your centre line and then fold two corners into that line, as shown.
2. Fold that top triangle down, as you see in the picture. It should look like an envelope.
3. Fold in the second set of corners. You should be able to leave a triangular point sticking out.
4. Fold the triangle over the corners to hold them down.
5. Fold in half along the spine, leaving the triangle on the outside, as shown.
6. Finally, fold the wings back on themselves, finding your halfway line carefully. The more care you take to be accurate with these folds, the better the plane will fly.

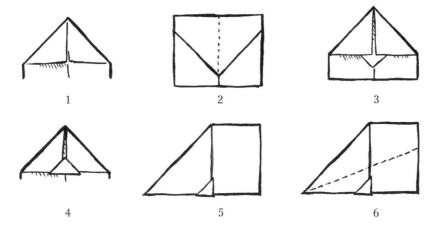

This plane does well at slower launch speeds. It can stall at high speed, but if you lift one of the flaps slightly at the back, it will swoop and return to your hand or fly in a great spiral. Fiddle with your plane until you are happy with it. Each one will be slightly different and have a character of its own.

THE SEVEN WONDERS
OF THE ANCIENT WORLD

⟶✻⟵

THE FAMOUS SEVEN WONDERS of the ancient world were: the Great Pyramid of Cheops at Giza, the Hanging Gardens of Babylon, the Temple of Artemis at Ephesus, the Mausoleum at Halicarnassus, the Colossus of Rhodes, the Statue of Zeus at Olympia and the Pharos Lighthouse at Alexandria. Only the pyramid at Giza survives to the modern day.

1. **The Great Pyramid** is the largest tomb ever built, created for the Fourth-Dynasty Egyptian pharaoh Khufu (2898–2875 BC), though he is better known by the Greek form of his name, Cheops.

THE GREAT PYRAMID OF CHEOPS.

   It is one of the three great pyramids at Giza near Cairo, the other two being constructed for the pharaohs Menkaure and Khafre. The largest, for Cheops, was the tallest structure on Earth for more than four thousand years, until the nineteenth century AD. Though the capstone was removed at some point, it would have stood at 146.5 metres (481 ft) high.
   The base is perfectly square – a feat of astonishing accuracy considering the sheer size of it. Each side of the base is 231 metres (755 ft, 8 in) long and each side slopes at 51 degrees, 51 minutes. It is composed of two million blocks of stone, *each one* weighing more than two tons. They fit together so well that not even a knife blade can be slid between them.

2. **The Hanging Gardens of Babylon** were built in what is now modern-day Iraq, on the banks of the river Euphrates. They were created by King Nebuchadnezzar for his queen between the seventh and sixth centuries BC.

Famously, they employed complex hydraulic systems to raise thousands of gallons from the river and keep the gardens blooming. We can only guess at the exact method, but an Archimedean screw, as shown here, may have been employed.

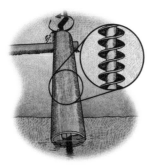

3. **The Temple of Artemis (Diana) at Ephesus** in what is modern-day Turkey is said to have awed Alexander the Great with its extraordinary beauty, though the citizens refused his offer to bear the cost of a restoration. Originally built in the sixth century BC, the temple was destroyed and rebuilt on more than one occasion, though the most famous was the night of Alexander's birth, when a man named Herostratus burned it so that his name would be remembered – one of the greatest acts of vandalism of all time. It finally fell into ruin around the third century AD.

THE HANGING GARDENS OF BABYLON.

TEMPLE OF DIANA AT EPHESUS.

4. **The Mausoleum at Halicarnassus** was created for King Mausolus of Persia, who ruled from 377 to 353 BC. Halicarnassus is now the city of Bodrum in Turkey. On top of the rectangular tomb chamber, thirty-six columns supported a stepped pyramid crowned by statues of Mausolus and his wife (and sister), Artemisia, in a chariot, reaching a height of approximately 42.5 metres (140 ft). It was destroyed in 1522 when crusading Knights of St. John used the stone to build a castle that still stands today. The polished marble blocks of the tomb are visible in the walls. From Mausolus, we have the word "mausoleum," meaning an ornate tomb.

5. **The Statue of Zeus at Olympia** is also lost to the modern world. Only images on coins and descriptions survive to tell us why the statue was considered so astonishing in the fifth century BC.

MAUSOLEUM AT HALICARNASSUS

STATUE OF ZEUS AT OLYMPIA.

Olympia was the site of the ancient Olympic games – giving us the word. The site was sacred to Zeus, and Phidias of Athens was commissioned to carve the statue. The statue was of wood layered in gold for the cloth and ivory sheets for the flesh. In his right hand stood the winged figure of the goddess Victory (Nike), made of ivory and gold. In his left, he held a sceptre made of gold, with an eagle perched on the end.

The Roman emperor Caligula tried to transfer the statue to Rome in the first century AD, but the scaffolding collapsed under the weight and the attempt was abandoned. Later on, the statue was moved to Constantinople and remained there until it was destroyed by fire in the fifth century.

6. **The Colossus of Rhodes** in Greece is perhaps the most famous of the seven ancient wonders. It was a statue of Helios, over 30 metres (100 ft) high.

    It did not actually stand across the harbour, but instead rested on a promontory, looking out over the Aegean Sea. The base was white marble and the statue was built slowly upwards, strengthened with iron and stone as the bronze pieces were added. It took twelve years and was finished around 280 BC, quickly becoming famous. An earthquake proved disastrous for the statue fifty years later. It broke at the knee and crashed to the earth to lie there for eight hundred years before invading Arabs sold it.

THE COLOSSUS OF RHODES.

7. **The Pharos Lighthouse at Alexandria** was built by the architect Sostratus of Cnidus for the Greco-Egyptian king Ptolemy Philadelphus (285–247 BC).

    Ptolemy's ancestor had been one of Alexander the Great's generals. His most famous descendant is Cleopatra, who was the first of her Greek line to actually speak Egyptian.

THE PHAROS OF ALEXANDRIA.

When Julius Caesar arrived in Alexandria, he would have passed by the great lighthouse on Pharos island. Its light was said to be visible for 55 kilometres (35 miles) out to sea. Its exact height is unknown, but to have shed visible light to that distance, it must have been between 121 and 182 metres (400 to 600 ft) high.

It was so famous that, even today, the word for lighthouse in Spanish and Italian is *faro*. French also uses the same root, with *phare*.

As you can see, even the greatest wonders can be lost or broken by the passage of millennia. Perhaps the true wonder is the fact that we build them, reaching always for something greater than ourselves.

THE FIVE KNOTS EVERY
BOY SHOULD KNOW

BEING ABLE TO TIE KNOTS in rope is extremely useful. It is amazing how many people only know a reef and a granny knot. Rather than naming hundreds, we've narrowed it down to five extremely useful examples.

However, they take endless practice. I learned a bowline on a sailing ship in the Pacific. For three weeks, I used an old bit of rope on every watch, night and day. On my return to England, I attempted to demonstrate the knot – and found it had vanished from memory. To be fair, it didn't take long to recall, but knots should be practised every now and then, so they will be there when you need them. There are hundreds of good books available, including expert levels of splicing and decorative knots. These are the standard basics – useful to all.

1. THE REEF KNOT

This knot is used to reef sails – that is, to reduce the amount of sail area when the wind is getting stronger. If you look at a dinghy sail, you'll notice cords hanging from the material. As the sail is folded on the boom, the cords are tied together using reef knots. It is symmetrical and pleasing to the eye.

The rule to remember is: left over right, right over left.

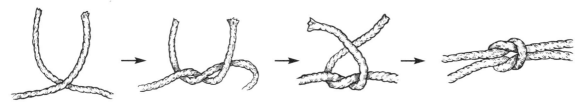

2. THE FIGURE OF EIGHT

This is a "stopper" – it goes at the end of a rope and prevents the rope from passing through a hole. A double figure eight is sometimes used to give the rope end weight for throwing. It's called a figure eight because it looks like the number eight.

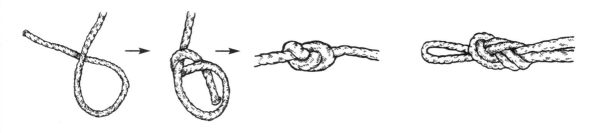

3. The Bowline (pronounced bow-lin)

This is a fantastically useful, solid knot. It is used whenever a loop on the end of a rope is needed – for a post, a ring, or anything else really.

i.   Make a loop toward yourself, leaving enough free at the end to go around your post, tree or similar object
ii. Now – imagine the loop is a rabbit hole and the tip is the rabbit. The other end of the rope is the tree. Feed the tip up through the hole – the rabbit coming up.
iii. Pass the rabbit round the back of the tree.
iv. Pass the rabbit back down the hole – back into the original loop.
v.   Pull tight carefully.

NOTE: You can make a simple lasso by making a bowline and passing the other end of the rope through the loop.

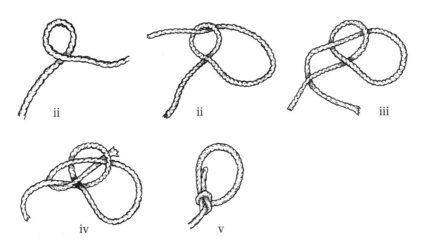

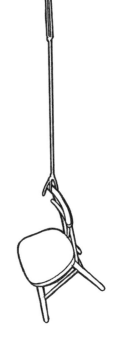

4. Sheet Bend

This is a useful knot for joining two ropes together. Reef knots fail completely when joining ropes of different diameters – but a sheet bend works very well.

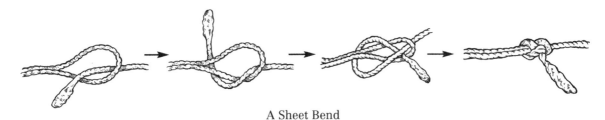

A Sheet Bend

5. A Clove Hitch – for hitching two things together very quickly

This is a short-term knot – the sort of thing you see used by cowboys in westerns to hitch their horses. Its main benefit is that it's very fast to make. Basically, it's wrapping a rope around a post and tucking an end into a loop. Practise this one over and over until you can do it quickly.

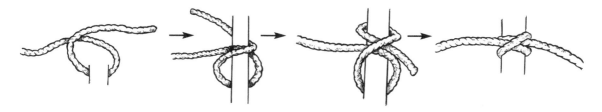

These five knots will be useful in a huge variety of situations, from building a treehouse to camping, to sailing, to tying up your horse outside a saloon. They will not come easily. They take practice and patience. Knowing knots will not impress girls, but it could save your life – or your horse.

QUESTIONS ABOUT
THE WORLD – PART ONE

1. **Why is a summer day longer than a winter day?**
2. **Why is it hotter at the equator?**
3. **What is a vacuum?**
4. **What is latitude and longitude?**
5. **How do you tell the age of a tree?**

1. Why is a summer day longer than a winter day?

In Australia, the shortest day is June 21, and the longest falls on December 21. In the northern hemisphere, June 21 is midsummer and midwinter falls on December 21. Christmas in Australia is a time for barbecues on the beach.

Although the North Pole points approximately at the star Polaris, the earth's axis is tilted twenty-three and a half degrees in respect to the path it takes around our sun.

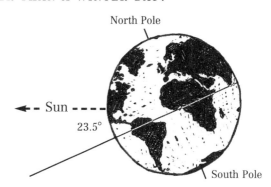

While the northern hemisphere leans towards the sun, more direct sunlight reaches us. We call this period summer. June 21 is the day when the North Pole points directly towards the sun, and the tilt is at maximum. The days are longest then, as most of the northern hemisphere is exposed. Down in the south, the days are shortest as the earth itself blocks light from reaching the shivering inhabitants.

As the earth moves around the sun, the tilt remains the same. The autumnal equinox (September 22 or 23) is the day when day and night are of equal length – twelve hours each, just as they are on the vernal equinox in spring on March 20. Equinox comes from the Latin for "equal" and "night."

When the northern hemisphere leans away from the sun, less light reaches the surface. This is autumn for us, and eventually winter. Longer days come to the southern hemisphere as shorter days come to the north. The summer solstice of June 21 is also the moment when the sun is highest in the sky.

The earth is actually closer to the sun in January rather than June. It's not the distance – it's the tilt.

The best way to demonstrate this is by holding one hand up as a fist and the other as a flat palm representing the earth's tilt. As your palm moves around the fist, you should see how the tilt creates the seasons and why they are reversed in the southern hemisphere. Be thankful that we have them. One long summer or one long winter would not support life.

At the midsummer and midwinter solstices, the conditions can become very peculiar indeed. The summer sun will not set for six months at the North and South Poles, but when it does set, it does not rise for another six. The Canadian arctic experiences the midnight sun effect, alongside countries such as Finland, Norway and Sweden.

2. Why is it hotter at the Equator?

There are two reasons why the equator is hotter than the rest of the planet. Strangely enough, the fact that it is physically closer to the sun than, say, the North Pole is not relevant. The main reason is that the earth curves less in the equatorial region. The same amount of sunlight is spread over a smaller area. This can be clearly seen in the diagram below.

Also, the sun's rays have to pass through less atmosphere to reach the equatorial band – and so retain more of their heat.

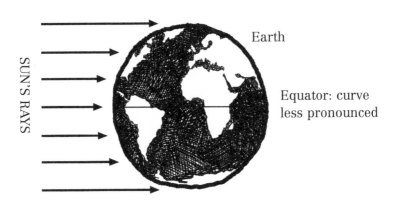

Earth

Equator: curve
less pronounced

SUN'S RAYS

3. WHAT IS A VACUUM?

A perfect vacuum is a space with absolutely nothing in it – no air, no matter of any kind. Like the temperature of absolute zero (–273.15 °C/0 Kelvin), it exists only in theory. The light bulbs in your home have a "partial vacuum," with most of the air taken out as part of the manufacturing process. Without that partial vacuum, the filament would burn far faster, as air contains oxygen.

The classic science experiment to show one quality of a vacuum is to put a ticking clock inside a bell jar and expel the air with a pump. Quite quickly, the sound becomes inaudible: without air molecules to carry sound vibrations, there can be no sound. That is why in space, no one can hear you scream!

4. WHAT IS LATITUDE AND LONGITUDE?

The earth is a globe. The system of latitude and longitude is a human-made system for identifying a location anywhere on the surface.

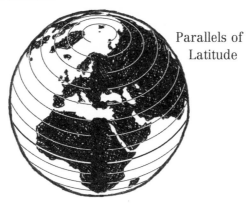

Parallels of
Latitude

Latitude takes the equator as a line of zero. If you cut the world in half at that point, you would have a horizontal plate. The centre point of that plate is at ninety degrees to the Poles above and below it.

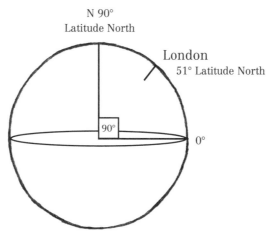

N 90°
Latitude North

London
51° Latitude North

90°

0°

Latitude is not measured in miles but in the degrees between ninety and zero in both hemispheres. London, for example is at 51° latitude north.The curve representing the ninety-degree change is split into imaginary lines called "parallels" – because they are all parallel to each other and the equator.

With something as large as the Earth, even a single degree can be unwieldy. For both longitude and latitude, each degree is split into sixty "minutes of arc." Each minute of arc is split into a further sixty "seconds of arc." The symbols for these are:

Degrees: °   Minutes: ′   Seconds: ″

With something as large as a city, the first two numbers would suffice. London would be 51° 32′ N, for example. The location of a particular house would need that third number, as well as a longitude coordinate.

There is an element of luck in the fact that a latitude degree turned out to be almost exactly sixty nautical miles – making a minute of latitude conveniently close to one nautical mile, which is 1,852 metres (6,000 ft).

The *longitude* of London is zero, which brings us neatly into longitude.

Longitude is a series of 360 imaginary lines stretching from Pole to Pole. London is zero, and 180 degrees stretch to the west or east.

If the world turns a full circle in a day, that is 360 degrees. 360 divided by 24 = 15 degrees. So the world turns fifteen degrees every hour. We call the fifteen-degree lines "meridians." ("Meridian" means "noon," so there are twenty-four noon points around the planet.)

Now, this is how it worked. On board your ship in the middle of nowhere, you took a noon sighting – that is, took note of the time as the sun passed its highest point in the sky. You could use a sextant and a knowledge of trigonometry to check the angle. If you were at noon and your ship's clock told you Greenwich was at nine in the morning, you would have travelled three meridian lines east or west – depending on the direction of your compass and watching the sun rise and set. You would be at longitude +/– 45°, in fact.

Having a clock that could keep the accurate time of Greenwich even while being tossed and turned on a ship was obviously crucial for this calculation. John Harrison, a clock maker from Yorkshire, created a timepiece called H4 in 1759 that was finally reliable enough to be used.

All that was left was to choose the prime meridian, or zero-degree point of longitude. For some time it looked as if Paris might be a possibility, but trade ships in London took their time from the Greenwich clock at Flamstead House, where a time ball would drop to mark 1 p.m. each day. Ship chronometers were set by it and Greenwich time became the standard. In 1884 a Washington conference of twenty-five nations formalized the arrangement. If you go to Greenwich today, you can stand on a brass line that separates the west from the east.

On the opposite side of the world, the two hemispheres meet at the International Date Line in the Pacific Ocean. It's called the International Date Line because we've all agreed to change the date when we cross it. Otherwise, you could travel west from Greenwich, back to 11:00 a.m., 10:00 a.m., 9:00 a.m., all the way round the planet until you arrived the day before. Obviously, this is not possible, and so crossing the line going west would add a day to the date. Complex? Well, yes, a little, but this is the world and the systems we made to control it.

Like latitude, longitude is broken down into a three-figure location of degrees, minutes and seconds. Common practice puts the latitude figures first, but it's always given away by the North or South letter, so they can't really be confused. A full six-figure location will look something like these:

38° 53′ 23″ N, 77° 00′ 27″ W   Washington DC
39° 17′ 00″ N, 22° 23′ 00″ E   Pharsalus, Greece, where Julius Caesar beat Pompey
and ended the civil war.
39° 57′ 00″ N, 26° 15′ 00″ E   Troy

5. HOW DO YOU TELL THE AGE OF A TREE?

You cut it down and count the rings. For each year of growth, a dark and a light ring of new wood are created. The two bands together are known as the "annual ring." The lighter part is formed in spring and early summer when the wood cells are bigger and have thinner walls which look lighter. In autumn and winter, trees produce smaller cells with thicker walls, which look darker. They vary in width depending on growing conditions, so a tree stump can be a climate record for the life of the tree – sometimes even centuries. The age of a tree, therefore, can be told by counting the annual rings.

MAKING A BATTERY

A BATTERY AT ITS SIMPLEST is a cathode (the positive end), an anode (the negative end) and electrolyte (the bit in the middle). There are quite a few different combinations out there. Electricity is the movement of electrons, tiny negatively charged particles. The anode tends to be made of a substance that gives up electrons easily – like zinc, which gives up two electrons per zinc atom. The cathode tends to be made of substances that accept electrons easily, like copper.

The electrolyte inside can be a liquid, a gel or a paste. All that matters is that it contains positive and negatively charged ions that flow when the anode and cathode are activated. When the Italian physicist Alessandro Volta made the first battery, he used copper for the cathode, zinc for the anode and an electrolyte of blotting paper and sea water. His name gives us the word "volt," as in a 12-volt car battery. If you think of electricity as a water pipe, a volt will be the speed of the water, but it also needs a big hole to flow through – or "amps." You can have enough voltage to make your hair stand on end, but without amps, it won't do more than cause a tiny spark. A house supply, however, has 240 volts and enough amps to kill you as dead as a doornail.

> You will need
>
> - Ten pennies.
> - Aluminum foil.
> - Blotting paper.
> - Two pieces of copper wire (taken from any electrical wire or flex).
> - Malt vinegar.
> - Salt.
> - Bowl.
> - LED – a light-emitting diode (available from model and hardware stores).
> - Masking tape.

The copper coins will be the cathode; the foil the anode.

Cut the foil and blotting paper into circles so they can be stacked on top of each other. The blotting paper will be soaked in the vinegar, but it is also there to prevent the metals touching – so cut those paper circles a little larger than the foil or coins.

1. Mix vinegar and a little salt together in the bowl. Vinegar is acetic acid and all acids can be used as an electrolyte. Sulphuric acid is found in car batteries, but don't fool around with something that powerful. It eats clothing and can burn skin – unlike vinegar, which goes on your french fries.

   Common salt is sodium chloride, a combination of a positive and negative ion ($Na+$ and $Cl–$). These will separate in the electrolyte, increasing its strength.

2. Soak your circles of blotting paper in the ion-rich electrolyte.

3. With the masking tape, attach the end of one wire to the bottom of a foil disc. This is the negative terminal. Now stack in this sequence – foil, paper, coin, foil, paper, coin. Each combination is its own tiny battery – but to light even an LED (light-emitting diode) you'll need quite a few. A car battery tends to have six of these, but with a much larger surface area for each "cell." As a general rule, the bigger a battery is, the more power it has. (Power measured in Watts = amps × volts.)

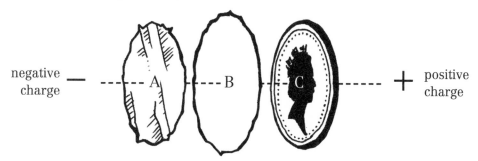

negative charge — ------ A ----- B ---- C ----- + positive charge

All the positive ions will go to one terminal, all the negative ions to the other. In effect, you are charging your battery.

4. When you have a stack, you can attach a wire to the last coin with tape. This will be the positive terminal. The coins can now light an LED, as in the picture below, or with enough coin batteries, even a small bulb.

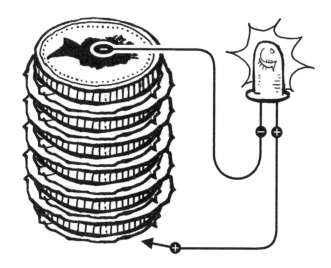

There may come a time when batteries go on to a new generation, but if you can understand the battery you have just made, you can understand every type of battery currently available, from nickel-cadmium, to lithium-ion, from rechargeable phone batteries, to the ones that drive toy rabbits. You won't hear acid sloshing in alkaline batteries, where a paste or gel is used, but the principles are identical.

BUILDING SNOW HOUSES

Winter can be a wonderful time to be outdoors – especially if there is a lot of snow. It invites snowball fights and making snowmen, but it also allows for some great construction projects. Snow is an extraordinary building material – lightweight, sturdy and, believe it or not, warm. Between the ice crystals in each snowflake are pockets of trapped air. A pile of deep snow can actually contain over 90 percent air. All that trapped air makes snow a great insulator because it regulates temperatures inside of a snow bank and keeps warm air surrounded by snow from cooling. Because of snow's unique properties, Arctic animals – including polar bears and sled dogs – cover themselves entirely with snow to stay warm while they sleep. The human population of the north has also learned how to take advantage of the cozy quality of snow.

The Igloo

Today, most residents of the far north live in contemporary homes built from materials shipped from the south. But for centuries, since no trees grow in the upper reaches of Canada and the Arctic Circle, snow was one of the few materials available for building shelters. In the summer months, the inhabitants of this northern territory, the Inuit, lived in tents and structures made from animal hide. In the winter months, however, these shelters would not have been warm enough. When the colder temperatures set in, the Inuit constructed homes out of snow and called them *igluviak,* or "igloos." The size and layout of the igloos varied. Some were just big enough to house one family. Others were large enough to function as com-munity halls where people gathered for dances and celebrations. Some Inuit communities joined their igloos together with tunnels so they could move from house to house without going outside. A family igloo might also have had a smaller igloo attached to it that served as a storage room. The insulating properties of snow kept the igloos warm inside, but of course, igloo dwellers had to take precautions against the snow houses getting too hot and melting away. Chimneys were inserted through the roofs to dispel the heat from cooking fires. But with the stoves and the heat generated by the people inside, walls did melt a bit sometimes. When the cooking stopped or people went outside, the wet interior would freeze again, creating a tough shell of ice. Once this happened, the igloos became extremely strong and could stand up to hurricane-force winds or support children playing on top of them. Eventually, however, an igloo would become too damaged to live in anymore, and a new one would be built.

Building an igloo quickly and well is a real skill – and not something you will likely master right away. Nor is it something you should do alone. But even your first time, you and your friends can achieve amazing results if you have the right snow and enough time (it will take you several hours). All you need (other than a good pair of mitts and some warm winter clothes) is a saw (a snow saw if you have one!) or a large knife.

To build an igloo, the snow has to be the right density – firm enough to hold its shape when you cut a chunk of it but not too hard and brittle. (Don't use ice.) Cut chunks out of the snow to see if they will hold their shape. You will need a lot of suitable snow to work with.

When you find a good patch, pace off a circle about 2 to 2.5 metres across. Cut blocks from inside the circle, creating a large hole in the snow. This will be the floor of your igloo. (You can dig out this floor further if you wish for more headroom.)

The blocks for the base of the igloo should be 60 centimetres to 100 centimetres wide, 15 to 20 centimetres deep and 38 to 47 centimetres high. Line the blocks along the edge of the circle that you've paced off. Placed all of your base blocks tightly together in a circle, making sure they are tilting inward toward the centre. (You may need to shape the sides slightly to do this – making the blocks a little narrower at the top than at the bottom.) Next, dig a small tunnel (just big enough for one person to crawl through) under one of the blocks, continuing it for several feet outside of the wall. This will be your entrance. (You can also carve out this tunnel later if you want, after more of your wall is built.) Now take your knife or your saw and shape the base wall into a spiral (like a curving ramp moving higher and higher) by cutting two or three blocks at an angle so that they start close to the ground and move upward to meet the height of the third or

fourth block. Once you've created your spiral base, place other blocks of snow along the top of it, gently tilting them in toward the centre of your hole so that a dome is created.

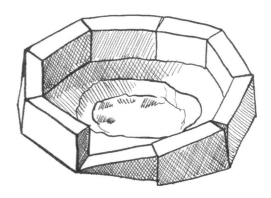

Cut the blocks into smaller trapezoid shapes (slightly shorter across the top than across the bottom) as you move up. Have one person patch the gaps between the blocks with handfuls of snow.

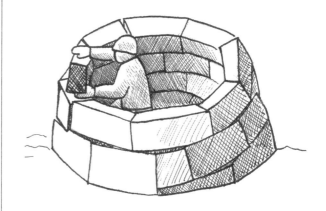

Pack smaller chunks of snow in any large gaps. The very last block must be put in place while you are standing inside the igloo. Cut it bigger than the hole and then shape it to size as you press it into place. To make a really firm seal, you can tilt the block and push it up through the hole and then lower it back down, shaping it until it fits snugly, like a cork in a bottle.

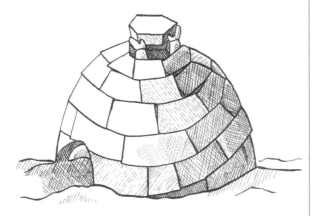

Crawl out of the igloo through the tunnel you've already dug under the wall, and fashion a roof over the tunnel with two or more blocks of snow. (You can place two big blocks in an inverted V-shape to create a peaked roof, or you can use two blocks for walls, and one for roof to fashion a rectangular roof.)

Smooth the inside surface of the igloo. Next, create some air holes for ventilation in the roof. Cutting small ventilation holes in the centre of blocks instead of leaving gaps between the blocks will make your igloo stur-

dier and less likely to collapse. You can use more blocks of snow to build sleeping platforms, benches and tables inside your igloo.

The Quinzhee

Igloos take time to build and also require a lot of the right kind of snow. Sometimes, therefore, the Inuit would build a temporary shelter called a "quinzhee." A quinzhee is simply a large pile of snow that is hollowed out to form a small snow hut. It is usually not as high as an igloo – you can sit or squat in one but there is not enough room to stand up, and unlike the igloo, the quinzhee is made from light, powdery snow. As the snow is piled up, it mixes, recrystalizes and hardens.

When building a quinzhee, work with at least one other person. Choose a site and then tramp down the snow in a circle about two to four metres across. With a shovel, a bucket or even your hands, pile snow in a large mound about two metres high. Make sure the snow is loose, breaking up any blocks you come across. Don't pack the snow down as you build your dome.

Next, gather a bunch of sticks about thirty centimetres long. Once you've finished the pile, take the sticks and insert them all over the pile so that only about ten centimetres of each stick is jutting out of the snow.

These sticks will help guide you as you hollow out the dome, allowing you to keep the thickness of the quinzhee walls uniform. Now let the snow sit for about three hours to firm up.

Start hollowing out the pile by digging a tunnel at the base of the quinzhee (make it just big enough for one person to crawl through). Then, hollow out the dome from the inside, moving snow out through the tunnel as you go. When you hit the end of each stick, you've removed enough snow in that direction and should dig out another spot on the inside of the quinzhee. If you don't have sticks, keep your eyes peeled for bright spots where the sun is shining through. If sunshine comes through the dome, the walls are too thin.

When the qunizhee walls are finished, smooth them out, and cut one or two two-to-three-centimetre ventilation holes in the top of the dome. You can dig out the floor to create extra height inside, but leave at least thirty centimetres of snow on the ground so that the quinzhee won't feel too cold. Now you can build sleeping platforms or benches inside out of snow.

A note of caution: Never build igloos and quinzhees alone. Large blocks of snow can be very heavy, so having someone else help you lift and place them is a good idea. But working in groups of two or more is also an important safety measure. If the structure collapses, the heavy snow could trap you and make it impossible to breathe. Work upright or on your hands and knees – never dig out your quinzhee or smooth out the inside of your igloo while lying on your back. If the snow does fall, being on your back would make breathing difficult. When building a quinzhee or igloo, make sure there is always one person working outside of the structure who can help dig the others out if the house crumbles. And because igloos and quinzhees can be very dangerous when they collapse, don't build them in areas where animals or other children may go into them unsupervised. And never forget to make holes for ventilation. Well-constructed igloos and quinzhees will be airtight – so you need to make sure that some fresh air can enter.

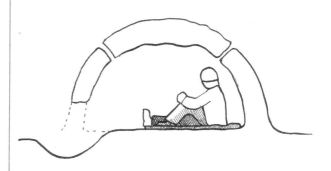

Snow Forts and Snow Houses
Snow forts and snow houses provide neither warmth nor practical shelter – with walls but no roof, they are built purely for fun.

Snow forts can be as simple as one wall or a U-shaped fortress for defence during snowball fights. You can build the walls out of blocks of snow or large snowballs. You can also pack soft, sticky snow into pails and pile it on the same way you would if you were building a large sandcastle. Remember: as you ready your snow battlements, leave a dip or window in your wall through which you can throw snowballs.

For snow houses, you can build walls in the same manner or simply carve your rooms out of deep drifts. Another way to make rooms out of deep snow is to tramp the snow down with your feet or lie on your back and roll back and forth until the soft snow is packed. An elaborate snow house might have many rooms connected with corridors. And don't forget that you can always furnish your fort with snow benches, chairs and tables.

If you want to get really fancy, "paint" your snow fort or house by mixing food colouring and water in a spray bottle and spraying the walls. If it is cold enough, spraying your walls with water (coloured or not) will make them firm and strong.

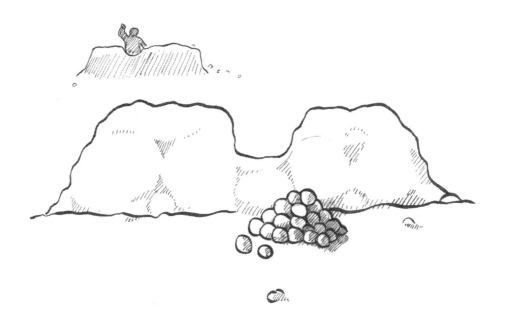

SLINGSHOTS

S LINGSHOTS HAVE INTRIGUED boys for as long as they have had access to strips of rubber. Before then, slingshots of leather were used right back to biblical times, as when David slew Goliath by hitting him in the forehead with a stone. Slingshots do have a serious use in hunting, of course, or for launching bait into a river while fishing. However, the classic images are more to do with Dennis the Menace and Bart Simpson. Slingshots can be astonishingly powerful and accurate, though this is not something to demonstrate by telling a younger brother "Run," and laughing in an unpleasant fashion. **Never** aim or fire a slingshot at someone else.

> You will need
>
> - A forked stick.
> - A piece of rubber – 60 centimetres (2 ft) long.
> - Twine to tie the ends.
> - A piece of leather, such as the tongue from an old shoe.

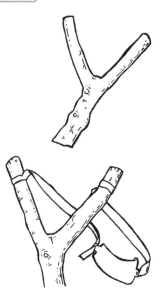

1. Find and cut a forked stick. We found our example in a large holly bush, but the "Y" shape can come from almost anywhere.

    A Swiss Army knife has a saw attachment that makes short work of small branches. You don't want the diameter of the wood to be any thicker than your thumb. If you are not confident in your "eye," cut a little more than you think you will need. A good top-to-bottom height is 15 to 17 centimetres (6 to 7 in).
2. Cut rings from the bark at the top of the 'Y' to anchor the rubber – a Swiss Army knife is perfect for this, too.
3. Finding the rubber is the hardest part. After a fruitless search in hardware and toy shops, we found that a strip cut from a bicycle inner tube works very well. Cut a 160-centimetre (2-ft) length of tube and then make two cuts lengthwise to remove a long strip. Some experimentation will be necessary to get the right pull tension and power.

    [Note that we have used two pieces of rubber. It was tempting to use one long piece, with the central pouch threaded through. In practice, we found that the pouch piece moved after one or two shots and suddenly we had a catapult that could fire almost anywhere without warning. It is far better to tie two pieces securely.
4. The central pouch piece is easy enough if you have an old shoe. Either the tongue of the shoe or some part of the body can be cut to produce a rectangle of material around 10 × 5 centimetres (4 × 2 in). Leather is best for this as it can be holed without splitting. Make two holes with a sharp point and attach the ends of the rubber. You now have a slingshot.

FOSSILS

Half a billion years ago, there was no life on land and only worms, snails, sponges and primitive crabs in the seas. When these creatures died, their bodies sank into silt and mud and were slowly covered. Over millions of years, the sea bottom hardened into rock and the minerals of the bones were replaced, molecule by molecule, with rock-forming minerals such as iron and silica.

Eventually, this process turns bones into rock – and they become known as fossils, a slowly created cast of an animal that died hundreds of millions of years ago. Other fossils are formed when dying animals fall into peat bogs or are covered in sand. As each new sedimentary layer takes millions of years to form, we can judge the age of the fossils from their depth. You can travel in time, in fact, if you have a shovel.

Those sea animals can move a long way in the time since they were swimming in dark oceans! Geological action can raise great plates of the earth so that what were undersea fossils can be found at the peak of a mountain or in a desert that was once a valley on the sea floor.

Canada has its own fossil treasure trove in the Badlands of southern Alberta. In Drumheller, you can see one of the world's most extensive fossil collections at the Royal Tyrrell Museum. And in nearby Dinosaur Provincial Park, you can see fossil displays and maybe even witness the discovery of a new skeleton.

In parts of New Zealand, you can see the fossilized remains of ancient prehistoric forests in visible black bands on the seashore. This particular compressed material is coal and it burns extremely well as fuel. Oil too is a fossil. It is formed in pockets, under great pressure, from animals and plants that lived three hundred million years ago.

It is without a doubt the most useful substance we have ever found – everything plastic comes from oil, as well as gas for our planes and cars.

By studying fossilized plants and animals, we can take a glimpse at a world that has otherwise vanished. It is a narrow view and the information is nowhere near as complete as we would like, but our understanding improves with every new find.

Even the commonest fossils can be fascinating. Hold a piece of flint up to the light and see creatures that last crawled before human beings came out of the caves – before Nelson, before William the Conqueror, before Moses. It fires the imagination.

Here are some of the classic forms of fossils.

Ammonite. A shelled sea creature that died out 65 million years ago (see Dinosaurs). Sizes vary enormously, but they can be attractively coloured.

Trilobite. These are also a fairly common find, though the rock must usually be split to see them. Fossil hunters carry small hammers to tap away at samples of rock.

Horseshoe Crab. In 2008, fossilized horseshoe crabs were found in Manitoba. Horseshoe crabs, despite their name, are more closely related to spiders and scorpions than to the crabs we know. The approximately four-centimetre-long creatures originally lived when plant and animal life was just beginning on the planet.

BUILDING A TREEHOUSE

L ET'S BE BLUNT. Building a decent treehouse is really hard. It takes something like sixty man-hours start to finish and costs more than $200 in wood and materials. In other words, it's a job for dads. You could spend the same amount on a games console and a few games, but the treehouse won't go out of date – and is healthier, frankly. We are well aware of the satisfaction gained from nailing bits of wood to a tree, but for something that looks right, is strong and safe and will *last* more than just a few months, you need a bit more than that.

Along with a canoe or a small sailing dinghy, a treehouse is still one of the best things you could possibly have. It's worth the effort, the sweat, the cost, even the blood if whoever builds it is careless with power tools. It is a thing of beauty. It really should have a skull and crossbones on it somewhere, as well.

You will need

- Thirty 6-inch (15-centimetre) lag screws with heavy square washers.
- Eight 8-inch (20-centimetre) lag screws with washers.
- Thirty-two 4-inch (10-centimetre) lag screws with washers.
- 4 × 3 inch (10 X 7.5 cm) beams – at least 4.8 metres (16 ft), but better to get 6 metres (20 ft).
- 2 × 6 inch (5 × 15 cm) pine planking – 19.5 metres (64 ft).
- 2 × 4 (5 X 10 cm) lumber for roof joists and walls – 10 metres + 46 metres (32 ft + 152 ft): 56 metres (184 ft).
- Exterior-grade plywood to cover the area of the platform – 4.5 square metres (49 square ft).
- Exterior-grade plywood for the ladder – 2.5 square metres (27 square ft).
- Jigsaw power tool, electric drill, rip saw (preferably an electric table saw).
- Spirit level.
- Large drill bits of 14, 16 and 18 mm.
- Stepladder and a long ladder.
- Safety rope.
- Bag of clout nails and a hammer.
- "Shiplap" planking – enough to cover four half walls with a total area of 7.8 square metres (84 square ft). Add in approximately 4.5 square metres (49 square ft) for the roof.
- Ratchet spanner with a set of heads to tighten the coach screws.
- Chisel to cut trenches for the trap-door hinges. Two hinges.
- Four eyebolts that can be screwed into the trunk.
- Cloth bag for trap-door counterweight.

To build the platform, you need some 2 × 6 inch (5 × 15 cm) pine planking, available from any large wood supplier. Our base was 2.1 metres × 2.1 metres (7 ft by 7 ft) and that worked out as eight 2.1 metre (7 foot) lengths, with one more for bracers. Altogether: 19.5 metres (64 ft) of 2 × 6.

Most dads will be concerned with making this as safe as possible. You really don't want something this heavy to fall down with children in it. Wherever possible, we went for huge overkill with materials, working on the principle that "in the event of nuclear war, this treehouse would remain standing."

Choose your tree and check if the treehouse will overlook a neighbour's garden. If it does and they object, you may be asked to take it down again. Choose the height of the base from the ground. This will depend in part on the age of the children, but we put ours at about 2 metres (6 1/2 ft) up. Higher ones are more impressive, of course, but are harder to make. If the ground is soft, use a board to stop the feet of the ladders from sinking in.

THE PLATFORM

The lag screws need to have holes pre-drilled, so make sure you have a suitable drill bit and a long enough extension cord to reach the tree. We ended up using three cords attached to each other and a double socket on the end. For a previous job, we had attached a table saw to an old table and it proved extremely useful to be able to cut wood as required.

Build the platform as shown in the diagrams below. Use the safety rope to support the planks until they are secure, putting the rope over a higher branch and tying it off when they are in position. Do not try to walk on the platform before it is supported at each corner. For it to drop, it would have to sheer off a number of steel coach screws, but the turning force of someone standing on a corner is immense and could be disastrous. Supporting the platform is technically the hardest part of the job.

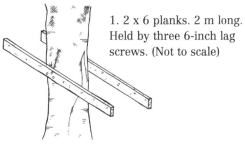

1. 2 x 6 planks. 2 m long. Held by three 6-inch lag screws. (Not to scale)

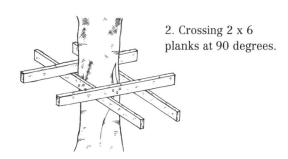

2. Crossing 2 x 6 planks at 90 degrees.

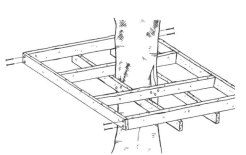

3. 7-ft square frame built around top pair of boards using 2 x 6. Two 6-inch lag screws to each corner.

Beams measuring 4 × 3 inches (10 × 7.5 cm) are immensely strong – probably far too strong for the job. Given that the trunk is likely to be uneven, they will almost certainly have to be different lengths. First cut them roughly to size, being generous. The hard part is cutting the joint where the top of the beam meets the platform.

The strength comes from the fact that the platform sits on a flat surface at all four corners. The joint for this looks a little like a bird's open mouth. Cut it by hand, marking it out carefully. The first task is cutting a 90-degree triangle with two saw lines.

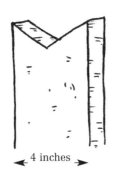

4 inches

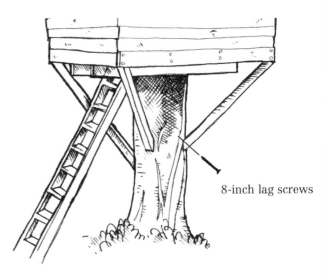

8-inch lag screws

Mark a point 10 centimetres (4 in) from the end on both sides, then draw a line to it from the opposite edge. Repeat to give you two diagonal lines. Where they meet is a neat centre point. Measure it all twice. Cut from the edge inwards.

The second and spatially trickier cut is straight down on one of the cut edges. Again, measure carefully and cut. It might be worth practising on a bit of scrap wood first. You should end up with four ends that fit neatly inside the corner of the main platform and support it as well.

Eight-inch (20-centimetre) lag screws might seem excessive to attach the four diagonals to the trunk, but everything rests on them.

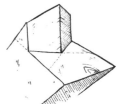

Drill through the 10-centimetre length of the diagonal beam, so another 10 centimetres of steel goes into the tree. Don't worry, you won't kill it. Trees are very resilient and a good gardener's pruning does more damage than this.

When the four diagonals are in place, the platform cannot tip without actually crushing one of them. This is practically impossible. We tested the strength by putting six adults up in the finished treehouse, with a combined total of more than 380 kilograms (838 lb).

We used offcuts of 2 × 6 lumber to add bracers to any spare gap in the platform. Rather than our usual overkill, this was to support the decking. Make sure you leave a gap for the trap door. We used exterior-grade plywood available from any DIY store. It has the advantage of being treated against damp – as was all the lumber here. Getting them treated is a little more expensive but makes the difference between a treehouse lasting ten years or twenty. We screwed the decking straight into the bracers and main beams of the platform, using a jigsaw to shape it around the actual trunk. Leave a little gap to allow for tree movement and somewhere to sweep dust and dead leaves.

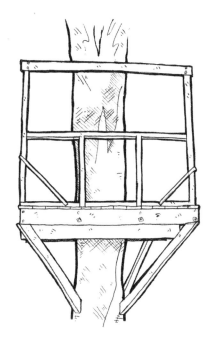

THE WALLS

It is easiest to assemble these rectangles on the ground, then hoist them into place. That said, they are extremely heavy, so use ropes and two people at least. Do not attempt to lift the section without it being held by a strong rope.

For each wall, 4 × 2 inch (10 × 5 cm) beams were used, with 4-inch lag screws holding them together. We planned to cover the lower half of each wall with over-lapping shed planking, except for one left open with just wire to stop the children falling through. It was absolutely crucial to have a drill powerful enough to send screws straight into the wood without pre-drilling. If we'd had to drill every hole first, we'd probably still be there now.

The shape was a simple rectangle with a ledge and a couple of support uprights. When you are deciding how tall it should be, remember that it is a treehouse for children. We went with 1.5 metres (5 ft), which was probably generous.

Each wall just sat on top of the decking and was screwed into it from above. Please note that it is going to feel wobbly at this stage. The four walls all support each other and when the last one is put in place, it becomes extremely solid. The roof will also add stability.

Also note that two of the walls will be shorter than the other two, so plan and measure these *carefully* or you'll have an awful time. You may also have trouble with the heads of the coach screws getting in the way. Although it's time-consuming, you may have to countersink these with a 16/18 millimetre (¾ inch) wood drill bit. As well as the 4-inch lag screws, we used four 6-inch bolts and nuts to bring the sides together.

THE ROOF

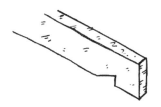

Once the four walls are in place and solid, you can think about the roof. We used eight joists of 2 × 4 lumber. The length will depend on the angles involved, but allow at least 1.2 metres (4 ft) for each one.

Cut them roughly to size, then take out a triangle near the end so that they will fit neatly over the top corner of the walls. In theory, this is the exact opposite of the lower diagonals, but we didn't think it was worth cutting more "bird-mouth" joints.

Measure and cut very carefully here as one end will be in contact with an uneven trunk. Use 6-inch lag screws (8) to anchor them to the tree. The roof supports only its own weight.

After placing the four diagonal joists for the corners, add four more between them, one to a side. Use a spirit level to be certain they are all at the same height, or your roof will be uneven.

There are various ways of finishing a roof, of course. We used a plastic roof membrane tacked to the eight joists with clout nails. Over that, we nailed strips of overlapping shed planking, known as "shiplap." It looked very natural, but each piece had to be cut to size and then taken up the tree. We also nailed very thin battens on the diagonals for cosmetic effect.

The roof was probably the most time-consuming part of the whole process – and a good safety rope at that height was absolutely crucial. In fact, to reach the highest point of the roof, we had to stand on the window ledges, make a loop out of the rope and sit on the loop

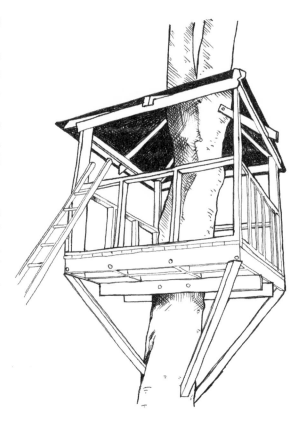

as we leaned out. To say the very least, this is extremely dangerous and for adults only.

Finally, we used the same overlapping planking to cover the lower half of the walls, then made a ladder out of decking planking. We attached the top of the ladder with loose bolts on the basis that it could be pulled up at some point in the future. It probably never will be, though – far too heavy.

We made the trap door from offcuts of decking and some exterior-grade plywood, screwing it all together. To pull the trap door closed behind you, a piece of rope hanging from an eyebolt is perfect.

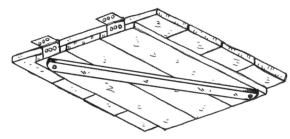

To prevent the trap door dropping on small fingers, it's worthwhile counterweighting it. To do this, get yourself a cloth bag of the sort you sometimes put marbles in. Run a rope through the trap door, with the knot on the underside. The other end should go through an eyebolt higher up the trunk and a third one out on the wall. Tie the bag of stones to the end and leave it dangling where the children can reach it. To open the trap door from below, they can pull on the bag. To close it, they pull on the knotted rope hanging down from the trap door. You'll have to adjust the weight of the bag to suit the child, of course, and it means the trap door has to be pressed shut with a foot when you're up there, but it's much safer.

The important thing when it's all done is to wait for a nice summer evening, take some cushions, blankets and a flashlight and spend the night up there under the stars. Take snacks – all that fresh air will give you an appetite.

THE RULES OF SOCCER

Neatly enough, there are only seventeen main rules for the most popular game on Earth. These are based on rules put together in England as far back as 1863 and formally ratified by the International Football Association Board in 1886.

1. **The pitch.** Length: 90–120 m (100–130 yd). Width: 45–90 m (50–100 yd). The two long lines are called touchlines, the two short lines are called goal lines. The pitch is divided by a halfway line, with a centre point where the "kick-off" occurs to begin the game. At each goal, there is a 5.5 metre (6-yd) box known as the goal area. Outside that, there is a 16.5 metre (18-yd) box known as the penalty area. A penalty spot is drawn 11 metres (12 yd) in front of the goalposts. The goalposts are 7.32 metres (8 yd) apart and 2.44 metres (8 ft) high.

2. **The ball.** Circumference: between 68–70 centimetres (27–28 in). Weight: between 410–450 grams (14–16 oz).

3. **The teams.** No more than eleven players can be fielded by each team, including the goalkeeper. Depending on the competition, between three and seven substitutes can be used. In addition, any player can change places with the goalkeeper provided that the referee is told and the change occurs while play has stopped.

4. **Clothing.** Players wear soccer shirts, shorts, shinguards under long socks and soccer shoes. Goalkeepers wear different-coloured uniforms.

5. **The referee.** All decisions by the referee are final. Powers include the ability to give a verbal warning, a more serious yellow card warning, or a red card, which results in immediate sending off. A second yellow card is equivalent to a red. The referee also acts as timekeeper for the game and controls any restarts after stopped play.

6. **Assistant referees** (linesmen). These indicate with a raised flag when a ball has crossed the lines and gone out of play, and let the referee know which side is to take the corner, goal kick or throw-in. They also raise their flags to indicate when a player may be penalized for being in an offside position.

7. **Duration.** Two halves of forty-five minutes, with a half-time interval of no more than fifteen minutes.

8. **Starting.** Whichever team wins a coin-toss kicks off and begins play. The ball returns to the centre spot after a goal and at the start of the second half. All opposing players must be in their own half at kick-off – at least 9.15 metres (10 yd) from the ball.

9. **In and out.** The ball is out of play when it crosses any of the touchlines or goal lines, or if play has been stopped by the referee. It is in play at all other times.

10. **Scoring.** The whole ball has to pass over the goal line. If a member of the defending team knocks it in by accident, it is an "own goal" and still valid. Whoever scores the most goals wins.

11. **Offside.** The offside rule is designed to stop players hanging around the goal of their opponents, waiting for a long ball to come to them. A player is given offside if the ball is passed to him while he is nearer to the goal than the ball and the second-last defender. Note that players are allowed to sit on the goal line if they want, but the ball cannot come to them without offside being called by the referee. An "offside trap" is when defenders deliberately move up the field to leave a forward player in a position where he cannot take the ball without being called offside. It is not an offside offence if the ball comes to a player from a throw-in, a goal kick or a corner kick.

12. **Fouls.** Direct and indirect free kicks can be given to the opposing team if the referee judges a foul has been committed. The kick is taken from where the foul occurred, so if it is close to the opponent's goal, the game can easily hinge on the outcome. Fouls can range from touching the ball with the hands to kicking an opponent. In addition, the player can be cautioned or sent off depending on the offence.

13. **Free kicks.** Direct free kicks can be a shot at goal if the spot is close enough, so are given for more serious fouls. The ball is stationary when kicked. Opposing players are not allowed closer than 9.15 metres (10 yd), which has come to mean in practice that the opposing team put a wall of players 9.15 metres (10 yd) from the spot to obscure the kicker's vision.
    Indirect free kicks cannot be directly at goal, but must first be passed to another player.

14. **Penalties.** These are awarded for the same offences as direct free kicks – if the offence happens inside the penalty area of the opposing team. This is to prevent what are known as "professional fouls," where an attacker is brought down deliberately to stop him scoring.
    The goalkeeper must remain on his goal line between the posts until the ball has been kicked. Other players must be outside the penalty area and at least 9.15 metres (10 yd) from the penalty spot – that's why there's an arc on the penalty area.
    The penalty must be a single strike at the goal. As long as it goes in, it can hit the posts and/or goalkeeper as well. In the normal run of play, a penalty kick that rebounds off the keeper is back in play and can be struck again. In a penalty shootout, this does not apply and there is only one chance to score.

15. **Throw-ins.** A player must face inwards to the field and have both feet on the ground, on or behind the touchline. Both hands must be used and the ball must be delivered from behind the head. The thrower must pass the ball to another player before he can touch it again.

16. **Goal kicks.** These are given when the opposing team kick the ball over the opposing goal line, after a missed shot at goal, for example. The goal kick is taken from anywhere within the goal area and the ball must pass out of the penalty area before another player can touch it.

THE RULES OF SOCCER

17. **Corner kicks.** These are given when a member of the defending team knocks the ball over his own goal line. The goalkeeper may do this in the process of saving a goal, for example, or a defender may do it quite deliberately to prevent a shot reaching goal. Many goals are scored from corner kicks, so the tension is always high when one is given.

Defending players must remain at least 9.15 metres (10 yd) from the ball until it is kicked. In practice, they group themselves around the goalmouth. Defenders work hard to prevent attackers finding a free space. Attackers work to drop their marking defender, get the ball as it comes in and either head or kick it into the goal. A goalkeeper is hard-pressed during corners. Visibility is reduced due to the number of people involved and the ball can come from almost anywhere with very little time to react.

OTHER POINTS OF INTEREST

The goalkeeper is the only player able to use his hands. However, apart from the lower arms and hands, any other part of the body can be used to help control the ball.

If the game must be played to a conclusion (in a World Cup, for example), extra time can be given. There are various forms of this, but it usually involves two halves of fifteen minutes each. If the scores are still tied at the end of extra time, a penalty shootout is used to decide the winner. Five pre-arranged players take it in turns to shoot at the goal. If the scores are *still* tied, it goes to sudden-death penalties, one after the other until a winner is found.

One advantage that soccer has over rugby and hockey is the fact that if you have a wall, you can practise football forever. The other games really need someone else. There are many ball skills that must be experienced to be learned. It's all very well reading that you can bend the ball from right to left in the air by striking the bottom half of the right side of the ball with the inside of your foot, or left to right by using the outside of your foot on the bottom half of the left side of the ball. Realistically though, to make it work, you'll have to spend many, many hours practising. This is true of any sport – and for that matter any skill of any kind. If you want to be good at something, do it regularly. It's an old, old phrase, but "practice makes perfect" is as true today as it was hundreds of years ago. Natural-born skill is all very well, but it will only take you so far against someone who has practised every day at something he loves.

DINOSAURS

THE TERM "dinosaur" means "terrible lizard," and was coined by a British scientist, Richard Owen, in 1842. These reptiles roamed the earth for over 150 million years, then mysteriously died out. They varied from fierce killers to gentle plant eaters.

The largest dinosaurs were also the largest land animals ever to have existed. In 1907, the immense bones of a Brachiosaurus were discovered in east Africa. When alive, the animal would have been 23 metres (75 ft) long and weighed between 50 and 90 tons. Its shoulder height would have been 6.4 metres (21 ft) off the ground. These giants rivalled the largest whales in our present-day oceans. In comparison, the largest living land animals today, elephants, weigh only 5 tons!

Brachiosaurus – the "Arm lizard."

The Age of the Dinosaurs

The age of the dinosaurs is known as the Mesozoic era. This stretched from 248 to 65 million years ago. It divides into three separate time spans: the Triassic, the Jurassic and the Cretaceous. At the start of the Mesozoic era, all the continents of today's Earth were joined

	Eras	Periods
0	Cenozoic	Quaternary Tertiary
50		
	Mesozoic	Cretaceous
100		
150		Jurassic
200		
		Triassic
250	Paleozoic	Permian
		Pennsylvanian
300		Mississipian
350		Devonian
400		Silurian
450		Ordovician
500		Cambrian

Millions of years ago

together in one super continent – Pangaea. This was surrounded by a massive ocean called Panthalassa. These names sound quite impressive until you realize they mean "the whole earth" and "the whole sea." The German geophysicist Alfred Wegener first came up with the theory of moving tectonic plates, or "continental drift," in 1912. He examined similarities in rocks found as far apart as Brazil and southern Africa and realized they came from a single landmass.

The Triassic world saw the first small dinosaurs, walking on their hind legs. This period lasted from 248 to 206 million years ago. Over millions of years Pangaea split into continents and drifted apart. After separation, different groups of dinosaurs evolved on each continent during the Jurassic period from 206 to 144 million years ago. This was the era of the giants. Huge herbivorous dinosaurs roamed in forests and grassland that covered entire continents.

The continental "plates" are still moving today. In fact, wherever an area is prone to earthquakes or volcanoes, the cause is almost always one plate pushing against another, sometimes deep under the sea. The vast mountain ranges of the Andes and the Rockies were formed in this way.

The Cretaceous period lasted from 144 to 65 million years ago. This age included armoured plant eaters like Triceratops, browsers like Hadrosaur and huge meat eaters like the Tyrannosaurus Rex.

Canada can claim its own dinosaur, the Albertosaurus, named for Alberta, the province where its remains were first discovered. The Albertosaurus existed in the late Cretaceous period, from 65 to 99 million years ago. It was a predecessor of the Tyrannosaurus, and though it had large, sharp, serrated teeth like its more famous relative, its frame was smaller (3.5 to 4 metres [11.5 to 13 ft] tall) and its arms were longer. The first evidence of the Albertosaurus— a skull—was discovered by Joseph Burr Tyrrell in 1844 while Tyrrell, who had little geological education or experience, was exploring the area around present-day Drumheller, Alberta.

Albertosaurus.

The seas too were filled with predators and prey that were very different from the inhabitants of today – except for sharks, oddly enough, who seem to have reached a perfect state of evolution and then stuck there for millions of years. Crocodiles are another example of a dinosaur that survived to the modern world. Modern crocodiles and alligators are smaller than their prehistoric cousins, but essentially the same animals. A crocodile from the Cretaceous period would have stretched to 15 metres (49 ft)!

The World of the Dinosaurs

The dinosaurs' world was hot and tropical, and dinosaurs of many shapes and sizes roamed prehistoric Earth. One of the most interesting things about studying dinosaurs is seeing how evolution took a different path before the slate was wiped clean in 65 million years BC. Carnivores developed into efficient killing machines, while their prey either grew faster or more heavily armoured as the eras progressed – the original arms race, in fact. Huge herbivores could nibble leaves from tree tops as tall as a five-storey building. The largest were so immense that nothing dared attack a healthy adult, especially if they moved in herds. The herbivores must have eaten huge amounts of greenery each day to fill their massive bodies – with stones, perhaps, to grind up the food in their stomachs.

As well as the giants, the age of dinosaurs overshadowed a smaller world of predators and

Compsognathus – meaning "pretty jaw."

Ornithomimids.

prey. Compsognathus was only about the size of a modern house cat. We know it ate even smaller lizards, as one has been found preserved in a Compsognathus stomach cavity.

The fastest group of dinosaurs was probably the two-legged ornithomimids – the "ostrich mimics." It is always difficult to guess at speed from a fossil record alone, but with longer legs than Compsognathus, these dinosaurs may have been able to run as quickly as a modern galloping horse. They have been found as far apart as North America and Mongolia.

Carnivores and Vegetarians

During the Cretaceous period, gigantic meat eaters such as Tyrannosaurus, Daspletosaurus

Tyrannosaurus – 15 metres (49 ft) of ferocious predator. Note that we have no idea of the actual skin colour.

and Tarbosaurus ruled the land. The Tyrannosaurus Rex had up to sixty teeth that were as long as knives and just as sharp. Although the T-Rex was a fierce hunter, its huge size may have prevented it from moving quickly. It is possible that it

Velociraptor claw and toe bones.

charged at and head-butted its prey to stun them, then used its short arms to grip its victims while it ate them alive – though behaviour is difficult to judge from a fossil record alone. Much of the study of dinosaurs is based on supposition and guesswork – and until time travel becomes a reality, it always will be!

The Velociraptor was made famous by the film *Jurassic Park* as a smaller version of Tyrannosaurus, hunting in packs. It may have used teamwork to single out and attack victims. Velociraptors were certainly well equipped to kill, with sharp claws, razor-sharp teeth and agile bodies.

Stegosaurus.

Our experience of evolution and the modern world suggests that carnivore hunters are more intelligent than herbivores. In the modern world, for example, cows need very little intelligence to survive, while wolves and leopards are capable of far more complex behaviour. We apply the patterns we know to fill the gaps in the fossil record, but intelligence is one of those factors that is practically impossible to guess. If it were simply a matter of brain size, elephants would rule the land and whales would rule the sea.

Armour

One aspect of the age of dinosaurs that has practically vanished from ours is the use of armour for defence. It survives in tortoises, turtles and beetles, but otherwise, it has vanished as a suitable response to predators. By the end of the Mesozoic era, the arms race between predator and prey had produced some extraordinary examples of armoured herbivores. The Stegosaurus, meaning "covered" or "roof lizard," is one of the best-known examples and evolved in the mid to late Jurassic period, some 170 million years ago.

Stegosaurus was a huge plant eater about the length of a modern sixteen-wheel truck. The plates along its back would have made it much harder for a predator to damage a Stegosaurus' spine. In addition, it had a viciously spiked tail to lash out at its enemies. Some dinosaurs, like the Ankylosaurus, even had their eyelids armour-plated.

Triceratops means "three-horned face" and was named by Othniel C. Marsh, an American fossil hunter. It looked armoured for both attack and defence. It weighed up to 10 tons and its neck protector was a sheet of solid bone – clearly designed to prevent a biting attack on that vulnerable area. It was very common 65 to 70 million years ago in the late Cretaceous period.

The camouflage dinosaurs used is unknown. Skin just doesn't survive the way bones do and, for all we know, some dinosaurs could have been feathered or even furred. Today's animals leave some clues, however. Living relatives of dinosaurs, such as birds and crocodiles show how some dinosaurs may have been coloured. Large plant eaters like Iguanodon probably had green, scaly skin, and predators would have found them hard to spot among the forest ferns, very similar to today's lizards. Some carnivores may have also had green or brown colouring, to help them sneak up on prey. Successful hunters like the Velociraptor may have evolved light, sandy skin if they hunted in desert regions or brown savannah, just as leopards have done today.

Like modern crocodiles, dinosaurs laid eggs. Some dinosaurs would look after these until they hatched, like the Maiasaur, which means "mother lizard." The evidence for this comes from the first one found in Montana, in a preserved nest containing regurgitated vegetable

Elasmosaurus.

matter – suggesting that the parents returned to feed their babies as modern birds do. In addition, the leg bones of the fossilized babies do not seem strong enough to support the infants after birth, suggesting a vulnerable period spent in the nest. In comparison, modern-day crocodiles leave the egg as a fully functioning smaller version of the parent, able to swim and hunt.

In the skies of the Mesozoic era, the reptile ancestors of birds ruled. There were many varieties, though most come under the species genus name of *Pterodactylus* – meaning "winged fingers." Of all species on earth, the link to birds from the Mesozoic era is most obviously visible, with scaled legs, hollow bones, wings and beaks. Many of them resembled modern bats, with the finger bones clearly visible in the wing. As might be expected, however, the Jurassic produced some enormous varieties. The biggest flying animal that ever lived may have weighed as much as a large human being. It was called Quetzalcoatlus – named after the feathered ser-

pent god of Mexican legend. To support its weight it had a wing span of 12 metres (39 ft) – like that of a light aircraft. It was almost certainly a glider, as muscles to flap wings of that size for any length of time would have been too heavy to get airborne.

There were no icebergs in Mesozoic seas. In the strict sense of the word, there were no dinosaurs either, as dinosaurs were land animals. However, pre-historic oceans brimmed with a variety of strange and wonderful reptiles, like the giant sea serpent Elasmosaurus. The neck alone grew up to 7 metres (23 feet) long and today people believe that "Nessie," the Loch Ness monster, is a surviving descendant of an Elasmosaurus or some other plesiosaur, a similar breed.

Extinction

Hundreds of different dinosaurs roamed the earth 75 million years ago, yet 10 million years later they had all but died out. Only the birds, their descendants, survived, and what happened is still uncertain. An enormous crater in the Gulf of Mexico was almost certainly caused by a giant asteroid hitting Earth. The impact occurred 65 million years ago, at the same time that the dinosaurs disappeared. Soil samples from the boundary between the Cretaceous and Tertiary periods – the moment of geological time known as the KT boundary – are found to be rich in iridium, an element commonly found in meteors and asteroids.

The asteroid would have hit Earth at an incredible speed and dramatically changed the planet's atmosphere. Huge clouds of rock and dust would have covered the sun, blocking out light and, crucially, warmth. Some animals lived through the changes; scorpions, turtles, birds and insects were just some of those resilient enough to survive. There is no definite explanation for why the dinosaurs vanished, although the asteroid strike is widely supported in the scientific community – at least for the moment.

MAKING A BOW AND ARROW

At some point, you may consider making a bow and arrow. Perhaps because of the British history of using longbows at Agincourt and Crécy, firing an arrow can be immensely satisfying – not to hit anything, even, but just to see it fly and then pace out the metres. The bow in this chapter sent a heavy-tipped arrow 41 metres (45 yd), landing point first and sticking in.

Despite the fact that English archers at the battle of Crécy fired arrows 275 metres (300 yd), it was a glorious moment. The current world record is held by Harry Drake, an American, who fired an arrow in 1971, while lying on his back, to a distance of 1,854 metres (2,028 yd) – more than a mile (more than a km).

Don't spoil such moments by doing something stupid with yours. The bow and arrow here could be used for hunting or target practice in a garden. Remember at all times that it is a weapon. Weapons are **never** pointed at other children.

Arrows and Arrowheads

> **You will need**
>
> - Flint or bone for arrowheads.
> - Baked bean can.
> - Strong scissors and penknife.
> - Straight 1.2 metre (4 ft) lengths of springy wood, such as oak, maple or birch.
> - Straight 0.9 metres (1 yd) lengths for arrows.
> - Thread, glue.
> - Crosshead screwdriver.
> - String.
> - Feathers, usually found, or bought from a butcher.
> - Strip of leather to protect fingers.

There are a number of ways to make an arrowhead. Stone-Age man used flint, and it is still intriguing to make a simple arrowhead with this material. Flint is the fossilized remnant of small organisms. Our selection came from a ploughed field that was absolutely littered with pieces bigger than a fist. It is usually found with chalk – on what was once the bed of an ocean millions of years ago.

Find yourself a good big piece like the one on the right of the picture. One of the very few benefits of wearing glasses is that your eyes are better protected from shards. If you don't wear glasses, look away as you bring it down sharply on another flint lump or wear goggles.

You'll find that with enough of an impact, flint breaks like glass, forming razor-sharp edges that almost instantly suggest axeheads and arrows to you. We found that with a bit of luck, five or ten of these impacts would give you a handful of suitable pieces – shards that look as if they could be shaped into an arrowhead.

You may have seen pictures of Stone-Age flints with a series of scalloped semi-circles around the edge. These circles are formed by "knapping" (some-

times spelled "napping"), which is a difficult skill. Many people still do it as a hobby, producing ornate as well as functional arrowheads.

Using a pointed implement such as a small crosshead screwdriver, it is possible to nibble away at the sharp edge of a flint until the right shape is achieved. Place the flint on a piece of soft wood, with the edge touching the wood, then press the screwdriver head downwards against the very edge.

It's a slow and tiring process, but it does work and if it was the only way to kill a deer to feed your family, the time would be well spent. A grindstone, patience and spit can also produce quite decent arrowheads, though without that classic look. A combination of the techniques would also work well.

Remember to leave enough of a "handle" to bind into the arrow shaft – and expect to have a few break in half and be ruined before you have one you like.

The next one we produced with only a grindstone. It is very small at 17 millimetres (¾ in) long – but much larger and the arrow range will be reduced.

Bone also works well – and can be shaped on a sanding block very easily. We found that if you give a lamb bone to a big dog, the splinters he leaves behind can be turned into arrowheads without too much trouble.

The easiest arrowheads to make come from tin cans – baked beans, spaghetti, anything. The base and lid will be a flat metal surface. Use a good pair of scissors, and you might find it is very easy to cut yourself and spend the rest of the day at your local hospital. Ask an adult to help with this bit. Leave a long "handle," as in the picture. It will help keep the head securely in place.

Note that these are not that useful for target practice – they bend. They are probably better for hunting rabbits, though we found the movement of drawing an arrow scared living creatures away for half a kilometre in every direction. For target practice, the best thing is simply to sharpen the wooden arrow tip with a penknife and use a soft target – an old sweater stuffed with newspaper or straw.

The arrows themselves are traditionally made out of very thin, straight branches, whittled, trimmed and sanded until they are perfectly smooth. Dowel rods, however, are already perfectly straight and smooth and can be bought from any large hardware shop. The arrow we made is from an English elm, but any wood that doesn't splinter easily will do.

There are three important parts to making an arrow – getting it straight, attaching the point and attaching the feathers. The old word for "arrow maker" was "fletcher," and it is a skill all to itself.

If you have a metal tip, simply saw a slit in the end of your arrow, push the head into place and then tie strong thread securely around the arrow shaft to keep it steady. Attaching a flint head like this is only possible if it is a flat piece.

Now to fletch the arrow, you are going to need feathers. We used pheasant ones after seeing a dead pheasant on the side of the road. If this isn't possible, you'll have to go to any farm, ask at a butcher's or look for pigeon feathers in local parks. Goose feathers are the traditional favourite, but are not easy to find.

Make sure you have a good stock of them to hand. Feathers are much lighter than plastic and are still used by professional archers today.

With a penknife, or just scissors, cut this shape from the feather, keeping a little of the central quill to hold it together. You can still trim it when it's finished, so it doesn't have to be fantastically neat at this stage.

You should leave 2 centimetres (about 1 in) of bare wood at the end of the arrow to give you something to grip with your fingers as you draw. We forgot this until actually testing the bow.

Also note that the three feathers are placed 120 degrees apart from each other (3 × 120 = 360). The "cock feather" is the one at 90 degrees to the string slot, as in the picture below. Use your eye to place them on the shaft for gluing. During a shot, the arrow rests on the outside of the hand gripping the bow and the cock feather points towards the face of the archer. The other two feathers can then pass the bow at speed without hitting it.

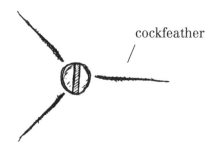

cockfeather

A touch of glue holds the feathers in place, but for tradition and for the look of the thing, you should tie a thread securely at one end, then wind it carefully through each of the three feathers until you reach the other end. This is a fiddly job, but strong thread will create an arrow that is a joy to behold. Tie both ends off carefully, trimming the ends of the thread.

It's a good idea to prepare five or six of these arrows. There is an excellent chance you are going to break a couple, or lose them. Use a little common sense here and don't fire them where they can disappear into someone else's backyard.

The Bow

Ideally, the wood for your bow should be straight and springy. It should be cut green and then left somewhere to dry for a year. However, our childhood experience of bow-making was that they were always made on the same day they were cut, so we did that again here. Oak works well, as do maple and birch. The most powerful bows come from a combination of yew sapwood and heartwood, the dense hedge tree found in every churchyard in Britain. In earlier times, Druids considered yew trees sacred and built temples close to them, beginning an association with places of worship that continues to this day. The red yew berries are extremely poisonous. Do not cut yew trees. They are ancient.

Freshly cut bows do lose their power after a day or two. They should not be strung unless you are ready to shoot and you should also experiment with different types of local woods for the best springiness.

The thing to remember is that the bow actually has to bend. It is tempting to choose a thick sapling for immediate power, but anything thicker than a couple of centimetres is probably too thick.

If you have access to carpentry tools, fix the bow gently into a vice and use a plane to taper the ends. Most ones you find in woods will have some degree of tapering, which can be redressed at this stage.

We cut all the notches and slots for this bow and arrow with a standard Swiss Army knife saw blade. However, a serrated-edge bread knife would do almost as well.

Cut notches in the head and foot of the bow, 5 centimetres (2 in) from the end. Use a little common sense here. You want to cut them just deep enough to hold the bowstring without slipping.

You'll need very strong, thin string – we found nylon to be the best. Fishing line snapped too easily. Traditional bowstrings were made from waxed linen or woven horsehair, forming miniature cables of immense strength. The Romans even used horsehair to form great springs for their war catapults!

The knot you'll need is a good all-rounder, from tying up a canal boat to stringing a bow. Its advantage is that the actual knot isn't tightened under pressure, so it can always be loosened when you need to move on. It is called "the round turn and two half-hitches."

First wind your rope fully around the bow end, as shown. This is the "round turn." Then pass the end under the bowstring and back through the loop – a half hitch. Pull tight. Finally, do another hitch in the same way: under the string, back through the loop and away. You should end up with a knot that doesn't touch the bow wood but is very solid.

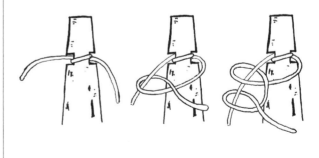

As a final note, it is a very good idea to wear a glove on the hand that holds the bow as you draw back the string. The arrow passes over it at speed and can take skin off. Also, we found it much easier to pull the string back if we had strips of leather wound around the second and third fingers. You can probably get a piece of leather from a furniture shop as a sample, or an upholsterer's offcut bin. Alternatively, you could just wear another glove. It may interest you to know that the rude gesture of sticking two fingers up at someone came from the English archers at Agincourt. The French had said that they would cut off the arrow-pulling fingers of those men when they beat them. Instead, the French were defeated and the archers mocked them by showing off their fingers – still attached.

Archery can be a fascinating and highly skilful sport and this isn't a bad way to start.

UNDERSTANDING GRAMMAR – PART ONE

I'T'S STRANGE HOW SATISFYING it can be to know right from wrong. Grammar is all about rules and structure. It is *always* "between you and me," for example. If you hear someone say "between you and I," it isn't a matter of opinion, they're just wrong.

The grammar of English is more complex than can be contained here, but a skeleton of basics is well within our reach. You wouldn't use a chisel without knowing how to hold it. In the same way, you really should know the sharp end from the blunt one in everything else you use – including your language. The English language is spoken by more people on Earth than any other, after all.

The first thing to know is that there are only nine kinds of words. Nine.

NOUN

1. **Nouns** are the names of things. There are three kinds. Proper nouns have capital letters: e.g. "Ottawa." Abstract nouns are the things that exist but you can't touch: "courage," "loyalty," "cruelty," "kindness." Common nouns are the words for everything else: "chair," "eyes," "dog," "car" and so on.

VERB

2. **Verbs** are words for action or change: "to become," "to wash," "to dissect," "to eat" and so on. There are six parts to each verb, known as first-person singular, second-person singular, third-person singular, first-person plural, second-person plural and third-person plural.

   Most verbs follow this simple pattern:

To deliver	
First-person singular:	*I deliver*
Second-person singular:	*You deliver*
Third-person singular:	*He/She/It delivers* – note the "s"
First-person plural:	*We deliver*
Second-person plural:	*You deliver*
Third-person plural:	*They deliver*

Irregular verbs such as "to be" and "to have" are not as . . . well, not as regular. They must be learned.

To be	**To have**
I am	*I have*
You are	*You have*
He/She/It is	*He/She/It has*
We are	*We have*
You are	*You have*
They are	*They have*

Note that the second person "you" is the same in the singular and plural. In older forms of English, you would have used "thou" as second-person singular. In modern English it makes no difference whether you are addressing one man or a thousand. You could still begin as follows: "You are responsible for your behaviour."

ADVERB

3. **Adverbs** are the words that modify verbs, adjectives and other adverbs. They are important as there is a huge difference between "smiling nastily" and "smiling cheerfully." Clearly the verb is not enough on its own.

   Most adverbs end in "-ly," as with the examples above.

   If you say, "I'll go to the store tomorrow," however, "tomorrow" is an adverb, because it adds detail to that verb "go." Words like "soon" and "often" also fall into this category. As a group, these are sometimes known as "adverbs of time."

   As mentioned above, an adverb can also add detail to an adjective. "It is really big" uses "really" as an adverb. "It is very small" uses "very" as an adverb. He walked "extremely quietly" uses "extremely" as an adverb for an adverb! This is not rocket science. Take it slowly and learn it all bit by bit.

ADJECTIVE

4. **Adjectives** are words that modify nouns. In "the enormous snake," "enormous" is the adjective. More than one can be used together, thus: "the small, green snake."

   As a general rule, adjectives come before the noun. However, as always with English, rules have many exceptions: "That snail is *slimy*!", for example.

PRONOUN

5. **Pronouns** are words that replace nouns in a sentence. It would sound clumsy to say "John looked in John's pockets." Instead, we say "John looked in *his* pockets." "His" is a pronoun.

   Here are some examples: *I, you, he, she, we, they – me, you, him, her, us, them – my, your, his, her, our, their.*

   "One" is also used in place of "people in general," as in the following sentence: "One should always invest in reliable stocks." The informal form of this is "you," but it does sometimes lead to confusion, which keeps this unusual use of "one" alive. The Queen also uses the "we" form in place of "I" during formal announcements.

CONJUNCTION

6. A **conjunction** is a word that joins parts of a sentence together. "I tied the knot *and* hoped for the best." Tying the knot is a separate action to hoping for the best, joined by the word "and." Conjunctions can also join adjectives, "short and snappy," or adverbs "slowly but surely."

   Examples: *and, so, but, or, if, although, though, because, since, when, as, while, nor.*

   The general rule is: "A sentence does not begin with a conjunction." Yes, you will find examples where sentences do begin with a conjunction. Professional writers do break this rule, but you should know it to break it – and even then, do it carefully.

   The examples above are fairly straightforward. It does get a little trickier when a conjunction is used to introduce a subordinate clause. (Clauses are covered in Grammar – Part Two.)

   "Although he was my only friend, I hated him." (Although)

   "As I'm here, I'll have a drink." (As)

   In these two examples, the sentences have been rearranged to change the emphasis. It would have been clearer, perhaps, to write, "I'll have a drink as I'm here," or "I hated him although he was my only friend." It's easier to see "although" and "as" are being used as joining words in that way, but many sentences begin with a subordinate clause.

ARTICLE

7. **Articles** are perhaps the easiest to remember: "a," "an" and "the." That's it.

   "A/an" is the **indefinite article**. Used when an object is unknown. "A dog is in my garden." "An elephant is sitting on my father."

   "The" is the **definite article**. "The dog is in my garden" can refer to a particular dog. "The elephant is sitting on my father" can mean only one elephant – one we already know: a family pet, perhaps.

   "An" is still sometimes used for words that begin with a clearly sounded "h": "an historical battle," "an horrendous evil" and so on. It is seen as old-fashioned, though, and using "a" is becoming more acceptable.

PREPOSITION

8. **Prepositions** are words that mark the position or relationship of one thing with respect to another. Examples: *in, under, over, between, before, behind, through, above, for, with, at and from.*

   "He fell from grace" demonstrates "from" as a preposition. Another example is "He lived *before* Caesar," or "I stood *with* Caesar."

INTERJECTION

9. This is another of the easier types of words. **Interjections** are simple sounds used to express an inward feeling such as sorrow, surprise, pain or anger. This can be a wide group, as almost anything can be said in this way. Obvious examples are: *Oh! What? Hell! Eh? Goodness gracious!*

   Note the last one – interjections don't have to be a single word. It could be a whole phrase such as "Holy Mackinaw!" or a complex oath. They tend to stand on their own and often have exclamation marks following them.

That is all nine.

Bearing in mind that English has more words than any other language on Earth, it is quite impressive that there are only nine kinds of words. The first part of grammar is to learn those nine well and be able to identify them in a sentence. If you have, you should be able to name each of the eight kinds of words used in the following sentence. If it helps, we didn't use a conjunction.

"No! I saw the old wolf biting viciously at his leg."

(Answer: "No!" – interjection, "I" – pronoun, "saw" – verb, "the" – definite article, "old" – adjective, "wolf" – common noun, "biting" – verb, "viciously" – adverb, "at" – preposition, "his" – pronoun, "leg" – common noun. Eight different types.)

TABLE FOOTBALL

T HIS IS A SIMPLE GAME, but it does require some skill and practice. It used to keep us occupied during French lessons.

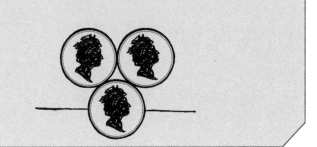

You will need

- A flat, smooth surface – a school table, for example.
- Three quarters are best.

1. Place the coins on the close edge of the table, as in the diagram. The first blow must be struck with the heel of the hand against the coin half over the edge. The three coins will separate. From then on, only the coin closest to the player can be touched.

2. The aim of the game is to pass the coins up the table by firing the closest through the two farther up. If you don't get the coin through, that's the end of your turn and your opponent begins again from his side of the table. Just one finger is usually used to flick the coins. They should always be in contact with the table, so a great deal of the skill is in judging the force as well as planning ahead.

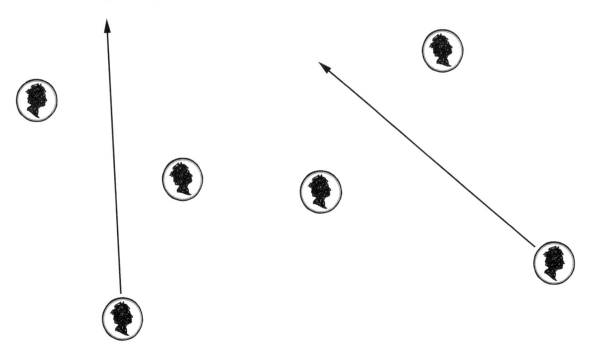

3. After a few of these "passes," the opposing goal comes into range. This is provided by the other player, as shown.

4. If the goal shot misses, the game is lost. If the shooting coin strikes one of the other two, the game is also lost.

In the rugby version of the game, tries are scored rather than goals, and they are worth five points. The scorer then has an opportunity to gain two more points by converting the try. This is difficult, to say the very least.

1. The opposing player rearranges his goal into a rugby-post formation, as in the picture.

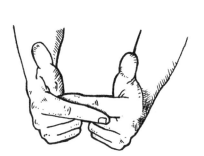

2. The goal or shooter coin must first be spun in place. *As it spins*, the coin must be gripped as shown in the picture and flipped over the posts in one smooth motion. No hesitation is allowed for aiming. This is not at all easy to do, which is as it should be.

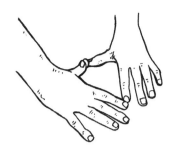

3. Play to an agreed number, or perhaps to win the coins.

FISHING

FISHERMEN ARE *NOT* PATIENT. Anticipation and concentration can make fishing an exhausting sport. It is a mainly solitary occupation. You hardly ever see people fishing in groups, laughing and chatting with each other, or drinking alcohol and singing. Fishermen can spend the day in silence. Even if you never catch anything, lazy afternoons spent fishing in the summer can be relaxing, rewarding – and addictive.

A simple starter kit—a rod, reel, bait, floats, lead weights and hooks—can be put together for less than forty dollars. As a legal requirement, you may need to purchase a fishing licence. Check your provincial and local laws to see what permits are required. The local fishing store will have the equipment and will be able to give you good advice about licences and local fishing grounds.

The classic fishing method is with a float. Maggots or worms are spiked on a hook suspended from a float that bobs on the surface. Push the hook through the blunt end of the maggot, taking care not to burst it, as it dies faster.

It tends to be necessary to place a couple of ball lead weights on the line to keep the float upright. Ask in the fishing shop if you're not sure how.

Cast carefully as a hook catching in your eyebrow is a deeply unpleasant experience. Watch out for overhead cables or tree branches. Your spool will have two settings – one for casting and one for retrieving the hook. Allow it to run loose and cast the hook and float upstream and allow the hook to come downstream towards you in the current. The first moment when that float dips is an experience to be treasured. Otherwise, wind back in slowly and try it again, replacing your maggots when they no longer move. If it's a nice day, find a place to sit and enjoy the peace that lasts until someone comes along and says, "Any luck?"

The second classic involves a heavier lead weight that keeps the hook on the bottom. Fish taking the bait feel no resistance. This works well with carp.

It should be clear that the method depends on the fish. Pike and perch tend to attack injured or dying fish. As a result, they can be caught using a "spinner," a device that resembles a wounded fish as it moves through the water. Many anglers use complex lures that mimic insects on the surface. In Canada, you're most likely to catch one of the following:

Bluegill (*Lepomis macrochirus*).
Bluegill are a member of the sunfish
family and one of the smallest game
fishes, but despite their small size,
they're fighters on the line, so don't
underestimate them! Sunfish like
warmer water and cover. Look for
them in shallow spots of a lake, pond
or slow-moving river, especially
around places they can hide, such as
in weed beds, under a floating dock or
near rocks.

Lake trout (*Salvelinus namaycush*).
Lake trout are the biggest trout in
North America. In the summer they
swim pretty deep, so you'll need special deep-water tackle. In the spring
and fall, though, they're closer to the
surface. And be on the lookout for big
ones—a 46-kilogram (102-lb) lake
trout was caught in Lake Athabasca,
Saskatchewan, in 1961!

Largemouth bass (*Micropterus
salmoides*). Largemouth bass are big
brawling fish and they like to eat!
Largemouth bass hide and ambush
their prey, so you should have luck
with most bait or lures in weedy,
slow-moving, warm water. Later in
the fishing season, largemouth bass
are more sluggish and remain closer
to the bottom.

Muskellunge (*Esox masquinongy*).
Commonly called "muskies," they're the largest freshwater game fish, but they're found mostly in Ontario and Quebec. Muskies are known for their leaping and fighting tactics, and because they can be big, they're not the easiest fish to catch.

Northern pike (*Esox lucius*).
Sometimes called the jackfish, some people also refer to them as the "wolf of the fresh waters" because they have an insatiable appetite and often hang out in weedy spots, attacking anything that swims by. Try fishing around sheltered areas and you might catch a big one—it's not unusual to catch one that is 9 kilograms (20 lb).

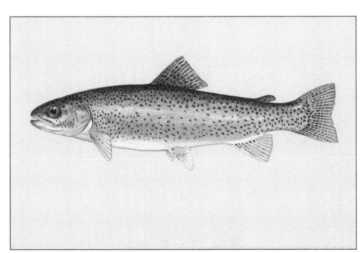

Rainbow trout (*Salmo gairdneri*).
Rainbow trout are found across Canada—and even in Newfoundland, where this fish was introduced in 1887. You can spot rainbow trout easily because of their distinctive look, but their colouring can change depending on their environment. The long, horizontal stripe on their side, for example, can vary from light pink to red to purple. Rainbow trout prefer cold, swift-flowing water, and on the Pacific coast, rainbow trout—known there as steelheads—sometimes head out to sea.

Smallmouth bass (*Micropterus dolomieu*). Not surprisingly, "smallies" have a smaller mouth than largemouth bass. The jaw of a smallmouth ends just below the eye, and the mouth in a largemouth can extend past its eyes. Smallmouth prefer cooler water than their cousins, and tend to like rocky and sandy areas of lakes and rivers.

Walleye (*Stizostedion vitreum*). Also called pickerel, walleye have a special membrane in their eyes that gives them very good eyesight in poor light conditions. They're often looking for food in the early morning and at sunset. Since they are sensitive to light, walleyes look for shelter and tend to be close to the bottom of the lake during the day.

Yellow perch (*Perca flavescens*). Yellow perch like the open water and often move in schools, so cast widely and chances are that if you find one, you can might catch a lot more. Perch prefer natural bait such as minnows, earthworms or insects, but since they're small (usually 100 to 300 grams) they're often prey to other bigger fish.

There are too many other types of fish to include here – the rivers and lakes teem with them.

"Game fishing" is a specific reference to the salmon family: salmon, trout, char and grayling. "Coarse" fish have five fins – ventral, anal, dorsal, pectoral and caudal. Members of the salmon family all have one extra fin close to the tail – known as the adipose fin. Salmon are born from eggs laid in rivers and swim to the sea, where they live for one to three years. After that, they return by instinct to the river where they were born to breed, in what is known as the "spawning season." They are caught as they travel upstream, with a lure containing a hook.

Catching a fish can be exciting – the real skill is not in hooking one but in bringing it in without breaking the line or losing the fish. As a final note, try reading the classic fishing tale by Ernest Hemingway – *The Old Man and the Sea*. Happy fishing.

TIMERS AND TRIPWIRES

You will need

- Old alarm clock.
- Bulb.
- Two pieces of insulated electrical wire with bare copper ends.
- Adhesive tape.
- Battery – C or D size.

These are very simple to make – and deeply satisfying. For the timer, any wind-up alarm clock will do – preferably one with plastic hands. The idea is to use the clock to complete a circuit and turn on a light. You want the bulb to turn on in twenty minutes – to win a bet perhaps, or to frighten your little sister with the thought that a mad axe murderer is upstairs.

First, remove the plastic front of the clock. Tape wire to each hand, so that when one passes under the other, the bare ends will touch. It should be clear that a circuit can now be made with a time delay of however long it takes the minute hand to travel around and touch the hour hand.

Attach one of the wires to a positive battery terminal. Tape a flashlight bulb to the negative terminal and the end of the other wire to the end of the bulb. Test it a few times by touching the hands of the clock together. The bulb should light as the wires on the hands touch and complete the circuit.

Bear in mind that the hour hand will have moved by the time the minute hand comes round, so it's worth timing how long it takes for the bulb to light after setting the minute hand to, say, fifteen minutes before the hour. You can then terrify your young sister with the threat of the murderer upstairs.

TRIPWIRE

This is almost the same thing, in that it uses a battery circuit with a bulb linked to a switch – in this case a tripwire. With a long enough wire, the bulb can be lit some way from the actual trip switch for longer warning times.

Wrap foil around the ends of the wooden or plastic clothes pins. Attach your wires with tape to those foil ends, running both to exactly the same battery and bulb set-up as the alarm-clock switch above.

The important thing is to have a non-conducting item between the jaws of the clothes peg. We found a wine cork worked quite well. The wire itself must also be strong enough to pull the cork out – if it snaps, the bulb won't light. Fishing wire is perfect for this as it's strong and not that easy to see. It is also important to secure the clothes peg under a weight of some kind. Only the cork should move when the wire is pulled.

When the cork is pulled out, the jaws of the peg snap shut, touching the foil ends together, completing the circuit and lighting the bulb to alert you.

This works especially well in long grass, but its main disadvantage is that whoever trips the switch tends to know it has happened. Enemy soldiers would be put on the alert, knowing they were in trouble. Of course, in a real conflict, the wire would have pulled out the pin to a grenade.

PRESSURE PLATE

One way of setting up a trip warning without the person realizing is with a pressure plate. Again, this relies on a simple bulb circuit, but this time the wires go to two pieces of cardboard held apart by a piece of squashable foam. A bit of sponge would also be perfect.

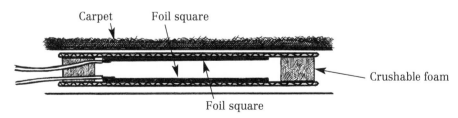

Carpet   Foil square

Crushable foam

Foil square

This time, tape foil squares over the bare ends of the wires on the inner surfaces of the cardboard and set up a simple bulb and battery circuit as before. With only light pressure from above, the two bits of cardboard come together, bringing the foil squares into contact. The circuit is made and the warning bulb comes on. Enjoy.

HOCKEY HIGHLIGHTS

———— ✤ ————

IT IS MORE THAN 130 YEARS since a group of McGill University students gathered at the Victoria Skating Rink in Montreal to play a game of hockey. *The Gazette* reported on that match, and this news story is the earliest known eyewitness account of a game in which the place, time, players and final score are all identified. Since then, there have been thousands of great moments and stories about outstanding players and games. Here are just a few of them.

1877 – *The Gazette* (Montreal) publishes the first-known rules of hockey a few weeks after a group of McGill University students found the world's first organized hockey club. Though similar games on ice have been developing for centuries, the sport as we know it begins to take real shape.

1880s – Rubber hockey pucks are introduced. Previously, hockey players used pucks made of wood, or lacrosse balls, stones, lumps of coal – and even frozen cow or horse poop.

1889 – The governor general of Canada, Lord Frederick Arthur Stanley of Preston, and his family witness a hockey tournament at the Montreal Winter Carnival. Several of his children – Arthur, Algernon, Edward and Isobel – become avid hockey players.

1890s – Players begin to wear shin pads.

1892 – Lord Stanley donates a trophy called the Dominion Hockey Challenge Cup, which becomes famous as the Stanley Cup. It is first awarded to the team members from the Montreal Amateur Athletic Association, players who are the champions of the Amateur Hockey Association of Canada. The Cup becomes property of the National Hockey League in 1926. It is the oldest trophy competed for by professional athletes in North America.

1895 – The first series of international matches is played between college players from the United States and Canada. Canada wins all four games.

1896 – George Merritt of the Winnipeg Victorias becomes the first goaltender to wear leg pads. During the Stanley Cup challenge game against the Montreal Victorias, he puts on a pair of cricket pads.

1900 – The goal net is introduced. Previously, goal nets consisted of a pair of posts at each end of the rink. And before that, rocks served as "goalposts."

1910 – Games change from two thirty-minute halves to three twenty-minute periods.

1911 – The National Hockey Association (NHA) switches from seven players per side to six.

1910s – Players begin to wear shoulder and elbow pads. Numbers begin to appear on hockey sweaters.

1917 – Four teams from the old NHA – Montreal Canadiens, Montreal Wanderers, Ottawa Senators and Quebec Bulldogs – form the new National Hockey League. When Quebec is unable to bring a team to the ice, a Toronto club is brought on board. After changing names and owners several times, this team becomes known as the Maple Leafs in 1927.

1918 – NHL players are allowed to pass the puck forward, as long as they are between the blue lines.

1919 – The Stanley Cup final, played in Seattle, Washington, is cancelled when players fall ill in the midst of an influenza epidemic. The Montreal Canadiens' star defenceman, "Bad Joe" Hall, dies in a Seattle hospital.

1920 – Hockey is introduced, strangely, at the Summer Olympics in Antwerp, Belgium. The Winnipeg Falcons, representing Canada, win the gold medal by defeating Sweden, 12–1.

1924 – Canada wins the gold medal in ice hockey at the first Olympic Winter Games in Chamonix, France.

1924 – In the first NHL game played in the United States, the Boston Bruins beat the Montreal Maroons, 2–1.

1937 – The first rule against icing the puck is introduced.

1945 – Maurice "The Rocket" Richard of the Montreal Canadiens becomes the first player in NHL history to score fifty goals in a single season.

Maurice "The Rocket" Richard, the legendary Montreal Canadiens player and the highest goal-scorer of his era.

1946 – The renowned player Gordie Howe, "Mr. Hockey," makes his NHL debut, playing for the Detroit Red Wings.

1949 – Ice rink owner Frank J. Zamboni receives a patent for a new apparatus. In 1955, the Zamboni ice-resurfacing machine makes its NHL debut during a game in Montreal on March 10.

1952 – In a game on March 23 against the Rangers, Bill Mosienko of Chicago scores three goals in twenty-one seconds—the fastest hat trick in history.

1952 – *Hockey Night in Canada* makes its CBC Television debut.

1959 – Canadiens goaltender Jacques Plante becomes the first goalie to wear a mask on a regular basis. (Clint Benedict of the Montreal Maroons wore a leather mask to protect a broken nose in a couple of games in 1930.) During a game on November 1, Plante is hit in the face by a puck shot from Andy Bathgate of the New York Rangers. Plante needs several stitches and refuses to re-enter the game without his mask.

1960 – The United States team wins the gold medal at the Olympic Winter Games in Squaw Valley, California.

1960 – The Montreal Canadiens win the Stanley Cup for a record fifth time in a row.

1961 – The Hockey Hall of Fame opens in Toronto, Ontario.

1962 – On November 7, goalie Glenn Hall of the Chicago Black Hawks leaves a game against Boston because of a back injury. It is his 503rd game in a row.

1963 – The NHL holds its first draft, in Montreal. The six teams select twenty-one amateur players in all.

1965 – All teams must have two goalies in uniform for each game. Previously, the home team would have had a spare goalie (an amateur or a practice goalie) standing by in case either team's goalie was injured too badly to play.

1966 – Bobby Hull scores fifty-four goals, breaking Rocket Richard's record.

1967 – In an expansion that doubles the size of the league, teams are added in Pittsburgh, Los Angeles, Minnesota, Oakland, St. Louis and Philadelphia.

1969 – Phil Esposito becomes the first NHL player to score 100 points in a season. Hull breaks his own record with fifty-eight goals.

Bobby Orr scores the Stanley Cup–winning goal against the St. Louis Blues in 1970.

1970 – Bobby Orr of the Boston Bruins wins the NHL scoring crown. He repeats the feat in 1975. To date, he is still the only defenceman in history to lead the league in points.

1971 – Esposito shatters the NHL records for goals and points in a season with 76 and 152.

1972 – The World Hockey Association (WHA) debuts with twelve teams, including the Miami Screaming Eagles, who never make it to the ice. The WHA lures several players away from the NHL. Bobby Hull leaves the Chicago Blackhawks for the Winnipeg Jets, who sign him to the game's first million-dollar deal.

Team Canada celebrates its victory against the Soviet Union during the Summit Series in 1972.

1972 – In the now-legendary Summit Series, Team Canada faces off against the Soviet Union in an eight-game series. Canada wins the last three games in a row to defeat the Russians.

1974 – On April 7, in a game against Atlanta, Andy Brown becomes the last NHL goalie to play without a mask. He signs with Indianapolis of the WHA the following season and continues to play maskless for three more seasons.

1979 – The World Hockey Association shuts down. The Quebec Nordiques, Hartford Whalers, Winnipeg Jets and Edmonton Oilers join the NHL.

1979 – All new NHL players must wear helmets. Those who are already in the league are given the choice of playing without one. Craig MacTavish is the last player to play without a helmet. He retires in 1997.

1980 – On February 24, Wayne Gretzky, a nineteen-year-old playing for the Edmonton Oilers, becomes the first player in history to score 100 points before turning twenty.

1980 – The American "Miracle on Ice" team wins the gold medal at the Olympic Winter Games in Lake Placid, New York.

1981 – Gordie Howe announces his retirement (for the second time) from the NHL. He has played twenty-six NHL seasons, along with six more in the WHA. He holds NHL records for goals (801), assists (1,049) and points (1,850) in a career. Gretzky scores 164 points, setting a new single-season record.

1982 – Gretzky scores 92 goals and 212 points in one season, shattering all previous marks.

1983 – A new rule calls for five minutes of sudden-death overtime to be played if the score is tied at the end of the third period. Overtime was an original feature of NHL games but was discontinued during World War II because of restrictions on train travel.

1984 – The Pittsburgh Penguins draft rookie Mario Lemieux. He becomes one of the greatest players in the game's history.

1988 – The hockey world is shocked when Wayne Gretzky is traded to the Los Angeles Kings after ten record-setting years with the Edmonton Oilers.

1989 – On October 15, Gretzky scores the 1,851st point of his career, breaking Gordie Howe's all-time record.

1990 – The first Women's World Hockey Championship is played. Canada wins.

1992 – Manon Rheaume becomes the first woman to play in the NHL. She tends goal for the Tampa Bay Lightning in an exhibition game.

1994 – Gretzky scores the 802nd goal of his career, breaking Gordie Howe's all-time mark.

1998 – The United States wins the first Olympic gold medal in women's hockey, beating Canada.

1998 – The NHL begins to use two referees in selected league games.

1999 – Considered one of the greatest players of all time, Wayne Gretzky retires after a twenty-year career in which he set records for goals (894), assists (1,963), and points (2,857).

2001 – The Michigan State University Spartans play the University of Michigan Wolverines outdoors at Spartan Stadium. The game, a 3–3 tie, is watched by 74,544 fans – the biggest crowd ever to watch a hockey game.

2002 – The NHL rules that, to honour Wayne Gretzky, no player will ever wear his number, ninety-nine, again.

Goalie Martin Brodeur celebrates the Canadian team's gold medal win at the 2002 Salt Lake City Winter Olympic Games.

2002 – NHL players compete for the first time in the Winter Olympics in Salt Lake City. Canada defeats the United States and wins the gold medal fifty years to the day after their last Olympic gold medal. The Canadian women's team wins gold too, also by beating the U.S. team.

2003 – For the first time, an NHL regular-season game is played outdoors. On November 22, the Edmonton Oilers and Montreal Canadiens face off before more than 57,000 fans at Commonwealth Stadium in Edmonton, where the temperature at game time is between –15 °Celsius and –20 °Celsius. The Canadiens win, 4–3.

2003 – Goaltender Patrick Roy retires. He holds the NHL records for games played (1,029) and victories (551) by a goalie.

2005 – Canada beats Russia in the World Junior Championship to win the gold medal. The Canadian Juniors win gold again in 2006 and 2007.

2005 – The NHL becomes the first major North American sports league to cancel an entire season because of a labour dispute. For only the second time in the trophy's history, there is no Stanley Cup champion.

2005 – The NHL introduces new rules, including the removal of the centre red line and a crackdown on obstruction, to entice fans back after the lockout.

2007 – Sidney Crosby becomes the youngest scoring champion in NHL history at age nineteen, with 120 points. Goalie Martin Brodeur sets a new record for victories in a season, with 48.

2008 – Brodeur racks up his seventh forty-win season (no other goalie has had more than three) and becomes the second goalie in the NHL to win 500 games.

THE IRON MEN OF HOCKEY

W HEN YOU CONSIDER that injuries are a fact of life in the NHL, it's no surprise that so few players get through an eighty-two-game schedule without missing at least one. In the 2007–2008 season, only eighty-nine team members had perfect attendance. The players on this list are even more special because they managed to string together season after season without a night off.

Two of these streaks were broken for reasons other than injuries. Andy Hebenton's run lasted for his entire nine-year NHL career and ended only when the Boston Bruins sent him to the minor leagues. Hebenton was an "iron man" in the minors too. According to hockey historian Patrick Houda, he played in 216 straight games for the Victoria Cougars before breaking into the NHL and another 216 for Portland and Victoria after he was sent back down – that comes to a total of 1,062 consecutive professional games.

Steve Larmer was just one season away from breaking Doug Jarvis' all-time record of 964 games played consecutively, but he couldn't agree on a new contract with his team, the Chicago Blackhawks, in time for the start of the 1993–1994 season, and he ended up missing the first several games.

Brendan Morrison of the Vancouver Canucks came close to making the "perfect attendance" list. In December 2007, a wrist injury ended his streak at 542. In February 2007, another lengthy streak ended when a knee injury sidelined Colorado defenceman Karlis Skrastins. He had appeared in 495 games in a row, more than any defenceman in NHL history.

What about goalies? Now we're talking about a record that may never be broken. Between 1955 and 1962, Glenn Hall played 502 straight games – more than 30,000 minutes of hockey. A back injury forced him onto the bench in the opening minutes of game number 503.

	Player	Years	Games
1.	Doug Jarvis	1975–1988	964
2.	Garry Unger	1968–1979	914
3.	Steve Larmer	1982–1993	884
4.	Craig Ramsay	1972–1983	776
5.	Andy Hebenton	1955–1964	630
6.	Johnny Wilson	1952–1961	580
7.	Billy Harris	1972–1979	576
8.	Mark Recchi	1991–1998	570
9.	Danny Grant	1968–1975	555
10.	Alex Delvecchio	1956–1964	548

HOCKEY DYNASTIES

The National Hockey League was formed in 1917 with just four teams, all of them from Canada. Various teams joined and disbanded until 1942, when the league settled down to the "Original Six" teams: Boston Bruins, Chicago Black Hawks, Detroit Red Wings, Montreal Canadiens, New York Rangers and Toronto Maple Leafs. In 1967, the NHL doubled in size to twelve teams, and six more were added between 1970 and 1974. In 1972 a second major pro league, the World Hockey Association, was launched with twelve teams, and people began to take it seriously when NHL star Bobby Hull signed with the Winnipeg Jets. The WHA folded in 1979 and four of its teams then joined the NHL. The NHL began growing again during the 1990s and today is made up of thirty teams.

EARLY YEARS

Boston Bruins
1924

Chicago Black Hawks
1926

Detroit Cougars 1926
(name changed to
Falcons in 1930, then
to Red Wings in 1932)

Montreal Canadiens
1917 (founded in 1909)

New York Rangers
1926

Toronto Arenas 1917
(name changed to
St. Patricks in 1919, then
to Maple Leafs in 1927)

'67 EXPANSION

Minnesota North Stars
1967

Los Angeles Kings
1967

Philadelphia Flyers
1967

Pittsburgh Penguins
1967

St. Louis Blues
1967

California Seals
(renamed Oakland Seals
and then the California
Golden Seals)
1967

1970s

Buffalo Sabres 1970

Atlanta Flames 1970

New England Whalers (WHA)
1967 (name changed to
Hartford Whalers when
team joined NHL in 1979)

Quebec Nordiques (WHA)
1972 (joined NHL in 1979)

Alberta Oilers (WHA) 1972
(renamed Edmonton Oilers
in 1973, joined NHL in 1979)

Kansas City Scouts 1974
(moved to Denver and
became Colorado Rockies in
1976)

New York Islanders 1972

Winnipeg Jets (WHA)
(joined NHL in 1979)

Vancouver Canucks 1970

Washington Capitals 1974

Cleveland Barons 1976
(moved from Oakland;
merged with Minnesota
North Stars in 1978)

1980S	1990S	NHL TODAY
Calgary Flames 1980 (moved from Atlanta)	Mighty Ducks of Anaheim 1993 (renamed the Anaheim Ducks in 2006)	Anaheim Ducks
		Atlanta Thrashers
		Boston Bruins
Chicago Blackhawks 1986 (spelling of name changed)	Atlanta Thrashers 1999	Buffalo Sabres
		Calgary Flames
		Carolina Hurricanes
New Jersey Devils (moved from Denver)	Carolina Hurricanes 1997 (moved from Hartford)	Chicago Blackhawks
		Colorado Avalanche
		Columbus Blue Jackets
	Colorado Avalanche 1995 (moved from Quebec)	Dallas Stars
		Detroit Red Wings
		Edmonton Oilers
	Columbus Blue Jackets 2000	Florida Panthers
		Los Angeles Kings
		Minnesota Wild
	Dallas Stars 1993 (moved from Minnesota)	Montreal Canadiens
		Nashville Predators
		New Jersey Devils
	Florida Panthers 1993	New York Islanders
		New York Rangers
		Ottawa Senators
	Minnesota Wild 2000	Philadelphia Flyers
		Phoenix Coyotes
		Pittsburgh Penguins
	Nashville Predators 1998	San Jose Sharks
		St. Louis Blues
		Tampa Bay Lightning
	Ottawa Senators 1998	Toronto Maple Leafs
		Vancouver Canucks
		Washington Capitals
	Phoenix Coyotes 1996 (moved from Winnipeg)	
	San Jose Sharks 1991	
	Tampa Bay Lightning 1992	

SOME EARLY NHL TEAMS THAT DIDN'T MAKE IT

During the "Roaring Twenties," it seemed that every city wanted an NHL team. Six new teams joined the league, while cities and team names changed frequently. The NHL shrank almost as quickly during the Great Depression of the 1930s, when money was tight. By 1942, there were just six teams, and that's the way things stayed until 1967. Here are the stories of those early NHL teams that didn't make it.

Quebec Bulldogs (1917–1920), Hamilton Tigers (1920–1925), New York Americans (1925–1941), Brooklyn Americans (1941–1942)

The Quebec Bulldogs' roots go all the way back to 1888, and they won the Stanley Cup in 1912 and 1913. The Bulldogs were original NHL members but the team's owner couldn't afford to put them on the ice. The Bulldogs finally played in the 1919–1920 season but finished last. A new owner brought them to Hamilton, where they became the Tigers.

In 1924–1925, the Tigers actually earned first place. But the players were upset that the season had been extended to thirty games while they were still paid for only twenty-four. They went on strike just before the Stanley Cup playoffs. NHL president Frank Calder disqualified the Tigers. That summer, a New Yorker, Bill Dwyer, took over the team and renamed them the Americans.

The next year, the New York Rangers joined the NHL. While the Rangers won Stanley Cup titles in 1928, 1933 and 1940, the New York Americans were never very competitive. In their last season, 1941–1942, they called themselves the Brooklyn Americans, hoping to attract fans from Brooklyn, but it didn't work.

Ottawa Senators (1917–1934), St. Louis Eagles (1934–1935)

The Ottawa Senators had a long history before joining the NHL – they first played as the Ottawa Hockey Club in 1889. In the early 1900s, they won the Stanley Cup several times, earning the nickname "the Silver Seven" – because the Cup was made of silver and teams had seven men on the ice in those days.

After joining the NHL, the Senators won the Stanley Cup in 1920, 1921 and 1927. But expansion to the U.S. meant that there were now richer owners in much bigger cities, and Ottawa could no longer keep up. The team sat out the 1931–1932 season and tried to get their affairs in order. They returned for two more seasons but finally gave up at the end of the 1933–1934 season, when they moved to St. Louis.

The Eagles didn't have any better luck in their new home, and they folded after just one year. The NHL put a new team in St. Louis in 1967. It didn't return to Ottawa until 1992.

Montreal Wanderers (1917–1918)

Founded in 1903, the Wanderers were an instant success – no surprise, since owner James Strachan raided the roster of the Montreal AAA (Amateur Athletic Association) team that had won the Stanley Cup in 1902. The Wanderers won the Cup themselves in 1906, 1907, 1908 and 1910. They won their first NHL game, 10–9 against Toronto, but lost each of their next three matches.

Then disaster struck on January 2, 1918, when the Montreal Arena – home to both the Wanderers and the Canadiens – burned to the ground. The Canadiens were able to find a new home and continue, but the Wanderers elected to call it quits.

Montreal Maroons (1924–1938)

The fire that destroyed the Montreal Arena left the city without a state-of-the-art hockey rink. Money was raised to build a hockey palace, the Forum, not far from the old arena. The builders of the Forum sought to launch a team that would appeal to English-speaking fans as much as the Canadiens appealed to French-speaking ones. In 1924, the Montreal Professional Hockey Club was born.

The team hoped to revive the Wanderers' name, but a former player owned the right to use the name. Before a new name could be selected, reporters began to call the team the Maroons because of the colour of their sweaters. The name stuck. The Maroons won the Cup in 1926 and 1935. Even when the team didn't win, it was often a contender, led by the high-scoring "S Line" of Nels Stewart, Albert Charles "Babe" Siebert and Reginald "Hooley" Smith.

The Canadiens began sharing the Forum with the Maroons in 1926, and games between the fierce rivals were played before sellout crowds. But during the Depression, Montreal could afford to support only one team. The Maroons withdrew from the NHL after the 1937–1938 season.

Pittsburgh Pirates (1925–1930), Philadelphia Quakers (1930–1931)

Professional hockey had been played in Pittsburgh as early as 1904, but it was the amateur game that paved the way for the city's first NHL entry. The Yellow Jackets won the U.S. amateur championship in 1924 and 1925, and the NHL made Pittsburgh the home of its third American team.

Named the Pirates, the team made a splash by placing third in the seven-team NHL. They made the playoffs twice in their first three seasons. But when player-coach Odie Cleghorn retired in 1928 to become a referee, the team's performance declined and fans grew scarce. In 1930, they moved to Philadelphia and called themselves the Quakers. The 1930–1931 Quakers were one of the worst teams in NHL history, winning four games, losing thirty-six and tying four. They did not return the next season.

STANLEY CUP CHAMPIONS

THE STANLEY CUP is one of the most famous trophies in the world, but its beginnings were quite humble. In 1892, Lord Stanley, the governor general of Canada, decided to donate what he called "a challenge cup which should be held from year to year by the champion hockey team in the Dominion." Accordingly, the cup was originally called the Dominion Hockey Challenge Cup.

In London, England, an assistant of Stanley's picked out a simple silver bowl measuring a little over 15 centimetres tall and a little less than 30 centimetres across. He paid ten guineas, or about fifty Canadian dollars.

At the end of the 1893 hockey season, the champions of the Amateur Hockey Association of Canada, the team from the Montreal Amateur Athletic Association, was presented with the trophy. Lord Stanley would never witness a Stanley Cup competition, as he returned to England that year.

Originally a trophy for amateur teams, the Stanley Cup has been symbolic of the best professional teams since the early 1900s. It has been awarded to many, but none as frequently as the Montreal Canadiens, who have won the championship twenty-three times. The longest

drought in Cup history belongs to the Chicago Blackhawks, who haven't won it since 1961.

Just as the Cup has grown in importance, it has grown in size. The original bowl was replaced in the late 1960s when it became brittle with age. The duplicate bowl sits atop a "neck" and a cylinder of bands engraved with the names of the players and staff of the winning teams. It takes about thirteen years to fill up each band. When the bottom band is full, the top one is removed, each of the others is moved up a level, and a blank one is inserted at the bottom. Used rings are displayed at the Hockey Hall of Fame in Toronto.

The Cup is also unusual in that it is the only professional sports trophy that travels around with members of the winning team after the season – in the last five seasons alone, it has logged over 600,000 kilometres of travel! In 2006, the Cup even returned to London for the unveiling of a commemorative plaque outside the building where it was purchased. Because the Cup is on the road for about 250 days out of each year, a replica is displayed for all to see at the Hockey Hall of Fame in Toronto.

Bob Gainey of the Montreal Canadiens hoists the Stanley Cup after defeating the New York Rangers in the 1979 finals and winning the cup for the fourth year in a row.

2007–2008	Detroit Red Wings	1961–1962	Toronto Maple Leafs
2006–2007	Anaheim Ducks	1960–1961	Chicago Black Hawks
2005–2006	Carolina Hurricanes	1959–1960	Montreal Canadiens
2004–2005	Not awarded (season cancelled)	1958–1959	Montreal Canadiens
2003–2004	Tampa Bay Lightning	1957–1958	Montreal Canadiens
2002–2003	New Jersey Devils	1956–1957	Montreal Canadiens
2001–2002	Detroit Red Wings	1955–1956	Montreal Canadiens
2000–2001	Colorado Avalanche	1954–1955	Detroit Red Wings
1999–2000	New Jersey Devils	1953–1954	Detroit Red Wings
1998–1999	Dallas Stars	1952–1953	Montreal Canadiens
1997–1998	Detroit Red Wings	1951–1952	Detroit Red Wings
1996–1997	Detroit Red Wings	1950–1951	Toronto Maple Leafs
1995–1996	Colorado Avalanche	1949–1950	Detroit Red Wings
1994–1995	New Jersey Devils	1948–1949	Toronto Maple Leafs
1993–1994	New York Rangers	1947–1948	Toronto Maple Leafs
1992–1993	Montreal Canadiens	1946–1947	Toronto Maple Leafs
1991–1992	Pittsburgh Penguins	1945–1946	Montreal Canadiens
1990–1991	Pittsburgh Penguins	1944–1945	Toronto Maple Leafs
1989–1990	Edmonton Oilers	1943–1944	Montreal Canadiens
1988–1989	Calgary Flames	1942–1943	Detroit Red Wings
1987–1988	Edmonton Oilers	1941–1942	Toronto Maple Leafs
1986–1987	Edmonton Oilers	1940–1941	Boston Bruins
1985–1986	Montreal Canadiens	1939–1940	New York Rangers
1984–1985	Edmonton Oilers	1938–1939	Boston Bruins
1983–1984	Edmonton Oilers	1937–1938	Chicago Black Hawks
1982–1983	New York Islanders	1936–1937	Detroit Red Wings
1981–1982	New York Islanders	1935–1936	Detroit Red Wings
1980–1981	New York Islanders	1934–1935	Montreal Maroons
1979–1980	New York Islanders	1933–1934	Chicago Black Hawks
1978–1979	Montreal Canadiens	1932–1933	New York Rangers
1977–1978	Montreal Canadiens	1931–1932	Toronto Maple Leafs
1976–1977	Montreal Canadiens	1930–1931	Montreal Canadiens
1975–1976	Montreal Canadiens	1929–1930	Montreal Canadiens
1974–1975	Philadelphia Flyers	1928–1929	Boston Bruins
1973–1974	Philadelphia Flyers	1927–1928	New York Rangers
1972–1973	Montreal Canadiens	1926–1927	Ottawa Senators
1971–1972	Boston Bruins	1925–1926	Montreal Maroons
1970–1971	Montreal Canadiens	1924–1925	Victoria Cougars
1969–1970	Boston Bruins	1923–1924	Montreal Canadiens
1968–1969	Montreal Canadiens	1922–1923	Ottawa Senators
1967–1968	Montreal Canadiens	1921–1922	Toronto St. Patricks
1966–1967	Toronto Maple Leafs	1920–1921	Ottawa Senators
1965–1966	Montreal Canadiens	1919–1920	Ottawa Senators
1964–1965	Montreal Canadiens	1918–1919	No champion
1963–1964	Toronto Maple Leafs	1917–1918	Toronto Arenas
1962–1963	Toronto Maple Leafs		

THE NHL'S HIGHEST-SCORING PLAYERS

HE HOLDS OR SHARES SIXTY-ONE DIFFERENT NHL SCORING RECORDS, but believe it or not, there was a season in which Wayne Gretzky, known to hockey fans as "the Great One," scored only one goal. Of course, it happened when he was six, and he was competing against ten-year-olds!

Notice that Gretzky had more assists (1,963) than Mark Messier had total points (1,887) in his career. That's a sure sign of just how dominant an offensive force Gretzky was.

One player who might have challenged Gretzky's astounding records was Mario Lemieux. Injuries and a battle with Hodgkin's lymphoma (a form of cancer) limited him to just 915 games over twenty-two seasons, compared with Gretzky's 1,487 games in twenty years. Had Lemieux been able to play as many games as Gretzky, he was on a pace to score 1,121 goals and 1,679 assists for a total of 2,800 points.

Could any of today's top players equal Gretzky's records? They would have their work cut out for them. Alexander Ovechkin scored 163 goals in his first three seasons – an average of fifty-four per year. He would have to keep up that pace for fourteen more years to eclipse Gretzky's total of 894. Sidney Crosby was the league's top point-getter in 2006–2007 season, scoring 120. Even if he could be that productive every year, it would take twenty-four years to catch the Great One.

The top European-trained player in all three categories – goals, assists and total points – is Jaromir Jagr, who is still adding to his totals. Mike Modano leads all American-born players in goals (528) and points (1,283), while Phil Housley is tops in assists among American-born players, with 894.

With this goal against the Buffalo Sabres in 1982, Wayne Gretzky, the Great One, earned a new NHL scoring record (beating Phil Esposito's record).

Top 25 NHL Goal Scorers (Career)

1.	Wayne Gretzky	894
2.	Gordie Howe	801
3.	Brett Hull	741
4.	Marcel Dionne	731
5.	Phil Esposito	717
6.	Mike Gartner	708
7.	Mark Messier	694
8.	Steve Yzerman	692
9.	Mario Lemieux	690
10.	Luc Robitaille	668
11.	Brendan Shanahan*	650
12.	Jaromir Jagr*	646
13.	Dave Andreychuk	640
14.	Joe Sakic*	623
15.	Bobby Hull	610
16.	Dino Ciccarelli	608
17.	Jari Kurri	601
18.	Mike Bossy	573
19.	Joe Nieuwendyk	564
20.	Guy Lafleur	560
21.	John Bucyk	556
22.	Mats Sundin*	555
23.	Teemu Selanne*	552
24.	Ron Francis	549
25.	Michel Goulet	548

Top 25 Assist Leaders (Career)

1.	Wayne Gretzky	1,963
2.	Ron Francis	1,249
3.	Mark Messier	1,193
4.	Raymond Bourque	1,169
5.	Paul Coffey	1,135
6.	Adam Oates	1,079
7.	Steve Yzerman	1,063
8.	Gordie Howe	1,049
9.	Marcel Dionne	1,040
10.	Mario Lemieux	1,033
11.	Joe Sakic*	1,006
12.	Doug Gilmour	964
13.	Jaromir Jagr*	953
14.	Al MacInnis	934
15.	Larry Murphy	929
16.	Stan Mikita	926
17.	Bryan Trottier	901
18.	Phil Housley	894
19.	Dale Hawerchuk	891
20.	Phil Esposito	873
21.	Denis Savard	865
22.	Mark Recchi*	859
23.	Bobby Clarke	852
24.	Alex Delvecchio	825
25.	Gilbert Perreault	814

Top 25 Point Leaders (Career)

1.	Wayne Gretzky	2,857
2.	Mark Messier	1,887
3.	Gordie Howe	1,850
4.	Ron Francis	1,798
5.	Marcel Dionne	1,771
6.	Steve Yzerman	1,755
7.	Mario Lemieux	1,723
8.	Joe Sakic*	1,629
9.	Jaromir Jagr*	1,599
10.	Phil Esposito	1,590
11.	Raymond Bourque	1,579
12.	Paul Coffey	1,531
13.	Stan Mikita	1,467
14.	Bryan Trottier	1,425
15.	Adam Oates	1,420
16.	Doug Gilmour	1,414
17.	Dale Hawerchuk	1,409
18.	Jari Kurri	1,398
19.	Luc Robitaille	1,394
20.	Brett Hull	1,391
21.	Mark Recchi*	1,381
22.	John Bucyk	1,369
23.	Guy Lafleur	1,353
24.	Brendan Shanahan*	1,340
25.	Denis Savard	1,338
25.	(tie) Dave Andreychuk	1,338

* Still playing in the NHL as of 2007–2008.

THE NHL'S HIGHEST-SCORING PLAYERS

THE "ZERO HEROES": HOCKEY'S GREATEST GOALIES

Martin Brodeur of the New Jersey Devils makes a brilliant glove save against the New York Rangers.

HOCKEY GOALIES HAVE OFTEN BEEN COMPARED TO ROCK 'N' ROLL DRUMMERS. Both groups have a reputation for being eccentric, so they're often hard to get along with – but equally tough to get along without. The similarities don't end there. Both are often hidden behind a battery of equipment. They're usually isolated from the action, remaining in one place while the others move all about the stage or the ice. They're both frequently misunderstood. And both have legions of adoring fans.

Listed here are some of the game's best-ever goalies, ranked by games won and by shutouts (games during which zero goals were made on the goalie). Some of the names on the second list may not be familiar: players such as Hainsworth, Thompson and Connell made their names during the 1920s when goals were scarce in the NHL. In one season, George Hainsworth racked up twenty-two shutouts in just forty-four games – it's still an NHL record.

Hainsworth is remarkable because he didn't turn pro – with Saskatoon of the Western Canada Hockey League – until he was twenty-eight. And he didn't make his NHL debut until the ripe old age of thirty-one!

His ten shutouts with Saskatoon give him 104 in leagues that competed for the Stanley Cup – one more than Terry Sawchuk's NHL shutout record. But New Jersey's Martin Brodeur will probably break both records within the next year or two to become the undisputed all-time champ.

Top 10 Goalies (ranked by winning games)

1.	Patrick Roy	551
2.	Martin Brodeur*	538
3.	Ed Belfour	484
4.	Curtis Joseph*	449
5.	Terry Sawchuk	447
6.	Jacques Plante	437
7.	Tony Esposito	423
8.	Glenn Hall	407
9.	Grant Fuhr	403
10.	Dominik Hasek*	389

Top 10 Goalies (ranked by shutouts)

1.	Terry Sawchuk	103
2.	Martin Brodeur*	96
3.	George Hainsworth	94
4.	Glenn Hall	84
5.	Jacques Plante	82
6.	Cecil "Tiny" Thompson	81
6.	(tie) Alex Connell	81
6.	(tie) Domink Hasek*	81
7.	Tony Esposito	76
7.	(tie) Ed Belfour	76

* Still playing in the NHL as of 2007–2008.

CANOEING

THERE ARE LARGER, FASTER and more complex boats than a canoe, but in none of those fancier boats can you feel the water so closely, touch the bulrushes that creep along the shoreline, or slip into creeks and shallow wetlands to drift silently alongside mallards, loons and herons to find the perfect fishing hole. Paddling a canoe is an art that, like most pursuits, just needs practice to master. Huck Finn may have floated the Mississippi on a raft, and white-water kayaking is a thrill, but short of those, nothing beats a canoe for a water adventure. Sometimes you need to be alone, and your canoe is there for you. Other times you want to go on an adventure with a friend, and canoeing together is an exhilarating lesson in teamwork.

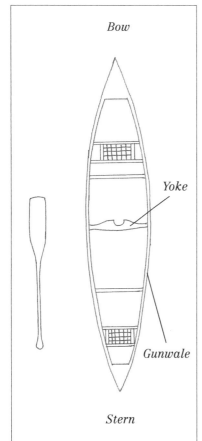

Bow

Yoke

Gunwale

Stern

As anybody who canoes can tell you, the very first thing you have to master is getting into the boat. It's not always as easy as it sounds – canoes can be pretty tippy. And because the bottoms can be damaged easily, it's best to climb in only when most of the canoe is already in the water (keeping just the end of the bow – the front – resting on shore). The safest way to climb into a canoe is to have someone hold the boat steady for you (on the shore or on the dock). You can manage on your own too, but you have to be that much more careful. When getting into a canoe, hold onto the sides (the gunwales). Make sure you step along the centreline of the boat. As you make your way to the front of the canoe, continue to hold onto the gunwales and keep low – crouching will help you maintain your balance and will keep the boat stabilized. And whatever you do, once you get out onto the water, don't stand up! If you need to move, stay low. You don't want to risk capsizing. Once everyone is in the boat (bow passengers – the ones at the front – enter last), use the back stroke to move the canoe away from shore.

You can sit in the seats, but you may find that you have more stability if your weight rests lower in the boat. You can kneel on the bottom of the canoe (resting your bottom on the edge of the seat if you want). You might want to place an extra life jacket or a foam pad under your knees for cushioning. Keeping your knees apart, and pressing them against the bottom of the canoe can give you increased stability and control.

If you are solo canoeing, you can sit either in the middle or in the stern (the back). If your canoe is pointed at both ends, the stern seat is much closer to the end of the boat than the bow seat is to the other end. Where you sit will largely depend on how heavy you are and what kind of canoe you have. Sitting in the stern will give you more control and make steering easier. But you may find that sitting in the back makes the bow end lift out of the water. If this happens, you need to move forward. You can use the middle seat, or, if the canoe is the same shape front and back, you can sit in the bow seat and face the stern (using the stern as the front of the boat). This will get you a little closer to the centre without being right in the middle. There are also certain strokes that make steering a canoe by yourself much easier and others that require you to sit in the centre.

With two-person or tandem canoeing, one person sits in the stern and one in the bow. (The middle seat, if there is one, is only used if you have a third passenger.) Tandem paddling is a delicate dance whereby the person at stern steers and gives directions while the person at bow paddles, changing sides at will to keep the boat in its line. It works best if both people paddle in unison, but the bow person sets the pace. The stern paddler watches the bow person and follows his or her rhythm.

There are a number of different strokes you can use to propel the canoe, but all require you to hold your paddle in the same way. To paddle on the right, grab the grip (or top knob of the paddle) with your left hand. Your hand should fold over the top of the grip. Your right hand holds the shaft of the paddle. You can tell how far down the shaft you should be placing your hand by tucking the paddle grip under your armpit and extending your arm down the length. Point your thumb straight along the paddle shaft. When you are paddling, your shaft hand should rest just below the spot where your thumb is when you are holding the paddle this way.

Much of the power of paddling should come from your torso and not your arms. To achieve this, turn your torso to the side on which you are paddling before you dip the paddle into the water, and twist back to face the front as you complete the stroke. Keeping your paddle within your field of vision will ensure that you don't raise the paddle too high at the beginning of the stroke. If you can see your paddle, you will also keep your stroke from extending too far behind your shoulders—where you lose power and control.

The ordinary canoe stroke is the **forward stroke**. Put the paddle into the water in front of you, with the blade of the paddle perpendicular to the side of boat. The paddle should slice deeply into the water with hardly any splashing or noise. As you pull the paddle back, the hand at the top of the paddle should be pushing forward toward the bow, while the shaft hand pulls back toward the stern. (At mid-point in the stroke, the shaft of the paddle should be more or less straight up and down.) As you do this, you should feel the pressure of the water against the blade. If you don't, your paddle blade may not be in deep enough or may be twisted so that it isn't at right angles to the side of the boat. Keep your arms straight and remember to turn your torso as you paddle. When you lift your paddle out of the water, give it a little twist so that the blade can slice out of the water easily. To paddle on the left, hold the grip with your right hand, the shaft with your left, and repeat.

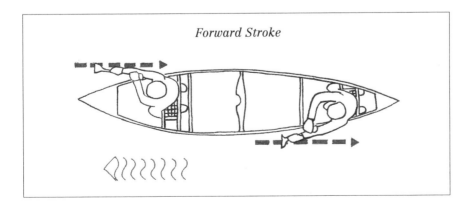

Forward Stroke

To change courses and return from whence you came, turn the boat around, and then paddle forward in the new direction. The **back stroke** causes the boat to slow or even stop. Put the paddle in the water slightly beside or slightly behind you, and push your paddle through the water toward the front of the canoe, and then out of the water.

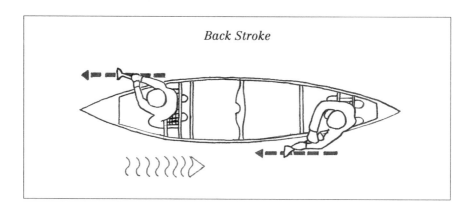

Back Stroke

It's important to remember that a canoe is not a bicycle. If you turn bicycle handlebars to the right, the bike will turn rightward. Not so in a canoe. When you paddle to the right, the boat will shift left. The opposite is true too: left paddling pushes the boat to the right. Rotate your body as you paddle, since the power comes not from your arms, exactly, but from your torso. With practice, you will learn to do this instinctively, using your hips and body weight to control the boat's direction.

When you paddle alone, it is essential to know the **J-stroke**, which, by means of a small turn of the paddle at the end, keeps the boat in a straight line. (When there are two paddlers in a canoe, the J-stroke can also be used by the stern paddler to correct the boat's direction.) As you paddle on the left side, draw the letter J. On the right side, it will look like a mirror-image J, or a fishhook. In other words, start with a standard forward stroke, but at the end of the stroke, turn the paddle out so that the blade is parallel to the side of the boat, and push it away from the canoe; that's the J. Then lift the paddle out of the water, and repeat.

A **draw stroke** is used to move your canoe sideways or to help you in making a turn. Turn your

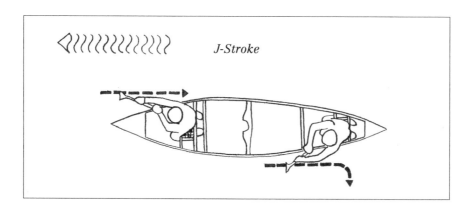

J-Stroke

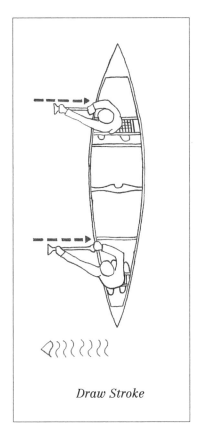

Draw Stroke

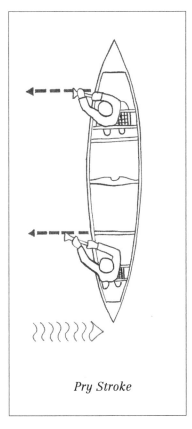

Pry Stroke

torso to the side and drop your paddle blade into the water as far away from the canoe as you can while keeping the paddle shaft vertical. The blade of the paddle should be parallel to the side of the boat. Now pull the paddle toward you until it reaches the side of the boat. The boat will move to the side on which you are drawing. To move in the opposite direction, place the paddle close to the side of the boat and push the blade away from you (the hand at the top of the paddle will move back, toward the centre of your body; the shaft can rest against the gunwales as you push). This stroke is called a **pry stroke**.

Some beginning solo canoers constantly move the paddle from right to left sides, but that's a quick way to tire your arms. Instead, try using a C-stroke. You should be sitting in the middle of the canoe to use this technique. Start as with a forward stroke, but trace a C (on the right, or its mirror image on the left) in the water. When you do this, turn the blade so it's nearly parallel to the side of the canoe at the beginning and end of each stroke. (You can also think of this stroke as beginning with a draw stroke, moving through a forward stroke and ending with a pry stroke, or starting with a draw stroke and ending with a J-stroke.)

For solo canoers, the **sweep stroke** can be used to make gentle turns in the boat. Dip the paddle into the water in front of you and pull it back in a wide arc toward the stern. Your torso should turn as you pull the paddle around, and the boat will turn to the opposite side of the one you are paddling on.

This next stroke has many names, crossback being one of them. It's a stop. Turning your torso

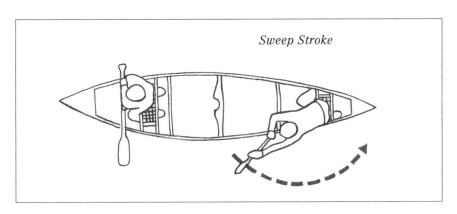

Sweep Stroke

to the side, drop the blade into the water so that it sticks out (at a right angle) from the side of the boat and hold it still. Really, really hold the paddle tight against the water's rush. This stops the boat when it's moving forward. It will also turn it to the paddle side, but this is not a suggested way to turn, since it slows the boat down too much.

One final stroke is perfect for when you find yourself in a river with no company other than beavers working industriously on their dams. The quietest possible stroke (sometimes called sculling) will break no water and make no sound. Put the paddle in the water beside you and keep it there, drawing a figure eight parallel to the boat, over and again. You will actually move forward without having to take your paddle out of the water.

And a final word about canoe strokes: In general, the closer to the boat you paddle, the straighter it will go. To turn the canoe, paddle farther from the boat.

Now, all you need is a boat and a paddle . . . and a few more pieces of essential gear, the first being a life jacket. It's itchy and annoying, and you'll be tempted to leave it on shore or take it off on the boat. Don't. It will save your life in a storm. In a less dangerous circumstance, if you tip, it will help you grab your paddle and pull yourself back into your boat.

Drinking water is necessary, and a small bailing bucket or scoop will come in handy if water gets in your boat. Last but not least, bring a rope. Ropes are key to canoe adventures. You might find a stray canoe that needs to be towed to shore or need to tie the canoe to a tree while you explore a riverbank. Perhaps the tide has gone out in a creek and you need to hop out and pull your roped canoe to deeper waters. Life jacket, water, bailer, rope, and you're set.

Portaging

Portaging is just a fancy word for walking while carrying something. Native Canadians taught the European explorers that canoes are the best way to work your way down rivers. But sometimes even the canoe can't travel through passages of rocks or rapids (safely that is). Then you have to paddle the canoe to the riverbank, haul it out of the water and carry it until the river is navigable again. You may also portage between two bodies of water. If you have a map of canoe routes to guide you (for example, those from provincial or national parks), the portages will be marked.

You may not be big enough to carry the canoe on your own. Most canoes weigh about 25 to

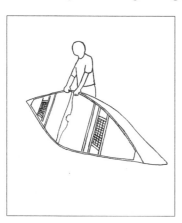 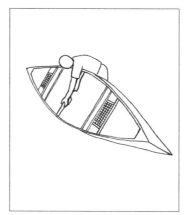

35 kilograms. You can portage a canoe with two people, but it is tricky unless you are well matched in height and strength.

If you are strong enough to portage on your own, prepare to lift the boat over your head by placing the canoe on the ground in front of you. Tip the canoe on its side, with the bottom facing you. Bend your knees, grab the centre thwart (the brace that runs from gunwale to gunwale), or, if there are two thwarts, grab the one closer to the stern (or yoke, if your canoe has one) and lift the canoe onto your lap. Next, balancing the canoe on your knees, grab the gunwale farthest from you with your right hand

and move your left hand to the gunwale nearest you. Now lift (with your knees as well as your arms) the canoe, turning it over your head. Lower the canoe so that the yoke or the thwart is resting on your shoulders.

 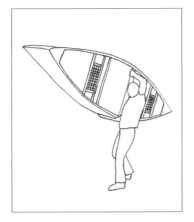 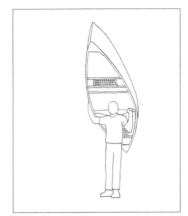

If you are portaging with another person, he can help you get the canoe into portaging position. First, turn the canoe upside down on the ground. While one person lifts the one end of the canoe up, the second person crouches down and gets under the canoe, positioning himself under the yoke or thwart. Then holding on to the gunwales, and bending his knees, the person under the canoe balances the canoe's yoke or thwart on his shoulders, straightens his knees and lifts the canoe up. The other person can help steady the canoe as the carrier lifts, but then lets go.

If you have a partner on your portage, and if it is very short, you can simply pick up the canoe

by the handles at each end or by the gunwales, and walk. Paddles and life jackets can stay in the canoe, but don't weight it down with anything else. For longer treks, you can try portaging in tandem. If two people are carrying a canoe, the stronger one should be positioned nearer the stern, which tends to be heavier.

If you have a lot of gear in your canoe (a backpack, etc.), you may have to do the portage at least twice – once with your pack and once with the canoe. Take the pack first – you can get a good sense of the trail and any rough spots before you carry the heavier canoe.

Here are a few final tips for portaging: Take all heavy items out of your canoe before pulling it gently to shore. Make sure you put your canoe down on the ground where there are no sharp rocks that may scratch or dent it. And keep your life jacket on while carrying the canoe – the padding will make the portage easier on your neck and shoulders. Spraying yourself with bug spray before you set out is another good idea. And finally, keep the front of your canoe up so you can watch the trail ahead of you.

And when you return to the water, breathe deeply, paddle well and enjoy your voyage.

FAMOUS BATTLES – PART ONE

IN THE MAIN, history springs from both noble and petty sources – from jealousy and murder as much as from the dreams of great men and women. As well as being formed in new laws and sweeping cultural movements, history is made on the battlefield, with entire futures hanging on the outcome. You will find further study of these examples both enlightening and rewarding. Each is an extraordinary story in itself. Each had repercussions that helped to change the world.

1. Thermopylae – 480 BC

Darius the Great ruled the Persian lands known today as Iran and Iraq, pursuing an aggressive policy of expansion. He sent his heralds to Greek cities to demand submission. Many accepted, though Athens executed their herald and Sparta threw theirs down a well. War followed and Darius' ambitions came to an abrupt end when he was beaten at the Battle of Marathon in Greece. Although he planned another great invasion, his death prevented his return. It would fall to his son, Xerxes, to invade northern Greece with a vast army of more than two million in the spring of 480 BC.

The Persian fleet had already won control of the sea and the Greeks could not hold the north against such a vast host. Instead, they chose to defend the pass at Thermopylae in the south. Here, the way through the mountains was a tiny path only four metres wide at its narrowest point. Thermopylae means "Hot Gates," named after thermal springs in the area.

The Spartan king, Leonidas, took his personal guard of 300 Spartans and about 7,000 other foot soldiers and archers to the pass. Of all the Greek leaders, he alone seemed to understand the desperate importance of resisting the enemy horde. When he reached the pass, his men rebuilt an ancient wall and 6,000 of them waited at the middle gate, the other 1,000 guarding a mountain trail above. They did not expect to survive, but Spartans were trained from a young age to scorn fear and hardship. They prided themselves on being elite warriors. The Royal Guard were all fathers, allowed to attend the king only after they had contributed to the gene pool of Sparta. They revered courage above all else.

The Persian king sent scouts to investigate the pass. He was surprised to hear that the Spartans were limbering up and braiding their hair for battle. Unable to believe that such a small group would honestly wish to fight, he sent a warning to withdraw or be destroyed. They made him wait for four days without a reply. On the fifth, the Persian army attacked.

From the beginning, the fighting was brutal in such a confined space. The Spartans and the other Greeks fought for three solid days, throwing the Persians back again and again. Xerxes was forced to send in his "Immortals" – his best warriors. The Spartans proved they were poorly named by killing large numbers of them. Two of Xerxes' brothers were also killed in the fighting.

In the end, Leonidas was betrayed by a Greek traitor. The man went to Xerxes and told him about a mountain track leading around the pass at Thermopylae. Leonidas had guarded one track, but for those who knew the area, there were others. Xerxes sent more of his Immortals to the secret path, and they attacked at dawn. The other Greek soldiers were quickly routed, but Leonidas and the Spartans fought on.

When Leonidas finally fell, he had been cut off from the rest of the Spartans. A small group of the guard fought its way into the heaving mass, recovered his body and carried him to where the others were surrounded,

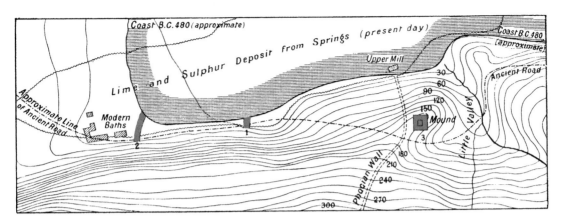

COAST AT MIDDLE GATE OF THERMOPYLÆ IN 480.

1, 2, 3, mark the three positions of the defenders of the Pass.

fighting all the way. The Persians simply could not break their defence, and finally Xerxes ordered them to be cut down with flight after flight of heavy arrows. He was so furious at the losses his army had suffered that he had Leonidas beheaded and his body nailed to a cross.

The Spartans went on to play a crucial part in the war against the Persians. Leonidas and his small guard had established an extraordinary reputation, and larger forces of Spartans struck terror into the Persians at later battles. They had seen what only 300 could do and no one wanted to face 10,000 or 20,000. The Greeks won classic sea battles at Salamis and Eurymedon, destroying the Persian fleet. Over the next eight years, they beat the Persian host on land with battles at Plataea and Mycale. They lost Athens twice to the enemy and saw it completely destroyed. Much of the war has been forgotten, but the battle at Thermopylae still inspires writers and readers today. When peace returned, the Spartans placed a stone lion at the Hot Gates to mark where Leonidas had created a legend. The epitaph reads: "Go tell the Spartans, Stranger passing by, that here, obedient to their laws, we lie."

2. Cannae – 216 BC

When the Latini tribe consolidated their hold on southern Italy, they joined two settlements on seven hills into a city named Rome. In the centuries that followed, they continued to explore their lands and boundaries, north and south, eventually crossing into Sicily. There, they came face to face with an outpost of the ancient and sophisticated Carthaginian empire. It was a clash of force and culture that launched generations of bitter conflict in what have come to be known as the Punic Wars and the first real test of Rome.

The Battle of Cannae is famous in part because the Roman legions were utterly annihilated. This is a surprisingly uncommon event. History has many more examples of battles where the defeated enemies were allowed to leave the field, sometimes almost intact. Cannae was a complete destruction of an army in just one day. It was very nearly the death knell for Rome herself.

The Romans had actually won the First Punic War, which lasted for twenty-three years (264–241 BC), but it had not been a crushing defeat for the Carthaginians. They had had a gifted general in Hamilcar Barca, who had brought southern Spain under the rule of Carthage. Yet it was his son Hannibal who would invade Italy from Spain, cross the Alps with elephants and threaten the very gates of Rome. He commanded Carthaginian forces for the Second Punic War (218–201 BC).

Cannae is in southern Italy, near the heel of the "boot." Hannibal had come south the previous year, after destroying Roman armies of 40,000 and 25,000. Rome was in real danger.

The senate appointed a Dictator, Fabius, who tried to wear Hannibal's forces down by cutting lines of supply. It was a successful policy, but unpopular in a vengeful city that wanted to see the enemy destroyed rather than starved to death. New consuls were elected: Gaius Terentius Varro and Lucius Aemilius Paullus. The senate mustered an army of 80,000 infantry and 6,000 cavalry over which the consuls assumed joint leadership.

Hannibal's army had very few actual Carthaginians. When he entered what is today northern Italy, his forces consisted of 20,000 infantry (from Africa and Spain) and 6,000 cavalry. He recruited more from Gallic tribes in the north, but he was always outnumbered. In fact, the Romans had every possible advantage.

The two armies met on August 2, 216 BC. Hannibal and his army approached along the bank of a river, so he could not easily be flanked. He left 8,000 men to protect his camp. His cavalry was placed on both flanks and his infantry took position in the centre.

Varro was in command on the Roman side that day. He was not an imaginative leader and marched the Roman hammer straight at Hannibal's forces, attempting to smash them. Varro thought he had protected his wings from flanking manoeuvres with his own cavalry. In fact, Hannibal's horsemen were far superior. They crushed one Roman flank almost immediately, *circling behind* them to destroy the other wing as well. They then wreaked havoc on Roman lines from behind.

Varro pressed on, however, his front line

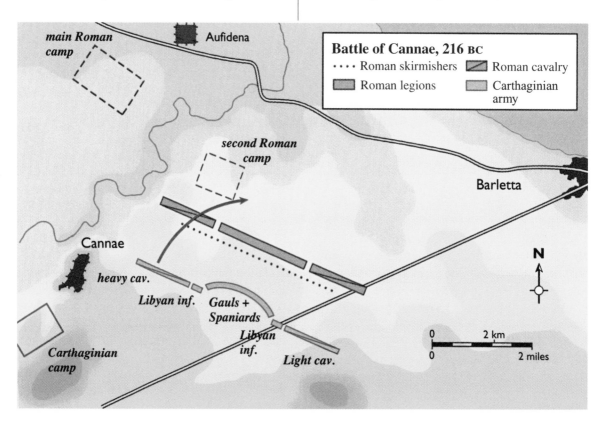

Battle of Cannae, 216 BC
- •••• Roman skirmishers
- ▨ Roman cavalry
- ▬ Roman legions
- ▭ Carthaginian army

main Roman camp

Aufidena

second Roman camp

Barletta

Cannae

heavy cav.

Libyan inf.

Gauls + Spaniards

Libyan inf.

Light cav.

Carthaginian camp

N

0   2 km
0   2 miles

pushing the forces of Carthage farther and farther back, like a bow bending. Hannibal's front
line had become completely concave and Varro
had no idea that it was part of the plan. The
Roman forces marched farther and farther into
the cup Hannibal had created for them. They
believed they were winning.

Hannibal signalled for the wings to move and
the cup began to close. Hannibal's cavalry completed the boxing-in of the Roman legions
behind. They were so compressed they could
hardly move, and their numerical advantage
had been completely cancelled out. More than
60,000 died over the next few hours as they
were butchered, unable to escape. Hannibal
lost 6,000 men.

One result of this battle was that the Romans
learned from it. Three years later they had
more than 200,000 men under arms and had
renewed the struggle. There were successes
and disasters on both sides, and Rome teetered
on the brink of destruction until they appointed
Publius Cornelius Scipio – known as Scipio
Africanus. He had the vision and tactical skill to
counter Hannibal. Though Rome was near
bankruptcy and Italy was starving, the fortunes
of Rome began to turn.

3. Julius Caesar's Invasions of Britain – 55 and 54 BC

Though neither invasion really came to anything, this has traditionally been the official
starting point of recorded British history. In
fact, Julius Caesar's own commentary is the
only written source for some of the information
that has survived today, such as the names of
tribes around the south coast.

The Romans' first landing was on the
beaches near Deal in Kent, having sailed from
Gaul (France). The Britons (meaning "painted
ones," as they painted themselves blue) fought
in the sea to prevent the landing, accompanied
by huge dogs. Caesar's reference to the dogs
makes the English mastiff the oldest recorded
breed. The Roman forces fought their way
onto dry land and made a truce with the local

inhabitants. It is important to remember that
Britain was practically off the edge of maps at
this time. The existence of "foggy islands" or
"tin islands" somewhere past Gaul was considered a myth in some places. Caesar was
overstretched and spent only three weeks in
Britain before heading back across the
Channel to Gaul.

The second landing in 54 BC was much better organized. Caesar returned with a fleet of
800 ships, five legions and 2,000 cavalry. As the
Spanish Armada would discover 1,500 years
later, the coast can be violent, and a storm
smashed a large number of his ships, scattering
many more.

Caesar marched north, destroying the tribes
who had gathered under their war chief,
Cassivellaunus of the Catuvellauni. Cassivellaunus
was forced to sue for peace near modern St.
Albans. Caesar accepted and returned to Gaul.

Events such as the great Gaul rebellion under Vercingetorix, a civil war in Rome, falling in love with the Egyptian queen Cleopatra and, finally, assassination would prevent him ever returning. The Romans did not come back to Britain until AD 43, under Emperor Claudius.

4. Hastings – 14 October 1066

This is one of the most famous dates in English history – the last successful invasion up to modern times. At first, after the Romans left, Britain was almost constantly invaded. First the Saxons proved bothersome, then just as everyone was settling down to being Anglo-Saxon, the Vikings arrived. The Danish king, Canute (sometimes written Cnut), created a small, stable empire early in the eleventh century, ruling England, Norway, Sweden and Denmark. He had taken the English throne from Ethelred the Unready and after Canute's death, his feckless sons lost it back to Ethelred's son Edward, known as the Confessor for his piety. He named Harold Godwinson as his heir, crowned King Harold in January 1066 – the last Anglo-Saxon king before the Normans arrived and spoiled it for everyone.

In fact, William of Normandy had probably been named heir by Edward the Confessor – as far back as 1051. William had also extracted a promise from Harold Godwinson to support that claim when Harold was shipwrecked off Normandy in 1064. In that sense, the 1066 landing was to protect his rightful throne, though that isn't the usual view. We don't know the exact size of his army and estimates vary enormously. It was probably around 12,000 cavalry and 20,000 infantry.

In September, Harold was busy repulsing Norwegian invasions. The Norwegians had promised Harold's brother Tostig an earldom for his aid. Harold marched north from London to relieve York from a Norse army. He met them at Stamford Bridge on September 25, fighting for many hours. Of the 300 ships the Norwegians had brought over, only twenty-four were needed for the survivors. Tostig was killed. Stamford Bridge resulted in heavy casualties among Harold's best soldiers, which was to prove of vital importance to the later battle at Hastings.

On September 28, William of Normandy landed on the Sussex coast. Harold heard of the landing by October 2 and immediately marched 321 kilometres (200 miles) south – which his army covered in less than five days. That is 64 kilometres (40 miles) a day with weapons and armour.

Harold rested his men in London from October 6 to 11, then marched to Hastings, covering 90 kilometres (56 miles) in forty-eight hours. Again we have only estimates of the size of his army, but it is believed to have been around 9,000 men. He was badly outnumbered and only a third of his men were first-rate troops. Still, it is difficult to see what else he could have done.

Harold took position on Senlac Ridge, about 13 kilometres (8 miles) north-west of Hastings. On October 14, the Norman army advanced in three lines: archers, pikemen and cavalry. William's archers fired first at too long a range, then fell back through their own lines to allow the pikemen to reach the enemy. The second line stormed forward, but were battered back from the ridge by rocks, spears and furious hand-to-hand fighting.

William then led a charge up the ridge, but it too failed to penetrate. The Normans' left wing fell back and Harold's soldiers rushed forward to take advantage of their weakness. Harold's army was set to crush the invaders as a rumour went around that William had fallen.

William threw off his helmet and rode up and down his lines to let his men see he was alive. As well as being a splendid moment, his action does show the importance of charismatic leadership at this time, a tradition going back to Thermopylae and beyond. When they saw William, the Normans rallied and crushed their pursuers. Seeing how this strategy had worked to his advantage, William used the technique again. He staged a false cavalry panic and succeeded in drawing more of Harold's men from their position, his cavalry returning to cut them down. Yet most of Harold's men remained on the ridge and the battle was far from over.

Many assaults by infantry, archers and cavalry followed. Harold's forces were exhausted by mid-afternoon, but their courage had not faltered and they had sent back every attack against them. At that point, a chance arrow struck Harold in the eye, wounding him mortally. Morale plummeted and the English lines began to fail.

In terms of historical effect, this battle was the seed that would flower into the largest empire the world has ever known. Countries such as Germany, Belgium and Italy have only existed as nation-states in the last couple of centuries, but England has maintained her identity through 1,000 years.

On Christmas Day, 1066, in Westminster Abbey, William I was crowned King of England.

5. Crécy – August 26, 1346

This battle was part of the Hundred Years' War. Fighting was not absolutely constant between 1337 and 1453, but there were eight major wars between France and England over the period. In addition, the French supported the Scots in their almost constant wars with England. It was a busy time and the period is fascinating and well worth a more detailed look than can be attempted here.

Edward III of England had declared himself King of France in 1338, a statement that did not go down well with the French king, Philip VI. In support of his claim, Edward invaded with a professional, experienced army of 3,000 heavy cavalry knights, 10,000 archers and 4,000 Welsh light infantry. An additional

3,000 squires, artisans and camp followers went with them. It is worth pointing out that the English longbow took more than a decade to learn to use well. It could not simply be picked up and shot, even after weeks of training. The strength required to fire an arrow through iron armour was only developed after years of building strength in the shoulders. It was necessary to start an archer at a young age to achieve the skill and power of those at Crécy.

Edward had failed to bring Philip to battle on two previous occasions. In 1346, he landed near Cherbourg and began a deliberate policy of the utter destruction of every French village and town he came to. In this way, Philip had to make an active response and his army marched against the English at the height of summer.

(The story of the early manoeuvres make excellent reading, especially Edward's crossing of the Somme river, made possible only by his

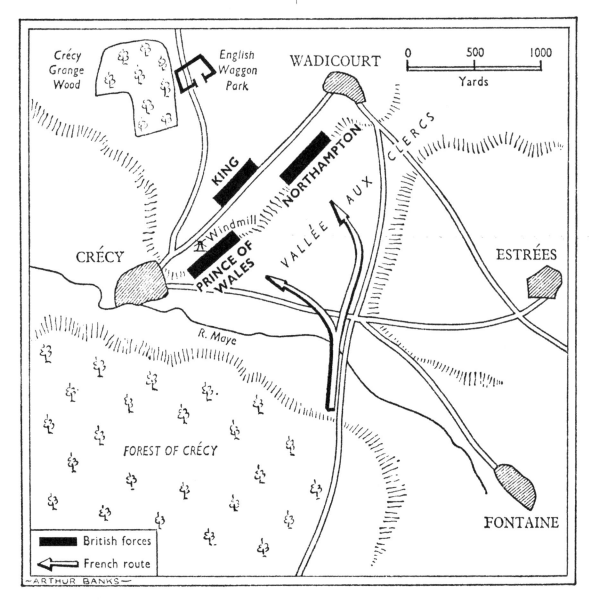

archers and neat timing. The Osprey Military book *Crécy 1346: Triumph of the Black Prince* by David Nicolle is well worth buying.)

To counter the English longbows, Philip did have Italian crossbowmen, but they needed a protective wicker shield while they reloaded, and these were still with the baggage train for this battle, leaving them vulnerable. Nevertheless, the French force outnumbered the English three to one, with 12,000 knights and men at arms, 6,000 crossbowmen, 17,000 light cavalry and as many as 25,000 foot conscripts. They were not well prepared when they came up against the English lines, however.

Philip's first action was to send his crossbowmen out to lay down fire. They moved forward and shot at 137 metres (150 yd). Most of the bolts fell short and they advanced to fire again. This brought them inside the killing range of the English longbows and a storm of arrows struck them.

The French knights saw the Italian crossbowmen falter and assumed they had lost their nerve. The knights were so keen to attack that they rode down their own allies to get through to the front, killing many. Then they too were in range of the English longbowmen and the thundering cavalry charge was torn apart. Those who did make it to the English lines were met by unsmiling veterans carrying axes and swords.

Charge after wild charge followed, and the French forces were destroyed by the archers and the grim men behind them. Edward's son, the Prince of Wales, played a part, though at one point his position was almost overrun by the maddened French. His father refused to send him aid, saying that he must win his spurs.

We know the exact number of French aristocracy killed, as careful records were kept: 1,542 knights died that day. The number of common dead is less certain – somewhere between ten and 20,000 is the best estimate. In comparison, the English forces lost 200 men, including two knights, forty men-at-arms and the rest from the Welsh infantry.

Crécy was a humiliation for the French king. It meant that Edward was able to go on to capture Calais on the north coast of France, which remained an English possession for almost two centuries.

Philip died in 1350, succeeded by his son, John, who was captured at the Battle of Poiters in 1356 by the Prince of Wales, then kept in London and held for a ransom of three million gold crowns. He never regained his father's throne.

This was not the last battle where cavalry played a part, far from it. After all, Winston Churchill took part in a cavalry charge in his youth some 500 years later. Yet Crécy does mark the end of the *dominance* of cavalry. It showed the future was with infantry and projectile weapons, at least until the tank was invented.

THE HISTORY AND RULES OF LACROSSE

HAVE YOU EVER NOTICED that when we talk about our favourite sports and teams, we use a lot of the same terms as when talking about war and the military? Teams have "captains" and they "battle" against other teams. Hockey players "shoot" the puck and spear and charge. But did you know that at least one sport actually played a part in war as a substitute for traditional battle? That sport is Canada's national game: lacrosse.

Lacrosse was developed by Native North Americans hundreds of years ago. Though Europeans named the game lacrosse, Natives called it *Baggataway* (Ojibwa) and *Tewaarathon* (Iroquois). One of the world's earliest known team sports, lacrosse uses sticks with netted pockets to catch and throw a ball. Each team tries to score goals on the opponent's net. There are a number of Native myths that describe the game's origins – a common tale is that lacrosse started as a sport between birds and land animals.

Because of the game's spiritual importance, the Huron Indians insisted that players undertake ritual cleansing before and after matches. Native tribes also believed that spirits and magic could influence the outcome of games. For that reason, Choctaw players put feathers of birds of prey in their hair to improve their eyesight. Bits of bat wings were sometimes woven into the netting of lacrosse sticks, and sticks and balls were often decorated with totemic patterns and symbols. Tribal medicine men also appealed to the spirit world before and during games, and they were frequently credited with securing victories. Failing to win a game was a bad sign to the players and the whole tribe. Sometimes, lacrosse was played to settle disputes between tribes. In the languages of many tribes of the American southeast, in fact, the word for lacrosse literally means "little brother of war."

When early European settlers first witnessed the game, they were awestruck by its size, energy and violence. Lacrosse fields could be huge – some were as big as 5 hectares (12 acres) – and there could be hundreds of players on each team. Games could last for days and were very physically demanding on the players. No protective equipment was used, and while some tribes used leather balls, others threw wooden ones that had been carved from the knots of trees – the hardest wood available. (The Ojibwa used a ball carved from a charred knot. They drilled two holes in the ball so it made a screaming whistle as it sailed through the air.) There were many injuries and even deaths during the hard-fought lacrosse contests.

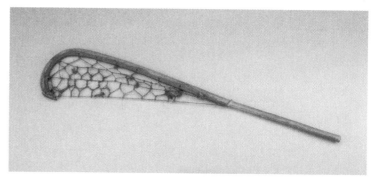

As European settlers built their own communities in Canada, they began to adopt the game as well. In 1840s, the first games were played between European Canadians and Native Canadians, and in 1859 parliament declared lacrosse Canada's national sport. As the country grew, so did the number of people playing the sport. By the late 1800s, most towns had lacrosse teams, and at the beginning of the twentieth century, it was the most popular sport in the country.

Today, four kinds of lacrosse are played – men's and women's field lacrosse, box lacrosse and inter-lacrosse. Men's field lacrosse is played with twelve players and women's with ten. Box lacrosse and inter-lacrosse are both played indoors, usually in hockey arenas (without the ice), with just six players (five runners and a goaltender).

Basic Rules of Box Lacrosse*
Box lacrosse is an exciting and fast-paced game in which the object, like in hockey and basketball, is to throw the ball into your opponent's net. Here are the basic rules. For the complete rules, visit **www.lacrosse.ca**.

Playing Area
The playing area or "box" for box lacrosse is surrounded by boards. At each end is a net 1.22 metres (4 ft) wide and 1.22 metres (4 ft) high with a semi-circular crease around the front of each net (and slightly behind).

Equipment
The regulation length of sticks can vary depending on your division. The goaltender's stick, however, can be of any length, as long as it is not more than 38.1 centimetres (15 in) at its widest. Regulation lacrosse balls are a solid rubber and about the size of a tennis ball.

Players and Positions
Lacrosse teams have a maximum of twenty players, with five players or "runners" (two crease-men, two cornermen and a centre) and a goaltender on the field at any time. As in basketball, all runners are involved in both offence and defence.

Play

There are three twenty-minute periods of play in a game. The home team decides which end the players will start the game on, and the ends are switched at the start of each new period. If the score is tied at the end of the third period, a ten-minute overtime period is played, but the teams do not change ends. If no goals are scored during overtime, the game is tied.

Each new period of play starts with a centre face-off. One player from each team crouches in the centre face-off circle. Then the centremen attempt to get the ball out of the circle by pulling their sticks back, parallel to the centre line, without touching the opponent's stick or the netted part of his own stick with his hand. The centre player is trying to get the ball out of the face-off circle toward one of his own team players.

Some kinds of checking are allowed. Players can make contact with a runner from the front or the side. Checking with arms fully extended is permitted. Players cannot, however, hit below the waist, on top of the shoulder or when the other player is not on his feet. They will also earn a penalty if, while in the defensive zone, they check any player who does not have the ball.

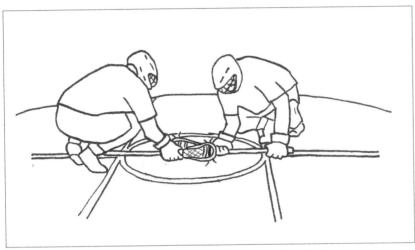
A centre face-off begins each new period of play.

Other Rules to Keep in Mind

- Once a team gains possession of the ball, one of its players must attempt a shot on goal within thirty seconds or forfeit possession to the opposing team.
- The ball is never out of bounds unless it first touches something that is out of bounds – so if a player is able to catch the ball as it sails over the boards or past the edge of the box, the ball is still in play.
- Players must not hold the pocket of the stick against their bodies or against the boards surrounding the box to prevent a player from the opposing team from getting the ball.
- Players must never fall upon the ball or otherwise withhold it from play (the goaltender can cover the ball temporarily as long as he and the ball are in the crease).
- With the exception of the goalie, players must never handle the ball with their hands. Goaltenders, however, can touch and catch balls with their hands as long as they are in their creases. If they throw the ball outside of the crease with their hands, however, possession of the ball will be given to the opposing team. Players can kick at a loose ball, but they cannot score a goal by kicking the ball into the net.
- No players can enter the crease with the ball. The stick or other parts of the body may cross

into the crease (as long as they don't touch the floor or another player), but a shooter's feet must stay outside the crease.

- The goaltender can come out of the crease to receive a pass from a team mate as long as both of his feet are outside of the crease and he doesn't re-enter the crease with the ball.
- The ball must enter the net from the front and go over the goal line. A goal will not be counted if an attacking player kicks the ball into the net or uses any other body part to get the ball in. If, however, a defending player or goaltender moves the ball into his own team's net in any way at all, this is counted as a goal.
- When a goal is scored, the play begins again with a centre face-off.
- Players will also be penalized for tripping, holding, high-sticking, elbowing and fighting, among other infractions.

(*Rules based on The Canadian Lacrosse Association's *Box Lacrosse Rule and Situation Handbook*, 2007.)

Lacrosse Techniques
Holding the Stick
If you shoot right, your right hand will be the "top" hand and the left will be the "bottom." (If you shoot left, it is the other way around.) To hold your stick properly, your top hand should be placed slightly below the mid-point of the shaft. Your bottom hand should be placed about 20 centimetres (8 in) from the top hand toward the butt end of the stick. The stick should be held loosely with your fingers so that you can easily rotate it when cradling, catching or passing. Your hands should not be too far apart as this will give less control over the stick. Holding the stick too close to the end will also lessen control; holding the stick too close to the pocket will make your passes choppy. Some players find it helpful to put their thumbs along the shaft of the stick to improve control and flexibility.

Cradling
When you are carrying a ball, your stick should never be still. Instead you need to be cradling the ball at all times. To cradle a ball, twist the stick in a continuous side-to-side or back-and-forth or up-and-down motion. Moving the stick in this way while holding the ball does three things:

1) It keeps the ball from falling out of the pocket while you are running.
2) It helps you feel the ball in the pocket and make sure you haven't dropped it.
3) It allows you to prepare for passes by moving the ball into the right spot before throwing.

For the small cradle, hold the stick over your shoulder, parallel to the floor, and use your top-hand wrist to twist the stick back and forth in small, semi-circular motions. Moving the wrist and therefore the stick up and down in short shakes is another way to do a small cradle. This motion will tell you where the ball is in the pocket when getting ready to pass or shoot.

Use a medium cradle when you are moving down the floor with the ball, especially when surrounded by a lot of other players. The medium cradle lets you know that you still have the ball in your stick as you are running. The rocking motion also keeps the ball in the pocket. For the medium cradle, the stick is held in front of your body, with your hands placed farther apart than they usually are when holding the stick. Using the top-hand wrist and forearm (and letting the stick turn in the loose grip of the bottom hand), the stick curls toward the upper body and rolls back again.

The large cradle prevents a ball from dropping out of your stick while you are being cross-checked by another player. Your top hand moves up to grip the stick at the throat (near the pocket). The bottom hand holds the stick loosely near the end. The stick is then raised so that it is held

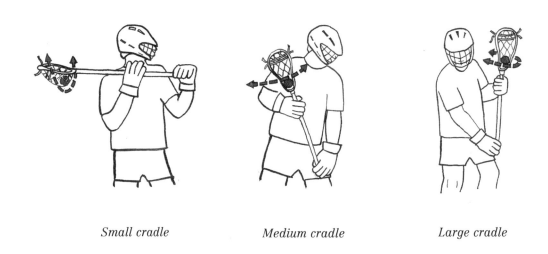

Small cradle   *Medium cradle*   *Large cradle*

vertically. Using the wrist, forearm and upper arm of the top hand, swing the stick back and forth in an almost complete circular motion. This swinging motion will help the ball stay in the pocket. The ball will be further protected if the open side of the pocket is facing the player who is checking you. When the cross-checker makes impact with you or the stick, the ball will be forced back into the netting rather than forward out of the pocket.

Catching

A good lacrosse player who plucks the ball out of the air makes catching looking easy. But using a lacrosse stick to catch a ball is much more difficult than throwing a ball with one. New players need to get plenty of catching practice to master the skill.

To catch the ball, your hands should be positioned on the lacrosse stick as described previously. Some beginners, however, find it easier to catch the ball if they move their top hand up closer to the throat of the stick. If you do this, remember to move that hand down just below the mid-point before you attempt to throw.

When preparing to receive a pass, you should hold your stick up, about 30 centimetres (12 in) away from your body, with the open face of the pocket toward the passer. Keeping the stick directly in front of you rather than to the side allows you to watch the play around you but still be able to line up your stick with the incoming ball. When the ball does reach you, position yourself and the stick so that the stick is vertical, lined up beside your head. Catch the ball over the same shoulder you throw with. Let your stick absorb the motion of the incoming ball, bringing the stick gradually back over your shoulder. Holding your stick very rigidly and "stopping" the ball as soon as it hits the netting makes the ball pop out of the pocket more easily.

You want to avoid reaching out in front of you to catch a pass. If your stick is extended in front of you, you will need to twist it back toward you and start cradling so that you don't lose the ball before you can get yourself in a position to throw. Catching the ball over your shoulder, with the stick lined up right beside your head, means that you will be able to pass or shoot right away if you need to. You also want to catch the ball so that it rests in the same spot in the pocket where you like to throw it from. Setting up the ball this way improves your passes and shots.

Passing

Once you've caught the ball, you've got to hold on to it. Turn so that you are standing sideways to any opposing team member who is trying to check you, protecting your stick with your body. Hold your stick over your shoulder, either horizontally or at a slight angle (your top hand should be near your head, the stick close to but not touching your body). Use the small cradle technique while preparing to pass. Bend your knees slightly and place the foot that is opposite your stick side in front of you. Put your weight on your back foot. Flex your wrists and dip your stick back slightly so that the butt end of the stick is raised a little and pointing in the direction of your target. Transfer your weight forward while taking a small step with your front foot. At the same time, bring your stick forward over your shoulder with your top-hand arm, snapping your wrists forward as you do so.

Timing the release of the ball from the stick is the key to a good pass. Releasing the ball while the stick is still behind your head will give the ball a high arc. Releasing it farther forward will reduce the height of the trajectory. As a general rule of thumb, it is better to release it earlier

Passing is one of the key skills of lacrosse.

rather than later, but most of the time, you want your passes to sail in a straight line rather than following a high, slow arc.

Once the ball is released, your top arm should be fully extended, while the arm holding the end of the stick remains flexed. The tip of the stick should be pointing toward the target during the follow-through, and the stick should be heading straight out and down. It should not come back toward your body. Your weight should now be over your front foot.

Before passing, it is a good idea to make eye contact with your intended receiver so he is ready for the ball. Focus on the head of your receiver's stick as a target, but aim slightly high and outside of the pocket so that the receiver can easily move his stick to catch the ball. Also keep in mind that your receiver will be moving. If you aim the ball slightly in front of him, once it reaches him, he will have moved forward to catch it at or behind his shoulder.

Remember that while you want your passes to be sharp and quick, throwing too hard can make it difficult for the receiver to catch. Accuracy is usually more important than power in passing. For that reason, try to make only overhand passes and avoid bouncing a ball to your team mate. A bouncing ball is likely to become a loose ball that can be scooped up by your opponents.

Ground Ball Scoops

This is key to winning any lacrosse game. The team that can scoop up the most loose balls has a definite advantage. When you see a ball bounce free, get to it as quickly as you can. Put your body between the ball and any opposing players. Move your top hand up the throat of your stick, crouch down and lower your stick so that it is almost parallel to the floor, with the pocket along the floor. Move the head of the stick toward the ball and scoop it into the netting. (Keep moving forward as you scoop the ball. Don't stop and try to shovel it up.) Once the ball is in the pocket, raise your stick, and immediately use the "large cradle" technique described above to protect the ball from being knocked free again by an opposing player.

One of the things that is most challenging about approaching a ground ball is the knowledge that members of the opposing team are also going after it and will likely check you if you pick it up. You cannot let thoughts like this slow you down or make you hesitant. Loose ball technique is more about attitude – the desire and drive to get to the ball – than it is about handling technique. What's more, if it appears that another player on your team or on the opposing team is going to get to the ball first, don't abandon your attempt. There is always a chance that the other player may drop the ball or fail to scoop it up. That's your chance to grab it.

Shooting

The set-up and positioning of the stick, arms and hands is more or less the same for the overhand shot as it is for the overhand pass. Your body, however, should be angled slightly so that your shoulder without the stick is closer to the net.

Another way to shoot is the side-arm shot. You need to slide your top hand farther down the stick toward the bottom hand. The stick is held out at your side, at waist level, parallel to the ground. Extend your arms to release the ball from the pocket with the "snapping" action of your wrists. Follow through with a swing that moves the stick around to the other side of your body – as you would when you swing a baseball bat. Where the ball goes depends on when you release it. If you let it go when the stick is farther back, it will stay on the stick side. Releasing it later will allow it to cross in front of you and head to the opposite side.

An underhand shot looks a bit like a golf swing. As in the side-arm shot, your hands should be close together, near the end of the stick. Hold the stick by your side so that the top of the pocket is near the floor. Then, swing the stick up, flexing the wrists to release the shot. Releasing the shot late in the swing will make the ball go higher in the air.

If there are no obvious open spots in the net, you can bounce a shot in. To do so, aim the ball near the goalie's feet so that once the ball hits the floor it bounces behind the goalie into the net.

An important trick to effective shooting is "faking." If the goalie figures you're about to shoot, he'll have a very good chance of blocking the shot. Taking him by surprise is important, so a little deception is often called for. Sometimes you can simply change the position of your body or the direction of your eyes to fool the goalie. Or you can pretend to make an overhand shot but then switch to a side-arm shot. You can also start a side-arm shot and switch to an overhand one. Whenever you fake this way, however, make sure that you twist your stick around during the switch so that the ball can't fall out.

One of the most important things to remember when getting ready to take a shot on the goal is that you have to be able to see how that ball might go into the net before you take the shot. Take a second to plan your shot, and if there is no spot to place the ball in the net or you are blocked by other players, pass it to a team mate who is in a better position. Keep in mind that accuracy in shooting (as in passing) is almost always more important than power.

Lacrosse is a game of considerable skill, but you can have a lot of fun playing even when you are just learning. If you are interested in joining a team, you can find one in your area by checking out the Canadian Lacrosse Association website (www.lacrosse.ca) and following the links. But you don't have to join a team to play. Gather a few friends; get a few lacrosse sticks and a ball; find a field, driveway or quiet road; then, begin your game. Pretty soon you'll discover why this amazing sport has been so popular with Canadians for so many centuries.

SPIES – CODES AND CIPHERS

THE PRACTICE OF SENDING secret messages is known as "steganography," Greek for "concealed writing." The problem with hiding a message in the lining of a coat or tattooed on the scalp is that anyone can read it. It makes a lot of sense to practise "cryptography," as well, Greek for "hidden writing." Cryptography is the art of writing or breaking codes and ciphers.

The words "code" and "cipher" are sometimes used as if they mean the same thing. They do not. A code is a substitution, such as the following sentence: "The Big Cheese lands at Happy tomorrow." We do not know who the "Big Cheese" is, or where "Happy" is. Codes were commonly used between spies in World War II, when groups of numbers could only be translated with the correct codebook. Codes are impossible to break without a key or detailed knowledge of the people involved. If you spied on a group for some months, however, noticing the president of France landed at Heathrow Airport the day after such a message, a pattern might begin to emerge.

"Ciphers," on the other hand, are scrambled messages, not a secret language. In a cipher, a plain-text message is concealed by replacing the letters according to a pattern. Even Morse Code is, in fact, a cipher. They are fascinating and even dangerous. More than one person has gone to his grave without giving up the secret of a particular cipher. Treasures have been lost, along with lives spent searching for them. In times of war, thousands of lives can depend on ciphers being kept – or "deciphered."

Edgar Allan Poe left behind a cipher that was only broken in the year 2000. The composer Elgar left a message for a young lady that has not yet been fully understood. Treasure codes exist that point the way to huge sums in gold – if only the sequence of symbols can be broken.

At the time of writing, the state-of-the-art cipher is a computer sequence with 2,048 figures, each of which can be a number, letter or symbol. The combinations are in trillions of trillions and it is estimated that even the fastest computers in the world couldn't break the code in less than thirty billion years. Oddly enough, it was created by a seventeen-year-old boy in Kent, named Peter Parkinson. He is quite pleased with it. To put it in perspective, it is illegal in the United States to export an encryption program with more than *forty* digits without providing a key. It takes three days to break a 56-bit encryption.

Combinations to computer locks are one thing. This chapter contains some classic ciphers – starting with the one used by Julius Caesar to send messages to his generals.

1. **The Caesar Shift Cipher**. This is a simple alphabet cipher – but tricky to break without the key. Each letter is moved along by a number – say four. A becomes E, J becomes N, Z becomes D and so on. The number is the key to the cipher here. Caesar could agree on the number with his generals in private and then send encrypted messages, knowing they could not be read without that crucial extra piece of information.

   "The dog is sick" becomes "WKH GRJ LV VLFN," with the number three as the key.

   As a first cipher, it works well, but the problem is that there are only twenty-five possible number choices (twenty-six would take you back to the letter you started with). As a result, people who really want to break the code could simply plod their way through all twenty-five combinations. Admittedly, they would first have to recognize the code as a Caesar cipher, but this one only gets one star for difficulty – it is more than 2,000 years old, after all.

2. **Numbers**. A = 1, B = 2, C = 3, et cetera, all the way to Z = 26. Messages can be written using those numbers. This cipher is probably too simple to use on its own; however, if you combine it with a Caesar code number, it can suddenly become very tricky indeed.

   In the basic method, "The dog is better" would be "20 8 5 – 4 15 7 – 9 19 – 2 5 20 20 5 18," which looks difficult but isn't. Add a Caesar cipher of 3, however, and the message becomes "3 23 11 8 – 7 18 10 – 12 22 – 5 8 23 23 8 21," which should overheat the brain of younger brothers or sisters trying to break the encryption. Note that we have included the key number at the beginning. It could be agreed beforehand in private to make this even harder to break. (With the Caesar combination, this cipher ranks at a difficulty of two stars.)

3. **Alphabet ciphers.** There are any number of these. Most of them depend on the way the alphabet is written out – agreed beforehand between the spies.

   A B C D E F G H I J K L M
   N O P Q R S T U V W X Y Z

With this sequence, "How are you?" would become "UBJ NER LBH?"

A	B	C	D	E	F	G	H	I	J	K	L	M	N	O	P	Q	R	S	T	U	V	W	X	Y	Z
Z	Y	X	W	V	U	T	S	R	Q	P	O	N	M	L	K	J	I	H	G	F	E	D	C	B	A

In this one, "How are you?" would become "SLD ZIV BLF?" It's worth remembering that even simple ciphers are not obvious at first glance. Basic alphabet ciphers may be enough to protect a diary, and they have the benefit of being easy to use and remember.

4. Most famous of the alphabet variations is a code stick – another one used by the Romans. Begin with a strip of paper and wind it around a stick. It is important that the sender and the receiver both have the same type. Two bits from the same broom handle would be perfect, but most people end up trying this on a pencil. (See picture.)

Here the word "Elephant" is written down the length of the pencil, with a couple of letters per turn of the strip. (You'll need to hold the paper steady with tape.) When the tape is unwound, the same pen is used to fill in the spaces between the letters. It should now look like jibberish. The idea is that when it is wound back on to a similar stick, the message will be clear. It is a cipher that requires a bit of forethought but can be quite satisfying. For a matter of life and death, however, you may need the next method.

5. **Codeword alphabet substitution.** You might have noticed a pattern developing here. To make a decent cipher, it is a good idea to agree on the key beforehand. It could be a number, a date, the title of a book, a word or even a kind of stick. It's the sort of added complexity that can make even a simple encryption quite fiendish.

    Back to one of our earlier examples:

A	B	C	D	E	F	G	H	I	J	K	L	M	N	O	P	Q	R	S	T	U	V	W	X	Y	Z
Z	Y	X	W	V	U	T	S	R	Q	P	O	N	M	L	K	J	I	H	G	F	E	D	C	B	A

If we added the word "WINDOW," we would get the sequence below. Note that no letters are repeated, so there are still twenty-six in the bottom sequence and the second "W" of "WINDOW" is not used.

A	B	C	D	E	F	G	H	I	J	K	L	M	N	O	P	Q	R	S	T	U	V	W	X	Y	Z
W	**I**	**N**	**D**	**O**	A	B	C	E	F	G	H	J	K	L	M	P	Q	R	S	T	U	V	X	Y	Z

This is a whole new cipher – and without knowing the codeword, it is a difficulty of three stars to crack.

6. **Cipher-wheels.** Using a pair of compasses, cut four circles out of cardboard, two large and two small – 12 centimetre (5 in) and 10 centimetre (4 in) diameters work well. For both pairs, put one on top of the other and punch a hole through with a butterfly stud. They should rotate easily.

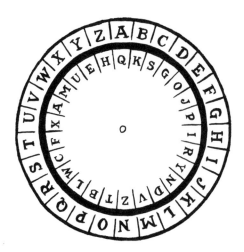

A circle = 360 degrees. There are twenty-six letters in the alphabet, so the spacing for the segments should be approximately 14 degrees. Mark off the segments as accurately as you can for all four circles. Next, write the normal alphabet around the outside of the large circles in the usual way – A to Z. For the inner circles, mark the letters in random order. As long as the matching code wheel is done in the same way, it doesn't matter where the letters go. The code sequence will begin with the two-letter combination that shows the positions of the wheels – AM or AF, for example.

You should end up with a cipher-wheel encrypter that can be read *only* by someone with the other wheel. Now *that* is a difficulty of four stars.

7. **Morse Code** is the most famous substitution cipher ever invented. It was thought up by an American inventor, Samuel F. B. Morse, who patented a telegraph system and saw it explode in popularity. He realized that a pulse of electricity could act on an electromagnet to move a simple lever – transmitting a long or short signal. He arranged a moving strip of paper to pass underneath the metal point, and a new method of communication was born. Using his cipher, he sent the first inter-city message in 1844 from Washington to Baltimore. The marvellous thing about it is that the code can be sent using light if you have a flashlight, or sound, if you can reach a car horn, or even a semaphore, though that is fairly tricky.

The first message Morse sent was "What hath God wrought?," which gives an idea of just how impressive it was to pick up messages as they were written on the other side of the country. In Morse's lifetime, he saw telegraph lines laid across the Atlantic.

The example *everyone* knows is SOS – the international distress call. ("May-day" is also well known. That one comes from the French for "Help me" – "M'aidez.")

The SOS sequence in Morse is dit dit dit – dah dah dah – dit dit dit.

MORSE CODE

A	• —	N	— •	1	• — — — —
B	— • • •	O	— — —	2	• • — — —
C	— • — •	P	• — — •	3	• • • — —
D	— • •	Q	— — • —	4	• • • • —
E	•	R	• — •	5	• • • • •
F	• • — •	S	• • •	6	— • • • •
G	— — •	T	—	7	— — • • •
H	• • • •	U	• • —	8	— — — • •
I	• •	V	• • • —	9	— — — — •
J	• — — —	W	• — —	0	— — — — —
K	— • —	X	— • • —		
L	• — • •	Y	— • — —		
M	— —	Z	— — • •		

This really is one worth learning. Rescuers have heard messages tapped out underneath fallen buildings, heard whistles or seen the flashes from a capsized dinghy. This cipher has saved a large number of lives over the years since its invention. *It has also sent quite a few train timetables.*

If you *do* have a flag handy, it's left for a dash, right for a dot. This is not so well known.

8. This last one is actually designed to make meaning clearer rather than to hide it. The **NATO Phonetic Alphabet** is just useful to know, so . . .

NATO PHONETIC ALPHABET

A	Alpha	N	November
B	Bravo	O	Oscar
C	Charlie	P	Papa
D	Delta	Q	Quebec
E	Echo	R	Romeo
F	Foxtrot	S	Sierra
G	Golf	T	Tango
H	Hotel	U	Uniform
I	India	V	Victor
J	Juliet	W	Whiskey
K	Kilo	X	X-ray
L	Lima	Y	Yankee
M	Mike	Z	Zulu

A previous RAF version (c.1924–1942) was Ace, Beer, Charlie, Don, Edward, Freddie, George, Harry, Ink, Johnnie, King, London, Monkey, Nuts, Orange, Pip, Queen, Robert, Sugar, Toc, Uncle, Vic, William, X-ray, Yorker, Zebra. This was more suited to British English accents, apparently. The NATO version was created in 1956 and has become the accepted standard phonetic alphabet. It is used to minimise confusion when reading letters aloud on the radio or telephone. "P" and "B" sound very similar – but "Papa" and "Bravo" do not.

MAKING CRYSTALS

Having a crystal growing on your windowsill can be good fun. With food colouring, you can make them any colour you wish.

The problem is finding a suitable chemical. You may have seen copper sulphate and potassium permanganate in school. Both can be quite toxic and are therefore not easily available. Your science teacher may allow you to have a sample, if you ask very politely.

For this chapter, we decided to use potassium aluminum sulphate, better known as alum powder. It is a non-toxic substance that used to be used to whiten bread. As with any household substance, you shouldn't get it in your eyes. One hundred grams is enough for crystal making, but alum can be also used for fireproofing and tanning skin – as discussed in other chapters. It works as an astringent on small cuts, or the crystals can be used as an underarm deodorant. Alternatively, you can grow crystals with common salt or sugar.

You will need

- 10 grams of potassium aluminum sulphate (alum).
  (You may use sugar or salt instead of alum.)
- A glass tumbler.
- A popsicle stick (clean).
- Warm water.
- Thread.
- Small stones, preferably with sharp edges.
- Food colouring (optional).

Method

1. Make sure the stones are clean – wash them thoroughly in running water.

2. Put enough warm water in the tumbler to cover the stones (about a third of the cup.) Do not put the stones in yet.

3. Add the alum and stir furiously with the popsicle stick until it stops dissolving easily. You may be left with a few grains at the bottom. Ignore them. You can either put the stones straight in or, for the classic look, tie a thread around a small stone and the other end around the popsicle stick, as in the pictures. We did both.

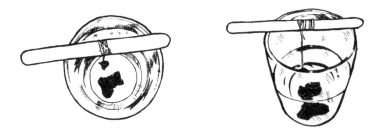

4. If you are intending to add food colouring, do it now. Show proudly to parents, who will pat your head for being a "little genius."

Evaporation is the key for these small crystals, so make sure the glass is in a warm place. It will take a few days for the first crystals to appear, and the full effect can take a few weeks. Larger crystals can be made by repeating the process – after tying a small crystal to the thread.

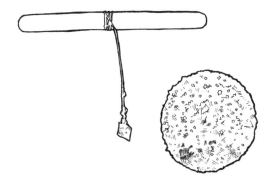

The crystal you see here is a picture of the one we grew – the one on the left, not the enormous thing. The huge circle came from the bottom of the glass and in many ways is more impressive than the actual crystal. It took about six weeks in total, and we refilled the alum once.

EXTRAORDINARY STORIES – PART ONE: SCOTT AND THE ANTARCTIC

STORIES OF COURAGE and determination are sometimes underrated for their ability to inspire. It is true that once-famous names can slip from the memory of generations, names like Charles George Gordon, Richard Francis Burton, Florence Nightingale, Robert Scott, Herbert Kitchener, Henry Morton Stanley, Rudyard Kipling, Isambard Kingdom Brunel and a host of others. Their lives, their stories, were once known to every schoolboy, held up as examples of fortitude and honour. These values have not ceased to be important in the modern world, nor have the stories become less moving. These are all tales worth knowing.

Robert Scott and the Antarctic

Robert Falcon Scott was born on June 6, 1868. All his life, he was known as "Con," a short form of his middle name. He came from a seafaring family, with uncles, grand-uncles and grandparents all serving in the Royal Navy. His father owned a small brewery in Plymouth that had been bought with prize money from the Napoleonic Wars.

"Con" Scott joined HMS *Boadicea* at the age of thirteen as a midshipman. It was a hard world, requiring instant obedience and personal discipline. By twenty-two, he was a lieutenant with first-class certificates in pilotage (steering/navigation), torpedoes and gunnery, with the highest marks in his year for seamanship.

He had met Sir Clements Markham, the president of the Royal Geographical Society, more than once in the course of his naval duties, impressing the older man with his intelligence and demeanour. When, at the turn of the century, the Royal Society wanted someone to head an expedition to the South Pole, Sir Clements Markham fought to have Scott lead the group.

Scott had no experience at that point in his career and little idea of the extremes he would be facing. He solved this problem by consulting those who had, travelling to Oslo to consult Fridtjof Nansen, a Norwegian explorer of Arctic regions who would later become the Norwegian ambassador to London. They became firm friends and Scott accepted Nansen's advice to get dogs to pull sleds, buying twenty dogs and three bitches in Russia for his first attempt to explore the South Pole.

By 1900, the first members of the team were appointed. Scott had insisted on personal

Robert Scott

approval of all appointments and was able to make quick decisions. With an idea of the hardship ahead, most of the men chosen were young and fit, though when Scott met Edward Wilson, a young doctor and artist, the man was suffering from an abscess in his armpit, blood poisoning and lungs weakened by tuberculosis. Nonetheless, Scott appointed him. He also chose one Ernest Shackleton, whose own courageous story would become famous later on.

With the money Sir Clements Markham had raised, the ship *Discovery* was built, costing £49,277, and was launched on March 21, 1901. Scott also purchased a balloon for the voyage, costing £1,300. The young king and queen, Edward VII and Alexandra, came on board to see the ship at Cowes. Sir Clements Markham said of the crew, "No finer set of men ever left these shores, nor were men ever led by a finer captain."

The trip south was slow and difficult. *Discovery* leaked and could not make more than seven knots under full steam. However, they reached New Zealand and had the leak fixed as well as took on supplies. They sailed on into the ice packs and the high southern latitudes. Scott and Shackleton were the first people ever to take a balloon trip in the Antarctic, though that ship too developed a leak and was used only once.

Their lack of experience showed in a number of ways, from misjudging distances and the difficulties of driving dogs, to protecting the skin and cooking in low temperatures. They had to learn vital skills very quickly in an environment where sweat froze and a blizzard could strike without warning. However, they did learn, spending a year in an icy landscape out of which their ship seemed to grow.

In November 1902, they made a push to the Pole, but the dogs sickened. They were the first to cross the 80th parallel, after which all maps were blank. They began to kill the dogs, feeding them to the others. Shackleton developed the first symptoms of scurvy due to a lack of vitamins in his diet, and the pain of snow blindness became so great for Wilson that he had to use a blindfold and follow Scott's voice. After an attempt lasting ninety-three days, the men were 772 kilometres (480 miles) from the Pole when Scott gave the order to turn back on December 31. More dogs died on the way back to the ship, but the men all survived to try again.

A support ship, the *Morning*, resupplied the expedition and took some members home, including Shackleton. Research trips continued, despite recording temperatures as low as −55°C. After two years, *Discovery* had become solidly wedged in ice, and it took a combination of relief ships and dynamite to free her. The men returned to Portsmouth in September 1904. Still on special leave from the Royal Navy, Scott was appointed captain on the strength of his achievements. There were exhibitions of drawings and scientific samples, lectures and tours. Scott became something of a celebrity, publishing a two-volume account of the expedition, complete with Wilson's dramatic pictures. Despite his relative success, the government ignored Scott's plea to save the *Discovery*, and she was sold.

In 1907, Scott went back to sea as captain on various ships, and met and married Kathleen Bruce in 1908. Shackleton tried a trip of his own, but his team turned back when they were only 156 kilometres (97 miles) from the Pole. The lure of the Antarctic had struck deep in both Scott and Shackleton, but it was Scott's second expedition of 1910 that was to become famous around the world.

Scott wrote that "the main object of the expedition is to reach the South Pole and secure for the British Empire the honour of that achievement." Science would play a lesser part in the second strike for the Pole.

Scott had learned from his previous experiences and consulted once again with Nansen while the money was raised and the team came together. Funds came slowly, and more than one member of the expedition collected money to earn their place. Captain L.E.G. Oates was in charge of ponies. Wilfred Bruce, Scott's brother-in-law, was sent to Russia to buy the vital sled-dogs and Siberian ponies. They also experimented with motor sledges.

The Norwegian explorer Roald Amundsen was also heading south. Originally, his intentions had been to explore the Arctic, but an American, Robert Peary, claimed to have reached the North Pole in 1909, and Amundsen now had his sights set on the unconquered southern pole. He had a hundred dogs with him and supplies for two years. He knew the conditions and he had planned the route. Scott was still struggling to collect funds in New Zealand and Australia. The final stores were loaded and the ship *Terra Nova* sailed on November 29, 1910. Two months before, Scott had received a telegram from Amundsen, sent after he had sailed. It had read only, "Beg leave inform you proceeding Antarctic. Amundsen."

Terra Nova entered the pack ice on December 9, smashing its way through and finally anchoring to solid ice in January 1911. The sledges, base equipment and supplies were unloaded – and the heaviest motor sledge broke through the ice, disappearing into the sea. The slow process of a pole attempt began, with camps established farther and farther south. The ponies did not do at all well and frostbite appeared very early on among the men.

Conditions were awful, with constant blizzards pinning them in their tents. The ponies were all dead by the time they reached the last camp, after dragging the sledges up a 3,048-metre (10,000-ft) glacier. Scott picked Wilson, Evans, Oates and Bowers for the final slog to the Pole, with each man hauling 91 kilograms (200 lb) on sledges.

The smaller team of five battled through blizzards to reach the 89th parallel, the last before the Pole itself. It was shortly afterwards that the men crossed the tracks of Amundsen and his dog teams. Scott and the others were touched by despair but went on regardless, determined to reach the Pole.

They finally stood at the southernmost point on Earth on January 17, 1912. There they found

a tent, with a piece of paper that bore the names of five men: Roald Amundsen, Olav Olavson Bjaaland, Sverre Hassel, Oscar Wisting and Hilmer Hanssen. The note was dated December 14, 1911. The disappointment weighed heavily on all of them – there have been few closer races in history with so much at stake.

The return journey began well enough, but Evans had lost fingernails to the cold, Wilson had strained a tendon in his leg, Scott himself

Captain L.E.G. Oates

had a bruised shoulder and Oates had the beginnings of gangrene in his toes. In such extreme conditions of exhaustion, even small wounds refused to heal. They had all paid a terrible price to be second.

Food began to run short, and every supply dump they reached was a race against starvation and the cold. Oil too ran low, and freezing to death was a real possibility. Evans collapsed on February 16 and never fully recovered. He struggled on the following day, but he could barely stand and died shortly afterwards.

Wilson too was growing weak, so Scott and Bowers made camp by themselves in temperatures of –42 °C.

On March 16 or 17, Oates said he could not go on and wanted to be left in his sleeping bag. He knew he was slowing the team down and that their only slim chance may have been vanishing. The next morning, there was a blizzard blowing. Oates stood up in the tent and said, "I am just going outside and may be some time."

Scott wrote in his diary, "We knew that poor Oates was walking to his death, but though we tried to dissuade him, we knew it was the act of a brave man and an English gentleman." Oates was not seen again and his body has never been found.

By March 20, Scott knew he would lose his right foot to frostbite. They were only 18 kilometres (11 miles) from a camp, but a blizzard prevented them from moving on, and staying still was a slow death for the three men remaining. They had run out of oil and had only two days of starvation rations left. They had run out of time and strength. Scott made the decision to try for the depot, but it was beyond them and they did not leave that last position. Scott's final diary entry was, "It seems a pity, but I do not think that I can write more. R. Scott. For God's sake look after our people."

With the diary ended, Scott wrote letters to the families of those who had died, including a letter to his own wife, where he mentioned their only son.

> I had looked forward to helping you to bring him up, but it is a satisfaction to know that he will be safe with you. . . . Make the boy interested in natural history if you can. It is better than games. They encourage it in some schools. I know you will keep him in the open air. Try to make him believe in a God, it is comforting . . . and guard him against indolence. Make him a strenuous man. I had to force myself into being strenuous, as you know – had always an inclination to be idle.

He also wrote a letter to the public, knowing that his body would be found.

> We took risks, we knew we took them; things have come out against us, and therefore we have no cause for complaint, but bow to the will of providence, determined still to do our best to the last. . . . Had we lived, I should have had a tale to tell of the hardihood, endurance and courage of my companions, which would have stirred the heart of every Englishman. These rough notes and our dead bodies must tell the tale, but surely, surely, a great rich country like ours will see that those who are dependent on us are properly provided for.

Scott knew that the expedition funds were crippled by debt and his last thoughts were the fear that their loved ones would be made destitute by what was still owed. In fact, enough donations came in when the story was known to pay all debts and create grants for the children and wives of those who had perished.

The men were found frozen in their tent by the team surgeon, Atkinson, in November of that year. The diaries and letters were recovered, but a snow cairn was built over their last resting place ready for the day when the moving pack ice would ease them into the frozen sea. The search party looked for Oates without success, finally erecting a cross to him with the following inscription.

HEREABOUTS DIED A VERY GALLANT GENTLEMAN, CAPTAIN L.E.G. OATES OF THE INNISKILLING DRAGOONS. IN MARCH 1912, RETURNING FROM THE POLE, HE WALKED WILLINGLY TO HIS DEATH IN A BLIZZARD TO TRY TO SAVE HIS COMRADES, BESET BY HARDSHIP.

> "For my own sake I do not regret this journey, which has shown that Englishmen can endure hardships, help one another, and meet death with as great a fortitude as ever in the past."
>
> — Robert Falcon Scott

MAKING A GO-KART

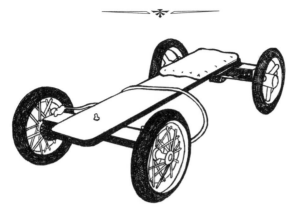

$\mathbf{T}$HE HARDEST PART of making a go-kart is finding the wheels. The sad truth is that most modern strollers have tiny wheels, so the classic idea of finding a baby carriage and removing the axles intact isn't really possible anymore. Those baby carriages that do survive are antiques and are too valuable for our purposes.

THE DESIGN

You will need:

- Two fixed axles with wheels attached.
- Plank to sit on – we used $^{3}/_{4}$-inch pine.
- Axle wood. Length will depend on your axles, but we used a plank of $3^{1}/_{2} \times 1^{1}/_{2}$ inches (88 mm × 40 mm).
- Rope for the handle.
- Two eye-screws to attach the rope.
- Four electrician's metal straps (see explanation on next page).
- Wood paint (colour of your choice).
- $1^{1}/_{2}$-inch screws (40 mm).
- Vinyl and foam if you intend to add a seat.
- A steering bolt (see explanation).
- Upholstery tacks for the seat.

However, the good news is that there are other things you can use. We found our two axles after many visits to three local waste management centres – dumps. It took many weeks to find our axles, so the best planning you can do is to go out now and make your face known to the employees in every dump or junkyard in your town. Our rear axle came from a golf cart and our front from a modern three-wheel stroller – used ones are just starting to appear curbside on garbage day, so you might find one faster than we did. The other possibility is to find a tricycle and use the rear wheels from that. As long as it has a fixed axle that doesn't turn with the wheels, you needn't worry. If at all possible, use metal wheels rather than plastic ones. Plastic is an awful material and has a tendency to shatter under stress – while going down a hill, for example.

First, cut the wood. We cut two lengths of 43 centimetres (17 in) for the axles, but this will be different for each project. We also cut quite a long central plank at 114 cm (3 ft, 9 in). Again, that depends on the length of your legs. Allow some growing room at least. It really is a good idea to let an adult cut the wood for you, especially if power tools are involved. If you ignore this advice and cut off a finger, please do not send it to us in the post as proof.

It is also a good idea to paint the wood – or varnish it – at this stage. We completely forgot to do this and painting it at a late stage was very fiddly. Better to do it now. We used a wood primer and black matte paint. As we had an old can of varnish in the shed, we then varnished it as well. You can, of course, buy paint, but digging out old cans with just a dab still wet at the bottom is somehow more satisfying.

When the painted wood is dry, attach the axles. Twenty years ago, we used U-shaped nails, and these were perfectly reliable. This time we found our axles were much wider and had to find an alternative. This is the sort of problem you might have to solve.

To the right is an electrical strap, available for less than a dollar from any electrical shop. These are also quite useful for attaching axles and come in a variety of sizes.

We used three of them on the front axle. The original plan was to use two, but one of the screw holes seemed weak and we wanted it to be reliable. Make sure you place the straps carefully so that the axle is straight on the plank. Given identical straps, we measured the distance from the top of each one to the edge of the wood. You can place this by eye, but it's better to measure and be certain.

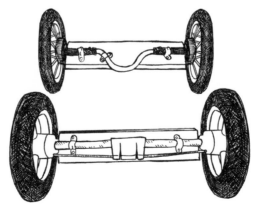

Screws measuring 1½ inch (40 mm) will secure the rear of the main plank, as shown below. It looks easy, but some careful measuring is necessary to make the angle between the main plank and the axle plank exactly ninety degrees. You must also make sure that the overhang on each side is the same. We clamped the pieces together quite loosely and then used a rubber mallet to tap them into place, measuring again and again until we were satisfied.

The steering is the only tricky thing left to do. We were extraordinarily lucky in finding that the single wheel bolt on a three-wheel pram is perfect for this job, but you can't depend on that kind of luck. You must find a bolt with a thread only part-way along.

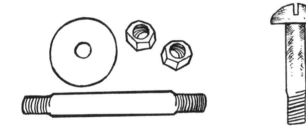

Bolt from a three-wheel stroller.　　　　　*More likely to use this one.*

The benefit of this is that a nut can be tightened on the bolt and yet the bolt can still turn freely in the hole. Bolts are available from any hardware store. Find one a little over the length you need and add a washer at both ends – or more if it's too long.

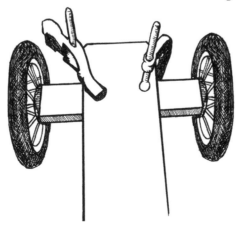

Getting the front position right wasn't as hard as the rear. It was crucial to have the same distance of axle poking out on either side as before, but it didn't have to be at ninety degrees, as the axle was going to pivot – otherwise there could be no steering. The nice thing about this design is that you sit with your feet on the steering bar, also holding onto ropes. As a result, it is extremely manoeuvrable.

We decided to put a seat on our go-kart. We asked in a carpet shop and were given a bit of carpet and a vinyl sample for free. We folded the vinyl around a piece of pine, using the carpet as padding between. We then tacked the carpet and vinyl down with upholstery nails from a hardware store and screwed the whole thing to the main plank from underneath. The rope was attached using a bowline knot on each end.

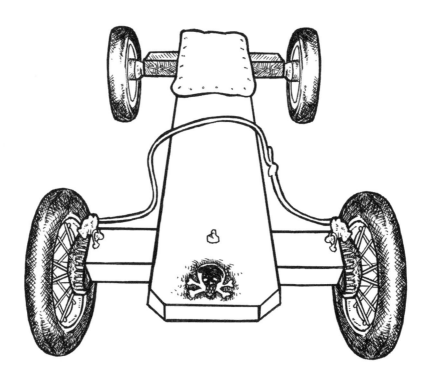

MAKING A GO-KART

INSECTS AND SPIDERS

INSECTS RULE. Millions of species and trillions upon trillions of individual little spineless creatures dominate our backyards – and the rest of the planet. They abound everywhere except the open ocean and account for more than half of all known species of living things. Insects have a head with a bunch of sensory structures and mouthparts, a thorax with jointed legs (and usually with wings) and an abdomen packed with digestive and reproductive "guts." Bug "blood" (most of the goo you see when you squash an insect) doesn't run in veins like our blood. Instead, it acts as a sort of multi-purpose hydraulic fluid that fills the insect's body cavity. The body is covered in a shell called an "exoskeleton." A few insects, like blister beetles, wasps and bees, can be dangerous, but most of those in your backyard are fair game for a good close look. Let's look at a few now.

A stink bug uses its straw-like beak to suck "blood" from a larva.

The brush-legged wolf spider, a fine – and hairy – hunter.

True Bugs (*Hemiptera*)

We routinely call all insects "bugs," but when an entomologist (insect scientist) uses the term, it means a "true bug": an insect with long, sucking mouthparts. Aphids, spittle bugs, ambush bugs, stink bugs and bed bugs are all true bugs. Look for the soft-bodied aphids in a garden to see how they connect to their host plant using long, straw-like beaks that suck up sap. Bright yellow ambush bugs so common on goldenrod use similar beaks to suck "blood" from other insects. (The best way to spot this super-common but superbly camouflaged bug is to look for a dead bee on a flower – it is usually connected to an ambush bug's beak!)

Other familiar bugs include the shield-shaped bugs you probably already know as stink bugs, whose powerful pong comes from glands that pump foul-smelling chemicals onto wick-like body surfaces. Some stink bugs impale other insects with their beaks; others use their beaks to suck berries and stems.

Spittle bugs are probably the strangest of all, since they begin life clinging to stems, sucking sap through their beaks and blowing bubbles out their bottoms to get rid of excess

The bubble-blowing spittle bug nymph surrounds itself in froth.

The long-legged water strider glides effortlessly across the surface of a pond.

sap. The whole sticky mess bubbles over their bodies, making white frothy masses that make it look like someone has been spitting in your back meadow. Only the young stages, or nymphs, live in these protective spittle shelters.

Spittle bugs are close relatives of cicadas, much bigger sap-sucking bugs that make that familiar loud buzz heard on hot summer days. Male cicadas fill the air with sound for a few weeks every August but spend seven years underground feeding on tree roots before emerging as adults. One kind of cicada found only in eastern North America appears only once every seventeen years and spends the rest of its life underground.

Many common water bugs, such as water striders, backswimmers and water boatmen, feed on aquatic organisms. Always handle aquatic bugs carefully as many are quick to use their beaks in self-defence.

Grasshoppers and Crickets (*Orthoptera*)

Grasshoppers and crickets are easy to spot. If an insect is bigger than your thumbnail and jumps, it's probably a grasshopper or cricket. Both groups have big, muscular hind legs and straight, paper-like wings that often double as musical instruments. In eastern North America, you can hear common field crickets and even Chinese fighting crickets, which were introduced accidentally from the Far East. If a cricket is male, its front wings, normally folded flat over its back, will

Chinese fighting cricket.

expand like drum skins, amplifying its song as wing rubs against wing. Male tree crickets and katydids have similar structures, and if you catch one and bring it inside for a night, it will probably sing loudly enough to drive your whole family crazy. Every kind of cricket and katydid (as well as other long-horned relatives like coneheads and meadow grasshoppers) has a unique song, and if your ears are good, you can identify different species by their night serenades.

Short-horned grasshoppers (with short antennae) are not noted for their singing talents. A few make crude scraping or clacking sounds, but that's about it. Some of the larger short-horned grasshoppers belong to a long-winged group called locusts because they occasionally form enormous swarms. True locust swarms no longer occur in Canada or the United States. The Rocky Mountain locust used to be a serious pest, but that species went extinct a hundred years ago. Now, you can find this species only in glaciers, where masses of them blundered over a century ago. If you want to see them, you had better go soon, because the glaciers are receding and the locusts are rotting away.

The bush katydid uses camouflage to blend with its environment.

Earwigs (*Dermaptera*)

Earwigs are unmistakable because of their forcep-like tails (cerci) and their very short, leathery front wings (the hind wings are usually folded away under the front wings). The tails act as pincers that grab other bugs, then spraying them with nasty chemicals. European earwigs are another accidentally introduced species that have become quite common. As omnivores, they'll eat almost everything, from your mother's prize dahlias to other insects, so they make easy-to-feed pets, though not very popular ones. Female earwigs are really unusual among insects because they take care of their young, wrapping their bodies around their eggs and newly hatched nymphs.

The European Earwig's distinctive feature is its pincer tail.

Praying Mantids (*Mantodea*)

Mantids are mostly tropical insects, but a few species of these spectacular predators are common in North America. These big insects, originally imported from China and Europe, spend the winter as insulated bunches of eggs that look like blobs of sponge toffee stuck to stems and twigs. If you bring the brown egg masses inside during early winter, they probably won't hatch since, like many insects, they need to be exposed to a certain number of cold days before they will behave like it's spring. If you bring the eggs inside, just before spring they will hatch into dozens of hungry nymphs that will promptly eat each other. Normally, the nymphs hatch in

Praying mantid.

the wild, and they disperse and eat small insects during spring and early summer, appearing as fully winged adults late in the summer. Mantids will eat just about anything, even each other, but they are harmless to you and me.

Mayflies (*Ephemeroptera*)

Mayflies appear near ponds, lakes and rivers, and their distinctive wings and tails make them instantly recognizable. The wings are triangular and clasped together above the body, and the two or three tails are long and trailing. Mayflies are really special among winged insects because they have two different winged stages and they are the only insects to shed their skins after attaining a full set of wings. For all other insects, growth stops when wings appear: little mosquitoes don't grow bigger, and tiny beetles will always be tiny. Because insects have an exoskeleton – a suit of armour that does not grow – they have to shed to get bigger.

A mayfly develops as a wingless nymph under water before emerging in the air as a fully winged insect without its nymphal skin. Newly emerged winged mayflies will cast off their skin one more time to grow into another winged stage.

Once mayflies reach their winged stage, they live only from less than an hour to a few days.

The scientific name *Ephemeroptera* refers to an ephemeral or short-lived winged stage, and indeed mayflies often have very brief adult lives, ranging from less than an hour to a few days. They don't even bother eating and some spend their entire adult lives flying. Look for swarms of male mayflies around dusk, especially if you live anywhere near a river or lake. The males are full of air (remember, they don't eat), and they seem to float up and down as they use their spectacularly large eyes to look for incoming females.

The big mayflies, locally known as fishflies or shadflies, often form huge swarms near lakes, and they sometimes end up in fishy-smelling piles near street lights. Shadflies only appear as adults for a couple of weeks in June; otherwise they spend their lives as burrowing nymphs that filter-feed on organic matter in lake bottoms.

Dragonflies and Damselflies (*Odonata*)

Dragonflies and damselflies are unmistakable because of their long, narrow abdomens and out-stretched wings. Like mayflies, dragonflies develop under water as wingless nymphs before emerging as aerial adults. Dragonflies and damselflies are voracious predators. As nymphs, they have fantastic hydraulic lower lips that shoot out in a fraction of a second to grab passing prey. Hold your hand cupped under your chin, then shoot your arm straight out to grab something with your fingers. Now imagine doing that just by squeezing your stomach muscles to force blood to your arm, in about one one-hundredth of a second. This gives you an idea of how dragonfly and damselfly nymphs attack small fish and other insects.

You can find dragonfly nymphs in any pond, and it is fun to put them in a dish to watch how they move. Try dropping some food colouring near a dragonfly nymph's tail, and then poke it gently. The nymph will fold its legs up, then blast across the dish as it shoots a coloured jet of water out its anus – hydraulic pressure in action again! Damselfly nymphs are more delicate and swim using paddle-like tails rather than jet propulsion.

Damselflies are voracious predators, and adults like this Rambur's forktail can be seen scooping victims from waterside foliage.

Adult dragonflies and damselflies are as remarkable as nymphs and fly with incredible speed and manoeuvrability using a muscle-packed thorax that drives four

wings. Their legs are held in front of the thorax to form a spiny basket into which prey (such as mosquitoes and blackflies) is scooped before being ground down by strong mandibles. Dragonflies scoop up their prey in flight, while the more slender and delicate damselflies pick their prey off stems and leaves

A dragonfly nymph grabs a fish with its hydraulic lower lip.

Butterflies and Moths (*Lepidoptera*)

Butterflies and moths belong to the *Lepidoptera* group, meaning "scaly wing." The name refers to the waxy powder that sticks to your fingers after you handle ones of these insects. That powder, which covers the wings and bodies, is made of microscopic scales.

You probably recognize the monarch, a bright orange butterfly that uses its colour to ward off potential predators. Predators see the colour and know that the butterflies taste awful. The monarch gets its defensive protection from poison-laced milkweed plants, which it eats when it's a caterpillar. Some other butterflies pretend to be monarchs to avoid being eaten, even though they aren't poisonous. Monarchs make an incredible one-way journey south every fall. Eastern monarchs fly all the way to Mexico to spend the winter; the next generation returns the following spring. Western monarchs migrate to wintering sites in California.

All *Lepidoptera* that are neither butterflies nor members of a similar group called skippers are referred to as moths. Most moths fly at night

The elegant cecropia moth.

rather than during the day. Some are tiny, with larvae that burrow into leaves, leaving telltale trails that you can see on many tree leaves. Look for a leaf with a trail and hold it up to the light to see what's inside. It could be a little caterpillar (a larval moth), but there are other insects (larval flies and larval beetles) that make similar burrows. Although most moths are small and obscure, the ones you are likely to notice are big ones, like the hand-sized, giant silkworm moths that occasionally appear around porch lights on early summer nights. Check out their heads – if their antennae look like broad feathers, they are males; if their antennae are thinner, they are probably females. If you stick a female in a screen cage where her powerful perfume can seep out into the night sky, you'll attract dozens of males! Common giant silkworm moths include the ethereal green luna and the fat-bodied brown

The giant green luna moth is hard to miss.

polyphemus and cecropia moths. Their fat larvae, often found feeding on tree leaves, are adorned with brightly coloured spikes, spines and decorations. Always handle brightly decorated caterpillars with great care, as their bristles are sometimes hollow and loaded with poisons.

Many moths spin silken cocoons in which to spend the pupal stage, and the silk from some moth cocoons can be spun into fine cloth. Most natural silk comes from the cocoons of the domestic silkworm moth. You can buy the larvae of this fat, flightless moth in pet stores, where they are sold as food. Feed them some mulberry leaves and they will soon spin out over two kilometres of fine silk thread and weave it into a cocoon. Another moth you can buy in stores spends its larval life in the seeds of a southwestern shrub, whacking its body against the inside of the seed when disturbed. You may recognize these as Mexican jumping beans.

A silkworm moth and its dome-shaped cocoon.

Beetles (*Coleoptera*)

The uniquely talented bombardier beetle can blast smelly chemicals out of its hind end.

A beetle is easy to recognize by the straight line that runs down its back where its armour-like front wings meet when closed. Like living transformers, beetles are tanks or submarines when they have their front wings closed and are totally different, aerial creatures when their wings are open. Water beetles store air in spiracles (air holes) beneath their armour; some terrestrial beetles can roll into an effectively impenetrable ball. Turn over rocks in your backyard and you'll probably uncover a beetle. Ground beetles are dark, shiny predators that will give you stinky fingers if you touch them. Bombardier beetles produce nasty-smelling, defensive chemicals that blast out of their bums at boiling temperatures. Other common beetles include the familiar lady beetles (commonly called "lady bugs"), many of which are aphid-eating beetles that advertise their poisonous blood by parading around in bright red and black. Our most common lady beetles, like the now widespread Asian lady beetle, were introduced to North America in the hopes that they would control pests. They do eat a lot of aphids, but they also displace native species and sometimes become nuisances when they gather in sheltered places to spend the winter – like in your house.

Many brightly coloured, inedible lady beetles spend the winter in dense clusters.

Weevils, with their often long, tubular snouts, are a large and diverse group of insects.

Beetles are everywhere – leaf beetles feed on plants; dung beetles eat poop; and fireflies light up the night. Weevils, long-snouted beetles, are more diverse than all vertebrates! Fireflies are not flies at all but bioluminescent beetles with constantly glowing larvae that often feed on snails. Adult fireflies switch their lights on and off at will to attract mates. Some fireflies fake the light patterns of other species to attract and then eat them. Like lady beetles, fireflies have toxic blood and are not normally eaten by other insects. Neither lady beetles nor fireflies, however, are dangerous to handle. But you should avoid blister and rove beetles. Blister beetles are soft-bodied and can pump toxic blood out of their leg joints. This blood may blister your fingers. Some bright red-and-black rove beetles excrete powerful chemicals that cause sores on the skin if you accidentally squish them.

Flies (*Diptera*)

Flies are unusual because they have only one pair of wings, with a pair of knobs on stems behind them. The knobs, called halters, work like the gyroscopic indicators of an airplane and make the flies master navigators in the air. Houseflies, blowflies, flower flies, horseflies, blackflies, midges and mosquitoes are among the most familiar flies, but there are tens of thousands of different kinds. Look around your house for slow-moving, dull-coloured flies covered with golden corn–silk hairs. Called cluster flies, because of their habit of clustering outside houses as they seek sheltered places (like attics) to spend the winter, these fat flyers feed on earthworms as larvae. Metallic flies called blowflies dump loads of plump, white eggs on any decaying meat they can find. Larval blowflies, or maggots, eat mixtures of decaying meat and bacteria, and play an important role in breaking down dead matter. Other flies prefer plants to carcasses and play an essential role in pollinating flowers. Drone flies – flower flies that look just like honey bees – are among the most common flies on flowers in North American gardens. You can tell them from bees by the two wings and the very different antennae, but you must look closely. Drone flies develop in puddles and pond margins, where their larvae, called rat-tailed maggots, feed on microbes in the muck while breathing at the water surface using a long, snorkel-like breathing

This parasitic fly develops inside another insect, eating it from the inside out.

tube. Some other common flower fly larvae are predators and can be found among almost any group of aphids, creeping around like little killer leeches (all fly larvae are legless).

One of the largest groups of flies, called the *Tachinidae*, is composed entirely of parasitic species that develop inside other insects, killing their hosts in the process. The biggest, most bristly flies seen visiting garden flowers are parasitic and develop as maggots inside the bodies of moth caterpillars.

The most dangerous flies, in fact the most dangerous of all animals, are mosquitoes, which carry diseases that kill millions of people every year. North America has relatively few mosquito-carried diseases, but it is best to avoid being bitten just in case.

Ants, Bees and Wasps (*Hymenoptera*)

Ants are probably the most widely recognized of all insects because wingless worker ants show up everywhere. These workers are females from a social colony in which a queen does all the

A solitary hunting wasp attacking a cicada.

egg-laying. Swarms of winged male and female ants appear periodically to establish new nests. Ants are actually a special kind of wasp, closely related to yellow jackets and hornets. Some have a sting similar to a hornet's but less powerful; others defend themselves with formic acid and other chemicals.

Hornets and yellow jackets form colonies each spring from queens that survive the winter. Social wasps use their stings to defend their colonies, but most wasps don't live in colonies and therefore rarely sting humans. Instead, they sting to paralyze insects and spiders they bring back to their nests to feed their larvae. Look under your eaves or in your garage rafters for the mud nests made by solitary wasps. If you break a nest, you'll find several cells, each containing paralyzed insects that are feeding an individual larva. The common mud nests are associated with two kinds of wasps: the yellow-and-black mud dauber that makes the nest and a shining, black one that takes over the nest the year after. Other kinds of solitary wasps make different kinds of nests, stocking them with different kinds of prey, carrying them back to the nest in different ways. Wasps are fun to watch and even the big, well-armed ones that tackle heavy prey such as cicadas are harmless insects that rarely sting in defence.

Bees are a special group of wasps that stock their nests with pollen rather than insects. Bees, especially the domestic honey bee, are common in gardens, where they play an important role in pollination. Most bees nest on their own, but honey bees and bumble bees are social insects and, like other

A mud dauber capping its mud nest.

The domestic honey bee.

social *Hymenoptera*, do use their stings for defence. If you get stung, watch carefully for effects other than a raised, sore bump. A few people are allergic to bee and wasp stings, and dozens of North Americans die every year from sting allergies. Yellow jackets and hornets, brightly banded social wasps that live in exposed or hidden paper nests, are certainly the most dangerous stingers in North America, and you should steer clear of them.

Spiders (*Arachnids*)

Spiders and their relatives are not insects but belong to a larger group called the *Arthropoda*, which means "jointed legs." They have external skeletons like insects, so they need jointed legs to move. (Think of the leg and arm joints in a suit of armour.) Spiders, scorpions, mites and ticks all have fangs, called chelicerae, used to impale prey and suck out their innards. Some spiders, like widows and recluse spiders, occasionally bite people and inject them with venoms that can cause excruciating pain, sores and swelling. It is worth learning to recognize and avoid black widows, which are distinctively fat, shiny, black spiders branded with a bright red warning mark in the shape of an hourglass. Despite the bad rap spiders get because of the few nasty ones, most are harmless (unless you are allergic), and you can safely find some really interesting kinds in any backyard.

A stealthy crab spider turns yellow to match its flower home. Here, it has caught a bee.

You have probably seen spiders that spin orb-like webs to capture prey, but there are lots of others that don't hang out in webs. Flowers, for example, are often home to crab spiders able to adjust their colour from yellow to white according to the flower they call home. Look for an awkwardly posed bee

The zebra spider is known for its acrobatic leaps and its curiosity.

or fly sitting still on the petals, and chances are it has been captured by a crab spider.

Closer to the ground, you might find wolf spiders, aptly named hunters that have the distinctive habit of carrying egg sacs under their abdomens and transporting newly hatched spiderlings on their backs. The other hunting spiders that are fun to watch are the big-eyed jumping spiders often found hunting in sunny, exposed spots or near your porch light. Many are brightly coloured, but the most common is the small black-and-grey zebra spider.

JUGGLING

THIS IS THE SKILL of tossing objects in the air and catching them. First of all, you will need three round balls, about the size of tennis balls. You can make excellent ones by putting a couple of handfuls of rice or flour into a balloon. If you use fruit, it will be very messy, so be prepared to eat them bruised. Alternatively, juggling balls can be bought from any toy shop. It looks difficult, but on average it takes about an hour to learn, two at most.

1

1. Hold one ball in your right hand and gently lob it into your left. Now lob it back in the direction it came. Go back and forth with this until you are comfortable.

2. Now let's add another ball! Hold one ball in your right hand and one in your left. As you lob the ball from your right hand to your left, release the ball in your left hand and catch the incoming ball. The hard part is releasing the left-hand ball so that you lob it back to your right hand and catch it. This will take some practice, or you might pick it up immediately. Make sure both balls are flowing in a nice arc from hand to hand. This will give you more time to release and catch.

3. Ball three! Hold two balls in your right hand. Hold the third ball in your left hand. Lob the first ball from right to left, and as you catch it in your left hand, release the second ball lobbing it back to your right. (This is just step 2, holding a third ball.)

2

3

The hard bit is releasing that third ball as you catch the second ball in your right hand, and lobbing the third ball back to your left hand. You must keep this lob-release-catch going from hand to hand. Practise, practise, practise!

Now for a fancy trick. Start in the beginning position (two balls in the right hand, one in the left), put your right hand behind your back and throw the two balls forward over your shoulder. As they sail over to the front, lob the left-hand ball up as normal and catch the two coming over in your left and right hand. Yes, this is as hard as it sounds. Quickly lob the right-hand one to your left and catch the one in the air coming down. You are into the routine. This is an impressive start to juggling three balls, but it *is* very hard, so the best of luck to you.

QUESTIONS ABOUT THE WORLD – PART TWO

1. **How do we measure the earth's circumference?**
2. **Why does a day have twenty-four hours?**
3. **How far away are the stars?**
4. **Why is the sky blue?**
5. **Why can't we see the other side of the moon?**
6. **What causes the tides?**

I. HOW DO WE MEASURE THE EARTH'S CIRCUMFERENCE?

The simple answer is that we use Polaris, the Pole Star. Imagine someone standing at the equator. From their point of view the Pole Star would be on the horizon – as in the diagram on the next page. If the same person stood at the North Pole, Polaris would be almost directly overhead. It should be clear, then, that in moving north, Polaris appears to rise in the sky. A sextant can confirm the changing angle.

The angle through which the Pole Star rises is equal to the change in the observer's latitude. If Polaris rises by ten degrees, you have travelled ten degrees of latitude.

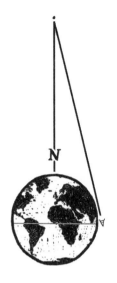

All the observer has to do is measure how far he has travelled when Polaris has risen by one degree. Multiply that distance by 360 and you have your circumference of the earth. Easy.

The actual circumference is 40,074 kilometres (24,901 miles) around the equator and 40,006 kilometres (24,859 miles) around the poles – or in rough terms 40,000 kilometres (25,000 miles) around, with a slightly fatter equator. As you can see, this is not a perfect globe. The correct term is "geoid," which just means "shaped like the earth." When you're a planet, you get your own word.

2. WHY DOES A DAY HAVE TWENTY-FOUR HOURS?

Well, because we say it does. The modern world uses the Roman system of measuring time from midnight to midnight – as opposed to the Greek system of measuring from sunset to sunset. The Romans also divided daylight into twelve hours. This caused difficulties, as summer hours would be longer than winter hours. When the system was made more accurate, it was sensible enough to double the twelve for the night hours. Most of the way we measure time is based on the number twelve, fractions and multiples of it, in fact – which is why we have sixty minutes and sixty seconds. The architects of the French Revolution were keen not only on introducing a decimal number system and metres to the world, but also a ten-day week, a hundred-minute hour and a hundred-second minute. Needless to say, no one else was quite as keen.

3. HOW FAR AWAY ARE THE STARS?

Light travels at 300,000 kilometres (186,000 miles) a second. In a year it would travel almost 6 million, million miles. (The American billion, or one thousand million, is now all-conquering in terms of usage.) A U.S. "trillion" is a thousand U.S. billion.

Using the American definition, a light year is 10 trillion kilometres. That is a long way by anyone's standards.

The closest star to us is Proxima Centauri – about four and a third light years away. That is even farther. To put it another way, the light from Proxima Centauri has taken four and a third years to get here. The actual star could have blown up yesterday, but we wouldn't know for almost five years.

The farthest stars we can see are more than 1,000 light years away.

4. Why is the sky blue?

To understand this, it's important to understand that colour doesn't exist as some separate thing in the world. What we call blue paint just means paint that reflects light in certain wavelengths we have learned to call blue. Colour-blind people have eyes that work perfectly well but are different from most other eyes in one way – how they register light wavelengths. Take a moment and think about this. Colour does not exist – only reflected light exists. In a red light, blue paint will look black, as there is no blue light to reflect. In a blue light, red paint will look black.

Now, the sky is blue because blue light comes in on a short wavelength and wallops into oxygen atoms of roughly the same size. When we look up and see a blue sky, we are seeing that interaction.

At sunset, we see more red because the sunlight is passing through many more kilometres of atmosphere at that low angle near the horizon. The blue light interacts with the oxygen and is scattered as before – but cannot reach the eye through the extra kilometres this time. Instead, we see the other end of the spectrum, the red light.

5. Why can't we see the other side of the moon?

Until the late twentieth century, humankind had no idea what lurked on the dark side of the moon. This is because the same face was presented to observers on Earth all the way through the lunar cycle.

The moon takes twenty-nine and a half days to go around the earth. It does actually rotate on its own axis, completing a full turn in . . . twenty-nine and a half days. As these two are the same, it always shows the same face.

The best way to demonstrate this is with a tennis ball and a soccer ball. Mark the side of the tennis ball and place the soccer ball somewhere where it can't roll away – or have someone hold it. Now move the tennis ball around your Earth, keeping the same side always inward. By the time you have gone all the way around, the tennis ball will also have turned on its own axis.

6. What causes the tides?

Following neatly on from the last question, the answer is *gravity* – from the moon and the sun. The moon's massive presence overhead actually pulls oceans out of place. These two diagrams are deliberately exaggerated to show the effect. They are *not* to scale!

 Spring Tide – New Moon

 Moon

 Sun

Spring Tide – Full Moon

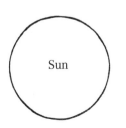

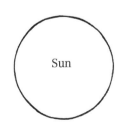 Sun

The seas move more easily than land, though the whole planet is actually affected. What happens in practice is that the earth's own spin produces two high and two low tides each day. It takes twelve hours to expose the other side of the earth to the moon's gravity, a little like squeezing a balloon twice around the middle in twenty-four hours. Both ends bulge to create high tides and then withdraw to create low tides.

The diagram on the previous page is actually of a "spring" tide, which occurs twice a month at the new and full moon. The name has nothing to do with the season. When the moon is in line with the sun and the earth, the tide is particularly strong. The weakest tides are known as "neap" tides and occur at the quarter moon, as in this diagram. The moon's effect is lessened by being out of line with the sun.

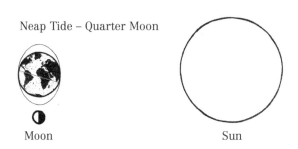

Neap Tide – Quarter Moon

Moon   Sun

ASTRONOMY – THE STUDY
OF THE HEAVENS

ASTRONOMY IS NOT ASTROLOGY. Astrology is nonsense. The idea that our lives can be affected by the flight of planets is not even slightly plausible. Venus may have been named after a goddess of love, but the planet's movement can have no bearing on our own chances for romance. The planet could equally have been called by another name, after all. The first (and last) point about star watching is that it is science and not superstition – but the stories of ancient heroes like Orion can be fascinating. Knowing Orion chases Taurus works as a mnemonic – an aid to memory.

There are eighty-eight constellations that can be seen in the night sky at different times of the year, and all the visible stars have names, or at least numbers. As the earth rotates, the positions of constellations change and you can follow them through the seasons (see Star-Maps that follow).

This chapter is an introduction to sky watching. Most of us live and work in noisy, artificial environments. Light pollution from cities hides the glories of the night sky, but those who are curious always find ways to explore them. Naked-eye astronomy is easy and fun and can be done alone or with friends. This chapter will make you more familiar with the wonders of the universe.

Look at the stars! look, look up at the skies!
O look at all the fire-folk sitting in the air!
The bright boroughs, the circle-citadels there!

Gerald Manley Hopkins

Since the dawn of time, humankind has grouped stars into constellations, filling the heavens with heroes, gods and fantastic creatures. The myths and histories of lost civilizations can be found above us and help us understand the legends and stories that chart our own time.

One of the most easily recognizable constellations, and a great way to start finding your way around the skies, is **Ursa Major**, the **Great Bear**.

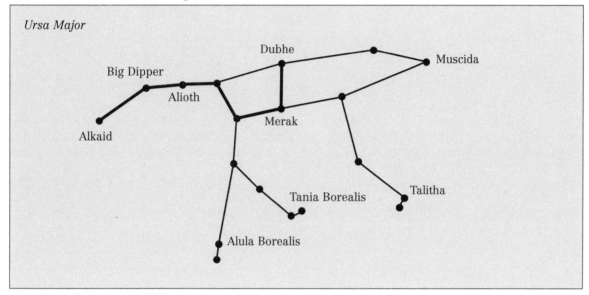

This constellation gets its name from the Greek legend of Callisto, a nymph transformed by Zeus into a she-bear. Many Native American tribes have also seen this constellation as a bear. Maybe the ancient Greeks sailed farther than we realize! Particularly famous is the group of seven stars often called the **Big Dipper** or the **Plough**. In Cherokee legend, the handle of the Big Dipper is seen as a team of hunters chasing the bear who is visible high in the sky in spring until he sets on autumn evenings. Each day, the hunters chase the bear farther west. Boys, you will need your compass.

This distinctive star system has been noted by Shakespeare and Tennyson. In Hindu mythology, the Big Dipper is seen as the home of the seven great sages. The Chinese saw these stars as the masters of heavenly reality; the Egyptians, as the thigh of a bull. The Europeans saw a wagon and the Anglo-Saxons associated them with the legends surrounding King Arthur.

In ancient times, north could be plotted using the star **Alkaid**, in the Big Dipper. Today north can be found in **Ursa Minor**, a constellation that lies almost alongside Ursa Major. In Greek legend this constellation was named after Arcas, the son of Callisto. He too was changed into a bear and left to follow his mother eternally around the north celestial pole.

Finding north, as with it all other points on the compass, is as important as knowing your address. It is one of the first steps to understanding where you are. The key star is called **Polaris** (see next page), the Pole Star for the northern hemisphere.

From the Big Dipper, mentally draw a line through the stars Dubhe and Merak, extend upward five times its length and you hit Polaris. Face Polaris and you are facing north. If there is light pollution, it may be the only star visible in Ursa Minor.

If you are in the southern hemisphere, then finding south is just as important, and almost as easy. First identify the **Southern Cross** (see right) and mentally extend a line down from the long arm. To the left are two stars, Rigil Kentaurus and Hadar, known as the pointers. Extend a line down from

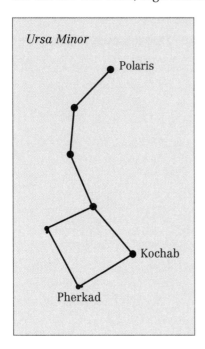

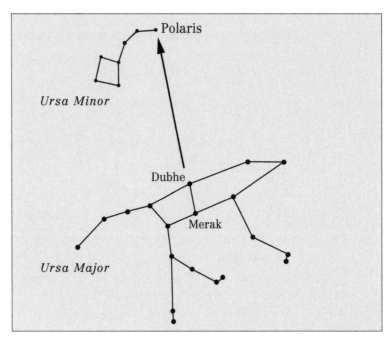

between them until it crosses the first line. This point is directly above south.

On a clear night in winter in the northern hemisphere if you face south, away from the Pole Star, the constellation of **Orion** is the chief attraction. It is characterized by its three belt stars with the red star Betelgeuse above and Rigel below.

In Greek mythology, Orion was a great hunter. Artemis, the goddess of the moon and the hunt, fell in love with him and neglected her duties of lighting the night sky. As punishment, her brother, Apollo, tricked her into slaying him from afar with an arrow. When she realized what she had done, she put his body in the sky with his two war dogs, Canis Major and Canis Minor. According to ancient Greek astronomers, her grief explains the sad, cold look of the moon.

The brightest star in the sky is in Canis Major – **Sirius**, the **Dog Star**. Sirius rises in the east in late summer, at the heels of Orion, hunting with him through the winter.

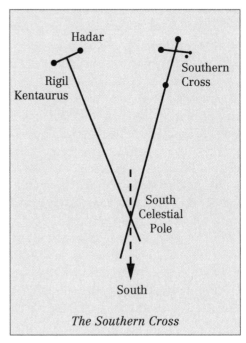

The Southern Cross

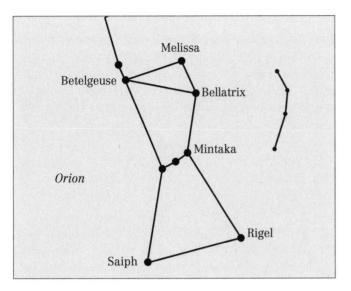

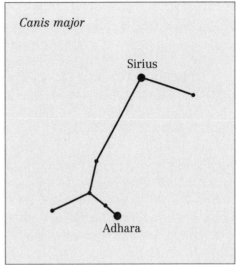

Above and to the right of Orion and his dogs is their prey, **Taurus**, the bull. Its red eye looks back nervously – the star Aldebaran. Since the time of the ancient Babylonians, some 5,000 years ago, this constellation has been seen as a bull. Bulls have been worshipped since ancient times as symbols of strength and fertility. The Greeks saw the constellation as Zeus disguised as a bull. In this form he seduced the princess Europa and swam to Crete with her on his back. Only the forequarters are visible in the constellation, as it emerges from the waves.

In the shoulder of Taurus is the most famous open star cluster in the sky, the **Pleiades**, also known as the **Seven Sisters**.

The legend tells that the sisters were being chased by Orion and called out to Zeus to protect them. Zeus turned them into doves and placed them in the sky. In a Native American tale, the Pleiades are seven girls who are walking through the sky and get lost, never making it home. They remain in the sky, huddled together for warmth. The seventh sister is hard to see because she really wants to go home and her tears dim her lustre. On a reasonably clear night, you should be able to pick out six of the sisters. The whole star cluster actually has more than 500 stars, but it is possible to see as many as nine with the naked eye.

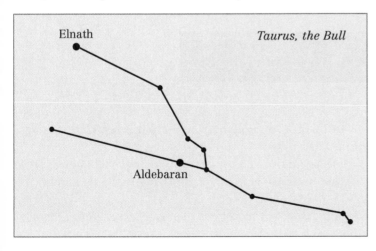

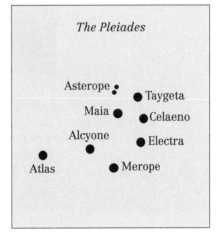

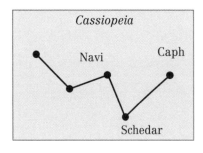

Cassiopeia

Navi   Caph

Schedar

On the other side of Polaris from the Big Dipper is the striking W-shaped figure of **Cassiopeia**. (be careful not to mix this up with the Little Dipper.) This is the most prominent constellation in the winter sky, visible all year round in the northern hemisphere. If the Big Dipper is low in the sky, then the W of Cassiopeia will be high. It is not as accurate in finding north, but it does point in the general direction of the Pole Star.

In Greek mythology, Cassiopeia was the Queen of Ethiopia. The Romans saw her as being chained to her throne and placed in the heavens to hang upside down, for boasting that her daughter, Andromeda, was more beautiful than Aphrodite. Arab cultures pictured the constellation as a kneeling camel.

In parts of Canada, you might see something else in the night sky, though it's not a constellation. Instead, it's a phenomenon that occurs in the earth's atmosphere. The aurora borealis, or "northern lights," is caused when electrons and protons from outside the earth's atmosphere interact with atoms in its upper atmosphere. The aurora borealis can take many forms, looking like a huge arc, band, or curtain of light in the sky. It is usually green, though sometimes tinged with red. And though we now have a scientific explanation for the northern lights, it wasn't always that way. A sixteenth-century drawing depicted them as coming from candles above the clouds, and some Native nations believed the lights were the dancing spirits of their ancestors.

The aurora borealis, or "northern lights," illuminate the night sky.

Finding your way around the night sky can be quite a challenge for the beginner. In this chapter, we have described a few of the brighter stars and constellations from which you will be able to explore further. There are many good periodicals about astronomy that will open up the sky to you. The stories that surround our heavens are wonderful and colourful and as easy as reading a road map, with a little work!

Remember that all stars twinkle – the light shifts and flickers as you concentrate on it. Planets do not. If you narrow your eyes, you can see the disc of Jupiter even without binoculars.

MAKING A PAPER HAT,
BOAT AND WATER BOMB

THERE IS SOMETHING ridiculously simple about these, but how to make them is something every boy should know. After all, with a little luck, you may one day have children of your own, and seeing a paper boat bobbing along on water is a pleasure.

THE HAT

First – the hat. The boat is just a few extra folds on the hat.

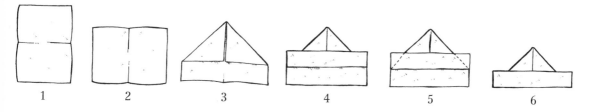

1. Fold a sheet of 8 1/2 x 11 in half, as shown.
2. Fold a central line in the half-page and open out again.
3. Turn down the corners to that central line.
4. Fold one long strip up.
5. Fold over the corners on the dotted lines.
6. Fold up the other edge and you now have a paper hat – open it. This also works well with newspaper, but blank printer paper can be painted or coloured. In theory, you don't need to fold the corners over if you're stopping at a hat – but we're going on to turn it into a boat.

THE BOAT

Turning this into a paper boat is only a fraction more complicated.

1. Holding the hat upside down, join the two ends together.
2. It will fold into a neat diamond that looks like the picture on the next page.
3. Next, fold each side of the diamond onto itself along the dotted line shown.
4. You will now have a triangle.
5. Open it as before and fold in the opposite corners.
6. Now this final bit doesn't look like it will work, but it does. Take hold of the two loose corners and gently pull them apart.
7. The boat will form. It might take a bit of tweaking to get exactly the right shape, but when the bottom is opened a little, it does float.

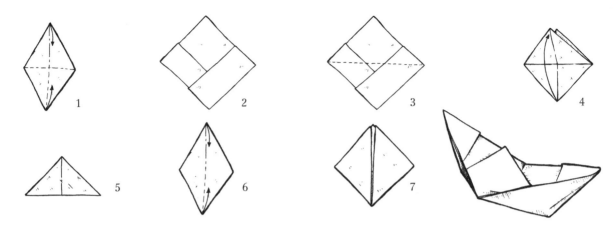

The Water Bomb

Finally, as we're folding paper, we might as well do the last one every boy should know – the water bomb.

Turn an 8 1/2 x 11 sheet of paper into a square piece by folding down a corner to the edge and tearing off a strip. When you have a perfect square of paper, fold it in half across both diagonals and horizontally as well. Concentrate – this is tricky to get right.

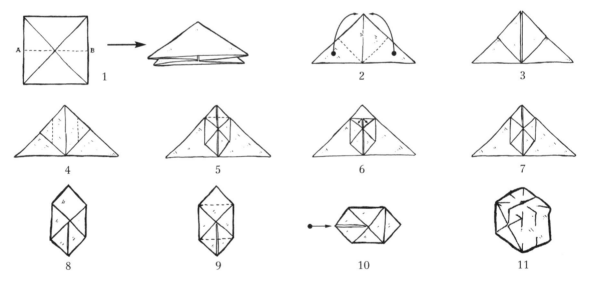

1. Put points A and B together, flattening the whole thing down so that it looks like the next diagram.
2. Fold upward on the line on the right and on the left.
3. Then it must look like this.
4. Fold on the lines.
5. Then it must look like this.
6. Fold the two little triangles on the lines downward. Put the triangles in the two pockets on the right and on the left. This is a little bit fiddly.

MAKING A PAPER HAT, BOAT AND WATER BOMB

7. Then it must look like this.

Turn the whole triangle over and repeat steps 2, 3, 4, 5, 6 and 7.

8. Then it must look like this.
9. Fold and unfold on the dotted lines to help with the last stage.
10. Take the folded cube in your hand and blow into the hole at the top to unfold the cube. It's pretty satisfying when it works.
11. The cube is ready.

Fill it with water – find a high place and drop it.

INTERESTING FACT: No piece of paper can be folded in half more than seven times. Try it.

TAKE A HIKE

What's the difference between going for a walk and going for a "hike"? We like to think of a hike as a good, long walk with plenty of adventure and discovery thrown in. A hike is a great way to explore a familiar area or strike out into new territory. But really, you can have a good hike just about anywhere – through the woods, in a park, along a beach, or even through city streets.

To prepare, decide how long you want to hike and find a route that you can walk in that time. If you are near a provincial or federal park or a conservation area, there may be plenty of interesting trails to choose from. There may also be great nature walks and hiking paths right in your town or city.

Make sure your parents, or other adults who are staying behind, know where you are going and when you plan to be back. Pack up your "Essential Kit" (see p. 1), including a compass. (See p. 150 for how to make your own compass.) You may want to add a few other items to your kit, such as the following:

Hat
Sunglasses
Sunscreen
Map of the area
Bug spray
First aid kit
Whistle for each person
Watch
Snacks or lunch
Full water bottle for each person

Small mirror
Light-coloured chalk
Rope – about three metres
Windbreaker or rain gear
Camera
Sketchpad and pencil
Medications that those in your group need – asthma inhalers, EpiPen, etc.
Backpack in which to carry all of this stuff

It's important to wear good, sturdy footwear, such as supportive running shoes or hiking boots, when you are heading out for a hike. Also make sure to wear a pair of thick, absorbent socks, even if it is a warm day. Athletic sandals will do for beach hikes or short walks, but they may be tough on your feet if you are covering rough terrain, rocks or gravel. Long sleeves and long pants will help protect you from insect bites, sunburn and scratches if you are moving through brush or dense woods. It's always a good idea to dress in layers so that you can add or remove clothes when you get too hot or too cold.

If you are hiking on a trail through a provincial or federal park, or a conservation area, there may be signs to tell you how long each route takes. You can cover between 1.5 and 4.5 kilometres an hour. (Only very brisk walkers who don't stop at all will cover 4.5 kilometres!) Remember, you will go slower if you are hiking uphill or if the ground is very rough. You also want to build in plenty of time for breaks and investigating along the way.

Before embarking on your hike, there are some safety measures you should take. It might, for example, be a good idea to read "First Aid" on p. 173 before you head out, although we sure hope you don't have to use that information! It's also important to have a plan or a meeting point in the event of an emergency or if someone gets lost.

Once you have set out, don't be tempted to find your snacks and refreshments in the wild. Water from creeks, rivers, ponds or lakes may look clean, but it could contain various parasites, including one that causes giardiasis, or "beaver fever," a nasty intestinal illness. And don't eat anything in the woods or fields unless you are very, very certain about what it is. There are a number of berries that look quite a lot like blueberries or raspberries but aren't. And a number of highly toxic wild mushrooms do a fine job of imitating their harmless cousins. And speaking of water, if you are carrying a backpack as you are crossing a creek or moving through water, unbuckle the waist strap, if there is one. If you leave it done up and you fall, the weight of the backpack could hold you under the water.

As you travel, always stick with your hiking companions and stay on well-marked trails. If someone gets separated from the group, he should stop and blow his whistle three times. The group can blow one of their whistles once to say, "We heard you. We're on the way." The separated person should blow his whistle again three times at intervals so the group can find him.

If your group has gotten off track or you are unsure if you are heading the right way, check your map. Place the map on the ground. Use your compass to find north, and then turn your map so that the arrow indicating north on the map (there should be one) is pointing in the same direction as your compass needle. Now the map is a miniature representation of the area around you. You should be able to figure out what direction you need to head in next.

If you think you've taken the wrong path, mark where you are by chalking a tree or making some other distinguishing sign. Then head back. If you see your mark again, you know you have been walking in circles. If you really are lost, stop walking and stay put. Blow your whistle to attract your friends (if you've become separated) or other hikers who can help. If you have a phone and there is service, call a nearby adult. Don't eat all your food or drink all your water right away. Hang your food from a tree at some distance from you so that it doesn't attract hungry animals to you. You can create a shelter for yourself (from the sun or rain) by tying a rope between two trees and draping a rain poncho, blanket or towel over it. Separate the ends of the cloth or plastic so the material forms an inverted V-shaped tent, and weight the ends with rocks.

If you are out for a long time, don't panic. Remain where you are. Continue to use your whistle. You can also hold a small mirror up and use it to reflect the sun. This could attract the attention of passing planes or helicopters.

But let's assume that nothing as dire as getting lost is going to ruin your adventure (and as long as you and your fellow hikers stay together and are careful, you'll be fine). To make your hike one of discovery, check out the sections in this book on insects and spiders (p. 113), trees (p. 277) and fossils (p. 24) before you head out. Depending on where your hike takes you, you may get a chance to see some of the things described there. You might also want to bring along a few compact field guides on plants, insects or minerals to help you identify the things you see on your walk. You could also use a sketch book or camera to record interesting plants or bugs and then do a little research when you get home to figure out what you've seen.

Winter Hiking

Hiking is a four-season activity, but you need to keep a few extra things in mind if you plan to hike in the winter.

Walking in snow will slow you down, so when planning your hike, build in a little extra time to cover your route. If you are walking where the snow is deep, you will need snowshoes, or you may want to cross-country ski instead. Remember, a blanket of snow does a very good job of making everything look level and flat, but the ground under the snow may dip and rise. Drifting also makes it impossible to know how deep the snow is – you may be able to walk quite comfortably for a while and then sink up to your waist in the powdery stuff. Following a well-marked path and having snowshoes with you, therefore, are good ideas.

Good boots and warm socks are a must for winter hiking. Avoid cotton socks or clothes. Once cotton gets damp (from sweat or from wet conditions), it no longer provides any warmth. Go for wool or fleece clothing when possible. Water-resistant outer garments will also keep you dry and therefore warm. And layering your clothes is even more important in winter than at other times of year. Your biggest enemy when you are outdoors in the winter is sweat! If your clothes get damp, you are going to get cold. You do need to dress warmly and to make sure your head and all exposed areas of your body can be covered. But you shouldn't let yourself get overheated. As soon as you feel too warm, shed a layer or two. You can always put them back on if you need to.

When you are hiking in cold weather, it is also important to bring plenty of water. The colder the air is, the less moisture it can hold. On a winter day, the air can be very dry, and you can get thirsty or dehydrated quickly. (If it's very cold outside, try this neat trick. Store your water bottle upside down in your knapsack. Ice will form at the bottom of the bottle instead of at the mouth, so when you take a drink, the water won't be blocked.)

Even on short winter hikes, it's a good idea to bring plenty of snacks. Your body has to work extra hard to keep you warm when it's cold outside, so eat often to provide yourself with all the extra fuel you need.

Animal Encounters 1

Nothing is more thrilling, as you are hiking through the woods, than spotting a deer moving through the foliage or a beaver working away on its den. If you want to see some wildlife – anything from birds to beavers to red fox – keep your voice down (except when you are in bear country, when it's really better to scare bears away). And don't bring your dog on a hike if you want to see other animals. Dogs generally frighten wildlife, and in some cases, they may agitate and provoke potentially dangerous animals such as bears and wolves. We like to think of dogs as great protectors, but if you are walking where there are bears, moose or other large animals, its best to leave Fido at home.

Watch the skies for birds, bats and flying insects. When passing through open fields, look for hawks swooping down on their prey. Wherever you go, keep your eyes peeled not only for animals but also for evidence of wildlife – bird nests, spider webs, cocoons, skins snakes have shed, feathers or claw marks on trees. Holes in the ground may be the entrances of burrows for rabbits, groundhogs or chipmunks. Tiny holes high in tree trunks might be indications that woodpeckers have been feeding on insect larvae under tree bark. (A persistent knocking sound is a hint that you should look up to spot woodpeckers.) Fallen trees with pointy, gnawed trunks or limbs are sure evidence of beavers in the area. As you near streams and rivers, look for beaver dams. (Use your ears too – beavers can be quite noisy as they chew on trees.)

Pileated woodpecker.

If you pay attention to the ground and the areas on either side of the trail, you may notice tracks of animals that have been in the area. Take a look at the illustrations below to familiarize yourself with the paw prints of various animals.

Red Fox
5.5 centimetres long/5 centimetres wide
Fox tracks tend to run along the edges of forests or along fences, so look for their prints in those locations. Their front paws are larger than the rear ones, and prints are usually smaller than those of most dogs.

Coyote
6.5 centimetres long/5.5 centimetres wide
Like the fox, coyotes tend to travel in straight lines when in open territory (as opposed to dogs, which like to amble about). The pad of the final paw print is quite faint compared to the pad of the print in front of it.

Wolf
12 centimetres long/10 centimetres wide

Wolves tend to travel in packs, so if you see one wolf print, you are likely to see many other prints from several different wolves. Like those of the fox and coyote, the front paws of a wolf are actually larger than the rear paws. Wolf prints are significantly larger than those of foxes or coyotes, and their toes are more spread out.

Black Bear
Front: 15 centimetres long/14 centimetres wide
Rear: 25 centimetres long/15 centimetres wide

When black bears walk, their feet turn slightly inward and their back feet tend to fall on their front paw tracks. Look for tracks in which larger prints overlap the smaller front paw prints.

Grizzly
Front: 11 centimetres long/10 centimetres wide
Rear: 18 centimetres long/9 centimetres wide

Look at the length of those claws – on average, they are over twice the length of the toe pads! The grizzly's claw prints distinguish its tracks from those of the black bear. The back paw prints are also significantly longer than a black bear's.

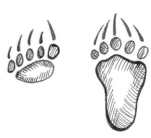

Deer
8.5 centimetres long/6.5 centimetres wide

Deer have cloven hooves, and their tracks appear as two pear-shaped impressions per leg. White-tailed deer tend to drag their feet as they bound, leaving grooves in the soil between each set of prints.

Moose
16 centimetres long/14 centimetres wide

Like the deer, moose have cloven hooves, but their tracks are twice as large as a deer's.

Cougar
8 centimetres long/8 centimetres wide

The cougar's prints look like those of a very large cat, except that their front paw prints are larger than their rear paw prints. Cougar tracks rarely show claw marks.

Rabbit (Cottontail)
Front: 2.5 centimetres long/2 centimetres wide
Rear: 8 centimetres long/2.5 centimetres wide

Since rabbits hop, you will see tracks in which the large back feet appear in front, with the smaller front feet slightly behind and between the back paws. Each set of prints will be about thirty centimetres apart for a rabbit on the move.

Jackrabbit (Hare)
Front: 4.4 centimetres long/3.8 centimetres
Rear: 15 centimetres long/6.4 centimetres

The hare's hind feet are longer than those of a rabbit, and the distance it can hop (therefore the space between each set of prints) can be anywhere from thirty to sixty centimetres.

Red Squirrel
Front: 3 centimetres long/3 centimetres wide
Rear: 4.5 centimetres long/2.5 centimetres wide

Red squirrel paw prints will appear side by side, rather than one in front of another. The tracks of black and grey squirrels are similar but larger than those of the red squirrel.

Skunk
Front: 3.5 centimetres long/3 centimetres wide
Rear: 5 centimetres long/3 centimetres wide

Like the black bear, the skunk's front feet are pigeon-toed – they point inward. The back paw prints will be quite close to the front prints, and you will usually be able to see clear claw marks above each toe.

Raccoon
Front: 7 centimetres long/ 7 centimetres wide
Rear: 10 centimetres long/ 6 centimetres wide

The front paw prints of a raccoon sometimes look like little handprints (but with small claws), and the back feet look a little like small versions of black bear tracks. Generally, raccoon tracks show the rear paw next to the front one on each side.

Beaver
Front: 8 centimetres long/7 centimetres wide
Rear: 15 centimetres long/12 centimetres wide

It's hard to find good beaver prints because beavers drag their tails and erase their tracks as they go. If you notice drag marks through the mud or dirt, look carefully to see if there are any full or partial paw prints on either side.

Porcupine
Front: 6 centimetres long/4 centimetres wide
Rear: 10 centimetres long/4 centimetres wide

Like the beaver, the porcupine drags its tail as it walks. Porcupine prints, therefore, will have the long, thin marks between them. These are made by the animal's quilled tail. The front paw prints turn inward, and since the porcupine drags its feet as well as its tail, you'll notice marks between each footprint.

Animal Encounters 2: Don't Be Dinner

We feel this is a good rule for life in general, but it's a rule that moves to the top of your list when you are on a hike. There are very few animals that will actually hunt down humans (cougars or mountain lions being two exceptions), but many creatures will attack if they feel threatened. If an animal is cornered or if it is hurt and can't run away from you, it may feel in danger. Animals that are protecting their young, are too sick or weakened to hunt their usual prey or are rabid can also be a threat to humans. Some animals that are very used to humans – such as those that live in or near towns, cities or campgrounds – can actually be more dangerous than ones that live in the wild because they are not as frightened by us and will not always flee when we're around. These animals may also associate humans with food, so you should be careful when you see wildlife – no matter where you are.

Black Bears

Black bears are sometimes called the "shadows of the forest" because they are so good at hiding. When black bears sense that humans are present, they usually walk away or even climb a tree to get out of sight. And since they have an extraordinarily keen sense of smell – they have

Black bear.

100 times more nasal area than we do – and good eyesight, they will most often become aware of us and move away long before we see them. Because of their strong senses, you don't have to worry too much about scaring them off by making noise as you walk, except when you are entering an area like a blueberry patch, where, since they're eating, they might not want to leave. If you find a great spread of wild blueberries on your hike and decide to pick yourself a snack, talk or sing loudly as you pick, or assign one person to bang rocks or sticks or otherwise make a racket, while the rest of your group gathers berries.

If you stop for a break anywhere on your hike and have food in your backpack, hang it from a tree – away from you – to avoid attracting hungry bears. (And never, ever feed a bear or leave food out for wild animals.) It's also a good idea, if you are travelling in an area inhabited by bears, to leave your dog at home, but if you did bring your pet, make sure it's on a short leash.

If you happen to see a bear and it doesn't see you, move away quietly, keeping an eye on it but not making eye contact, which may be seen as a challenge. If the bear notices you and gets up on its hind legs, it is usually doing so out of curiosity – not aggression. If it feels threatened, it may act aggressively, huffing, panting, growling or swatting its paws on the ground or at vegetation. These actions are all meant as a warning for you to stay away. Slowly back away, keeping your eye on the bear and talking in a calm even tone. If there are bear cubs around, make sure you are moving away from the cubs, not toward them.

In the rare event that a black bear comes toward you, drop your pack (particularly if it has food in it), and back away at an angle. If the animal continues to approach you, stay close to your group and make yourselves seem threatening by raising your arms or jackets over your heads, banging sticks or rocks, shouting, blowing your whistles, stamping your feet and clapping your hands. Move uphill if possible or stand on a log or rock to make yourselves look bigger. Don't climb a tree in the hopes of escape – black bears are better climbers than we are and will follow you up. (The same holds true for moving into water – black bears are strong swimmers.)

If a bear comes at you silently, without the huffing and puffing warning signs, it usually means that it is intent on doing you harm. Luckily, these silent "predatory" attacks are extremely rare – there have only been forty cases in all of North America in the last 100 years. If a bear does make contact with you – with or without warning – the best thing to do is to fight back with all your might. (Most experts do not recommend that you play dead during a black bear attack.) Use anything you can as a weapon, and aim for the bear's eyes, nose and ears.

Grizzly Bears

While black bears can be found across most of Canada, grizzly bears are found only in British Columbia, Alberta, the Northwest Territories and the Yukon. Grizzlies are significantly bigger than black bears and are often more dangerous. Like black bears, they have an excellent sense of smell, great hearing and good eyesight, which means they are usually aware of us before we are aware of them. But compared to black bears, grizzlies are more likely to attack human beings who get in their way. There's a good reason for this. Grizzlies evolved in areas where the tree coverage was minimal. When one of their predators approached, there were few places to hide and few trees to climb in order to escape. Survival often depended on being the first to attack. Grizzlies don't often attack unprovoked, but any surprise or any approach toward their territory can be perceived as threatening. Grizzlies that are used to the presence of people and to getting food from people (from garbage, campsites, etc.) may also be more likely to attack. Be especially careful if you are hiking around campsites or populated areas where grizzlies are known to live.

In grizzly country, it's a good rule to hike in groups

A grizzly mother and her cubs.

of four or more, and always hike with an adult at the front of the line. Grizzlies are not as likely to attack a group, so stay together. Be aware of your surroundings and look for signs of bears, like tracks or scat (poop) or animal carcasses.

Using binoculars is also a good idea. If you see a grizzly bear off in the distance, don't get any closer to it. Most attacks happen when people are about sixty metres or less away from the bear. Your best bet is to never get that close. Wait until the grizzly moves away or off the trail, or make a very wide detour around it.

When you can't see what's ahead or when visibility is poor, make noise as you hike. You can talk loudly, ring bells, bang rocks or blow whistles.

If you encounter a bear and it does come at you, stay together with your group and don't move. The bear may stop short of attacking. If it does halt, wait to see if it moves off. If it remains, move extremely slowly at an angle away from it while talking in a calm voice. Stop if your actions appear to upset it. If the bear comes toward you, follow the same response as you would for a black bear attack – behave in a threatening manner by making yourself look bigger than you are, shout, stamp your feet, blow your whistle and so on. Never turn and run.

Grizzlies can climb trees, but they are not nearly as good at it as black bears. Escaping up a tree may provide you with more protection from a grizzly than it would from a black bear, but this is only worth trying if you are directly under a tree and can get up it very quickly. If a grizzly does make contact with you, playing dead may end the attack. Curl up in a tight ball or lie on your front (to protect your stomach and face) with your legs spread apart and your hands behind your head. Do your best not to struggle or cry out. If the bear manages to flip you over, roll back onto your stomach. Once the bear is convinced that you are no threat at all, it is likely to leave.

·

Cougar (*Mountain Lion*)

Found primarily in the Yukon, Alberta and British Columbia, cougars – also called mountain lions – are Canada's largest cat. And while these creatures are beautiful to look at, it's way better to see them on TV or in a nature preserve than to meet them in the wilderness. That's because cougars are skilled predators that don't seem to distinguish between tasty wild deer and tender young boys. In fact, although cougar attacks are extremely rare, cougars looking for their next meal have been known to track down people of all genders and ages. They seem, however, to prefer children to adults (children under a metre tall are most at risk), probably because they sense that smaller people are easier to overpower.

So, the very first rule when you are in cougar country is never to hike alone or without adults. Groups of hikers should always stay together. Adults should walk at the front of the line of hikers (as in bear country) but also at the back, since cougars stalk their prey and attack from behind.

Cougar (also known as mountain lion).

Luckily for us, cougars are most active at night, but they may still be on the prowl at dusk and dawn – so schedule your hikes for midday.

Make noise as you walk – it's never a good idea to surprise a cougar. You might also want to carry a big walking stick that you can use for defence if necessary. And your dog won't be able to protect you from a cougar. In fact, it's more likely to excite and attract one!

As you walk, pay attention for signs of cougars – like tracks or scat – and leave the area if you see one. If a cougar has killed an animal, it will sometimes cover the carcass with dirt and come back later to feed on it again. If you see any dead animals in the woods, stay well away from them. Watch also for flocks of ravens or magpies overhead. They could be circling a recent cougar or bear kill, meaning the predator is likely close by.

If you meet up with a cougar, stay calm. Don't turn your back (remember, the cougar prefers to attack from behind), don't run (that will encourage the cougar to pursue) and never play dead. Instead, face the cougar. Talk to the cougar in a firm voice, make noise and try to make yourself look big by stretching your arms over your head. You want to make yourself appear as a threat rather than as prey (some people even recommend showing your teeth so that you look aggressive). At the same time, move slowly back, leaving a path or space for the cougar to escape. If the cougar comes closer to you, throw rocks or sticks at it. If the cat attacks, fight back, using anything you can as a weapon. Aim for the cat's eyes, nose, ears and face.

Coyotes

Coyotes resemble medium-sized dogs and have bushy tails. Coyotes in the wild are more likely to avoid us than to attack us, but coyotes that live in populated areas and are used to being fed by people (or by their garbage) are more dangerous. If you see a coyote but it doesn't see you, back away quietly, keeping an eye on the coyote as you move away. In the unlikely event that a coyote approaches you (probably looking for food), make loud noises, stamp your feet or throw things at it to scare it away. If the coyote moves toward you, back away slowly in the direction of other people or buildings. Don't turn and run – the coyote may see this as a good reason to give chase.) If the coyote attacks, fight back, aiming at the animal's nose, eyes and ears.

Coyote.

Wolves

Wolf attacks on people are rare. Like coyotes, wolves generally pose a threat to people only if the animals are used to human presence or associate people with food. Be careful if you are hiking near campgrounds, and never feed wolves or any other wild animals.

One situation that sometimes causes people to get wounded by wolves occurs when they try to get between their dog and the wolves. Wolves are very territorial, and they will see dogs as rivals on their turf. To avoid injury to your pet and to yourself, it's best to leave dogs at home when hiking in parks, conservation areas or other places that wolves are known to inhabit.

Grey wolf.

Moose

A grazing moose.

If you see a full-grown moose lumbering along in the distance, it may be hard to believe that he could be dangerous. He looks a bit like a lumpy, ungainly horse. And while moose are gentle most of the time, they can nevertheless have mighty tempers. Weighing up to 725 kilograms and able to run forty-eight to fifty-six kilometres per hour, moose have been known to charge cars, animals and people, with little provocation. If you see a moose, don't approach it. If you encounter a moose calf, be especially careful – a protective mother moose is sure to be close by (and a 100-kilogram calf can be dangerous all by itself). Avoid getting between the mother and her babies. Move away, taking a route that not only puts distance between you and it but also gives the moose an escape route.

If you are close to the moose and it lowers its head and seems ready to charge, climb a tree or get behind a large object. Keep in mind that wolves often prey on moose and their calves. A moose will not distinguish between its enemy, the wolf, and your family dog. Keep your dog away from areas where you might encounter moose.

Skunk

Skunks only spray when frightened or when they feel they have to protect their babies. If you come across a skunk on your hike, back off and give the skunk plenty of room to get out of your way. If you are walking with a dog, the dog is much more at risk than you are, as many dogs think chasing skunks is a great game – until they are sprayed. Your best bet to avoid skunk spray is to leave your dog at home or keep it on a short leash while you are hiking.

Striped skunk.

ORIENTEERING

THE FIRST THING TO understand is that a compass points north because it is magnetic and the earth has a magnetic field caused by the rotation of a liquid metal core. The magnetic north pole happens to correspond reasonably well with the true pole – but they are not the same. Magnetic south is off Antarctica and can be sailed over. Magnetic north is near the Canada/Alaska border. They are both very deep within the core of the planet and move over time.

If you are interested, a compass will actually jam on the magnetic poles as it tries to point either "up" or "down" – ninety degrees to the surface. A gyroscopic compass is invaluable in such circumstances – that is, a gyro that has been set to point north and then holds its position regardless of changes in direction. Pilots find gyroscopic compasses invaluable. The International Space Station (ISS) has thirteen of them.

Admiralty charts plot the lines of "magnetic variation" across the globe, showing whether the variation from true north is to the east or west and increasing or decreasing. As you can imagine, this is crucial for navigation. A compass in New York will be approximately 14° W off true north. If you were plotting a course north, you would have to subtract 14 degrees from your compass direction. If the difference was 14° E, 14 degrees would have to be added.

The compass is the universal means of finding your position anywhere on the surface of the planet. The earth rotates east, so in *both* hemispheres, the sun rises in the east and sets in the west. It is true, however, that water swirls the other way down plugholes and toilets in the southern hemisphere.

The figure below shows the thirty-two points of the compass. In the northern hemisphere when the sun is at its highest point in the sky, it will be due south. In the southern hemisphere this noonday point will be due north.

KEY: Read the word "by" for the symbol –, so N–NW is north *by* north-west.

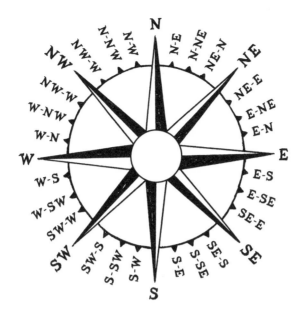

The hemisphere can be indicated by the movement of the shadow cast by the sun: clockwise in the north and anti-clockwise in the south. This shadow can also be a guide to direction.

SHADOW STICK

Place a metre stick upright on flat ground and mark where the tip of the shadow falls – point "a."

Wait fifteen minutes and mark where the tip of the new shadow falls – point "b."

Now draw a line from "a" to "b" and you have east–west, "a" being west. Bisect this line at right angles and you have north–south with "a" on your right and "b" on your left, you are facing south. This works in both hemispheres – feel free to heat your brains up trying to explain why.

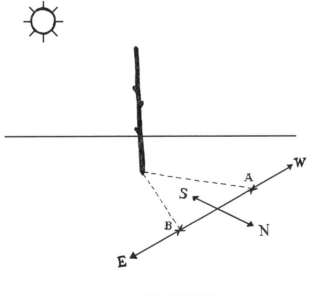

A watch with two hands can tell the direction. It must have the correct local time (excluding daylight saving: this is when you put the clocks back and forward – "spring forward and fall back" – so in summer you should *subtract* an hour and in autumn *add* one to use this technique). The nearer to the equator you are, the less accurate this is.

In the northern hemisphere, hold the watch horizontally. If it's summer, wind it back an hour; if it's winter, wind it on an hour. Point the hour hand at the sun. Bisect the angle between hour hand and 12 to give you a north–south line. In the southern hemisphere point 12 at the sun, and the midpoint between 12 and the hour hand will give a north–south line.

Northern

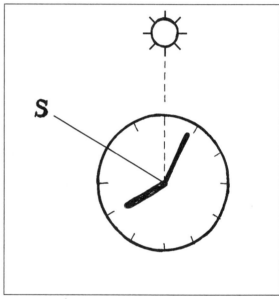

Southern

NEEDLE COMPASS

Get a piece of ferrous (meaning iron) wire – a sewing needle is ideal – and stroke it in one direction repeatedly against silk. This will magnetize it. Suspend the needle on a length of thread and it will point north.

Stroking the wire with a magnet in one direction will work better than silk. This aligns the atoms in the needle. Heating the needle also works, though not as reliably. Try it and see.

If you have no thread then you can also float the magnetized needle on a piece of tissue paper or bark on the surface of water and it will turn to indicate north.

An old-style razor blade can also be used as a compass needle. Rub it against the palm of your hand (carefully!) to magnetize it, then suspend it to get the north–south line.

Use as many methods as you can to get your bearings, then mark out your compass, check all your readings against the sun and keep your needle magnetized.

To find north in the night sky you need to find Polaris, the Pole Star. This is discussed in the astronomy chapter. There are other indicators in the night sky which can be used. The rising of the moon can give a rough east–west reference. If the moon rises before the sun has set, the illuminated side will be on the west. If it rises after midnight, the illuminated side will be on the east.

Stars themselves can also be used to indicate direction. If you cannot find Polaris or the Southern Cross, get two sticks, one shorter than the other. Stick them in the earth and sight along them as shown to any star except the Pole Star. From the star's apparent movement, you can work out the direction you are facing!

If the star you are lined up on appears to be rising, you are facing east. If it appears to be

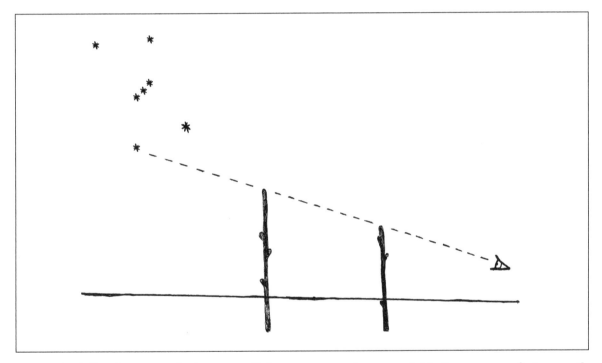

setting (or falling), you are facing west. If the star seems to move right, then you are facing south and if it moves left, you are facing north. These are only approximate directions and will be reversed in the southern hemisphere.

Being able to find your bearings at any time of day and night is a pretty impressive thing to know, but try not to show off your knowledge. Keep it safe for a time when you may really need it. As the Scouts say, "Be prepared."

UNDERSTANDING GRAMMAR – PART TWO

GRAMMAR DOES BECOME more complicated when you look at sentences, as you might expect. However, there are, in fact, only four *kinds* of simple sentences.

The Four Kinds of Sentences

1. **Imperative** (Command) – "Get out of my office!"
2. **Interrogative** (Question) – "Did you take my keys?"
3. **Exclamatory** (Exclamation) – "Fantastic!"
4. **Declarative** (Statement) – "You are not my friend."

As you see, a simple sentence can be very simple indeed. It needs a subject and a verb to be a sentence – so you need to know what a subject is.

Subject and Object – Nominative and Objective

The **subject** of a sentence is the person or thing acting on the verb. "The man kicked the dog" has "the man" as the subject. It does get a little harder to spot with the irregular verbs – "John is sick" still has "John" as the subject. The **nominative** forms of words all have to do with the subject. This is crucial when it comes to pronouns, as the pronoun you use will depend on whether it is the subject or object in a sentence.

The **object** of the sentence is the person or thing on which the verb acts. "The man kicked the dog" has "the dog" as an object. The **objective** forms of words all have to do with the object.

Before we go on to explaining nominative and objective in more detail, you should know that imperative or exclamatory sentences often have an invisible or implied subject. "Get out!" does have a subject – the person doing the getting out, though the word isn't included. "Fantastic!" as an exclamation implies "That is ..." The verb is there in a sense, but not seen. All other sentences have a subject and a verb. Easy.

Nominative/
Objective
Pronouns

When a pronoun is in the subject part of a sentence, we use nominative case pronouns. These include: *I, you, he, she, it, we, they, who* and *which*.

He went home.	*not*	"Him went home."
He and I were good friends.	*not*	"Him and me were good friends."
She and Susan were going home.	*not*	"Her and Susan were going home."
We went to the park.	*not*	"Us went to the park."
Who struck Tim?	*not*	"Whom struck Tim?"

In the above examples, the pronouns are all acting on the verbs, making it correct to use the nominative or subjective form.

The objective is the object part of a sentence. In the case of a pronoun, if it has the verb acting on it, we use *me, you, him, her, it, us, them, whom* and *which*, among others.

Susan went with him.	*not*	"Susan went with he."
John loved her.	*not*	"John loved she."
David enjoyed playing chess with them.	*not*	". . . chess with they."
Why not come with us?	*not*	"Why not come with we?"
We did not know whom to thank.	*not*	". . . who to thank."

Some of these examples are blindingly obvious. No one with the most casual knowledge of language would say "John loved she." However, "who" and "whom" cause problems still. It is worth giving those two words a small section of their own.

Who and Whom

Learn this: If the word in question is acting on a verb (nominative), use "who." If it is being acted upon (objective), use "whom." Be careful – this is tricky.

Examples:

1. *The man who walked home was hit by a bus.* Correct or incorrect? Well, the "who" in question is doing the walking, so it is in the nominative form = subjective = correct. (You would not say "Him was hit by a bus," but "He was hit by a bus.")

2. *The man whom we saved was hit by a bus.* Correct or incorrect? This time, the man has been saved. The verb is acting on him. He is not doing the saving, so it is in the objective form = correct to use "whom" here. (You would not say "We saved he," but "We saved him.")

3. *He was walking with his mother, whom he adored.* Correct or incorrect? She is not doing the adoring. The "who" or "whom" in question is being acted upon by the verb and therefore should be in the object form: objective = correct.

Finally, for the "who" and "whom" section, prepositions must be mentioned. Most examples of "whom" are used when it is the object of a preposition. Note that it is still the objective form. There is nothing new here, but this one gives a great deal of trouble. The form often comes as sentences are rearranged so as not to leave a preposition at the end. It has the added bonus of putting a key word at the end of the sentence, which works very well for emphasis.

1. *He was a man for whom I could not find respect.* If this had been written, "He was a man I could not find respect for," it would have been wrong. "For" is a preposition and you just don't end a sentence with them. Note that it could have been written "He was a man I could not respect" – to avoid the problem.

2. *To whom it may concern* – a formal opening in letters. Note that such a letter should be ended, *Yours faithfully*. If the letter begins with a name, *Dear David*, for example, it should end with *Yours sincerely*.

A final mention of pronouns in the objective must be made. It should now be clear enough why it's "between you and me" – the "me" is in the objective, acted on by the preposition "between." You would not say, "He gave the car to I," which has "to" as a preposition, or "Come with I." Similarly, you don't say, "Between you and I."

As You Now Know Nominative and Objective . . .

For the record, **Genitive** has to do with possessive words: *mine, my, his, hers, ours*, etc. Easy.

Dative is the term used to describe an indirect object. In the sentence "Give me the ball," "the ball" is the object. However, "me" is also in the objective, as if the sentence had been written "Give the ball to me." The word "me" is in the dative – an indirect object.

Note that dative is of very little importance in English. In Latin, sentence word order is less important. "The man bites the dog" can be written as "The dog bites the man" – and only the endings will change. As a result, the word endings become crucial for understanding. English has evolved a more rigid word order and so the dative, for example, has become less important. It's still satisfying to know it though and most modern English teachers can be made to glaze over with a question on this subject. That said, if you try it on a Latin teacher, you'll be there all day. . . .

The **Ablative** case is another one more relevant to the study of Latin than English. It involves words that indicate the agent or cause of an event, its manner and the instrument with which the action is done. The ablative case is likely to be used in sentences with the words "from," "in," "by" and "with" – prepositions. "They proceeded *in silence*," for example, shows the manner in which they proceeded. "He was beaten *with sticks*," shows how he was beaten. Those phrases are "in the ablative."

Clauses and Phrases

Simple sentences are not the whole story, of course. A complex sentence is one that has two or more clauses, but what is a clause?

The simplest working definition of a **clause** is that it has a subject and a verb. Sometimes the subject is understood, or implied, but the verb should always be there. The following example is a sentence with two clauses, joined by the conjunction "so": "I could not stand the heat, so I leaped out of the window.'

In a sense, clauses are mini-sentences, separated either by conjunctions or punctuation.

This sentence has four clauses: "Despite expecting the voice, I jumped a foot in the air, I smashed a vase and I rendered my daughter speechless."

"Despite expecting the voice" is a subordinate clause, separated by a comma from the rest. (Subordinate means that the clause cannot function as a sentence on its own.) "I jumped a foot in the air" is the second clause, "I smashed a vase" is the third, and "I rendered my daughter speechless" is the last. The final two are joined with the conjunction "and."

Subordinate clauses cannot stand on their own. Main clauses such as "I jumped a foot in the air" are complete sentences, but "Despite expecting the voice" is not. On its own, it would beg the question "Despite expecting the voice . . . what?"

Phrases are groups of words that do not necessarily contain a verb and a subject. Expressed simply, they are every other kind of word grouping that is not a clause or main sentence. A phrase can even be a single word.

The main kinds of phrases are: Adjectival (which work like adjectives); Adverbial (which work like adverbs); Nouns (which work like nouns); Prepositional (which work like a prepositions); and Verb (which work like . . . um, verbs). If you want to impress an English teacher, ask if part of a sentence is using an adjectival or prepositional phrase.

Examples:

1. "I lived *in France*." "In France" is a prepositional phrase, as it is a group of words indicating position.

2. "I thought you wanted to leave *early tonight*." "Early tonight" is an adverbial phrase, as it modifies the verb "leave."

3. "It was an elephant *of extraordinary size*." "Of extraordinary size" is an adjectival phrase as it adds information to the noun "elephant."

4. "*The bearded men in the room* stood up and left." "The bearded men in the room" is a noun phrase – it's just a more complicated name for the men, using more than just one word.

5. A verb phrase is a group of words often containing the verb itself – an exception to the general rule that phrases won't have verbs. "You *will be going* to the play!" has "will be going" as a phrase of three words combining as the verb.

GIRLS

Y OU MAY ALREADY have noticed that girls are quite different from you. By this, we do not mean the physical differences, more the fact that they remain unimpressed by your mastery of a game involving wizards, or your understanding of Morse Code. Some will be impressed, of course, but as a general rule, girls do not get quite as excited by the use of urine as a secret ink as boys do.

We thought long and hard about what advice could possibly be suitable. It is an inescapable fact that boys spend a great deal of their lives thinking and dreaming about girls, so the subject should be mentioned here – as delicately as possible.

ADVICE ABOUT GIRLS

1. It is important to listen. Human beings are often very self-centred and like to talk about themselves. In addition, it's an easy subject if someone is nervous. It is good advice to listen closely to a girl – unless she has also been given this advice, in which case an uneasy silence could develop, like two owls sitting together.

2. Be careful with humour. It is very common for boys to try to impress girls with a string of jokes, each one more desperate than the last. *One* joke, perhaps, and then a long silence while she talks about herself . . .

3. When you are older, flowers really do work – women love them. When you are young, however, there is a ghastly sense of being awkward rather than romantic – and she will guess your mother bought them.

4. Valentine's Day cards. Do *not* put your name on them. The whole point is the excitement a girl feels, wondering who finds her attractive. If it says "From Brian" on it, the magic isn't really there. This is actually quite a nice thing to do for someone you don't think will get a card. If you do this, it is even more important that you never say, "I sent you one because I thought you wouldn't get any." Keep the cards simple. You do not want one with padding of any kind.

5. Avoid being vulgar. Excitable bouts of wind-breaking will not endear you to a girl, just to pick one example.

6. Play sports of some kind. It doesn't matter what it is, as long as it replaces the corpse-like pallor of a computer programmer with a ruddy glow. Honestly, this is more important than you know.

7. If you see a girl in need of help – unable to lift something, for example – do not taunt her. Approach the object and greet her with a cheerful smile, while surreptitiously testing the weight of the object. If you find you can lift it, go ahead. If you can't, try sitting on it and engaging her in conversation.

8. Finally, make sure you are well-scrubbed, your nails are clean and your hair is washed. Remember that girls are as nervous around you as you are around them, if you can imagine such a thing. They think and act rather differently from you, but without them, life would be one long hockey locker room. Treat them with respect.

MARBLING PAPER

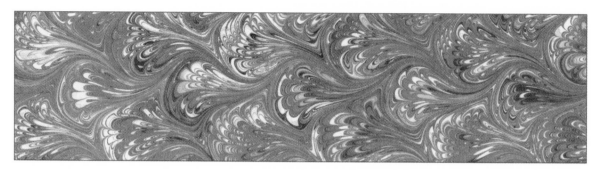

IF YOU'VE EVER WONDERED how the marbled paper inside the covers of old books is created, here it is. It is a surprisingly simple process, but the results can be very impressive. Once you have the inks, there are all sorts of possibilities, like birthday wrapping paper or your own greeting cards.

You will need

- Marbling ink – available from any craft or hobby shop and some large stationery stores.
- A flat-bottomed tray – a baking tray, for example.
- 8 1/2 x 11 paper for printing and newspaper ready to lay out the wet sheets.
- Small paintbrush, a toothpick, comb or feather to swirl ink.

Marbling ink is expensive, but you only need a tiny amount for each sheet, so it lasts for years. We began with red, blue and gold.

We used printer paper, as it was handy, but almost any blank paper will do. You could do this in the bath, but remember to clean it later or you will have a blue father or mother the following morning. The paper must not have a shiny surface, or the inks won't penetrate.

1. Fill the tray with water to the depth of about 25 millimetres (1 in). It is not necessary to be exact.
2. Using the small brush, or a dropper, touch the first colour to the water surface. It will spread immediately in widening circles.
3. Speckle the water with circles of your colours, then when you are satisfied, swirl the colours with a toothpick, a comb or a feather. Anything with a point will do for the first attempt.
4. When the pattern is ready, place the sheet of paper face down onto it and wait for sixty seconds. That is long enough for printer paper, though times may vary with different types.

5. Take hold of one end of the paper and draw it upward out of the liquid. There really isn't any way to do this incorrectly, as far as we could tell – it really is easy. Wash your paper under the tap to get rid of excess ink. Place the wet sheet on newspaper and leave it to dry.

If you have access to a colour photocopier or printer, you could make a copy with certain sections blanked off. The spaces could then be used for invitation details, or the title of a diary or story – perhaps an old-fashioned Canadian ghost story, with an old-fashioned marble-paper cover. Dark green, gold and black is a great combination.

CLOUD FORMATIONS

I T REALLY IS AMAZING just how many times you can look up at the sky in a lifetime and say "I can never remember, is that cumulocirrus, or strato-whatsit?" Everyone is taught them at school and, frankly, we all forget. You'll read them now, and when you *really* want to know, you'll have forgotten. The solution is to get spare copies of the book, so that you always have one with you.

THERE ARE ONLY THREE BASIC TYPES OF CLOUDS

This image is of **cirrus** – light, wispy clouds, which can be as high as 4,500 metres (15,000 ft) and are made of ice crystals. The formation is sometimes referred to as "mare's tails."

After that comes the most common – **cumulus**. These are the fluffy cotton-wool clouds you can see on most days.

The last member of our big three is **stratus** – a dark, solid blanket of cloud at low level.

All cloud formations are combinations of these three basic forms. The only other word that crops up is **nimbus** – meaning a dark grey rain cloud. You could, for example, see cumulonimbus, which would be large and fluffy, but dark and look just about to rain. The leading edge of a storm is usually cumulonimbus. Nimbostratus would be a heavy, dark layer covering the sky and again have the appearance of a raincloud just about to pour down.

Cirrus

Cumulus

THE MAIN CLOUD FORMATIONS

HIGH ALTITUDE
(above 5,500 metres/18,000 feet)

Cirrus – high and wispy

Cirrostratus – high thick layer

Cirrocumulus – high cotton wool

Cumulonimbus – cotton-wool storm clouds

MEDIUM ALTITUDE
(5,500–6,500 metres/ 18,000–20,000 feet)

Altostratus – medium-height heavy band

Altocumulus – medium-height cotton wool

LOW ALTITUDE
(up to 2,000 metres/6,500 feet)

Stratus – heavy, flat layer

Stratocumulus – fluffy and flat combined

Cumulus – cotton wool

Nimbostratus – raining flat layer

Stratus

You know a storm is coming when you see stratus and stratocumulus cloud formations getting lower. If the clouds descend quickly into nimbostratus, it is time to find shelter as the rain will be coming at any moment. If you happen to have a barometer, check the mercury level. A sudden drop in pressure indicates a storm is on the way.

These ten formations can be further subdivided, with names such as cumulonimbus incus, an anvil-shaped storm cloud often called a "thunderhead." For most of us, however, just remembering and identifying all ten major types would be enough.

FAMOUS BATTLES – PART TWO

1. Waterloo – June 18, 1815

NAPOLEON HAD OVERREACHED himself by 1814. He had lost more than 350,000 men in his march on Russia, one of the most ill-advised military actions in history. Wellington had beaten his armies and their Spanish allies in Spain. In addition, the armies of Austria and Prussia stood ready to humble him at last. Yet Napoleon was not a man to go quietly into obscurity. When he abdicated as emperor, he was exiled to rule the tiny island of Elba off the west coast of Italy. Perhaps cruelly, he was allowed to keep the title he claimed for himself. Many lives would have been saved if he and his honour guard had stayed there. Instead,

eleven months after his arrival, a frigate picked him up and he returned to France.

The French king, Louis XVIII, sent troops with orders to fire on him. Famously, Napoleon walked fearlessly out to them, threw open his coat and said, "Let him that has the heart, kill his Emperor!" The soldiers cheered him, and Napoleon turned them round and marched on Paris. By March 20, 1815, the French king had fled and Napoleon was back. The period of March to June is still known as the Hundred Days war.

With extraordinary efficiency, Napoleon put together an army of 188,000 regulars, 300,000 levies (conscripts) and another 100,000 support

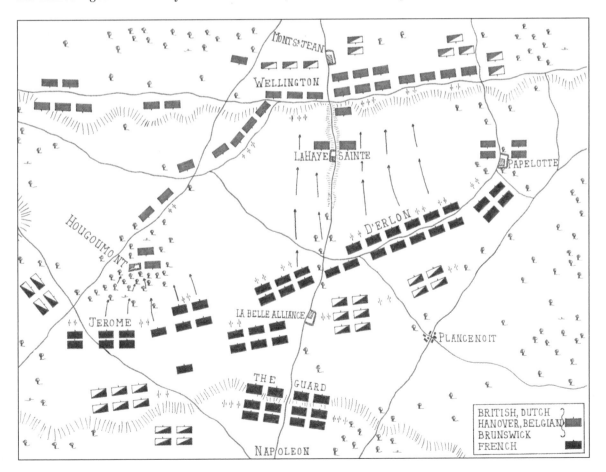

personnel. In addition, he had his veteran army of the north around Paris – 124,000 men.

Wellington's Anglo-Dutch army of 95,000 was in Flanders (Belgium) at this point, with the Prussian army of 124,000 under Marshall Blücher. The Austrians had 210,000 men along the Rhine and another army of 75,000 in Italy. The Russian army of 167,000 under Barclay was coming through Germany to attack France. In many ways, Napoleon had overreached himself in 1815, as well.

Napoleon moved quickly against the armies in Belgium, attempting to crush his enemies one or two at a time. Unfortunately for his hopes, Wellington's forces stopped one of his marshals at Quatre-Bras, south of Brussels, counterattacking and preventing the support Napoleon needed to destroy the Prussians. Blücher's men did take terrible casualties when they met Napoleon at Ligny but were still able to retreat in good order. Napoleon did not follow up his advantage and Wellington was able to move from Quatre-Bras to a better position, ready for battle. He chose a ridge named Mont St-Jean, to the south of the village of Waterloo. It was the evening of June 17 and that night it rained in torrents.

Blücher had given his word to Wellington that he would reinforce the British position. His deputy Gneisenau was convinced Wellington would fail to hold the ridge and would be gone by the time the Prussians arrived. He wanted to abandon their allies and return to Prussia. Despite exhaustion and being wounded himself, the seventy-two-year-old Blücher overrode him and gave orders for his men to support Wellington. It is an interesting detail that Gneisenau arranged the Prussian marching order so that the units farthest away from Wellington would go first. It seems he knew this would delay their arrival. The farthest unit, however, was General von Bülow's IV Corps, one of the best units the Prussians had. The eventual arrival of the Prussians would force Napoleon to respond, just as he should have been attacking the British centre. This was a vital part of the victory.

The ground was a quagmire after the downpour of the night before, and Napoleon delayed the attack until it began to dry. At noon on June 18, he attacked at last with 72,000 against Wellington's 67,000. Napoleon's troops moved forward in a feint attack, while his "belles filles" (beautiful daughters) guns hammered at Wellington's army for an hour. At 1:00 p.m., 20,000 veterans moved in line formation towards the British-held ridge. They too had to march through artillery fire and the carnage was horrific. Yet two of the veteran divisions made it to the crest through fierce hand-to-hand fighting. This was a crucial point in the battle, but it was saved by the Household Brigade and Union Brigade cavalry under the Earl of Uxbridge, who smashed the French attackers with a charge over the ridge.

The two brigades continued on across the valley, attacking the French guns. They took about twenty and most of them were exhausted as they were broken in turn by the French cavalry reserves. The damage was done, however. The only truly formidable French infantry left on the field was Napoleon's Imperial Guard, his elite.

There were some confused orders in the French lines at this point. Wellington ordered his men to pull back 30 metres (33 yd) out of range of the French guns. Marshal Ney thought they were retreating and ordered a brigade of French cavalry to attack. His order was queried and in an angry response, Ney led them himself, taking around 4,000 cavalrymen forward without support. If Napoleon had sent in his Imperial Guard at this point, Wellington could well have lost the battle. Napoleon had become aware of the approach of the Prussians and refused to commit them. Unsupported, the cavalry failed to damage the British square formations in any significant way. Volley fire repulsed them and the survivors eventually retreated. The heavy French cannons opened up again and more on the ridge began to die.

By four in the afternoon, the Prussians were there in force, led by the IV Corps. They took a strategic position on Napoleon's right flank and had to be dislodged by vital troops from the Imperial Young and Old Guard regiments. By the time that was done it was getting on for seven in the evening. So close to midsummer, the days were long and it was still light when Napoleon sent in his Imperial Guard at last to break the British centre. They wore dark blue jackets and high bearskin hats. In all their history, they had never retreated.

The Imperial Guard marched up the hill towards a brigade of British Foot Guards under Colonel Maitland and a Dutch brigade under Colonel Detmer. Volley fire and a bayonet charge made the Imperial Guard retreat. Wellington sent in more men after them as they tried to re-form and they were finished. The British Guard regiments were well aware of the reputation of the Napoleonic elite and took their hats as souvenirs. The high bearskin headgear is still worn today by the Grenadier, Welsh, Irish, Scots and Coldstream Guard regiments.

Blücher attacked the French right as Wellington counterattacked in force. The French army collapsed. Afterwards, Blücher wanted to call the battle "La Belle Alliance," but Wellington insisted on his old habit of naming battles after the place where he'd spent the night before. As a result, it became known as the Battle of Waterloo.

Napoleon returned to Paris and abdicated for the second time on June 22, before surrendering to the British. HMS *Bellerophon* took him on board, one of the ships that had fought at the Nile and Trafalgar with Nelson. Ironically, *Bellerophon* (known as "Billy Ruffian") was one of those that had fired on Napoleon's flagship *L'Orient* before she exploded at the Battle of the Nile.

Napoleon was taken to the island of St. Helena and would not leave it until his death. Waterloo was Wellington's last battle, though he did become Prime Minister in 1828.

Blücher died in his bed at home in 1819.

France was forced to pay damages to Britain, Austria, Prussia and Russia. Those countries met in Vienna to settle the future of Europe. A neutral country, or buffer zone, was created from those talks, its peace guaranteed by the others. It was later known as Belgium when it became completely independent in 1830. Interestingly, it is true that the "Wellington boot" takes its name from a leather boot style popularized by Wellington. Originally, it was made of leather and only later produced in the rubber form we know so well today.

2. *The Battle of Vimy Ridge, April 9–12, 1917*

The German army seized Vimy Ridge in Northern France in October 1914 and turned it into an earthen fortress, with snaking tunnels, barbed wire–lined trenches and elaborate fortifications. They even equipped it with makeshift telephone and electrical lines, and rail lines for transporting weapons. The ridge was dotted with machine-gun platforms and artillery.

Having control of Vimy Ridge gave the German army a distinct advantage. Because Vimy Ridge was so high, the soldiers could keep watch on the surrounding countryside and battlegrounds, and protect the coal fields to the north that helped fuel their war effort. Their enemies could not advance past the ridge or around it without being left wide open. Twice, in 1914 and 1916, the British and French had tried to take control of the land, but each assault had been defeated. The failed attacks had exacted a high price – over 200,000 French and British soldiers had been wounded or killed.

In October 1916, with the help of British artillery forces, the newly formed Canadian Corps, under the command of Lieutenant-General Sir Julian Byng and Major-General Arthur Currie, replaced British soldiers along the western slopes of Vimy Ridge. They were told to take Vimy Ridge. Many doubted that the Canadians could achieve more than other soldiers had. The ridge was securely held by the Germans, and the Allied forces had suffered a number of stinging defeats – including the disastrous Battle of the Somme. The Canadians' attack on Vimy, however, changed everything. It was carefully planned, with six months of cunning strategy and rigorous training.

The stable, chalky ground around Vimy was good for building tunnels. With the help of infantry units, tunnelling companies built passages to connect different units. Like the Germans, they installed light rail and electrical lines, and communications centres. The tunnels concealed hospitals, stores of ammunitions, and reserves of water. Using the tunnels, the Canadians moved under the German positions to eavesdrop or plant mines (explosives) that they would later detonate. Telephone and telegraph lines were also strung between the observation posts and the artillery.

While all this work was being done to prepare for the battle, many infantry units were raiding German trenches. This risky and dangerous activity required soldiers to move through "no man's land" in the dead of night. During these raids, the Canadians captured as many enemy soldiers as they could in order to get information from them.

While the infantry harassed the German trench soldiers, the commanders and officers got ready for the big push. They had built a full-scale mockup of the Vimy battlefield in the hilly areas behind the Canadian positions. On the mock battlefield, troops worked in platoons to practise their innovative battle tactics. Over 40,000 topographical trench maps were distributed to the men so that everyone could learn the layout of the entire battlefield.

Soldiers were drilled in a new tactic called the "creeping barrage." The artillery were instructed to aim their shells directly ahead of the Canadian troops as they moved toward the frontline. This way, the bombs would create a wall of explosions behind which the army could move forward while the enemy was pinned in the trenches. But in order to work, the timing of the shelling and the advance of the soldiers had to be coordinated precisely. The Canadian Corps practised until the operation was perfect.

Preparation for the battle also included strikes to weaken the German fighting positions. Before the major assault, the Balloon Company of the Royal Flying Corps found enemy gun positions and fired at them.

Canadian colonel Andrew McNaughton had also developed a way to locate enemy guns by measuring the difference in time between a gun's flash and its sound. With this knowledge, McNaughton's soldiers were able to destroy more than 80 percent of German guns before the Allied troops advanced.

After months of painstaking work, on March 20, 1917, phase one of the attack began with a steady, constant bombardment of the enemy position. The intensity of the shelling varied from heavy to light to confuse the German soldiers. The Canadians and the British used only half of their artillery, hiding the rest of their firepower from the enemy. Then, on April 2, the Allied forces unleashed their full power. The artillery assault beat down German morale. But the German soldiers had no idea how bad it was about to get.

On Easter Monday, April 9, 1917, the long-rehearsed final attack began. It was a day of fighting like no one had ever seen. At 5:30 in the morning, the sun was hardly up and it was icy cold, with sleet driving down across the plains, obscuring the soldiers' view of the ridge. Out of the frozen stillness, the shells and machine guns exploded, creating a curtain of molten metal, fire, dirt and debris behind which tens of thousands of Allied soldiers began their long-awaited charge to the ridge. Many of the soldiers emerged from the tunnels toward the German line.

Even though the men had practised the creeping barrage technique for months, no amount of training could have prepared them for the sights and sounds of so many soldiers moving together in unison, surrounded by so much destruction. Over 1,100 artillery and machine guns fired continuously. Six million shells blasted through the sky in an hour and forty minutes – that's 3,000 shells per second raining down in front of the troops. Mines that had been planted in underground tunnels exploded like fiery volcanoes. The air was filled with a wave of noise so loud and thick that one soldier said it felt as though the sound was a solid ceiling above him. Later, there were reports that the pounding of shells was heard all the way to England.

An Allied plane flying too close to the firestorm burst into flames from the heat of the explosions. And all the while, the soldiers pressed forward, through the mud and muck, past the dead and dying, over the heaps of ruined equipment, the shards of metal, the litter of wood and wire. Those who got too far ahead of their units were killed or wounded by the creeping barrage's gunfire and shells. Before long, much of the ridge had been churned into a seething mass of wet earth, old bones, bleeding bodies and mangled equipment.

It took just under three hours for the first three Canadian divisions to take their sections of the ridge. The fourth division had more trouble; they had been held back by German machine-gun fire coming from the highest point along the slopes. In one battalion, half the men had been wounded or killed. Troops that had been serving as supply or construction units were called in to help, and by the end of the

Canadian soldiers advancing through German barbed wire and heavy fire during the Battle of Vimy Ridge.

day, they had captured this section of the ridge as well. By April 12, the Canadian Divisions had driven the Germans from the entire ridge, severely weakening the enemy's position in the war.

In total, over 100,000 men fought to take Vimy that day; 3,598 of them were killed and 7,004 were wounded. The German army suffered heavy losses, and the battle marked a turning point for the Allied forces.

Despite Canada's lack of war experience, Vimy and other World War I battles earned Canadians a reputation as fierce soldiers. British prime minister David Lloyd George wrote in his memoirs, "Whenever the Germans found the Canadian Corps coming into line, they prepared for the worst." But perhaps more important, the Battle of Vimy Ridge helped to shape Canada's idea of itself as a nation. As Lieutenant Gregory Clark would later say, "As far as I could see, south, north, along the miles of the Ridge, there were the Canadians. And I experienced my first full sense of nationhood." Here, on the battlefields of Europe, the men from nine provinces (Newfoundland had not yet joined Canada) fought as one, proving to themselves – and to everyone back home – what their country could achieve when its people worked together. The words of one Canadian war veteran sum up the experience best: "We went up Vimy Ridge as Albertans and Nova Scotians. We came down as Canadians."

3. The Plains of Abraham – September 18, 1759
In the history of war, battles are won and lost because of many different things: the size of the armies, the weaponry, the planning and strategy, the skill and strength of the soldiers. Sometimes, however, it is sheer luck that shifts the advantage from one side to the other. And there may be no better example of this than the battle that changed the future of Canada: the battle of the Plains of Abraham.

In 1759, England and France were battling for control of New France, which occupied large parts of what we now call Cape Breton (Nova Scotia) and the province of Quebec.

Under the command of the Canadian-born governor general of New France, Pierre de Rigaud de Vaudreuil, and defended by the French General Louis-Joseph, Marquis de Montcalm, the walled city of Quebec sat high atop the embankment of the St. Lawrence River. Protected by its geography and also by its impressive military fortifications, the city seemed to be unassailable.

In late spring of 1759, General James Wolfe was appointed by Britain to lead the assault on the French stronghold at Quebec City. Wolfe made a number of attempts to bombard the city and the French bases around Quebec but to little effect. Wolfe was stumped. There was no obvious way for him to gain access to the city. For months, he had to satisfy himself with disrupting supplies coming up the river and attacking the small communities of Canadians who lived along the shore lines. He thought that such raids might discourage the settlers from providing militia support or supplies to Montcalm's men, but more importantly, he hoped that his constant assaults would force Montcalm and his troops out from inside the heavily fortified city and into open battle. Montcalm, however, was in no hurry to co-operate – he knew that if he just waited, Wolfe would have to leave the area before the St. Lawrence River froze in the fall.

And so Wolfe's siege dragged on throughout the entire summer, sapping the morale of both armies and deeply discouraging each commander. Montcalm was worried about the dwindling supplies to the French colony – the food shortage inside and outside the city was getting desperate. He was also worried about the strength of Wolfe's army. While the French had more soldiers available to them, a great many of that force were Canadian militia (ordinary settlers who had volunteered to fight) and Native warriors. These men were largely untrained, and Montcalm feared they would be undisciplined and unreliable in battle. And the fact that Wolfe could attack at any time kept Montcalm on pins and needles. He and his soldiers slept clothed and booted; the general's horse was always saddled.

But Wolfe was feeling desperate too. He knew his best chance for victory was to get Montcalm and his men out onto an open battlefield. But so far, nothing he'd tried had worked. And time was not on his side. What's more, illness had swept through the British boats: Wolfe got so sick that he feared he would not be able to lead his men.

Finally, he decided that the only thing he could do was to try to land upriver, at Anse-aux-Foulons, a cove three kilometres to the west of the city of Quebec. Even if he could not draw Montcalm into battle, he might cut off Quebec's connection to Montreal in the west, crippling the city for good. Above the cove was a sheer cliff leading to a small road that ran along the top of a plateau – the Plains of Abraham.

Quebec was situated to the east on this plateau. If Wolfe's vessels managed to pass by the city without being bombarded by artillery fire, if his army managed to land without being noticed and if his soldiers managed to climb to the plateau, they would be on a flat stretch of land just outside the walls of the city – the perfect spot for a traditional European field battle. They would also be within the French's line of defence, meaning that many of their soldiers would be too far away to join the battle quickly. But the British soldiers would have to climb the fifty-three-metre-high cliff walls (about the height of a 15-storey building), dragging their guns, cannons and all their gear with them. At the top of the cliff, they would be met by armed French sentries guarding the road. There would also be a military encampment close by that they would have to overcome before gaining access to the plateau. It seemed an impossible plan of attack. In fact, Wolfe was so doubtful that it would succeed, he even confided to one of his officers the night before the assault that he expected to die in battle the next day. But the British general was determined not to return to England without one serious attempt to take Quebec. He planned his attack for September 13.

Despite the fact that Wolfe's boats had made it as far as Quebec and beyond, Montcalm was convinced that the general would attack down river, east of the city. Wolfe played upon Montcalm's assumption by leaving some ships down river of the city. These men fired all night on September 12, as if to clear the shores for their landing. And they lowered small boats filled with troops into the water to make it look like they were about to launch an attack from that spot. Many of these soldiers, however, were too sick to fight.

But even if Wolfe had not planned these deceptions, it's unlikely that Montcalm would have been prepared for the Anse-aux-Foulons attack. Governor General Vaudreuil and General Montcalm had been in constant disagreement over how to proceed against Wolfe. When Vaudreuil had suggested that Anse-aux-Foulons might be vulnerable, Montcalm dismissed the idea. "It is not to be supposed that the enemies have wings so that they can in the same night cross the river, disembark, climb the obstructed acclivity [the cliffs], and scale the walls, for which last operation they would have to carry ladders," he said.

Montcalm did miscalculate, but how could he have anticipated all of the unlikely things that would make Wolfe's attack possible? Wolfe's first stroke of fortune, for example, was to be told by a couple of French deserters that a French supply ship planned to sail upriver in the middle of the night, hoping to get supplies through without drawing the attention of the British fleet. Wolfe's boats started up the river first. When they were hailed by French sentries twice along the route, Wolfe had a French-speaking British officer respond. It was enough to fool the guards.

The British had managed to get past two sets of sentries, but once they attempted to land, surely the mounted sentry who patrolled the cliff top above Anse-aux-Foulons would sound the warning. Indeed he might have—if he had been on duty that night. His horse, however, had just been stolen.

Wolfe's ships slipped unnoticed into the cove. Boats carrying the first wave of British soldiers were sent ashore. As one group of soldiers struggled up the embankment, another

Wolfe's troops struggle up cliff walls to reach the Plains of Abraham.

party cleared a slanting path that led up the incline so that later troops could climb the hill more easily.

When the first group reached the top, fortune once again shined on them. The sentries weren't standing guard; they were sleeping. Wolfe's men easily overpowered them. Next, the soldiers had to contend with the militia unit that protected the plateau. This too turned out to be a good deal easier than it should have been. The commanding officer had just allowed half the Canadian militia to go home to their farms for

harvest. The British took control of the rest without much struggle. One soldier, however, did manage to escape and make it back to the city to warn Montcalm. But once again, the British were in luck. Montcalm's aides thought the man sounded crazy and ignored him.

Once Wolfe's soldiers had gathered on the plateau, they became targets for the Canadian and Native militia men who were watching from the woods that lined the plateau. Wolfe told most of the soldiers to lie flat to avoid being shot; others engaged the snipers in skirmishes. During the fighting, several houses that bordered the plateau were set on fire. Eventually, the commotion drew the attention of the French commanders. When Montcalm finally rode out of Quebec on his black horse to survey the situation, he was shocked to see thousands British soldiers waiting for him on the Plains of Abraham.

The French had troops stationed both to the east and the west of Quebec – Montcalm might have been able to trap Wolfe's men on the plateau if he had waited for these units to arrive. But Montcalm did not want the English to have any more time to prepare for battle, and he feared that Wolfe might have even more troops on the way to the battlefield (he didn't). Montcalm ordered the French troops to leave the protected city and meet the British on the battlefields. He also asked Vaudreuil to send more troops from the Beauport area, but Vaudreuil, once again disagreeing with his French general, kept them where they were. And it got worse. When Montcalm requested that the garrison inside the city walls send some of its artillery to the battlefield on the plateau, its commander gave only three pieces, saying he needed the rest to defend the city itself.

In the ensuing battle, Montcalm's concerns about his fighting forces proved to be well grounded. His men charged the British, firing as soon as they got into range. The militia who had joined the French troops were armed with rifles, not with muskets topped by bayonets. Each time the Canadians had to reload their rifles, they would throw themselves to the ground, creating confusion and distraction among the rest of the advancing men. And without bayonets, they tended to scatter and retreat when they got close enough for hand-to-hand combat. Wolfe's troops, on the other hand, maintained a rigid discipline. Standing in just two rows (a standard formation would have had the men standing many rows deep), they were able to string themselves along the entire width of the plateau. They were instructed not to fire until the enemy was within 18 metres. As the French troops rushed toward them, firing wildly, they stood firm. Then Wolfe gave the order to shoot. The front row fired in unison, the volley of bullets so heavy that the explosion of guns sounded like a cannon going off. Then the first row stepped back and the second row moved forward and fired. When the smoke cleared, the battlefield was littered with the mangled bodies of French soldiers. Now close enough for hand-to-hand combat, the British soldiers rushed forward with their deadly bayonets.

The bloody melee lasted only fifteen minutes. But during the fighting, well over a thousand soldiers were killed (about the same number on both sides). What's more, both generals were shot. Wolfe received a bullet to the wrist but was able to keep fighting until he was hit again, in the stomach and then in the chest. As Wolfe lay dying on the battlefield, one of his men standing nearby looked at the retreating French soldiers and said, "They run, see how they run." Upon hearing this, Wolfe said, "Now, God be praised, I will die in peace." And so he did.

During the battle, Montcalm continued to ride across the battlefield on horseback. But as he and his battle-bruised soldiers retreated to the safety of the city, the general was shot in the lower abdomen and thigh. As Montcalm passed through the city walls, a woman, seeing his wounds cried, "The Marquis has been killed!" Montcalm responded, "It's nothing, it's nothing. Don't be troubled for me, my good friends." But it wasn't nothing – Montcalm died the next day. The battle on the Plains of Abraham had left the French command in disarray. On September 18, Quebec was turned over to the British. It would be a death blow for the colony of New France.

Both Wolfe and Montcalm had held great disdain for the Canadians and the Natives they had led. And each had been accused of arrogance in their leadership. But the battle of the Plains of Abraham made General James Wolfe a hero both in Britain and in English Canada. Montcalm's legacy, however, was more controversial. His defence of Quebec had been a difficult task – but had his own behaviour ensured that he would not receive co-operation from the men on his side of the conflict? Could he have avoided the many mistakes his troops and militia made? Would the results have been different if he hadn't decided to meet Wolfe on the plains? Perhaps. But it is hard to blame him entirely for a battle in which Lady Luck seemed so clearly to favour the British.

4. The Somme – July – November, 1916

One of the many and complex reasons that World War I began was that Germany invaded Belgium. Britain was bound by treaty to defend the country. Similar alliances across Europe drew in all the great powers one by one. It may have begun with the assassination of Archduke Franz Ferdinand in Serbia, but that was merely the spark that set the world on fire.

The Somme was the river in France that Edward III crossed just before the battle of Crécy. The area has had a great deal of British blood soaking into its earth over the centuries, but never more so than on the first day of the Battle of the Somme, July 1, 1916.

Before the British army marched into the machine-gun tracks criss-crossing the battle-field, General Sir Douglas Haig had ordered eight days of artillery bombardment. This had not proved a successful tactic over the previous two years and it did not on that day. One flaw was that the barrage had to stop to allow the allies to advance, so as soon as it stopped, the Germans knew the attack was coming and made their preparations. They had solid, deep bunkers of concrete and wood that resisted the

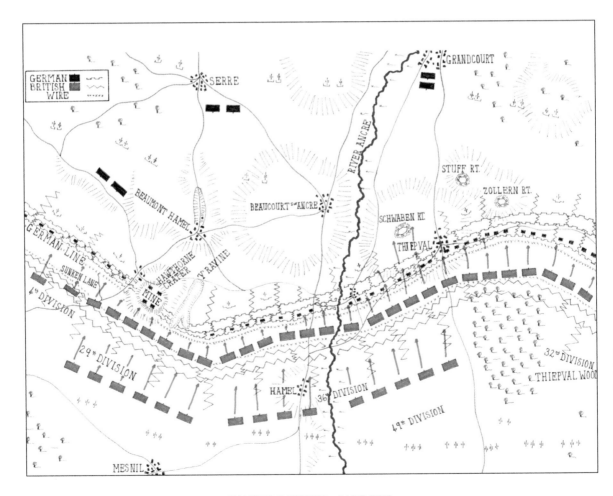

barrage very well indeed. Their barbed-wire emplacements were also still intact after the shells stopped.

At 7:28 in the morning, the British forces detonated two huge mines, then three smaller ones near German lines. The idea was probably to intimidate the enemy, but instead, they acted as a final confirmation of the attack.

The slaughter began at 7:30, when the British soldiers rose up out of their trenches and tried to cross 730 metres (800 yd) in the face of machine-gun fire. A few actually made it to the German front line in that first surge before they were cut down. There were more than 60,000 British casualties and over 19,000 dead. An entire generation fell on a single morning, making it the worst disaster of British military history. Who can say what their lives would have meant and achieved had they survived?

There is a touching poem called "For the Fallen" written by Laurence Binyon in 1914 that is quoted at many Remembrance Day services. This is an extract from it, remembering those who gave their lives for their country. The second verse is particularly poignant.

They went with songs to the battle, they
*   were young,*
Straight of limb, true of eye, steady and
*   aglow.*
They were staunch to the end against
*   odds uncounted:*
They fell with their faces to the foe.

They shall grow not old, as we that are
*   left grow old:*
Age shall not weary them, nor the years
*   condemn.*
At the going down of the sun and in the
*   morning*
We will remember them.

MAKING CLOTH FIREPROOF

PERHAPS THE MOST impressive use for alum (potassium aluminum sulphate) is in fireproofing material. This could be very useful for tablecloths where there is a fire hazard, as in a laboratory or on a stage. It works with any porous cloth, but should not be considered foolproof. To demonstrate it, we used household dusters.

First prepare a solution of alum and water. Hot water works best in dissolving the powder. 500 grams (1 lb, 1 oz) of alum dissolves easily in half a litre of water. Dip the material you wish to fireproof in the solution and make sure it is completely covered. Remove immediately and leave to dry. Be careful not to let it drip onto valuable carpets. If you leave it outside and it happens to rain, it will probably still work.

Once dry, the cloth should be a little stiffer than usual but otherwise unchanged. An untreated duster burned almost completely in twenty seconds. The treated duster could *not be lit*, though there was some light charring after thirty seconds of applied flame.

FIRST AID

ACCIDENTS ARE GOING TO HAPPEN. You can't spend your life worrying about them or you'd never get anything done. However, using common sense and taking a few simple precautions is well worth a little of your time. Really, everyone should have a basic knowledge of first aid. If you were injured, you'd want someone close to you who doesn't panic and knows what to do. It's not being dramatic to say a little knowledge can be the difference between life and death.

When dealing with more than one casualty, a decision has to be made about which person to treat first. This process is called triage. One rule of thumb is that if someone is screaming, they are clearly alive, conscious and almost certainly in less danger than someone silent and still.

These are your priorities:

1. Checking breathing and heartbeat
2. Stopping bleeding
3. Bandaging wounds
4. Splinting fractures
5. Treating shock

When dealing with blood and wounds, there is a risk of AIDS infection. Wear gloves, if you have them, or put plastic bags over your hands. Avoid touching your mouth or face with bloody hands. Wash thoroughly as soon as possible. This advice is almost always ignored in high-stress situations, but it could save your life.

When you approach an injured person, make sure whatever hurt them isn't likely to hurt you – falling debris on a building site, for example.

ARE THEY BREATHING?

If they are breathing, turn them on their side and bend one leg up away from the body for support. This is the "recovery position." It helps to prevent choking caused by vomit or bleeding.

If breathing is poor, use a finger to remove any obstructions from the mouth and throat. Check that they have not swallowed their tongue and if they have, pull it back into the mouth. If breathing is blocked, put them onto their back, sit astride them, place your hands just above their navel and thrust upward into the ribcage. If this does not work, grasp them around the chest under the armpits from behind, joining your hands in front if you can. Then grip hard, compressing their chest. This is the Heimlich manoeuvre.

Once the blockage is clear, if they are still not breathing, start artificial respiration.

Note that babies require special delicacy. If a baby stops breathing, support them face down on your forearm. The pressure alone is enough in some cases, but if not, press three or four times between the shoulder blades with the heel of your hand. If there is still no response, support the head and turn the baby face up, then use just two fingers to press down on the chest four times. Repeat this action. Finally, cover the baby's mouth and nose with your mouth and breathe into their lungs.

IS THE HEART BEATING?

To take the pulse at the wrist, press your fingers on the wrist, just below the thumb at the lower end of the forearm. To take the pulse at the neck, turn the face to one side and press your fingers under the jaw next to the windpipe.

The normal pulse rate for the relaxed adult is 50 to 100 beats per minute. For a child it is 80 to 100 beats per minute. In high-stress situations, it can spike as high as 240, though a heart attack is very close at that point.

Use your watch to count the beats in thirty seconds and then double it. If you cannot feel a pulse and the pupils of the eyes are much larger than normal, start CPR. (See CPR section.)

ARTIFICIAL RESPIRATION

The first five minutes are the most crucial, but keep going until the person starts to breathe on his or her own or medical help arrives. This can be exhausting, so take turns if there are others to help.

1. Lay the patient on their back.
2. Tilt the head back.
3. Check for breathing by placing your ear next to the patient's nose and mouth.
4. Place mouth over patient's mouth and blow firmly twice. It takes more effort than you might expect to inflate someone else's chest.

Watch for the chest to rise, and take your mouth away and check for a pulse at the neck. Repeat this five or six times in succession. If there are signs of air circulation, continue checking for further signs every minute. After that, get a rhythm going of one breath every five seconds. After ten or twelve, begin cardiac compression.

With a baby, put your mouth over the nose and mouth and use short gentle breaths twenty times a minute. A baby's lungs can be damaged by too forceful treatment.

With an animal, such as a dog, hold the mouth closed with both hands and blow into the nose to inflate the chest. Whether you do this will of course depend on how much you love the dog. Use a strong mouthwash afterwards.

CPR (CARDIOPULMONARY RESUSCITATION)

1. If the patient's pulse has not returned from artificial respiration, begin CPR.
2. Place heel of hands on the bottom end of the ribcage.
3. With arms straight, push down about 4 centimetres ($1\frac{1}{2}$ in).
4. Do this in cycles of fifteen compressions to two breaths, as with artificial respiration.

Never try compression when the heart is beating, even if it is very faint. This could stop the heart.

Check for a pulse after one minute and then at three-minute intervals. Do not give up.

As soon as a pulse is detected, stop compressions but continue mouth-to-mouth until the patient is breathing normally, then put them into the recovery position.

BLEEDING AND INJURY

If anything is embedded in the wound, you will need a ring pad bandage. Roll a piece of cloth into a tube, then join the ends to make a doughnut shape. Put this around the wound before bandaging, so the bandage won't press glass or other fragments in deeper.

An adult has up to eleven pints of blood. Losing three of them will cause unconsciousness. Even a loss of half a litre can cause someone to faint, which is why blood donors are asked to sit down and have a biscuit and orange juice after donating.

Immediate steps must be taken to stop the flow of blood. Pressure is the key. It slows down the blood flow enough to allow the body's own repair mechanisms to start vital clotting. Apply pressure for five to fifteen minutes and don't keep checking it. Talk to the patient as you do, keeping an eye on their state of mind and alertness. If you have no dressing, make a pad of a shirt or any other cloth.

Raise the injured part above the heart to aid clotting. Squeeze the edges of a gaping wound together before applying the pad.

Apply a tourniquet only if you cannot otherwise control the bleeding. Tie a bandage above the wound, tightening it until the blood flow slows. You cannot leave this on for any significant length of time, so if help is delayed, loosen the tourniquet with each passing hour.

If you don't have anything to tie it, apply pressure on the main artery above the wound. To do this, find a pulse in the side of the jaw or wrist, underside of upper arm, crook of the elbow, top of the shoulder (clavicle), the temples on the side of the head, top of the thighs by the groin, back of the knees and the front of the ankles. Find the closest one and press it hard into the bone. It is a good idea to try to find these on yourself, before you try to do it in real life with someone screaming in your ear.

Soap is an antiseptic and can be used to wash a wound to avoid infection. Hot water or boiled wine will also sterilize the site, though the application will be extremely painful. In an emergency, fresh urine will also work, as it is sterile.

Serious internal bleeding may be indicated by cold clammy skin, a rapid pulse, restlessness and rapid bruising under the skin. Try to minimize shock by elevating their legs, keeping the patient warm and getting help fast.

BREAKS

If someone fractures a bone in an accident, it may be necessary to splint the damaged limb before trying to move them. This is done by placing two pieces of firm material along the damaged area and securing them with bandage.

A wrist or a dog's leg can be secured in a rolled-up magazine and held with shoelaces. Damaged arms will need to be put in a sling and secured against the body.

A sling can be formed by a large triangular bandage which folds over the arm and is secured at the neck.

BURNS

Burns destroy the skin and carry a risk of infection. Run cold water over a heat burn until the pain begins to subside. Try not to break any blisters that form. Give the injured person lots to drink. Remove any jewellery and clothing from the burned area, but do not remove clothing that is stuck to the burned area. Do not apply ointments to the skin. Cover with a loose bandage if you have one, or if not, a plastic bag. Put dressings between burned fingers and toes to stop them from sticking together.

SHOCK

This can occur after any serious accident and can be fatal. The symptoms are loss of colour from the lips, dizziness, cold and clammy skin, and a rapid pulse.

Reassure the patient and talk to them. If they can talk, ask them their name and then use it often. Keep them warm and check their breathing and pulse. Lay them down and elevate their legs. Be ready to give mouth-to-mouth and cardiac compression if they fall unconscious.

Hot sweet tea is useful if they are conscious and alert. Try not to leave a shock victim on their own, however.

Staying calm is most important for your own safety and other people who may be relying on you. It helps to prepare. When the injury occurs, the first thing you should do is take a deep breath and reach for the first-aid kit you have prepared long before. Remember the ABC of "Airway, Breathing, Circulation" and check one at a time.

Make sure you have considered methods of contact in the event of an emergency. A mobile phone is a good idea, but is it in a waterproof bag? Is it charged? Remember that the best captains look after their men.

Nausea

Nausea from some external cause, like car sickness, sea sickness or morning sickness, can sometimes be eased with an acupressure point in the wrists. To find it, lay the other hand at right angles to the wrist.

The point lying underneath the index finger between the first and the second joints can relieve nausea after about five minutes of pressing. It is possible to have each hand press on the other's nausea point. It does not work for everyone, but it can be very useful to know.

Frostbite

Frostbite has two stages. When tissue is exposed to freezing temperatures for long enough, superficial frostbite may develop. The skin will look white and waxy and be firm to the touch, and though touch will be painful, numbness will follow. This means that the skin is frozen. In deep frostbite, which follows, the skin and all tissue below it freezes, sometimes down to the bone. Skin will feel cold and hard, and a person won't feel anything. To treat frostbite, first cover the frostbitten area—ears, nose, toes—with warm hands. If your own hands are frost-bitten, breathe warm breath on them or put them under your armpits. For deep frostbite, get medical help immediately. If it's not available, remove any jewellery and put the frostbitten part in warm water until it turns pink. This might be painful, but it's the right thing to do. Then, seek medical help.

Hypothermia

Hypothermia is a condition that results when your body's temperature drops well below where it should be. It is usually associated with freezing weather but can happen any time the body is exposed to chilly temperatures. Someone with hypothermia may have a slow pulse or slow breathing, or they may be shivering, stumbling or confused. Hypothermia can easily be mistaken for drunkenness, so be on the lookout for the signs. To help someone who has been exposed, cover the person and make sure the head is warm. Ideally, wrap the person in something wind-proof—like space blankets or garbage bags— and make sure his or her clothes are dry. If possible, move the person to a warmer place, and then get medical help.

Heatstroke (Sunstroke)

Heatstroke can be very dangerous. It occurs when someone has been in a hot, humid environment for a long time. The body literally overheats and your natural cooling processes—like sweating—stop, causing your temperature to rise quickly. The symptoms include skin that is hot to the touch and flushed, a rapid pulse, loud breathing and vomiting. You should immediately move someone with heatstroke to a cooler and shaded place and remove outer clothing. If possible, put the person in a cool bath, cover them with wet sheets or sponge them with cool water.

Insect Bites

Look closely at the site of an insect bite or sting, as there may be a stinger remaining in the skin. If so, remove it by scraping it out carefully with tweezers. Apply rubbing alcohol or ice to the bite. Some people are severely allergic to insect bites and stings, and carry prescription medicine. You may need to help them get their medicine if the reaction is particularly strong.

Medical Kits

Whether this kit is intended for a house or for emergencies will alter the contents. There isn't much point putting athlete's foot powder in an emergency kit. However, the basics are:

1. BAND-AIDs and scissors. Cloth BAND-AIDs or dressings are the best and can be cut to any shape.
2. Antiseptic cream and TCP antiseptic liquid.
3. Needle and thread. Stitching cuts is possible if the patient is unconscious. (Dogs will occasionally let you do this, though most of them struggle like maniacs.)
4. Painkillers. Ibuprofen also works as an anti-inflammatory drug but can be dangerous to asthmatics. Acetylsalicylic acid (ASA) is useful in cases of heart attack or a stroke as it thins the blood. Paracetamol is good for pain and to bring down a high temperature. Oil of cloves can be dabbed on for tooth pain.
5. Antibiotic eye ointment. Available in drug stores, it is good stuff for any eye soreness or infection. Works brilliantly on dogs as well.
6. Bandages. Including one large square that can be folded diagonally into a sling.
7. Gauze pads to go under the bandage and soak up blood.
8. Lip balm.
9. High-factor sun block.
10. Tweezers and safety pins.
11. A couple of pairs of latex gloves.
12. Antihistamine pills for insect stings or allergic reactions.

If there is a chance of you needing antibiotics away from civilization, such as on a mountaineering trip, your dctor may supply a prescription. It will probably be a general-purpose antibiotic, like amoxicillin.

THE COMMONWEALTH

FACTS AND FIGURES

THE COMMONWEALTH IS AN ORGANIZATION OF FIFTY-THREE NATIONS. With the exception of Mozambique, which joined at the end of the twentieth century, the other fifty-two were all part of the British Empire. In fact, the Commonwealth was created as the peaceful twilight organization of that empire. It has been largely successful, remaining a surprisingly influential group today. More than 1.8 billion people live in Commonwealth countries and Queen Elizabeth II broadcasts an address to them on Commonwealth Day (the second Monday in March) each year. All fifty-three take part in the Commonwealth Games.

1. Antigua and Barbuda*
2. Australia*
3. The Bahamas*
4. Bangladesh
5. Barbados*
6. Belize*
7. Botswana
8. Brunei Darussalam
9. Cameroon
10. Canada*
11. Cyprus
12. Dominica
13. Fiji Islands
14. The Gambia
15. Ghana
16. Grenada*
17. Guyana
18. India
19. Jamaica
20. Kenya
21. Kiribati
22. Lesotho
23. Malawi
24. Malaysia
25. Maldives
26. Malta
27. Mauritius
28. Mozambique
29. Namibia
30. Nauru
31. New Zealand*
32. Nigeria
33. Pakistan
34. Papua New Guinea*
35. St. Kitts and Nevis*
36. St. Lucia*
37. St. Vincent and the Grenadines*
38. Samoa
39. Seychelles
40. Sierra Leone
41. Singapore
42. Solomon Islands*
43. South Africa
44. Sri Lanka
45. Swaziland
46. Tanzania
47. Tonga
48. Trinidad and Tobago
49. Tuvalu*
50. Uganda
51. United Kingdom*
52. Vanuatu
53. Zambia

The * symbol indicates the constitutional monarchies where Queen Elizabeth II is head of state. Up to 1947, there were no republics in the British Commonwealth. To allow India to remain a member while becoming an independent republic, the word *British* was dropped from the description. Today, thirty-two members are republics and five (Brunei, Lesotho, Malaysia, Swaziland and Tonga) have national monarchs of their own. All, however, accept the British monarch as "Head of the Commonwealth." In addition, Crown Dependencies like Guernsey, Jersey and the Isle of Man can take part in the Commonwealth Games.

This is an extract from a speech on the Commonwealth by the Right Honourable Owen Arthur, prime minister of Barbados:

> It is the oldest living political association of states, yet in many ways the most adaptable to modern realities and thus the most responsive to the changing needs of its membership. It is rich in its diversity, yet remarkable in its cohesiveness, forged in no small measure by the sense of common identity we derive from our shared historical experience and the administrative, legal and institutional structures.

The Commonwealth promotes democracy, equality and good governance not only among its own members, but also throughout the world. It gives aid and disaster relief to its members and provides funds for development and the eradication of poverty.

MAPS OF CHANGING CANADA

CANADA'S BOUNDARIES, like those of many countries, have changed over time. By studying the maps on the next page, you will see the story of this country emerging, from its roots as a colonial holding to the fully independent nation we know today.

Our settlement history reflects two distinct patterns of boundaries. The eastern boundaries, from Ontario all the way to the Maritimes, trace natural features such as drainage basins. That's why there are fewer straight boundary lines in the central and eastern provinces. In the west, however, treaties often used latitude and longitude divisions – especially the 49th and 60th parallels – to mark out provincial and territorial limits.

Canada began as a nation of four provinces, but it has since grown to include ten provinces and three territories. It is now the second-largest land mass in the world. The most recent change to Canada's map occurred on April 1, 1999, when Nunavut officially separated from the Northwest Territories to become the third and largest territory of the country.

Map 1

France successfully establishes the first French settlement in North America. The city of Port Royal is founded in present-day Nova Scotia and the city of Quebec on the St. Lawrence River.

Map 2

With the Treaty of Paris (1783), the United States of America becomes its own country, independent from Britain.

Map 3

The 49th parallel extends westward, marking the international boundary between the United States and what would later become part of Western Canada. Upper and Lower Canada are formed following the Constitutional Act of 1791.

Map 4

Upper and Lower Canada unite to form the Province of Canada. The Oregon Treaty of 1846 extends the international boundary of the 49th parallel westward.

Map 5	Map 6

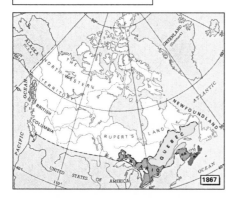

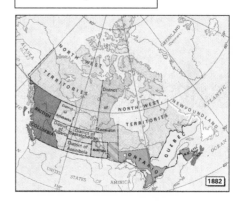

The Dominion of Canada becomes a country on July 1, 1867. This is why we now celebrate Canada Day on July 1 of every year. The newly formed nation includes Ontario, Quebec, New Brunswick and Nova Scotia. Manitoba (1870), British Columbia (1871) and Prince Edward Island (1873) are the next three provinces to confederate.

Canada gains control of the Arctic islands. The districts of Assiniboia, Saskatchewan, Athabaska and Alberta are formed.

Map 7	Map 8

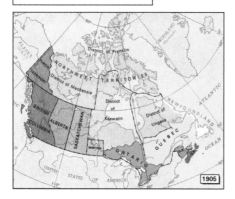

Alberta and Saskatchewan become provinces, making Canada a nation of nine provinces. The boundaries of the Northwest Territories are redefined, and in 1898 the Yukon becomes a territory.

Ontario and Manitoba extend their present-day boundaries, and Quebec extends northward.

Map 9

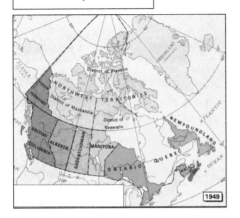

Newfoundland joins Canada as the country's tenth province.

Map 10

Nunavut becomes Canada's third and largest territory.

MAPS OF CHANGING CANADA

EXTRAORDINARY STORIES – PART TWO: THE VOYAGEURS

CANADIAN HISTORY almost bursts at the seams with tales of danger. The early days in this country were not for the weak or the faint of heart. Whether it was the Native Canadians' thunderous buffalo hunts, perilous explorations by the early Europeans or the treacherous work in lumber camps, mines and seas, the labour that fashioned this country required bravery, brawn, fortitude and stamina. And perhaps no other men demonstrated this physical and mental toughness better than the voyageurs of the fur trade.

The fur trade in North America was propelled in the eighteenth and nineteenth century by a European fashion craze for beaver hats (actually constructed from a felt-like material that was made from beaver pelts). For a time, the hat's popularity made this rodent's hide the most valuable fur in the world.

In the early days of the trade, the English Hudson's Bay Company used posts in the north, accessible from James Bay, to collect furs from Native trappers and traders. But French merchants in Montreal also collected furs to export to Europe. They hired *voyageurs* ("travellers") who made their way by canoe into the north to collect pelts from Native trappers. (Renegade traders who worked by themselves were called *coureurs des bois* or "runners of the wood.")

In the late eighteenth century, the Scottish North West Company realized that if it too used voyageurs and had these men travel from the Montreal area to the tip of Lake Superior and beyond to collect furs, they could challenge the Hudson's Bay Company's stronghold on the trade. And they were right. The voyageurs who worked for the North West Company were so swift and effective in bringing the furs to market that by 1783 the NWC controlled 78 percent of the fur trade.

That sounds fairly simple, doesn't it? Travel by canoe to Lake Superior, pick up a few furs, maybe have a little break while you're there, then turn around and come home with your cargo. Well, it was a lot more difficult than that.

The North West Company voyageurs, almost all of whom were French-speaking, would meet in Lachine outside of Montreal in the spring. They needed to make it to the company head-quarters in Grand Portage (later called Fort William) on Lake Superior in eight weeks. Their canoes would be loaded down with provisions for the journey and with huge quantities of goods to trade for furs.

The voyageur canoes were made of birch bark and cedar, and were held together with tree roots and tar. The boats varied greatly in size, from small, nimble ones that could take only a few paddlers, to eleven-metre "freighters" that could hold as many as sixteen passengers and paddlers. The typical canoe trekking from Montreal to Lake Superior, however, was big enough to seat eight to twelve paddlers and their cargo.

The voyageurs were under constant pressure to make good time on their journey. The lakes and streams were only navigable for a short time every year – the voyageurs had to get to the trading posts quickly so they could get home again before the end of the warm weather. What's more, traders from the far north and the west would be travelling to meet them at the company headquarters. They too would have to get back to their homes before the cold temper-atures and the harsh storms of the fall and win-ter. Every daylight hour was a working hour for the voyageurs. They would get up before the sun even cracked the horizon – generally about 4:00 a.m. but sometimes earlier. They would move into their boats as quickly as possible and then work their way through the rivers and lakes until the sun began to set that evening. They paddled at least fourteen hours a day, although sometimes many more hours than that.

As the day progressed, they might take short breaks every hour – usually just long enough to smoke a small pipe of tobacco. The breaks were well earned – voyageurs had to paddle between forty-five and fifty-five strokes a minute. They often sang as they dug their paddles in and out of the water. This helped to break the monotony of the work and to set the rhythm of their strokes so that they all worked in unison.

When the sun began to drop below the hori-zon, they would find a spot along the shore to make camp. After unloading their boats and pulling them ashore, they would make a fire, and then eat and repair their canoes by firelight.

Despite the fact that they were travelling through a wilderness rich in game, they had no time to hunt or fish for their meals. Instead, they ate only the things they had brought with them. On the journey from Montreal, they brought flour, corn, pork and fat. On the return trip, they carried staples they had picked up at the post: fish, dried meat, flour, corn and sometimes wild rice. When they travelled farther west and north, they relied on the Native populations for food supplies, such as pemmican. Pemmican is made from dried buffalo meat, fat and Saskatoon berries, and has the advantage of not spoiling on long journeys. The voyageurs would eat it plain, fried or in a soup called "rabaloo."

While a diet of corn and fat may not sound too appetizing to us today, it's clear that pem-mican was also an acquired taste. An early chronicler of the fur trade, H. M. Robinson, described pemmican in his book *The Great Fur Land*: "Take the scrapings from the driest out-side corner of a very stale piece of cold roast beef, add to it lumps of rancid [rotten] fat, then garnish all with long human hairs and short hairs of dogs and oxen, and you have a fair imi-tation of common pemmican."

But the voyageurs were grateful for all the corn, fat and pemmican they could get. The physical exertion of the voyage required an enormous amount of fuel. David Thompson, one of the managers of the North West Company, commented that some voyageurs would eat eight pounds of meat a day while at the posts. It was quite easy to run out of food on their journey (either because the provisions were too small or because food had been lost to rough water), so many voyageurs faced hunger and even starvation.

Back at camp, after the voyageurs had eaten, they would settle down for a few hours of sleep. Their bed was the hard ground – their overturned canoes their only shelter from wind or rain.

But the long days, relentless paddling and bad food were only the beginnings of the voyageurs' hardships. When the rapids got too rough or they needed to get from one lake to another, the voyageurs had to portage. After finding a spot along the shore to land their boats, they emptied them and then carried all of their packs and canoes over land. Each pack weighed 41 kilograms (90 lb), and each voyageur was required to carry two packs. One pack hung from a tumpline (a strap) that was stretched across his forehead and down his back. As the voyageur leaned forward slightly, the other pack was balanced on top of the first. The tumpline left the voyageur's hands free to swat away the swarms of mosquitoes and blackflies that plagued him as he walked.

As if carrying 82 kilograms (181 lb) wasn't enough, many voyageurs actually carried more, since they could earn extra money by doing so. There were reports that some men carried as much as 227 kilograms (500 lb). Carrying the packs was such a physical strain that strangulated hernias – in which the muscles of the abdomen separate, allowing the intestines to bulge out against the skin – were the most common injury for the voyageurs. In fact, the bright red, woven sashes that were a standard part of the voyageurs' clothing were worn to support their backs and to keep their intestines in place. Unfortunately for the voyageurs, portages were not a rare occurrence. Between Montreal and Fort William, there were thirty-six of them!

Paddling was hard work, but portaging was worse, so voyageurs were often willing to shoot through heavy rapids to avoid the long haul across land. (They were sometimes forced to run the rapids because the cliffs or steep riverbanks were too difficult to climb.) But running rapids was extremely dangerous. Canoes overturned and broke, and most voyageurs could not swim. If a man died on route, his companions buried him on the shoreline and erected a small wooden cross. After one of his trips along the fur trade route, an NWC clerk noted that at "almost every Rapid that we have passed since we left Montreal, we have seen a number of Crosses erected, and at one I counted no less than thirty!"

A voyageur's work was gruelling indeed. Colonel George Landmann's description of these men is tinged with awe: "No men in the world are more severely worked than are these Canadian voyageurs," he wrote. "I have known them to work in a canoe twenty hours out of twenty-four and go on at that rate during a fortnight or three weeks without a day of rest . . . but it is not with impunity they so exert themselves; they lose much flesh in the performance of such journies. . . ."

The voyageurs themselves were well aware of the extraordinary difficulty of their work. They took great pride in their own courage and their endurance. They were largely unschooled and illiterate, and few could ever hope to move up in the ranks of the companies for which they toiled. They therefore contented themselves with creating a world of their own, with its own culture, customs, dress and legends. They developed many religious and spiritual rituals that helped them through their travels. They created and adapted countless songs to entertain themselves and to accompany their paddling. And they told many stories and tall tales about their fellow adventurers and the world through which they travelled.

They also established a unique social order. Where you sat in the canoe, for example, said a lot about your status among your fellow voyageurs. Middle paddlers were at the bottom of the ladder. The ends (the foresmen and steersmen) were next up, and guides were considered more important still. Clerks or businessmen from the company were considered the most superior, though they were passengers, not paddlers.

But the pecking order went far beyond where you sat in the canoe. While many voyageurs travelled from Montreal to Lake Superior and back (and therefore worked for the company only in the spring and summer), others continued west after the rendezvous at the trading post and spent the winters working in the bush or collecting furs from trappers as far away as Lake Winnipeg and Great Slave Lake. These men called themselves *hommes du nord* ("northmen") or *hivernants* ("winterers"). They thought that part-time voyageurs were lightweights, and they dubbed them *mangeurs de lard*, or "pork eaters."

Eventually, Hudson's Bay Company also began using voyageurs, and after a period of intense competition with the North West Company, the two companies merged. But the fur trade would soon be on the decline. The War of 1812 disrupted trade at many posts, and the beaver populations across Canada started to shrink. And finally, when men and women in Europe began favouring silk hats to felt hats, the demand for beaver pelts petered out.

While many hommes du nord continued to guide, trap and trade, the dangerous world of the voyageur eventually disappeared. It lives on, however, through history, legends and paddling songs, such as this voyageur favourite:

My Bark Canoe (Mon Canoe d'Écorce)

(final verse)

You are my voyageur companion!
I'll gladly die in my canoe.
And on the grave beside the canyon
You'll overturn my canoe.

His cart is beloved of the ploughman,
The hunter loves his gun, his hound;
The musician is a music lover
To my canoe I'm bound.

BUILDING A WORKBENCH

Bᴇꜰᴏʀᴇ ᴡᴇ ᴄᴏᴜʟᴅ ᴍᴀᴋᴇ a number of the things in this book, it was obvious we needed a workbench. Even the simplest task in a workshop becomes difficult without a solid vice and a flat surface.

We kept this as simple as possible. Pine is easiest to cut, but it also breaks, dents and crushes, which is why classic workbenches are made out of beech – a very hard wood.

Complete beginners should start with pine, as mistakes are a *lot* cheaper. Planning is crucial – every table is different. Ours fitted the wall of the workshop and is higher than almost any workbench you'll ever see. Both of us are tall and prefer to work at a higher level. Draw the plan and have an idea of how much wood you will need.

The suppliers cut the wood square to save time, and we spent two days cutting mortice and tenon joints before assembling it.

RULE: Measure twice and cut once. Carpentry is 80 percent care and common sense, 20 percent skill, or even artistry. You do not have to be highly skilled to make furniture, as long as you *never* lose your temper, plan carefully and practise, practise, practise. The reason a professional is better than an amateur is because the professional cuts joints every day.

Mᴏʀᴛɪᴄᴇ ᴀɴᴅ Tᴇɴᴏɴ Jᴏɪɴᴛꜱ

A mortice is a trench cut into wood. The tenon is the piece that fits into the trench.

NOTE: Using sharp tools is not to be undertaken lightly. A chisel will remove a finger as easily as a piece of wood. Don't try this unless you have an adult willing to show you the basics. There are hundreds of fiddly little things (like how to hold a chisel) that we couldn't fit in here.

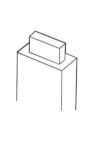

We started by making two rectangular frames to go at each end of the table workbench. This is a very simple design, but mortice and tenon joints are strong on the corners.

Make sure that the top of your tenon is not too close to the top of the upright. When it comes to cutting the mortice, you do not want to break through.

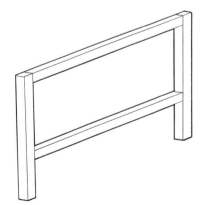

For simple "through" joints, the tenon length is the same as the width of the upright. To create the tenon, you have to make four saw cuts (accurately!) down to a marked line that is equal to the depth of the upright. Only the middle rectangle will remain. After the four cuts, you saw away the waste pieces and use a chisel to trim any splinters or roughness.

When you have your tenons cut, number them in pencil. Use the tenons as the template for the mortice trenches, also numbered. We also pencilled a cross on the top side so we wouldn't lose track. Obviously, they should all be identical, but it's odd how often they aren't. Mark the mortices with extreme care, taking note of the exact position. The first upright will be relatively easy, but the second has to be absolutely identical – and that's where the problems creep in.

Next, cut the mortice. Great care is needed here – and some skill with the chisel. Take care also not to crush the edges as you lever backwards. Ideally, you should use a chisel as wide as the mortice itself – though some prefer to use narrower blades.

Once you have your pair of end pieces, you need bars running lengthways to prevent wobble. We used mortice and tenons again, as the beech joints seemed easily strong enough for our needs.

In the picture, you can see that we put both beams on one side. We wanted to have access for storage underneath, so we left the front open.

The rope arrangement in the picture is called a "windlass." It is used when a piece of furniture is too long to be clamped. Most tables will have this problem and it's good to know you can overcome it with nothing more than a double length of rope and a stick to twist it tighter and tighter. The same technique has even been used to pull wooden ships out of the sea. Be sure to protect the wood with cloth, or you'll cut grooves into your uprights.

The top planks can be glued together if they have perfect edges, or simply screwed in place. The simplest possible method is to screw down into the end pieces, but this does leave ugly screw heads visible. We used a corner piece underneath, screwing across into the end piece and also up into the underside of the top. It worked well enough for our purposes.

To finish, we sanded like madmen for the best part of a day, used filler for the gaps we could not explain in the joints, then wiped it all over with linseed oil. The oil soaked in very nicely to seal the wood – just in case we spill paint on it in the future.

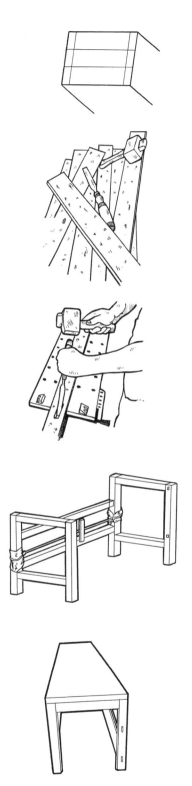

MAKING A POCKET LIGHT

※

THIS IS AN EXTREMELY simple circuit toy that will be instantly recognizable. It is also fun – and portable. You will need a tobacco tin – and they're not easy to find these days. Ask at any garage sale, or badger the elderly. Try to get more than one, in fact, as they are fantastically useful. Otherwise, an Altoids tin will work.

> You will need
>
> • A battery – ideally one of the square 9V ones.
> • A flashlight bulb.
> • Two pieces of bare wire about the length of a ruler.
> • Duct tape.

If you have access to a soldering iron, soldered connections are more reliable, but this can be made without.

1. Attach one wire to the positive terminal of the battery (+). If you do use a soldering iron, make sure the battery is firmly held and don't rush – it isn't easy to place a blob of solder where you want it without it cooling down too fast.

2. Attach the end of the other wire to the end of the bulb, as in the picture. We soldered it.

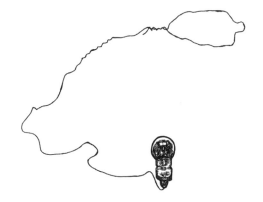

Using small strips of tape, you could hold it steady, but try not to cover the barrel of the bulb – you'll need it for the last connection. Make a loop out of the other end, as shown.

3. Attach the barrel of the bulb to the other terminal. Note that the bulb should go sideways rather than be pointing up, or the tin might not close properly. This a good point to try the circuit. With the bulb in contact with the anode (–), the bulb should light when the wires touch. If it doesn't, check every connection – and make sure the bulb works.

You now have a circuit that will light a bulb when two wires touch. Install it in the tin with more tape.

To use, bend one wire into an assault course of curves and use the loop to go from one end to the other without touching. Here is where you need the steady hand. The whole thing can be carried in a pocket.

There is a slight chance the wires will form a circuit through the metal of the tin, so it's not a bad idea to line it with the tape. At the time of writing, our pocket light has lasted more than a year without breaking or the battery wearing out – despite regular use.

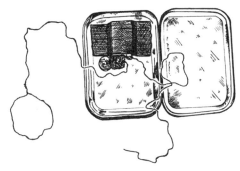

FIVE PEN AND PAPER GAMES

1. HANGMAN

This is the classic word game for two or more players. Think of a word and mark out the number of letters in dashes – – – – – – –. The other player guesses letters one at a time. If they guess correctly, write the letter. If they get one wrong, draw a line of the hanged man and write the letter on the page. Incorrect guesses of the whole word also cost a line.

There are twelve chances to get the word right. If the hanged man is completely finished, they lose. Take it in turns and try some really hard words, like "paella," or "phlegm."

2. HOUSES

This one is silly, but enjoyably frustrating. It looks very easy. Draw six boxes anywhere on the page. Mark three of them with G, W and E – Gas, Water and Electricity. Number the others 1, 2 and 3. The object of this puzzle is to provide vital services to the three numbered houses. You do this by drawing a pipe line from one to the other. Lines are not allowed to cross and they may not go through a house or a vital service.

In the example, you can see one of the houses has Gas and Water but no Electricity. Try moving the squares around but remember you are not allowed to cross any lines. This puzzle looks possible, but it actually isn't. No matter where you put the boxes you cannot connect all three services without crossing a line. It is perfect to give to someone who thinks they are

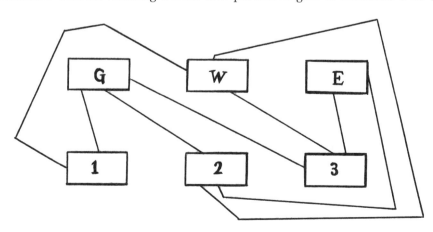

really clever (like an older brother). It will completely stump them. Pretend you know the answer, refuse to tell them and watch them struggle. (There is a cheating way to complete the puzzle. You take the last pipe line out to the edge of the paper, run it back on the other side and then punch a hole through to the house. This does not impress onlookers.)

3. SQUARES

This is a very simple game for two players that can be fiendishly difficult to win. Draw a grid of dots on a piece of paper, say nine by nine or ten by ten. Each player can draw a line between two dots as his or her turn. The aim is to close a box, making a square. If you can do this, you get another turn.

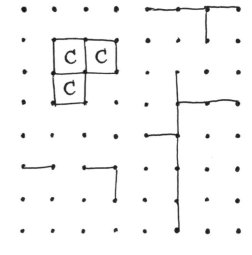

The game tends to follow a pattern of easy steps as most of the lines are filled, then sudden chains of boxes are made, one after the other, until the grid is complete. It may be a good idea to sacrifice a small line of boxes so that a larger one is yours. Mark the boxes clearly so they can be counted – either with different colours or with a symbol. The player with the most boxes at the end wins.

4. BATTLESHIPS

This is a classic. Two grids are drawn, with x and y axes numbered 1–8 and A–H. Larger grids will make the game last longer. Draw ships on your grid – an aircraft carrier of five squares, a battleship of four, two destroyers of three, a submarine of two and another cruiser of two. Any reasonable combination is possible as long as both players agree.

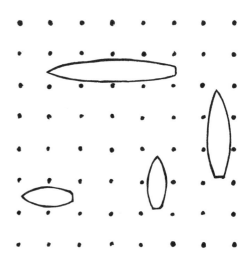

Once these have been drawn in private, each player then calls out shots in turn, using the grid references – A4, C8 and so on. The aim is to sink your opponent's ships before yours are sunk.

An interesting alternative is to replace the ships with words chosen by each player – of two letters, three letters and so on. The aim is still to find and "sink" the words, but with a score of five points for every word – or *ten* points if the word can be guessed before the last letter is hit. The winner then is the one with the most points at the end.

5 · OTHELLO

Another game that looks easy, but this one is in fact fiendish. Begin by drawing a grid – school exercise books always make these things easier, which may be why an awful lot of these games are played at school.

Three by three is not enough of a challenge but will do for the explanation. Five by five is much better.

The player using *O* fills in two corners, while the opponent puts an *X* in the other two. Decide who moves first by flipping a coin.

Each player can only place a symbol on adjacent squares to the ones he already has. You can't move diagonally.

Any of the opponent's adjacent symbols are changed into yours by the move – including diagonals. In diagram number 2 it would make sense for *O* to put one in the middle-right square.

You'll need an eraser! The *X* in the corner will be erased and turned into an *O*.

Of course, now *X* can respond. If they put their *X* in the middle of the top row, it will win two more *X* squares.

. . . and so on. In fact, *O* must win this one.

The game ends when one player has nothing left, or when the grid is filled. This is just a taster. With larger grids, the game can be fascinating and complex.

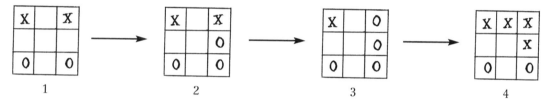

1   2   3   4

THE GOLDEN AGE OF PIRACY

THERE HAVE BEEN PIRATES for as long as ships have sailed out of sight of land and law. The period known as "the golden age" of piracy began in the seventeenth century and continued into the early eighteenth. The discovery of the New World and vast wealth there for the taking caused an explosion of privateers – some, like Francis Drake, with the complete authority and knowledge of Queen Elizabeth I.

The word "buccaneer" comes from European sailors who caught wild pigs on the islands of Haiti and Tortuga in the Caribbean and smoked the meat on racks to preserve it. The French *boucaner* means to dry meat in this fashion. The men referred to themselves as the "Brethren of the Coast" and it is from their number that the most famous names came, like Calico Jack Rackham and Blackbeard. Perhaps the most astonishing thing about the golden age is the fact that many pirates were given pardons, sometimes in exchange for military aid or a cut of the loot. The Welsh privateer Henry Morgan was not only pardoned, but knighted by Charles II, made acting governor of Jamaica, a vice-admiral, commandant of the Port Royal Regiment, a judge of the Admiralty Court and a Justice of the Peace!

Although the skull and crossbones, or "Jolly Roger," is by far the most famous pirate flag, there were different versions and many other flags that would send fear into the hearts of merchant sailors and their captains. Here is a selection of the most famous, as well as the men who sailed under them.

Walter Kennedy

Bart Roberts

Henry Every

Edward England

Richard Worley

Christopher Moody

Stede Bonnet

Edward Low

Bart Roberts (2nd Flag)

Jack Rackam

Blackbeard (Edward Teach)

Emanuel Wynne

Christopher Condent

Thomas Tew

A SIMPLE ELECTROMAGNET

An ELECTROMAGNET is just a copper coil with a current running through it. The classic use is the junkyard crane, lifting cars into the crusher. Ours lifted two iron screws.

You will need a couple of metres of copper wire and something iron to wrap it around – a piece of metal coat hanger or a nail. You will also need a battery and preferably one of the plastic battery holders you can see in the picture. Model shops sell them for very little. It is possible to attach batteries to a circuit using no more than duct tape and elastic bands, but it's fiddly and the connections are unreliable.

1. Insulate the iron nail with tape. It still works without, but the battery terminals heat up and can burn.

2. Wrap the copper wire around the nail, leaving several centimetres of the first end free to attach to the battery later. The more turns of wire, the stronger the magnet, so use the longest length you can find. The one in the picture has more than one layer of wire, up then down the rod. Each layer should be insulated from the next with electrician's tape.

3. Make a switch if you like – it's less fiddly than poking wires through the battery terminals, even when you have a holder. We used a couple of black screws – one attached to positive (+), one to negative (–). It is crucial to complete the circuit, or this won't work.

Now use the iron tip to pick up paperclips! In theory, with enough wire, or stronger batteries, the magnet could become quite powerful – a car battery would work very nicely – and then you have applications like dangling the magnet into dark spaces to retrieve screws and iron tools.

SECRET INKS

———✳———

ANYTHING ORGANIC (animal-based) that is clear or almost clear can be used as a heat-activated secret ink. Put simply, organic means a substance contains carbon and carbon things will burn. Milk, lemon juice, egg white and, yes, urine will work as a secret ink. In the picture, we used milk.

In our first attempt, we wrote a sentence down the side of a letter. Unless you were looking for it, it wasn't easy to see. The letter on top helped to disguise it. We let this dry and then applied a flame directly to the hidden words. Try to avoid setting fire to the paper or your clothing. The letters appeared as if by magic.

You can read the words "the army lands at midnight." Though it sounds very dramatic, this is a clumsy sort of message. Far better to have your spy waiting for a time, then put "mid" somewhere on the piece of paper. That would be much harder to find.

The trouble with this sort of thing is that the cover letter must look real, but not so real that your spy doesn't look for the secret message. As with the section on codes, some things work better with a little planning. Invent a sister – and then they will know that every letter that mentions the sister by name contains secret words.

Secret inks allow you to send confidential information by post. If it's not expected, it's not at all likely to be spotted.

THE ARMY LANDS AT MIDNIGHT

Hello David,

Just a quick note to say
how much we enjoyed
the party.
See you in the new year

Susan

SAMPLING SHAKESPEARE

NO WRITER OF ANY AGE has come close to rivalling the creative genius of William Shakespeare. He was born in 1564, on April 23 – St. George's Day, in Stratford-upon-Avon. Anyone alive should know *Macbeth*, *Romeo and Juliet*, *A Midsummer Night's Dream*, *King Lear*, *Othello* and *Hamlet*, or have seen them in a theatre.

Here are a few of the better-known quotations. Shakespeare has added countless commonly used phrases and words to English – so common, in fact, that we often hardly recognize them as Shakespearean. He really did write "I have not slept one wink" before anyone else, as well as "I will wear my heart upon my sleeve" and hundreds more.

1.

What's in a name? that which we call a rose
by any other word would smell as sweet.

Romeo and Juliet, Act 2, Scene 2

2.

This royal throne of kings, this sceptered isle,
This earth of majesty, this seat of Mars,
This other Eden, demi-paradise,
This fortress built by Nature for herself
Against infection and the hand of war,
This happy breed of men, this little world,
This precious stone set in the silver sea,
Which serves it in the office of a wall,
Or as a moat defensive to a house,
Against the envy of less happier lands,
This blessed plot, this earth, this realm, this England.

Richard II, Act 2, Scene 1

3.

If music be the food of love, play on.

Twelfth Night, Act 1, Scene 1

4.

But screw your courage to the sticking-place,
And we'll not fail.

Macbeth, Act 1, Scene 7

5.

Out, out brief candle!
Life's but a walking shadow, a poor player

That struts and frets his hour upon the stage,
And then is heard no more; it is a tale
Told by an idiot, full of sound and fury,
Signifying nothing.

❀

Macbeth, Act 5, Scene 5

6.

Cry "Havoc!" and let slip the dogs of war.

Julius Caesar, Act 3, Scene 1

❀

7.

Once more unto the breach, dear friends, once more;
Or close the wall up with our English dead!

Henry V, Act 3, Scene 1

❀

8.

Neither a borrower, nor a lender be;
For loan oft loses both itself and friend.

Hamlet, Act 1, Scene 3

❀

9.

All the world's a stage,
And all the men and women merely players.

As You Like It, Act 2, Scene 7

❀

10.

Uneasy lies the head that wears a crown.

Henry IV, Part 2, Act 3, Scene 1

❀

11.

The lady doth protest too much, methinks.

Hamlet, Act 3, Scene 2

❀

12.

To be, or not to be: that is the question:
Whether 'tis nobler in the mind to suffer
The slings and arrows of outrageous fortune,
Or to take arms against a sea of troubles,
And by opposing end them?

Hamlet, Act 3, Scene 1

❀

13.

Let me have men about me that are fat;
Sleek-headed men and such as sleep o'nights.
Yond Cassius has a lean and hungry look;
He thinks too much: such men are dangerous.

Julius Caesar, Act 1, Scene 2

14.

                            We are such stuff
As dreams are made on, and our little life
Is rounded with a sleep.
(Usually rendered as ". . . dreams are made of")

The Tempest, Act 4, Scene 1

❀

15.

Why, then the world's mine oyster,
Which I with sword will open.

The Merry Wives of Windsor, Act 2, Scene 2

❀

16.

                    I am a man
More sinn'd against than sinning.

King Lear, Act 3, Scene 2

❀

17.

There's a divinity that shapes our ends,
Rough-hew them how we will.

Hamlet, Act 5, Scene 2

❀

18.

There are more things in heaven and earth, Horatio,
Than are dreamt of in your philosophy.

Hamlet, Act 1, Scene 5

❀

19.

Something is rotten in the state of Denmark.

Hamlet, Act 1, Scene 4

❀

20.

Double, double toil and trouble;
Fire burn and cauldron bubble.

Macbeth, Act 4, Scene 1

❀

21.

Is this a dagger which I see before me,
The handle toward my hand?

Macbeth, Act 2, Scene 1

❀

22.

Yet do I fear thy nature;
It is too full o' the milk of human kindness.

Macbeth, Act 1, Scene 5

23.

Why, man, he doth bestride the narrow world
Like a Colossus.

Julius Caesar, Act 1 Scene 2

24.

Et tu, Brute?

Julius Caesar, Act 3, Scene 1

25.

This was the most unkindest cut of all.

Julius Caesar, Act 3, Scene 2

26.

Good-night, good-night! parting is such sweet sorrow.

Romeo and Juliet, Act 2, Scene 2

27.

A plague o' both your houses!

Romeo and Juliet, Act 3, Scene 1

28.

Now is the winter of our discontent.

Richard III, Act 1, Scene 1

29.

We few, we happy few, we band of brothers.

Henry V, Act 4, Scene 3

30.

I thought upon one pair of English legs
Did march three Frenchmen.

Henry V, Act 3, Scene 6

EXTRAORDINARY STORIES – PART THREE: TOUCHING THE VOID

I<small>N</small> M<small>AY</small> 1985, two young English climbers set off to conquer the unclimbed west face of Siula Grande – a 6,400-metre (21,000-foot) peak in the Andes. There are no mountain rescue services in such a remote region, but Joe Simpson (age twenty-five) and Simon Yates (age twenty-one) were experienced, confident and very fit. Their story is an extraordinary one. Apart from being made into a book and a film, it has inspired intense debate among that small group of expert climbers with experience enough to judge what happened.

The two men tackled the face in one fast push, roped together and taking everything they needed with them. They carried ice axes and wore boots with spikes (crampons), using ice screws and ropes for the ascent.

They climbed solidly that first day until darkness fell and they dug a snow cave and slept. All the second day, they climbed sheet ice, reaching 6,100 metres (20,000 ft) when high winds and a blizzard hit them on an exposed vertical slope. At that point, they were climbing flutes of powder snow, the most treacherous of surfaces and incredibly dangerous. It took five to six hours to climb just 61 metres (200 ft) in the dark before they found a safe place for a second snow cave.

The third morning began with a clear blue sky. By 2 p.m., they reached the north ridge at last – the first men ever to climb that face of Siula Grande. Both men felt exhausted after some of the hardest climbing of their lives, but they decided to follow the ridge toward the peak.

They reached it, but with the weather uncertain, they couldn't stay for long. Only half an hour into the descent, clouds came in and they were lost in a whiteout on the ridge, completely blind. On one side was a drop of hundreds of metres and the ridge itself was made of overhanging cornices of snow that could break off under their weight. Yates saw the ridge through a break in the clouds and climbed back up to it. The cornice broke under his weight and he fell, saved by the rope attached to Simpson. He shouted up that he had found the ridge. In such conditions, progress was very slow. By the time darkness came, they were still at 6,100 metres (20,000 ft).

❈

The fourth day began with good weather once more. The two men came to a cut in the ridge and Simpson started to climb down a face of sheer ice. He hammered in one of his ice axes and didn't like the sound it made. As he pulled one out to get a better contact, the other gave way without warning and he fell.

He hit hard, his shinbone going through his knee and into the upper leg. As Yates climbed down, Simpson tried to stand on his leg, appalled at the pain and grating of the bones. The two men looked at each other in desperation. Simpson expected his friend to leave him. There was no other choice – a broken leg so far from civilization meant that he was dead. Instead, Yates stayed and they discussed a plan to lower Simpson on two ropes, knotted together. Yates would dig himself a seat in the snow and lower Simpson the first 46 metres (150 ft). The knot wouldn't pass through the lowering device, so Simpson would dig in until Yates had retied it and could lower away once more.

The laborious process began, with Simpson face down. His broken leg jarred constantly, but it had to be fast as neither their endurance nor the light would last for long. Yates' snow seat crumbled quickly in the time it took to lower his friend. As the hours passed, a full storm hit the mountain with wind chill of −80 degrees. Darkness came upon them and both men were exhausted. They had no gas to make tea or get warm. They continued on in the dark, one rope at a time.

Simpson felt the powder snow change to hard ice and called out to stop. His voice wasn't heard and he slipped over the edge of an overhang, dangling below it. He couldn't reach a surface and, crucially, was unable to take his weight off the rope. Above him in the dark, Yates waited alone and freezing, with the wind roaring around him.

At first, Simpson attempted to climb back up the rope using a "prussic loop," a knot that locks solid once pressure is applied. He needed two and managed to fix the first with frozen hands. The second one escaped his numb fingers and he watched it fall with his last hopes. He waited then to drag Yates to his death.

Yates waited and waited as his seat began to crumble under the unrelenting weight. All he could do was hang on until he began to slide down. He remembered he had a penknife and made a decision in an instant, using it to cut the rope. The rope snaked away and below the overhang, Simpson fell into darkness, losing consciousness. Yates dug himself a snow cave out of the storm and waited for daylight.

❋

Simpson awoke in pitch blackness on a narrow slope, sliding. He had fallen more than 30 metres (100 ft) into a crevasse, ending up on an ice ledge next to another drop into infinite darkness. He screwed in an ice screw anchor very quickly.

His helmet flashlight revealed the rope going up to a small hole 24 metres (80 ft) above. He thought Yates was on the end of it, dead. Simpson thought the rope would come tight on Yates' body. He pulled it to him and it fell. When he saw the end, he knew it had been cut and guessed what had happened. He was pleased Yates was alive, but realized his own chances of survival had dropped to almost nothing.

In the dark, he turned off the flashlight to save the batteries. Alone, he despaired.

❋

Yates continued to climb down the next day, feeling desperately guilty about cutting the rope. He lowered himself past the overhang and the crevasse, convinced that Simpson was dead. He went on numbly, following tracks back to the base camp that he had made with Simpson only days before.

When no one answered his shouts, Simpson tried to climb out of his crevasse, but 24 metres (80 ft) of sheer ice was impossible with only one working leg. He didn't believe anyone would ever find him. His only course seemed to be to sit and wait to die – or to lower himself into the crevasse to see if there was another way out in the darkness below. He took this terrifying decision, but didn't put a knot on the end of the rope. He decided that if he reached the end and there was nothing beneath him, he would rather fall than be stuck and slowly freeze.

Joe lowered himself 24 metres and found he was in an hourglass-shaped crevasse. He reached the pinch point and found a crust of snow there that had a chance of taking his weight. He heard cracking and movement beneath him, but there was light nearby, at the top of a slope he thought he could climb, bad leg or not. This was the way out.

Though every jarring step brought him close to fainting, he made it onto the mountainside to see a blue sky and bright sunshine. He lay there and laughed with relief at his deliverance.

❋

After the initial exhilaration, he looked farther down and realized that he still had kilometres of glacier to cross as well as a treacherous maze of crevasses. He thought at first that he couldn't do it, but there was no point in simply sitting and waiting. He could see Yates' tracks and knew that they would lead him through the crevasse field.

He made progress sitting down, with his legs flat on the snow and pushing himself along backwards. Snow and high winds came again, and he kept going as darkness fell, terrified at losing sight of Simon's tracks.

The tracks had gone by the morning of the sixth day, but Simpson struggled on, reaching at last the jumbled boulders that meant the end of the glacier. He wrapped his sleeping mat around the broken leg, using his ice axes to try to support himself over the broken ground. He fell at almost every step and each fall was like breaking the leg again. Somehow, he kept going. He ate snow for water, but there was never enough to quench a brutal thirst. He could hear streams running under the rocks, but maddeningly he could not find them. He pushed himself on and on until he collapsed and lay looking at the sky as it grew dark once more.

❋

As Day Seven dawned, he could barely move at first. He believed he was going to die, but kept crawling. He found a trickle of water and drank litres of it, feeling it make him stronger. Despite this, he was becoming delirious.

Simpson reached the lake by the camp by four in the afternoon of the seventh day. He knew the camp was in a valley at the far end, but he had no idea if Yates would be there. He tried to make faster progress, plagued by the thought that he would get there too late.

Clouds came down as the day progressed and by the time he looked into the valley, it was white with mist. He lay there for a long time, delirious and hallucinating. Eventually, he moved on as night fell and it began to snow once more.

He dragged himself through the latrine area of the camp and the sharp smell acted like smelling salts, bringing him back. He began to call for Yates and when no one came at first, he believed he had been left behind.

Yet Simon Yates had stayed and he woke as he heard his name called. When he heard his name again, he went out and began to search. He found his friend 183 metres (600 ft) from the camp and dragged him back to the tent. Yates could not believe it. He had cut the rope and seen the drop and the crevasse. He *knew* Simpson could not have survived.

As Joe Simpson became conscious, he sought to ease his friend's guilt. His first words were,

"Don't worry, I would have done the same."

Adapted from *Touching the Void* by Joe Simpson, published by Jonathan Cape.

GRINDING AN ITALIC NIB

ALTHOUGH THE PEN we used is an expensive model, this should absolutely not be tried with a valued pen. There is a reasonable chance of destroying the nib completely and the nib is usually the most expensive part to replace. The rest, after all, is just a tube.

The first thing to know is that *almost all* italic nibs are hand-ground. In theory, there is no reason why you should not be able to grind a nib to suit you, with a little common sense and care.

Before you begin, it is a good idea to get hold of an italic nib and try writing with it. The writing style is quite different and they tend to be "scratchier" than regular pens. It is extremely satisfying knowing you have ground your own nib – and the handwriting is attractive.

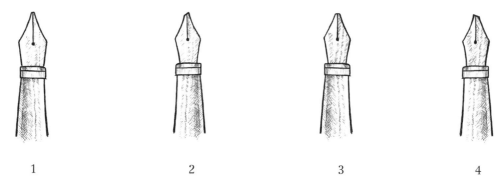

1	2	3	4

Picture 1 shows a standard nib. Picture 2 would be best suited to a left-handed writer. Picture 3 is suitable for both, and 4 is best suited for right-handers. It's difficult to change from one to the other if you are not happy with the result – which is why you should try a shop-bought italic nib first.

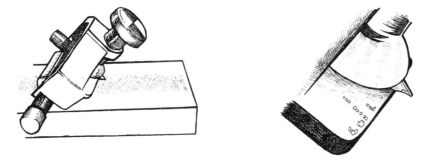

We used a sharpening gig – a useful little gadget that helps to hold chisels at the required angle. It can be done completely by hand, but no matter how you choose to do it, stop often, dip the nib in ink and try it out. Do not be discouraged by scratching at this stage. A fine sharpening stone will take longer, but as delicate as this is, it is probably a good idea.

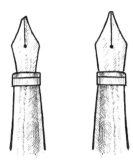

You should arrive somewhere near the nib on the left – if you are left-handed. It was identical to the nib on the right before grinding. Attempts at writing with the new angle were initially discouraging. Very fine sandpaper (or wet and dry paper) was needed to smooth away roughness and dust from the grindstone. It is a matter of personal preference how far you smooth the corners, but I found it helped the easy flow of ink.

All the King's horses and all the King's men

All the King's horses and all the King's men

NOTE: This is not italic or copperplate lettering. Those alphabets have to be learned, though they are based on the wide and narrow strokes of an italic nib.

U.S. NAVAL FLAG CODES

EVEN IN THESE DAYS of radio and satellite communications, the U.S. Navy uses the international alphabet flags, numeral pennants, numeral flags, and special flags and pennants for visual signaling. These signal flags are used to communicate while maintaining radio silence. Navy Signalmen transmit messages by hoisting a flag or a series of flags on a halyard. Each side of the ship has halyards and a "flag bag", containing a full set of signal flags. Signals unique to the Navy are used when communicating with other U.S. Navy or allied forces. When communicating with all other vessels, the International Code of Signals is used. The code/answer pennant precedes all signals in international code.

Flag	Name	Phonetic Pronunciation	Navy Meaning	International Meaning
	ALFA	*AL-fah*	I have a diver down; keep well clear at slow speed.	
	BRAVO	*BRAH-voh*	I am taking in, discharging, or carrying dangerous cargo.	
	CHARLIE	*CHAR-lee*	"Yes" or "affirmative".	
	DELTA	*DELL-tah*	I am maneuvering with difficulty; keep clear.	
	ECHO	*ECK-oh*	I am directing my course to starboard.	
	FOXTROT	*FOKS-trot*	I am disabled; communicate with me.	On aircraft carriers: Flight Operations underway
	GOLF	*GOLF*	I require a pilot.	

Flag	Name	Phonetic Pronunciation	Navy Meaning	International Meaning
	HOTEL	*hoh-TELL*	I have a pilot on board.	
	INDIA	*IN-dee-ah*	Coming alongside.	I am directing my course to port.
	JULIET	*JEW-lee-ett*	I am on fire and have dangerous cargo; keep clear.	
	KILO	*KEY-loh*	I wish to communicate with you.	
	LIMA	*LEE-mah*	You should stop your vessel immediately.	
	MIKE	*MIKE*	My vessel is stopped; making no way.	
	NOVEMBER	*no-VEM-bur*	No or negative.	
	OSCAR	*OSS-kur*	Man overboard.	
	PAPA	*pah-PAH*	All personnel return to ship; proceeding to sea (Inport).	
	QUEBEC	*kay-BECK*	Boat recall; all boats return to ship.	Ship meets health regs; request clearance into port.
	ROMEO	*ROH-me-oh*	Preparing to replenish (At sea). Ready duty ship (In port).	

Flag	Name	Phonetic Pronunciation	Navy Meaning	International Meaning
	SIERRA	*see-AIR-ah*	Conducting flag hoist drill.	Moving astern.
	TANGO	*TANG-go*	Do not pass ahead of me.	Keep clear; engaged in trawling.
	UNIFORM	*YOU-nee-form*	You are running into danger.	
	VICTOR	*VIK-tah*	I require assistance.	
	WHISKEY	*WISS-kee*	I require medical assistance.	
	XRAY	*ECKS-ray*	Stop carrying out your intentions and watch for my signals.	
	YANKEE	*YANG-kee*	Ship has visual communications duty.	I am dragging anchor.
	ZULU	*ZOO-loo*	I require a tug.	
	ONE	*WUN*	Numeral one.	
	TWO	*TOO*	Numeral two.	
	THREE	*TREE*	Numeral three.	

Flag	Name	Phonetic Pronunciation	Navy Meaning	International Meaning
	FOUR	*FOW-er*	Numeral four.	
	FIVE	*FIFE*	Numeral five.	
	SIX	*SICKS*	Numeral six.	
	SEVEN	*SEV-en*	Numeral seven.	
	EIGHT	*AIT*	Numeral eight.	
	NINE	*NIN-er*	Numeral nine.	
	ZERO	*ZEE-roh*	Numeral zero.	

EXTRAORDINARY STORIES –
PART FOUR: JOSIAH HENSON

Born into slavery in 1789 in Maryland, Josiah Henson escaped to Canada and freedom in 1830. His work and accomplishments in his new home would make him an important historical figure in Canada (and the first African Canadian to be featured on a postage stamp), but like so many of his fellow refugees, Henson's journey to a new life was an act of courageous rebellion, fraught with heart-stopping danger.

Josiah Henson's early years were marked by the horrors of slavery. His only memory of his father was seeing him drenched in blood after he'd been whipped and had his ear cut off for defending his wife from an attack by a white man. Shortly after this, Josiah's father was sold to another slave owner. Josiah never saw him again.

When Josiah was about five or six, his family's "owner" died and Josiah, his mother and his siblings were sold off at auction. The man who bought Josiah's mother, Isaac Riley, refused to buy any of her children. But Josiah, the youngest, soon fell ill, and his new owner sold him to Riley for almost nothing.

Josiah grew up to be a strong young man. He eventually became the superintendent of Riley's estate and was put in charge of the other slaves and selling the plantation's crops at market. But even this relative independence could not save Josiah from the cruelties of slave life. One day when he was returning from an errand, he was attacked by the white overseer of another estate who felt that Josiah had treated him with disrespect during an earlier encounter. With three other men, the overseer beat Josiah unmercifully, breaking his arm and both shoulders. Josiah would never again be able to move his arms fully.

Josiah married and had children while on Riley's estate, but he had no control over the life they led. When Riley fell into financial trouble, he instructed Josiah to take all of the slaves from his plantation to his brother Amos in Kentucky. As the group travelled west, they passed through Ohio, where slavery had been abolished. African Americans there encouraged Josiah to allow his group to abandon the trip – to escape from slavery by staying in Ohio. Josiah was tempted (he knew his owner, and slavery itself, to be heartless and unjust), but his honour prevented him. He wanted to buy his freedom from his master – so that he could feel he had done the right thing.

Josiah managed to earn money preaching, and after a short time in Kentucky, he returned to Maryland with $350 to buy his freedom from Riley. Riley took the money, but Josiah received a bitter blow in return. When he returned to his wife and children in Kentucky, he discovered that Riley had cheated him – raising his price to $1,000. Josiah was still a slave. And it would get worse. Amos had decided to separate Josiah from his wife and children and sell him "down river" in New Orleans. The plight of slaves in the southern states was even more brutal and harrowing than that of slaves in Maryland or Kentucky. As Josiah sailed down the Mississippi River with Amos Jr., his feelings of desperation and despair were overpowering. He saw along the shores a number of slaves he had once known in Maryland. Their half-starved and broken bodies were a grim reminder of the fate that was in store for him in the south. He could think of only one thing left to do: "I resolved to kill my four companions, take what money there was on the boat . . . and escape to the north. . . ."

One black and rainy night a few days before they had reached New Orleans, Josiah crept down below deck where the white men were sleeping. He took an axe and had raised it, about to strike a fatal blow on young Amos, when he was seized by the reality of what he was about to do: "Commit murder!" He had never thought of it as murder before – only self-defence – but now he knew he could not go through with the violent act.

In New Orleans, Josiah received a stroke of luck. Amos fell ill, so instead of being sold, Josiah had to help the sick man return home. Once back home, however, he realized that he would likely be sent south again. Josiah had heard about the "underground railroad" – the men and women who helped escaped slaves travel to freedom in Canada. While there were states in which slavery was illegal, slaveowners regularly visited these areas, attempting to recapture escaped slaves. Canada, Josiah decided, was the only real chance for freedom for himself and his family.

We have to marvel and admire the courage it took for men and women like Josiah Henson to make a bid for freedom. Josiah must have thought back to the ghost of his father, covered in blood, punished for simply defending his wife, not utterly disobeying the man who "owned" him by running away. What's more, Josiah had no map and no knowledge of the land he would be travelling. He would be guided only by the vague directions to follow the Northern Star. And if he or his family were noticed by suspicious people along the way (never mind the slave hunters), they would be thrown in jail and returned to their former owners.

One dark, moonless night a short time later, Josiah, his wife and his four young sons slipped away from the Kentucky plantation. A fellow slave took them in a small boat across the river to Indiana. "You will not be brought back alive, will you?" asked the man. "Not if I can help it," Josiah answered. As the skiff sailed off, the family was left utterly alone on the shore. Josiah's wife was trembling with fear and would have headed back to Kentucky had Josiah not stopped her.

For over a month, Josiah and his family trudged along the roads, mostly at night so there would be less chance of getting caught by slave hunters and their snarling dogs. The family found shelter and rest in Cincinnati, Ohio, before continuing their journey to Canada along what Josiah had been told was a military trail. What Josiah hadn't realized, however, was that it was not really a road but simply a rough path blazed through the wilderness. There were no houses or any places where he could get food for his family – and he had not brought any supplies with him, other than a few tiny scraps of dried beef.

Once in the woods, the family travelled all day without seeing a soul. The trail was overgrown and rough, obstructed with fallen trees. The brush tore at their clothing. At one point, Josiah's wife fainted from hunger and fatigue. At night, they lay down in the woods to sleep on empty stomachs. The howls of wolves broke their slumber – terrifying them all. Eventually, they happened upon a Native encampment. The Native Americans treated them well, fed them and gave them shelter for the night. The next day, they led Josiah and his family farther along the route and pointed them in the direction of Lake Erie. The kind treatment they received marked a turning point in the family's journey. While they had to make their way across a deep and dangerous stream (Josiah carried each member of his family across on his back), they eventually arrived in the town of Sandusky, Ohio, on the southern shore of Lake Erie. While Josiah's wife and children hid, he screwed up his courage and approached a group of men working on a boat at the water's edge. While the few people Josiah had encountered in the early days of his escape had treated him with hard-hearted suspicion, here the boat captain generously offered to take his family to Buffalo, New York. He even gave Josiah enough money to pay for a ferry to cross the Niagara River to Canada. When the ferry docked on the other side, the family's long and terrifying journey of more than 800 kilometres was finally over. They had landed on Canadian soil. Josiah cried out and threw himself on the ground in sheer happiness.

After seeing the brutal effects of enslavement on so many he loved, Josiah resolved to build a haven for others who sought freedom. He established Dawn, a community for escaped slaves, near Dresden, Ontario. He built a school for the education of children and labourers; he oversaw the operations of the town's farms and industries, and he travelled across North America, speaking out for the abolition of slavery. Josiah Henson's story became the inspiration for Harriet Beecher Stowe's bestselling 1852 novel *Uncle Tom's Cabin*, a book that inspired many in both Canada and the United States to join in the fight against slavery.

Josiah Henson 1789-1883   Canada 32 postage/postes

"From my earliest recollection, freedom had been the object of my ambition."

THE MOON

Through all human history, the moon has drawn the gaze upward. It was there in ancient myths; it was the light for a million romantic evenings – and it was our first stepping stone to the darkness beyond it. The gravity well of Earth is crushingly powerful. Without the moon as a launching stage, regular space flight may never be possible. While it sails above, we can dream of lunar bases and leaving the earth behind.

The first landing on the moon was on July 20, 1969, one date *everyone* should know. It is the only object in space that we have visited, after all. The *Apollo 11* spacecraft reached the moon and fired braking rockets to take up orbit around it. Neil Armstrong and Edward "Buzz" Aldrin descended to the surface in a landing module named "Eagle." Michael Collins remained in the command module. After announcing to the watching Earth that "the Eagle has landed," Armstrong stepped out onto the surface of the moon.

There have been many momentous events in our history, from Caesar crossing the Rubicon to the first use of an atomic bomb, but having a human being set foot on another, stranger soil may be the most extraordinary.

Armstrong's first words were, "This is one small step for man, one giant leap for mankind." Famously, he had intended to say "a man." Without the "a," he seemed to repeat himself.

The two men spent twenty-one hours on the surface and brought back 21 kilograms (46 lb) of moon rock. The moon has no atmosphere – and therefore no protection from meteorites. Its surface has been battered and melted by these strikes over billions of years, resulting in a soil called a "regolith" – made of dust, rock and tiny beads of glass that are slippery underfoot.

The *Apollo 11* landing was the first of six successful landing missions during the twentieth century. In sequence, they are: *Apollo 11*, *12*, *14*, *15*, *16* and *17*, ending in December 1972. *Apollo 13* suffered technical problems and had to return to Earth without landing on the moon. There will be others. An unmanned probe named *Lunar Prospector* found ice in 1998 at both moon poles – one of the most important requirements of a future colony since it means water is available!

The Phases of the Moon – as Seen from Earth

The phases of the moon are such a part of our world that they should be common knowledge.

1. This is a new moon. The moon is between the earth and the sun and shows no light. This position creates the strong vernal tides on Earth.

2. A waxing (growing) crescent. This use of the word "waxing" is now almost completely restricted to describing the phases of the moon. As the moon moves on its cycle, we see the sunlight reflecting on its surface. The crescent will grow as it moves around the earth.

3. First quarter moon. Quarter of the way around the earth, one clear half of the moon is visible.

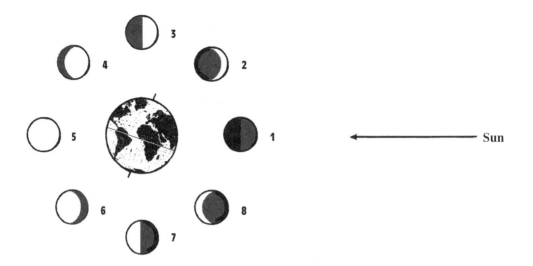

4. Waxing gibbous. The word "gibbous" is another one that tends to be used only in descriptions of the moon. It means convex, or bending outwards. This is a good time to take pictures of the moon. Surprisingly sharp images can be made by the simple action of putting a camera up against the lens of a telescope on a tripod.

5. Full moon – also a time of strong tides, as both the sun and moon pull at the earth's oceans.

6. Waning moon – beginning the path back to the new moon.

7. Last quarter, with a perfect half of the moon again visible.

8. Waning crescent.

Moon Facts

1. Distance from earth: because of an elliptical orbit, this varies, but on average is 386,000 kilometres (240,000 miles).

2. Gravity: about 1/6 of Earth.

3. Day length: 27.3 Earth days.

4. Time to orbit earth in relation to a fixed star (sidereal month): 27.3 Earth days.

5. Time in relation to the sun (new moon to new moon/synodic month): 29.5 days.

6. Because it takes 27.3 days to orbit earth *and* turn on its own axis, we always see the same face. (See Questions About the World – Part Two.) However, there is no dark side in the sense of lacking light. Like Earth, there is a night and day side, but both receive light during the cycle. The "dark side" of the moon just doesn't exist!

7. The moon has no atmosphere, which means no wind, so Neil Armstrong's original footprint will still be there exactly as it was in 1969 – unless Buzz Aldrin or one of the others scuffed it over.

THE MOON

8. Daytime temperatures can reach up to 134 °C (273 °F). That is almost three times as hot as the Sahara Desert on earth. Night-time temperatures can be as low as –152 °C (–243 °F). Needless to say, human beings cannot survive such an extreme range without a great deal of protection.

9. The American flag planted by the *Apollo 11* astronauts had to be made out of metal. Without an atmosphere, a cloth flag would have hung straight down.

10. The moon is silent. Without air or some other medium, sound waves cannot travel.

11. We owe many of the beautifully named parts of the moon to Galileo. It was he who thought he saw oceans on the moon in 1609, giving us Mare Tranquillitatis (Sea of Tranquillity), Mare Nectaris (Sea of Nectar), Mare Imbrium (Sea of Showers), Mare Serenitatis (Sea of Serenity) and many more. Sadly, they are dry depressions and not the great oceans of his imagination.

SOME KEY FEATURES

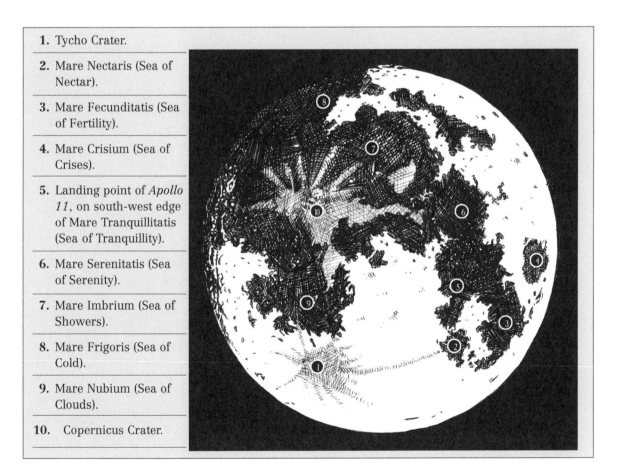

1. Tycho Crater.

2. Mare Nectaris (Sea of Nectar).

3. Mare Fecunditatis (Sea of Fertility).

4. Mare Crisium (Sea of Crises).

5. Landing point of *Apollo 11*, on south-west edge of Mare Tranquillitatis (Sea of Tranquillity).

6. Mare Serenitatis (Sea of Serenity).

7. Mare Imbrium (Sea of Showers).

8. Mare Frigoris (Sea of Cold).

9. Mare Nubium (Sea of Clouds).

10. Copernicus Crater.

Every month, at full moon, the earth goes between the sun and the moon. However, the exact line-up required for a lunar eclipse is not so common. Usually, the moon's tilted orbit takes it out of alignment. At most, there are only two or three full eclipses of the moon each year. You might expect to see around forty in a lifetime.

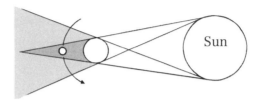

If you were standing on the moon at the time of a lunar eclipse, you would see the earth slowly blotting out the sun. In a lunar eclipse, the earth's shadow falls across the moon, though red sunlight scattered from the earth's atmosphere sometimes means a red moon can still be seen. Given the relative sizes, the earth's cone of shadow completely covers the moon and the eclipse can be seen from anywhere on the earth's surface.

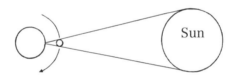

A solar eclipse is a far rarer event. In these, the full eclipse can only be seen along a narrow track, never more than about 321 kilometres (200 miles) wide. Obviously, these can only take place at the time of a new moon, when the shadow of the moon falls onto earth.

There are two kinds of solar eclipse, "annular" and "total." Annular eclipses are about twice as common and far less impressive. They occur when the moon is too far from Earth to block the sun completely. The sky will not darken as completely and a bright ring will still be visible around the moon. Annular means "ring-shaped."

A total solar eclipse is well worth travelling to see. It is one of the marvels of the natural world. First, a tiny bite appears in the ring of the sun, which deepens until the sun becomes a crescent and the day darkens towards an eerie twilight. The corona of the sun can then be seen around the black disc. The temperature drops and birds often return to trees to roost. Then the light begins to reappear and the world as we know it returns.

SKIPPING STONES

THIS IS QUITE A TRICKY skill, but it is possible to bounce a stone on water five or six times without too much trouble. Barnes Wallis used the same principle when designing the bouncing bomb for raids on the Ruhr Valley in Germany. You will need several things in your favour to skip stones.

First of all, you need to pick your stone, as flat as possible without being too thin. It needs some weight to carry, but if it weighs much more than an apple, you won't get the range. Most beaches will have a variety of stones to choose from but if you find the perfect "skipper" in the park, hang on to it.

Skipping stones on the sea is harder because of the waves. If you try it on a lake, watch out for swimmers, who object to having stones thrown at them.

The skill is in the grip and the angle. Curl your forefinger around the stone, resting it on your middle finger. Secure it with your thumb.

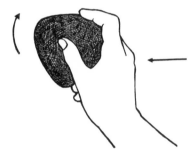

The action of throwing the stone is all important – too steep and the stone will just plonk into the water. Bend your knees to keep the angle of descent around twenty-five degrees and try to get the flat side to hit the water when you release, to help it bounce on the surface.

The power you use to throw the stone can be increased once you get the hang of the technique.

More than one bounce and you are skimming, though you will have a way to go to beat the current world record of *thirty-eight*.

PINHOLE PROJECTOR

THE SUN IS A BRIGHT shining star that gives life to our planet. It is also very dangerous to look at directly and can damage your eyes. How then do we study the eclipses and transit of planets across its surface? With a pinhole projector, one of the best tools to view solar events as they take place.

As the name implies, a pinhole projector projects an image (upside down) of the sun so you can watch an eclipse without actually looking at it.

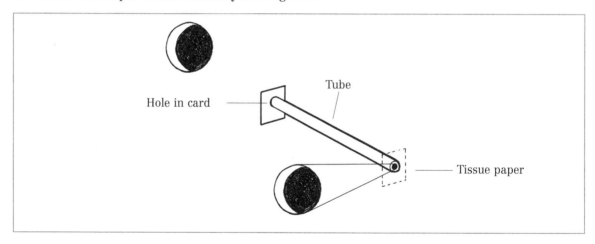

To build the projector, use glue or adhesive tape to attach the sheet of bristol board at one end of the tube, as shown in the diagram. Make a small hole in the bristol board over the tube. Attach a thin sheet of tissue paper to the other end with glue.

To make it work, simply lift the bristol board end toward the sun and an image will be projected onto the tissue paper "screen" at the other end. Remember, only look at the projected image.

You can also build a projector with a magnified image, which is far more impressive and can be focused. You will need a telescope or binoculars and two pieces of white bristol board.

First cut a hole in one of the pieces of card so that it fits over the end of your telescope or one side of your binoculars to shield the image from unwanted light. Now, aim the telescope (or binoculars) at the sun and hold the other piece of white bristol board about half a metre from the eyepiece. An image of the sun should appear, which you can sharpen by changing the focus or moving the card. Never, *ever* look through a telescope while focusing or aiming it at the sun.

With a similar contraption, we saw the transit of Venus cross the sun in 2004. These transits usually come in pairs and the next is due on June 6, 2012. Partial eclipses are not particularly rare, though whether you can see one depends on where you are in the world. Here is a list of the more impressive total solar eclipses coming up in the next few years. Each date is followed by the latitude and longitude that will give the best view.

1. 01/08/2008	Latitude: 65.6N	Longitude: 72.3E
2. 22/07/2009	Latitude: 24.2N	Longitude: 144.1E
3. 11/07/2010	Latitude: 19.8S	Longitude: 121.9W
4. 13/11/2012	Latitude: 39.9S	Longitude: 161.3W
5. 20/03/2015	Latitude: 64.4N	Longitude: 6.6W
6. 09/03/2016	Latitude: 10.1N	Longitude: 148.8E
7. 21/08/2017	Latitude: 37.0N	Longitude: 87.6W
8. 02/07/2019	Latitude: 17.4S	Longitude: 109.0W
9. 14/12/2020	Latitude: 40.3S	Longitude: 67.9W

In 2038, there will be seven solar and lunar eclipses. A total lunar eclipse is a strange and wonderful sight, as light is scattered by the earth's atmosphere to turn the moon a dark red, as if it were made of copper.

Set up your pinhole projector and enjoy the sights.

CHARTING THE UNIVERSE

———✦———

THE ANCIENT GREEKS were the first recorded people to try to explain why natural events took place without reference to supernatural causes. Astronomy started to become a science and began its long journey from superstition to enlightened understanding. They were beginning to uncover the "rules" of the universe but these often conflicted with the prevailing beliefs and the conflict between faith and science continues even today.

Thales was a Greek philosopher and explorer who lived in the sixth century BC. He travelled to Egypt to study geometry. On his return, he demonstrated a high level of mathematical skill, even predicting the eclipse of 585 BC. His legacy is the belief that natural events could have natural causes. It is true that he thought the world was flat and floated on water – but, on the other hand, he realized earthquakes could be explained as more than a bad-tempered Poseidon.

Aristotle (384–322 BC) was one of the most influential of all Greek philosophers. He was a student of Plato, and became the teacher of Alexander the Great in Macedonia. He constructed three experimental proofs to show that the earth was round. He was the first to classify plants and animals. He thought that the earth was at the centre of the universe and that all the planets and stars were fixed in the heavens in a sphere around the earth. He believed earthquakes were caused by winds trapped beneath the earth.

Aristarchus flourished in the century after Aristotle and made a model to show that the sun was at the centre of things and not the earth. His theories were more scientific but history only briefly records his heliocentric ideas. However, no less a figure than Copernicus (see entry that follows) gives him credit in *De revolutionibus orbium coelestium*, writing, "Philolaus believed in the mobility of the earth, and some even say that Aristarchus of Samos was of that opinion."

Ptolemy of Alexandria was another gifted Greek astronomer. In AD 150, he published an encyclopedia (the *Almagest*) of ancient science with details and workings of the movements of the planets, showing an intricate mathematical system of circles within circles that buttressed his arguments for an earth-centred universe surrounded by unchanging spheres. This Ptolemaic system was to rule the world of astronomy for 1,500 years.

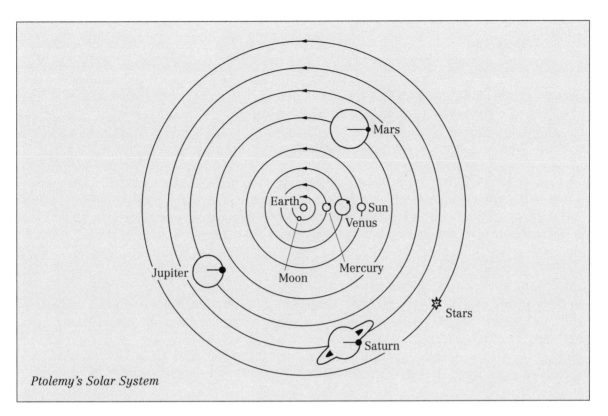

Ptolemy's Solar System

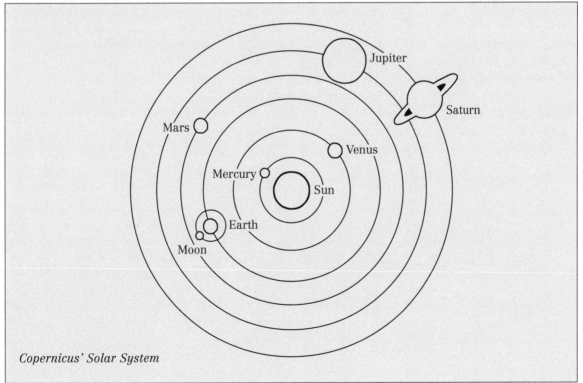

Copernicus' Solar System

Nicolaus Copernicus (1473–1543) was a Polish astronomer. Just before his death, he published his masterwork, *De revolutionibus orbium coelestium* – "On the Revolution of the Celestial Spheres," which was to change humanity's view of the cosmos. Copernicus claimed that the sun was at the centre of the universe. This met with great hostility from the Christian church, which had adopted the Ptolemaic geocentric (earth-centred) system.

Tycho Brahe (1546–1601) was a Danish astronomer who in 1572 saw a brilliant new star in Cassiopeia. This was a supernova – the explosion of a dying star, and in 1604 another supernova blazed forth in the sky. These events shattered a cornerstone of Ptolemaic thinking: that the outermost sphere was unchanging. The heavens had joined the renaissance.

Johannes Kepler (1571–1630) was Tycho Brahe's assistant and with his combined notes produced three laws of planetary motion. This enabled him to predict the positions of planets more effectively than Ptolemy.

Galileo Galilei (1564–1642) was an Italian scientist, who in 1609 took a telescope – then a new invention – and pointed it at the night sky. He discovered that the giant planet Jupiter had four moons clearly revolving around it in simple orbits, a miniature version of the Copernicus system. He published his discoveries, and in 1616 was warned by the church to change his views. In 1632, he published *Dialogue Concerning the Two Great World Systems*, ridiculing the Ptolemaic system. He was forced to recant and abandon his beliefs that the sun was at the centre of things and lived out his days under house arrest.

The Catholic church later absolved Galileo from any wrongdoing. In 1989, a spacecraft was launched to study Jupiter and its moons; it was called *Galileo* and those moons are still collectively known as the Galilean moons.

These names should be known to all.

DOG TRICKS

TEACHING A DOG simple tricks helps the bond between you. Dogs enjoy pleasing their owners and a well-trained dog is a happy dog! The only difficulty is in making the dog understand what you want. Commands should be given in a firm, low voice. Don't expect them to understand perfectly the first time. Be prepared to come back to the same commands again and again, leaving a few days between. Most dogs are perfectly willing to jump through hoops (literally) for their owners.

1. Speak.
This comes under the group of tricks from observed behaviour. If a dog does something and a command word is uttered and a treat given every time, they will quickly associate the treat and the pat with the command word. Say "Speak!" when they bark and in a short time, they will bark on command. Saying "Are you sleepy?" when they yawn works in exactly the same way.

2. Sit.
Everyone is familiar with this one. It is important that a dog should know to pause at every curb rather than rush across. Sitting helps to mark the importance of roads. Repetition is the key here – even bright dogs like collies can take two years to become well trained. Do not expect overnight results with any of these. Press the dog's hindquarters down firmly, while saying "Sit." Then give a treat – a fragment of biscuit, for example. It doesn't have to be much. A pat on the head will probably do, but you'll find training easier with some sort of small reward to hand out.

3. Down.
Always follows "Sit." Point firmly at the floor in front of the dog's head. As with teaching them to "speak," you might try this when they are on their stomachs naturally. Otherwise, you can try placing them in the "down" position manually, then express delight and give them a treat. They should remain upright, like a sphinx.

4. Play dead.
Usually follows "Down." "Play dead" involves lying completely flat on their side. You may have to press your hand gently against the dog's head to indicate what you want it to do. Dogs love this and though they lie still, their tails wag madly. Keep your voice very low and touch the tail, saying slowly, "Dead dogs don't wag. . . ." Hold it for two or three seconds, then get them up and give them a pat and a treat.

5. Paw.
This is one you have to demonstrate. Simply lift the dog's paw in your hand and shake hands gently before giving them a treat. Follow with the command "Other paw" for them to swap over. It won't be long before they offer paws on command. I had a terrier who took forever to get this, but he managed it in the end.

6. Over.
This is used when you want the dog to run – to cross a road swiftly is the most common use. Train the dog by holding their collar and raising your tone in excitement, holding them back. When all is clear, say "Over!" loudly and let them run. They will probably not cross neatly the first few dozen times, so don't train them near cars.

7. Heel.
Crucial when walking a dog on the lead. It is tiring and annoying to have a dog pull as it walks along. Curb the habit early with a sharp jerk of the lead and a very firm tone as you say the command word. Puppies are excitable and curious. They often take a long time to learn this. Be careful not to hurt them and do not worry about looking a fool. Anyone who has ever had

a puppy has walked along a road saying "Heel" over and over and over again without any clear effect. To state the obvious, the dog does not understand why you are calling out parts of your feet. You are setting up a link in their minds between the word and the action of being jerked back. It will probably take a good year for this to work, depending on how young the puppies are when you get them. Be patient. It's good practice for controlling your temper when you have children later on. Seriously. Like a lot of things in life, early work bears fruit when it really matters.

8. Stay.

This is another important one to teach early. Most dog owners have been surprised by a situation where the dog is far away and suddenly there's a car coming toward you. If you can tell the dog to "Stay" and have it remain still, a serious accident can be avoided. This is taught with the aid of a pocketful of treats and many afternoons. You have the dog sit and say "Stay!" in your deep command voice. You hold up your hand at the same time, showing the dog a flat palm. You take a step back. If the dog follows you, return it to the same spot and begin again. Begin with three steps and then give it a treat and a pat, making a big fuss of the dog. When they can remain still for three steps, try six, then a dozen and so on. You should be able to build up to quite long distances in only a short time. Dogs do like to be able to see you, however. If you turn a corner, almost all dogs will immediately move forward to find you again.

9. Gently.

This is usually said with the second syllable elongated. A dog must be taught not to snap at food, though their instincts tell them to grab things before another dog gets it. You must never tease a dog with food – they will learn to snap at it and someone will be hurt. Always present food firmly on a flat palm. If they lunge at it, say the word "Gently!" in a firm, low voice. They will hear the tone and hesitate.

10. Begging.

I'm not really sure if this is a trick or not. Small dogs do this almost automatically. If you hold a biscuit slightly out of reach of a terrier, he'll probably sit back on his haunches rather than leap for it. Collies are almost all hopeless at begging and fall over when they try. If you do want to try teaching it, the same requirement of treats, patience and common sense applies. Have the dog sit and hold the treat just out of reach. If you have taught them the command word "Gently . . . !" it could be used to stop them snapping at your fingers. Let them have the first treat just by stretching, then move the next a little higher so their front paws have to leave the ground. Repeat over months.

11. Drop!

This is a very important command. Puppies in particular are very playful and as soon as you touch something they are holding, they will pull back and enjoy the game as you desperately try to save your shoes from destruction. It's best to take them by the collar to prevent them tugging too hard and say "Drop!" in a loud, fierce voice. Repetition, as with all of these, is crucial.

12. Over! Over!

Different families will have different command words, of course. This one is probably not that common. Our dogs are always taught to jump at hearing this. You may be out walking and need them to jump a low fence, for example, or jump up onto a table to be brushed. Begin with a higher surface and simply pat it firmly, saying "Over! Over!" to them in an excited voice. If this doesn't work, do not pull them up by the collar. They could be frightened of being off the ground and that won't help. If you can, lift them to the higher level and then make a huge fuss of them, giving a treat. Repeat pats and lifts until they are comfortable with the higher position.

This is quite fun to see. Like cats, dogs can really jump, but they aren't taught to do it on command very often.

13. Pee.

Police dogs are taught to evacuate their bowels and bladder on command. It's done by using the command word – or make your own one up – at the time when the dog is going to the toilet, and then the usual routine of making a fuss and giving a treat. In all honesty, this is only useful when, say, a dog will spend most of the day inside an airport and must not pee on luggage. For pets, it isn't worth it.

14. *Jumping through your arms.*

Not all dogs can do this – the terrier absolutely refused point-blank. The command "Over! Over!" is useful as the dog knows it is for jumping. Begin by making a circle on the floor with your arms and having the dog called through for a treat. You need two people for this. After a few successful repetitions, raise your hands from the floor, so the dog has to step up a little to pass through. They're probably far too excited by then, so try it again the next day. Raise your hands higher and higher, then stand upright, holding your arms out in the largest circle you can make. Dogs the size of collies can do this, though some will thump you in the body or hit your hands as they go through. They improve with practice and it is a great trick to impress other dog owners.

15. *Attack commands.*

There is no secret to having an attack word for a dog. Be aware, however, that unless it was absolutely justified, the dog is likely to be destroyed. Children accompanied by dogs are *much* less likely to be troubled by strangers, regardless of the breed of dog. Dogs are known to be aggressive and territorial, especially with strangers – men in particular. They do not need to be taught higher levels of aggression.

The opposite of this is what to do if you come into contact with an aggressive dog. First of all, it is a risk to put your hand out to pat any strange dog. If you must take the chance, let the dog smell your hands first, coming in slowly and low down so as not to startle them. If they show their teeth, move away. Humankind is the only animal on the planet who shows his teeth to smile. The rest of them are saying "Go away or I will attack." The same applies for growling. It is never playful. Never growl back. That is what another dog would do and the aggression will increase dramatically. Most dogs have the courtesy to warn you. Take the warning and back away.

If the dog does attack, remain on your feet and protect your face. Don't scream. Break eye contact if you can, as dogs see a direct gaze as aggressive. Dogs are almost never interested in serious damage. They simply want to remove you from the area. Do not run, however. Walk slowly away. Big dogs like German shepherds will hit you hard in the chest or back to try to knock you down. On the ground is not a good place to be in a full attack.

If you do end up on the ground, curl up to protect your face and neck. Again, they will do a lot more barking than actual biting in almost every case. Remain as still as you can and don't call for help or scream. The noise may excite them.

A well-trained dog will not be aggressive with other dogs or people, or at least they'll bring the poodle back when you call them. They will guard your home, force you to remain active to walk them, play with you whenever you have the slightest interest and adore you with complete trust in all weathers, on all days.

WRAPPING A PARCEL IN
BROWN PAPER AND STRING

NOT A VERY "DANGEROUS" ACTIVITY, it's true, but it is extremely satisfying to know how to do this. There are two main ways: one without sticky tape of any kind and a more ornate one that needs the ends held with tape. I think they both have a place when sending a present or something thoughtful to someone else – just to give them the old-fashioned pleasure of tearing it open. It is true that you could simply cocoon a parcel in tape, but there is a certain elegance in doing it without.

1

2

You will need brown paper and string, available from most post offices and all stationery stores.

Place the item to be posted on the sheet and cut a piece to fit it. Leave as much as half the height again and three times the width. Be generous with that paper. If it really is too much, you can cut some off later, but you can never put it back on.

If you were using sticky tape, you'd use less paper, fold one sheet under the other and then tape the edge. Here, we are going to fold the edge down over itself in strips. This will create a "spine" of paper that is very useful for rigidity and finishing it off. It also looks quite good, if you are careful with the folds.

Take a little time getting the ends right. Fold in a middle piece on each side so that you end up with a duck's bill in brown paper, as in the picture. This is not the classic "folding triangles in on themselves" technique. It is better.

Fold that duck's bill over itself into a neat point on both ends. You don't need to tape it, just leave it loose. The folded spine will prove very useful to hold it all together while you tie the string.

3

4

5

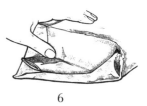

6

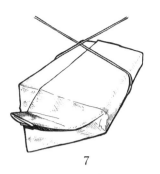

7

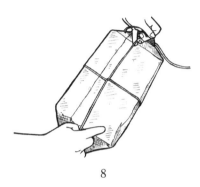

8

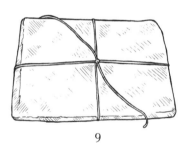

9

Now for the string. Cut a good long bit – about 1 metre (3 ft). Once again, you can always shorten it. Begin on the side where the final knot or bow will go. Take the string around to the other side and then cross the two pieces as shown above, changing directions at ninety degrees. Take the two lines round the other ends of the parcel and back to the middle of where you started, for tying. It is helpful to have someone put their finger on the knot to stop it slipping.

One useful tip is to tie an extra knot before tying the final bow, linking the two lines together on top. This makes it more secure and is a good habit to get into.

The spine of folded paper is underneath. The parcel is neatly wrapped. Well done.

The only drawback to this method is that the crossed strings go right through where you would usually put the address. It is possible to tie the string so that it doesn't, but we found this way needed a bit of tape to hold those ends down.

Instead of starting in the middle of the parcel, start at one end, running the middle point of a long piece of string underneath. For this method, there is nothing more annoying than running out of string halfway through, so we suggest 150 centimetres (5 ft).

Wrap the string around, but this time cross at the three-quarter mark rather than at halfway. Run the strings around the other side and do it again and again, crossing at the corners until you can finally tie it off. As you'll see from the picture, the ends are not held by the string, but this is robust – and it leaves a space for the address.

10

11

WRAPPING A PARCEL IN BROWN PAPER AND STRING

STAR MAPS: WHAT YOU SEE
WHEN YOU LOOK UP...

Facing south in the **northern hemisphere**, turn the book so the current month of the year is at the bottom. This will be accurate at around 11:00 at night.

STAR MAPS: WHAT YOU SEE WHEN YOU LOOK UP

228

Facing north in the **southern hemisphere**, turn the page again to put the correct month at the bottom, and these are the constellations visible on a good clear night at 11:00 p.m.

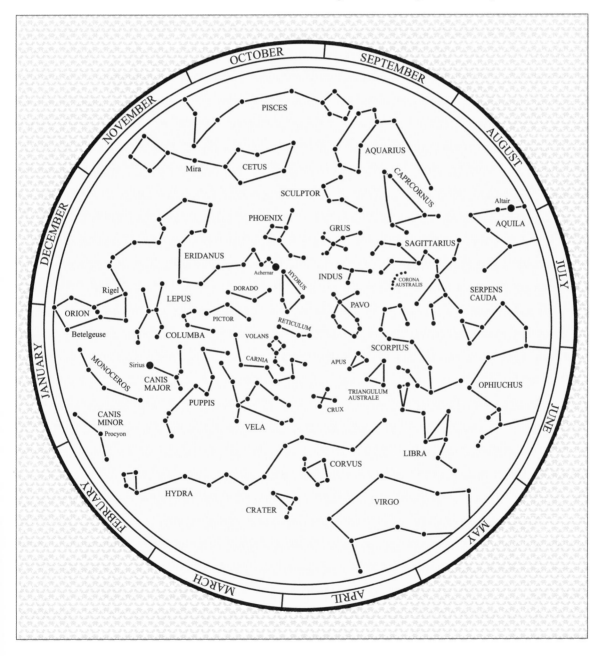

STAR MAPS: WHAT YOU SEE WHEN YOU LOOK UP

MAKING A PERISCOPE

You will need

- Saw, hammer, glue, small tacks.
- Two mirrors – 5 x 5 centimetres (2 x 2 in).
- Plywood – three-ply or five-ply. Cut two pieces of 45 x 5 centimetre (18 x 2 in), two pieces of 40 x 5 centimetre (16 x 2 in), two end pieces of 5 x 5 centimetres (2 x 2 in).
- Duct tape.
- Tacks.

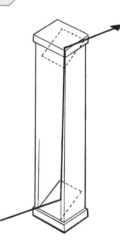

THIS IS A QUICK and easy one. It took just over an hour to put together once we had everything in hand. It does, however, involve work with a saw, hammering and glue, so if you are unsure, ask for help.

First, get yourself two small square mirrors. Any glass shop will cut a couple of bits for you. For the actual periscope tube, we used plywood we had lying around. Ours was five-ply, which is more robust than you actually need. Three-ply would be better and is also easier to cut.

A periscope works by reflecting from one mirror to another and finally to the eye. Its simple effect is the ability to look higher than your head. It can be used to peer over fences or check enemy positions without exposing yourself to sniper fire. The classic use is in submarines.

We used small tacks to create the box, leaving a space (at the top of one side and the bottom of the other) for the mirrors. We kept ours simple and fairly rough, though obviously your periscope can be smoothed, painted or even joined and glued properly if you wanted one that will survive a generation or two. As a woodwork project in mahogany with brass corners, it would be very impressive.

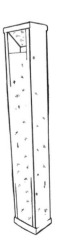

The only difficulty was in securing the mirrors. By far the best way is to glue tiny wood strips in place on the inner surfaces, like runners. The mirrors slide between the strips and lock neatly into place against the end pieces. We used heavy insulation tape, however, and that seemed to do the job almost as well.

Having relied on the tape, it seemed sensible to cut one of the 40-centimetre (16-in) sides down to 36 centimetres (14 in), so that the top mirror could actually rest on its edge. Obviously, if it sat in neat little wooden runners, it would be perfectly all right to leave the piece at 40 centimetres (16 in), a neater look.

The angle of the mirrors should be 45 degrees for the right reflection. This isn't easy to judge, however, and the easiest way is just to position the first mirror until you can see the other end of the periscope tube in it. Once that is secured, position the second by hand, marking lines so you can find the correct position easily. Then either tape it or glue the wooden runners.

In theory, you could build quite a long periscope. We found 45 centimetres (18 in) was about right for our mirrors, but you could use larger pieces and experiment with a longer box.

SEVEN POEMS EVERY BOY SHOULD KNOW

YES, A BOY SHOULD BE able to climb trees, grow crystals and tie a decent bowline knot. However, a boy will grow into a man and no man should be completely ignorant of these poems. They are the ones that spoke to us when we were young. Find a big tree and climb it. Read one of these poems aloud to yourself, high in the branches. All the authors are long dead, but they may still speak to you.

IF –
BY RUDYARD KIPLING (1865–1936)

If you can keep your head when all about you
Are losing theirs and blaming it on you,
If you can trust yourself when all men doubt you,
But make allowance for their doubting too;
If you can wait and not be tired by waiting,
Or being lied about, don't deal in lies,
Or being hated, don't give way to hating,
And yet don't look too good, nor talk too wise:

If you can dream – and not make dreams your master;
If you can think – and not make thoughts your aim;
If you can meet with Triumph and Disaster
And treat those two impostors just the same;
If you can bear to hear the truth you've spoken
Twisted by knaves to make a trap for fools,
Or watch the things you gave your life to, broken,
And stoop and build 'em up with worn-out tools:

If you can make one heap of all your winnings
    And risk it on one turn of pitch-and-toss,
And lose, and start again at your beginnings
    And never breathe a word about your loss;
If you can force your heart and nerve and sinew
    To serve your turn long after they are gone,
And so hold on when there is nothing in you
    Except the Will which says to them: "Hold on!"

If you can talk with crowds and keep your virtue,
    Or walk with Kings – nor lose the common touch,
If neither foes nor loving friends can hurt you,
    If all men count with you, but none too much;
If you can fill the unforgiving minute
    With sixty seconds' worth of distance run,
Yours is the Earth and everything that's in it,
    And – which is more – you'll be a Man, my son!

We recommend *Puck of Pook's Hill* as an example of Kipling's prose. Tragically, his only son, John, was killed in the First World War, in 1915.

Ozymandias
BY PERCY BYSSHE SHELLEY (1792–1822)

I met a traveller from an antique land
Who said: Two vast and trunkless legs of stone
Stand in the desert ... Near them, on the sand,
Half sunk, a shattered visage lies, whose frown,
And wrinkled lip, and sneer of cold command,
Tell that its sculptor well those passions read
Which yet survive, stamped on these lifeless things,
The hand that mocked them, and the heart that fed:
And on the pedestal these words appear:
"My name is Ozymandias, king of kings:
Look on my works, ye Mighty, and despair!"
Nothing beside remains. Round the decay
Of that colossal wreck, boundless and bare
The lone and level sands stretch far away.

This poem was written as a commentary on human arrogance. It is based on a broken statue near Luxor, Egypt. The actual inscription (translated) reads "King of Kings am I, Osymandias. If anyone would know how great I am and where I lie, let him surpass one of my works."

Invictus

BY WILLIAM ERNEST HENLEY (1849–1903)

Out of the night that covers me,
* Black as the pit from pole to pole,*
I thank whatever gods may be
* For my unconquerable soul.*

In the fell clutch of circumstance
* I have not winced nor cried aloud.*
Under the bludgeonings of chance
* My head is bloody, but unbowed.*

Beyond this place of wrath and tears
* Looms but the Horror of the shade,*
And yet the menace of the years
* Finds, and shall find, me unafraid.*

It matters not how strait the gate,
* How charged with punishments the scroll,*
I am the master of my fate:
* I am the captain of my soul.*

Invictus is Latin for "unconquerable." As a child, Henley suffered the amputation of a foot. He was ill for much of his life and wrote this during a two-year spell in an infirmary. He was a great friend of Robert Louis Stevenson and the character of Long John Silver may even be based on him.

In Flanders Fields

BY JOHN MCCRAE (1872–1918)

In Flanders fields the poppies blow
Between the crosses, row on row,
That mark our place; and in the sky
The larks, still bravely singing, fly
Scarce heard amid the guns below.

We are the Dead. Short days ago
We lived, felt dawn, saw sunset glow,
Loved, and were loved, and now we lie
In Flanders Fields.

Take up our quarrel with the foe:
To you from failing hands we throw

The torch; be yours to hold it high.
If ye break faith with us who die
We shall not sleep, though poppies grow
In Flanders fields.

Written in 1915 after John McCrae witnessed the death of a close friend in the First World War, *In Flanders Fields* quickly became a long-lasting tribute to bravery, love and heroism and a part of many Remembrance Day ceremonies. The first stanza of the poem is printed on the ten-dollar bill, and the line "The torch; be yours to hold it high" was painted on the wall of the Montreal Canadiens dressing room in the old Montreal Forum.

Sea-Fever
BY JOHN MASEFIELD (1878–1967)

I must down to the seas again, to the lonely sea and the sky,
And all I ask is a tall ship and a star to steer her by,
And the wheel's kick and the wind's song and the white sails shaking,
And a grey mist on the sea's face and a grey dawn breaking.

I must down to the seas again, for the call of the running tide
Is a wild call and a clear call that may not be denied;
And all I ask is a windy day with the white clouds flying,
And the flung spray and the blown spume, and the sea-gulls crying.

I must down to the seas again, to the vagrant gypsy life,
To the gull's way and the whale's way where the wind's like a whetted knife;
And all I ask is a merry yarn from a laughing fellow-rover,
And quiet sleep and a sweet dream when the long trick's over.

Masefield, who later became Poet Laureate, wrote "Sea-Fever" when he was only twenty-two. It contains some fantastic examples of onomatopoeia – words that sound like their meaning. You can hear the wind in "wind like a whetted knife," for example.

There are hundreds more poems that have stayed with us as we grow older. That is the magic perhaps, that a single line can bring comfort in grief, or express the joy of a birth. These are not small things.

The Cremation of Sam McGee
BY ROBERT SERVICE (1874–1958)

There are strange things done in the midnight sun
By the men who moil for gold;

The Arctic trails have their secret tales
That would make your blood run cold;
The Northern Lights have seen queer sights,
But the queerest they ever did see
Was that night on the marge of Lake Lebarge
I cremated Sam McGee.

Now Sam McGee was from Tennessee, where the cotton blooms and blows.
Why he left his home in the South to roam 'round the Pole, God only knows.
He was always cold, but the land of gold seemed to hold him like a spell;
Though he'd often say in his homely way that he'd "sooner live in hell."

On a Christmas Day we were mushing our way over the Dawson trail.
Talk of your cold! through the parka's fold it stabbed like a driven nail.
If our eyes we'd close, then the lashes froze till sometimes we couldn't see;
It wasn't much fun, but the only one to whimper was Sam McGee.

And that very night, as we lay packed tight in our robes beneath the snow,
And the dogs were fed, and the stars o'erhead were dancing heel and toe,
He turned to me, and "Cap," says he, "I'll cash in this trip, I guess;
And if I do, I'm asking that you won't refuse my last request."

Well, he seemed so low that I couldn't say no; then he says with a sort of moan:
"It's the cursed cold, and it's got right hold till I'm chilled clean through to the bone.
Yet 'tain't being dead – it's my awful dread of the icy grave that pains;
So I want you to swear that, foul or fair, you'll cremate my last remains."

A pal's last need is a thing to heed, so I swore I would not fail;
And we started on at the streak of dawn; but God! he looked ghastly pale.
He crouched on the sleigh, and he raved all day of his home in Tennessee;
And before nightfall a corpse was all that was left of Sam McGee.

There wasn't a breath in that land of death, and I hurried, horror-driven,
With a corpse half hid that I couldn't get rid, because of a promise given;
It was lashed to the sleigh, and it seemed to say: "You may tax your brawn and brains,
But you promised true, and it's up to you to cremate those last remains."

Now a promise made is a debt unpaid, and the trail has its own stern code.
In the days to come, though my lips were dumb, in my heart how I cursed
  that load.
In the long, long night, by the lone firelight, while the huskies, round in a ring,
Howled out their woes to the homeless snows – O God! how I loathed the thing.

And every day that quiet clay seemed to heavy and heavier grow;
And on I went, though the dogs were spent and the grub was getting low;

The trail was bad, and I felt half mad, but I swore I would not give in;
And I'd often sing to the hateful thing, and it hearkened with a grin.

Till I came to the marge of Lake Lebarge, and a derelict there lay;
It was jammed in the ice, but I saw in a trice it was called the "Alice May."
And I looked at it, and I thought a bit, and I looked at my frozen chum;
Then "Here," said I, with a sudden cry, "is my cre-ma-tor-ium."

Some planks I tore from the cabin floor, and I lit the boiler fire;
Some coal I found that was lying around, and I heaped the fuel higher;
The flames just soared, and the furnace roared – such a blaze you seldom see;
And I burrowed a hole in the glowing coal, and I stuffed in Sam McGee.

Then I made a hike, for I didn't like to hear him sizzle so;
And the heavens scowled, and the huskies howled, and the wind began to blow.
It was icy cold, but the hot sweat rolled down my cheeks, and I don't know why;
And the greasy smoke in an inky cloak went streaking down the sky.

I do not know how long in the snow I wrestled with grisly fear;
But the stars came out and they danced about ere again I ventured near;
I was sick with dread, but I bravely said: "I'll just take a peep inside.
I guess he's cooked, and it's time I looked"; . . . then the door I opened wide.

And there sat Sam, looking cool and calm, in the heart of the furnace roar;
And he wore a smile you could see a mile, and he said: "Please close that door.
It's fine in here, but I greatly fear you'll let in the cold and storm –
Since I left Plumtree, down in Tennessee, it's the first time I've been warm."

There are strange things done in the midnight sun
By the men who moil for gold;
The Arctic trails have their secret tales
That would make your blood run cold;
The Northern Lights have seen queer sights,
But the queerest they ever did see
Was that night on the marge of Lake Lebarge
I cremated Sam McGee.

Robert Service was born in England and worked in a bank in the Yukon for eight years during the Klondike gold rush. Although the poem is fictional, it was based on the experience of a friend of Service, a doctor who was sent to care for a sick prospector, only to find him frozen stiff. He cremated the man in the boiler of a ship since he didn't have the tools to bury him.

The Road Not Taken

BY ROBERT FROST (1874–1963)

Two roads diverged in a yellow wood,
And sorry I could not travel both
And be one traveler, long I stood
And looked down one as far as I could
To where it bent in the undergrowth.

Then took the other, as just as fair,
And having perhaps the better claim,
Because it was grassy and wanted wear;
Though as for that the passing there
Had worn them really about the same.

And both that morning equally lay
In leaves no step had trodden black.
Oh, I kept the first for another day!
Yet knowing how way leads on to way,
I doubted if I should ever come back.

I shall be telling this with a sigh
Somewhere ages and ages hence:
Two roads diverged in a wood, and I –
I took the one less traveled by,
And that has made all the difference.

The famous American poet Robert Frost wrote one stanza of this poem on a sofa in the middle of England. He found it four years later, and he felt he just had to finish it. "I wasn't thinking about myself there," he told a group of writers in 1953, "but about a friend who had gone off to war, a person who, whichever road he went, would be sorry he didn't go the other. He was hard on himself that way."

COIN TRICKS

COIN TRICKS ARE EASY to do and very effective. Here, we will show you some simple sleight-of-hand "vanishes."

Any coin will do, the bigger the better, though I would suggest nothing smaller than a quarter or a loonie.

Most tricks are over quite quickly but a little "patter" (spoken introduction) is still required. The speed of the trick is not important. It's all about the smoothness of movement and that takes practice. Misdirection and the final flourish will make you seem like a seasoned magician. When performing, let your hands move smoothly and confidently.

One of the oldest coin sleights is called "the French Drop," a simple, effective "vanish." The reappearance is also important and we will suggest some examples such as taking it from behind a spectator's ear, but with a little ingenuity and practice you will come up with some ideas of your own to keep the spectators captivated.

THE FRENCH DROP

If you are right-handed, hold the coin by the edge in your left hand between your first two fingers and your thumb. Make sure the hand is turned palm up and the fingers are curled in.

With the right hand palm down, go to grab the coin, with the thumb of the right hand going underneath the coin and the fingers above it. Close the right hand into a fist to take the coin.

At this point, release the coin, letting it fall into the cupped fingers of the left hand. The right hand now moves forward, supposedly holding the coin. The left hand drops to your side with the real coin.

This sleight is quite elegant and needs to be performed smoothly and naturally. A good way to practise is to alternate between the French Drop and actually taking the coin, so when you perform the sleight you precisely duplicate the action of taking the coin.

Check occasionally in the mirror to see if it looks natural. Do not try to hide the coin in your left hand, just let the hand drop to your side. You could point at the right hand with a left finger, to misdirect the attention of the spectators. Always keep your eyes on the right hand, and then drop the left hand to your side.

Everyone watching will think the coin is in the right hand, so hold it out straight, focus on it and open the hand finger by finger. It will have vanished! Now reach toward a spectator with your cupped left hand and produce the coin from behind their ear! They can't see the approach around the back, so this is fairly easy.

The Easy Vanish

The Easy Vanish is simple to perform yet very deceptive. Hold both hands palms up with a coin on the second and third fingertips of the right hand. Hold the coin in place with the right thumb.

Now turn that hand over and slap the coin into the palm of the left hand. Close the fingers of the left hand over the fingers of the right; withdraw the right hand, but hang onto the coin, using your thumb. Drop your right hand down by your side and reveal an empty left hand!

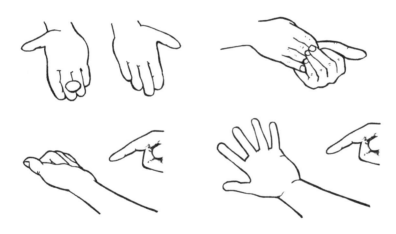

The Basic Vanish

Hold both hands out, palms up, with a coin in the centre of the right hand. The right hand approaches the left hand from below so the palm of the right hand touches the fingertips of the left hand.

The legitimate move is to drop the coin into the left hand as the right hand passes over it, closing the fingers of the left hand over the coin and dropping the right hand to one side.

Now to create the sleight, place the coin in the centre of your right hand and close the fingers and thumb slightly, gripping the coin with your palm. This is called "palming." As you pass over the left hand with the back of the right hand to the audience, you can retain the coin in your right hand. This will take some practice. Getting the coin in the right position for the palm needs confidence and a little patter to bounce it around until it's right.

As before, practise the sleight and check in the mirror so it looks natural.

Outlined above are three easy vanishes, but as I said at the beginning, it is the reappearance that is important. One great reappearance that can be used for any of the vanishes is called "cough up." It involves a little patter and a flourish.

At the beginning of the sleight, let the people watching know that you have a hole in the top of your head. Lean forward and let them look. Ask them if they can see it. They should say no and when they do, look a little confused and state that you can prove it. Smoothly perform one of the vanishes above, let's say the French Drop, but do not reveal the empty right hand. Instead, slap the top of your head with it. Then move your left hand to your mouth and cough, letting the coin drop. Catch it with your right. This really does look as if you have passed a coin through your head! Remember, it's smoothness that counts and if people ask you to do it again always decline. Don't give your tricks away too easily.

LIGHT

W HAT IS LIGHT? Without the human sense of sight, the word "light" would have no meaning. Light enters our eyes and we "see" things. Seeing things is a mental sensation and light is the physical cause of this. The mental effect that light causes is still one of the mysteries of the mind, but we do understand a great deal about light on the physical side.

The thing we see might have its own light source – like a light bulb, or light might be reflected off it from somewhere else – like the sun. We see most things by this reflected or borrowed light.

The origin of any light source will begin with the vibration of atoms. A light bulb, for example, uses electricity to heat a filament to the point where it gives out energy in the form of white light. That light travels at about 300,000 kilometres per second (186,000 miles per second) in empty space. It travels in waves or a steady flow of waves, like ripples on a pond. The waves have a very short wavelength (this is measured from the crest of one wavelength to another): 0.00006350 centimetres (1/40,000 in) to 0.00003175 centimetres (1/80,000 in), depending on the colour.

When light shines on a non-luminous body (like a table), it stimulates the atoms to varying degrees. Some atoms absorb all the light that falls upon them, while other atoms absorb some of the light but allow the rest to be reflected. The light finally reaches the eye, producing on the retina an image of the object viewed. Thus we "see" and recognize the different parts of an object.

Light waves of various wavelengths create the sensation of colour when they fall on the eye. These waves can be identified by passing light through a prism, a coloured strip called "the spec-

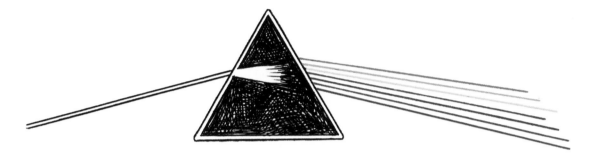

trum" being produced, red at one end and passing through orange, yellow, green, blue and indigo to violet at the other end. "**Roy G. Biv**" is a good way to remember the colours of the spectrum. Each letter in this made-up name stands for a colour in the spectrum.

By mixing colours, using coloured glass and a white background, any colour whatever can be produced, including some that are not present in the spectrum, like brown. The eye cannot tell the composition of the light that produces any given colour; for example, the colour yellow is a simple colour, but may be produced by mixing red and green in the correct proportions. Whiteness is caused by a mixture of all the simple colours. The classic way to see this is to colour a carboard disc with the shades of the rainbow and punch a pencil through the middle. When spun quickly, the colours will blur into whiteness.

When we look at a raindrop, we call it transparent, and think that the light goes straight through. Actually, some of it is reflected from the inner surfaces. The light is bent or "refracted" as it enters the raindrop and again when it leaves.

Raindrops act in the same way as rough prisms of glass or ice and cause rainbows. The drops of water split up the sunlight into the colours of the rainbow by "refracting" each of the different colours of light to a different degree.

You will always find that your shadow points directly to the middle of the rainbow. You might also hear of a "pot of gold" where the rainbow ends. Unfortunately, a rainbow has no end. As you move your position so the rainbow will move with you. Curiously no two people will ever see exactly the same rainbow. They generally appear when the sun is fairly low in the early morning and afternoon. The lower the sun, the higher the bow.

Colour is an affair of the mind, while light is purely physical, but you cannot have one without the other.

LATIN PHRASES EVERY
BOY SHOULD KNOW

=⟩—✳—⟨=

THERE ARE HUNDREDS OF THOUSANDS of Latin roots in English. If that wasn't enough, some Latin words have become so common they are often believed to *be* English! "Agenda" (things to be done), "alter ego" (other self), "exit" (he/she leaves), "verbatim" (word for word) and "video" (I see) fall into that group. There is satisfaction in understanding your own language – and that includes its origins.

Latin phrases crop up in conversation as well as the law courts. It is still the gold standard of education, but be warned – showing off is not a suitable reason for learning this list.

The precision of Latin can be a pleasure, but the main reason for this chapter is cultural. The three pillars of English culture are the King James Bible, the complete works of Shakespeare – and Latin. If you know English, you should know a little Latin. What follows can only ever be a small sample of the whole.

Learn one a day, perhaps. After each phrase, you'll find a homemade phonetic pronunciation guide. Stressed syllables are in capitals (SCIssors, DINosaur.) For some, you'll find an example of it being used.

1. **Ad hoc** (ad-hok). Literally "to this." Improvised or made up. "I wrote an ad hoc poem."
2. **Ad hominem** (ad HOM-in-em). This is a below-the-belt, personal attack, rather than a reasoned response to an argument.
3. **Ad infinitum** (ad in-fin-EYE-tum). To infinity – carried on endlessly. "And so on and so on, ad infinitum . . ."
4. **Anno Domini** (AN-no DOM-in-eye). In the year of our Lord. Example: "This is the year of our lord, 1492 – when Columbus sailed the ocean blue."
5. **Ante meridiem** (AN-tay Mer-ID-ee-em). Before noon – 4:00 a.m., for instance.
6. **Aqua vitae** (AK-wa VIT-eye). Water of life. Most often used to refer to whisky or brandy.
7. **Audio** (ODD-i-o). I hear. Romans would probably have pronounced this like Audi cars.
8. **Bona fides** (BONE-uh FIDE-eez). Bona fides are credentials establishing good faith or honesty. Technically, it is a singular term, though it is usually heard with a plural verb these days, because it ends in "s."
9. **Carpe diem** (CAR-pay DEE-em). Seize the day, or use your time.
10. **Cave canem** (CAV-ay CAN-em). Beware of the dog. Found preserved in a mosaic floor in Pompeii, to name one place.
11. **Circa** (SUR-ca). Around – approximately. Julius Caesar was born circa 100 BC.
12. **Cogito ergo sum** (COG-it-o ER-go sum). "I think, therefore I am" – a famous conclusion form René Descartes, the French philosopher. He considered the statement to be the only defensible proof of existence. All else could be fantasy.
13. **Curriculum vitae** (cur-IC-you-lum VEET-eye). The course of life – or school and work history. Usually abbreviated to CV.
14. **Deus ex machina** (DAY-us ex MAK-in-a). Literally, a god out of a machine, as when Greek

playwrights would have Zeus lowered on wires to solve story problems. It has come to mean poor storytelling, where some outside force makes it all end well.

15. **Dulce et decorum est pro patria mori** (DOOL-chay et de-COR-um est pro pat-ri-ya MORE-ee). "It is sweet and fitting to die for your country." A line from Horace. Later used ironically by Wilfred Owen in a World War I poem.

16. **Ergo** (UR-go). Therefore.

17. **Exempli gratia** (ex-EM-pli GRA-ti-ya). For (the sake of) example – usually abbreviated to "e.g."

18. **Fiat lux!** (FEE-at lux). Let there be light!

19. **Habeas corpus** (HABE-e-as CORP-us). Literally, "You must have the body." This has come to mean that a person cannot be held without trial – the "body" must be brought before a court.

20. **Iacta alea est** (YACT-a Ali-ya est). The die is cast. Julius Caesar said this on the Rubicon river, when he was deciding to cross it. He meant "It's done. The decision is made."

21. **In camera** (in CAM-e-ra). In secret – not in the open. "The meeting was held in camera."

22. **In flagrante delicto** (in flag-RANT-ay de-LICT-o). In "flaming crime" – caught red-handed, or in the act.

23. **Ipso facto** (IP-so FACT-o). By the fact itself. "I have barred my house to you. Ipso facto, you are not coming in."

24. **Magna cum laude** (MAG-na coom LOUD-ay). With great praise and honour. "He graduated magna cum laude."

25. **Modus operandi** (MODE-us op-er-AND-ee). Method of operation – a person's professional style of habits.

26. **Non compos mentis** (non COM-pos MEN-tis). Not of sound mind. Cracked.

27. **Non sequitur** (non SEK-wit-er). Does not follow – a broken argument. "He never takes a bath. He must prefer cats to dogs."

28. **Nota bene** (NO-ta BEN-ay). Note well. Usually abbreviated to "n.b." Note that "Id est" is also very common and means "that is." "Id est" is usually abbreviated to "i.e."

29. **Paterfamilias** (PAT-er-fam-IL-i-as). Father of the family – paternal figure.

30. **Persona non grata** (Per-SONE-a non GRAT-a). An unwelcome person.

31. **Post meridiem** (POST me-RID-ee-em). After noon – usually abbreviated to p.m.

32. **Post mortem** (post MOR-tem). After death. Usually taken to mean investigative surgery to determine cause of death.

33. **Postscriptum** (post-SCRIP-tum). Literally, "thing having been written afterwards"– usually abbreviated to p.s.

34. **Quis custodiet ipsos custodes?** (kwis cus-TOAD-ee-yet IP-soss cus-TOAD-ez). Who guards the guards?

35. **Quod erat demonstrandum** (kwod e-rat dem-on-STRAN-dum). Which was to be demonstrated. Usually written as QED at the end of arguments.

36. **Quo vadis?** (kwo VAD-is). Where are you going?

37. **Requiescat in pace** (rek-wi-ES-cat in par-kay). "May he or she rest in peace" – usually abbreviated to RIP.

38. **Semper fidelis** (SEMP-er fid-EL-is). Always faithful. The motto of the United States Marines Corps. The motto of the Royal Canadian Air Force is "Per ardua ad astra" – through adversity to the stars.

39. **Senatus populusque romanus** (sen-AH-tus pop-yool-US-kway rome-AN-us). The senate and the people of Rome. Imperial legions carried SPQR on their banners. Oddly enough, it is still to be found on drain-hole covers in modern Rome.

40. **Status quo** (state-us kwo). "The state in which things are." The existing state of affairs. Example: "It is crucial to maintain the status quo."

41. **Stet** (stet). Let it stand. Leave it alone. Often used in manuscripts, to indicate that no editing change is necessary.

42. **Sub rosa** (sub ROSE-a). Under the rose – secret. From the custom of placing a rose over a doorframe to indicate what was said inside was not to be repeated.

43. **Tabula rasa** (TAB-yool-a RA-sa). Literally a "scraped tablet." Blank slate. A state of innocence.

44. **Terra firma** (TER-a FIRM-a). Solid ground.

45. **Terra incognita** (TER-a in-cog-NIT-a). Land unknown. Used on old maps to show the bits as yet unexplored.

46. **Vade retro satana!** (VA-day RET-ro sa-TAN-a). Get behind me, Satan. This is an order to crush desires or temptations to sin.

47. **Veni, vidi, vici** (WAYN-ee WEED-ee WEEK-ee). I came, I saw, I conquered. Said by Julius Caesar after a rebellion in Greece that he defeated in one afternoon.

48. **Versus** (VER-sus). Against – usually abbreviated to "v" or "vs."

49. **Veto** (VEE-tow). I forbid. Another one so commonly used as to appear English.

50. **Vox populi** (vox POP-yool-ee). Voice of the people. Often abbreviated to a "Vox Pop" – a short interview on the street.

AND THE NUMBERS...

There are only seven kinds of Roman numerals. These are: I, V, X, L, C, D and M (1, 5, 10, 50, 100, 500 and 1,000). From just those seven, all other numbers can be made. The only difficulty comes in recognizing that some numbers, like four and nine, are made by IV and IX – one less than five, one less than ten. This pattern is used all through Roman numerals, so 99 will be IM. That's it. Spend ten minutes on this page and then go and read any gravestone you wish.

I   II   III   IV   V   VI   VII   VIII   IX   X   **(1–10)**

XI   XII   XIII   XIV   XV   XVI   XVII   XVIII   XIX   XX   **(11–20)**

XXX **(30)**   XL **(40)**   L **(50)**   LX **(60)**   LXX **(70)**   LXXX **(80)**   XC **(90)**   C **(100)**

The year 1924, for example, is MDCCCCXXIV.

HOW TO PLAY POKER

EVERY BOY should know how to play this game – but be warned. Luck has very little to do with it. High rollers in Las Vegas stay clear of poker because playing against experts is a humiliating way of giving money to strangers. In many cases, the roulette wheel is more attractive to those people – at least when they are thrown out wearing nothing more than their underpants, they have only themselves to blame.

There are dozens of variations of poker, so we're going to cover only two popular games: Five-Card Draw and Texas Hold-'em. It is worth mentioning at this point that poker is a game that must be played for money. There is no *risk* in throwing all your matchsticks into the pot – and therefore no chance to bluff. It *is* possible to limit the bets to a level where it doesn't mean you have to sell the dog, but you can still feel as if you've won something.

FIVE-CARD DRAW

The aim is to beat the other players and that can be done by sudden changes in betting, bluffing or simply having a better hand. The very first thing to learn is the value of hands. Here they are, in order:

The best hand possible is the **royal flush** – all cards in sequence, from ace to 10, and of the same suit. The odds against being dealt this hand are 650,000/1. It would be a lifetime event to see one of these in the first five cards. Below that is a **straight flush** – again, all the cards in sequence and of the same suit, but lower down the line: 4, 5, 6, 7, 8 in spades, for example. Even that has odds of 72,000/1.

Four of a kind. Odds against being dealt it: 4,000/1.

Full house. Three of a kind and a pair. Into the realms of possibility, perhaps, at 700/1.

   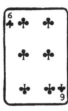 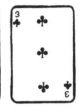

Flush. All cards of the same suit but of mixed ranks. Odds: 500/1.

   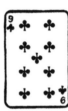 

Straight. All five cards in sequence, but of different suits. 2, 3, 4, 5, 6 for example, or the high one seen in the picture. Odds: 250/1.

Three of a kind. Three cards of the same rank. Odds: 50/1.

Two pairs. Odds: 20/1.

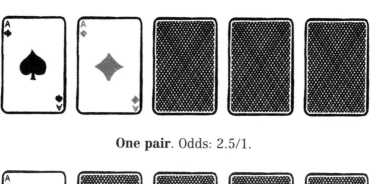

One pair. Odds: 2.5/1.

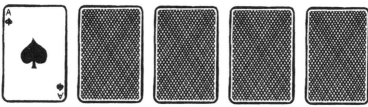

High card or **no pair**. Odds: 2/1.

Memorize these rankings and what they mean. You really can't check them while playing.

Four players is the classic home game number, but five or even six can be accommodated.

Begin by placing an agreed amount in the pot. This is to prevent weak hands being automatically folded. If one player does nothing but hold on, he may scoop the pot – and that should be worth something.

A dealer is nominated to start. Whoever is dealer will go clockwise round the table. It is common practice for the dealer to shuffle the cards, then slap the shuffled pack onto the table for the person on his right to cut.

When the dealer is ready, he deals five cards face down to each player. These are examined without showing them to anyone.

A round of betting follows. Betting also goes in a clockwise direction, so the person to the left of the dealer puts an amount of money into the pot. For the sake of the example, we'll say the bet is ten cents.

Going round the circle, each player now has three choices.

1. They can pay ten cents to stay in, saying "I'll see that ten." The word "call" is also used.
2. They can raise the bet, saying "I'll see that ten and raise you another ten."
3. They can fold their cards, saying "Fold," and drop out of the hand.

The person opening the betting has a further choice of saying "Check," meaning "No bet." It could be a bluff, or it could be a weak hand. Other players can also say "Check" in response, but if someone puts money in, everyone has to match it or fold.

If the ten-cent bets go around the table, the betting round ends. It cannot be raised by the first better.

If someone *does* raise it, saying "I'll see that ten cents and raise you another ten," they are showing their confidence in their hand. To stay in now, everyone else will have to match the combined bet of twenty cents.

When the round of betting is over, the dealer offers the person to his left the chance to exchange up to three cards. If the player already has an excellent hand, he might refuse the offer. Most players will exchange, though, keeping the pair of sevens they were dealt and hoping to be given another one.

If you are thinking that mathematics is your weakness, you really should not be considering playing poker for money. Give it to charity instead – it will be better used than ending up as someone else's pocket money.

A FEW USEFUL IMPROVEMENT ODDS

- Three of a kind, change two cards: odds on four of a kind or full house –   9/1
- Three of a kind, change one card: odds on four of a kind or full house –   12/1
- One pair, change three cards: odds to improve to two pairs –   6/1
- One pair, change three cards: odds to improve to three of a kind –   9/1
- One pair, change three cards: odds to improve to a full house –   98/1

There are dozens more – and the good players know them all.

Another calculation that comes in is whether winning a particular pot is worth the bet.

$$\frac{\text{size of pot x "probability of winning"}}{\text{potential loss}} = \text{investment odds}$$

If the answer comes to more than one, it's probably a good bet to make – but note the fact that "probability of winning" is expressed as a fraction and could be guesswork.

$$(50 \text{ cents x } 0.4) / 10 \text{ cents} = 2.0 = \text{good bet}$$

The final aspect of poker is the ability to read other people – not just their expressions, though this is the game that created the phrase "poker face" – someone who hides their emotions. Patterns of betting can also be read. Perhaps when you sit with Jim you notice that whenever he has a good hand, he puts in a very big bet at the first opportunity. You might avoid hands where he does this, but there is always a chance he is deliberately setting up a pattern on good hands, to then do it on a bad hand and watch everyone else fold . . . that's bluffing.

In essence, that's about it for draw poker, except for invaluable experience. The chances of good hands are increased by "wild" cards. If you get these in a hand, you can call them anything you like, which throws the odds right out of the window. Suddenly, unheard-of hands become possible, like five aces.

This is the type of poker used at the world championships. First, the two players to the dealer's left put up "the small blind" and the "blind" – usually half the minimum bet and the minimum bet. This becomes more significant as the game goes on and bet limits increase.

Two cards are dealt face down to each player. These are the "hole cards."

A round of betting takes place, exactly as described above, with raises, folds, etc. It is customary to say "Call" when matching the current bet without a raise.

When betting comes to an end, the dealer deals the "Flop" – three more cards, this time face up where everyone can see them.

After the Flop, another round of betting takes place, beginning with the player to the left of the dealer. He has the choice to bet, fold or check, as with Five-Card Draw. If he checks and the next person bets, he will have to match it – but will now have a better idea of the sort of hands held. As a result, checking can be tactically useful.

The dealer plays another card face up – the "Turn," beginning another round of betting from the left. When that ends, the final card is dealt – the "River."

Now there are five cards face up on the table and two face down in each player's hand. Although seven cards are available, the aim is to make the best five-card hand.

Bluff plays a large part in this version of poker – and the betting tends to be much higher than five-card draw, as players hang on to see if later cards help their hand.

The final round of betting starts with the player to the dealer's left, as before.

SOME OF THE ODDS FOR TEXAS HOLD-'EM

1. HOLE CARD ODDS

• Any pair –	16/1
• Ace, king of different suits –	110/1
• At least one ace –	5.7/1
• Two cards of same suit –	3.25/1

2. IMPROVING ON THE FLOP

You hold	Flop gives you	Odds against
A pair	Three of a kind	10/1
Any two	Two pairs	48.5/1
Two cards of same suit	Flush	118/1

3. IMPROVING ON THE TURN

From	To	Odds against
Four cards of a flush	Flush	4.2/1
Three of a kind	Four of a kind	46/1
Two pairs	Full house	10.8/1
One pair	Three of a kind	22.5/1

4. IMPROVING ON THE RIVER

From	To	Odds against
Four cards of a flush	Flush	4.1/1
Three of a kind	Four of a kind	45/1
Two pairs	Full house	10.5/1
One pair	Three of a kind	22/1
Nothing	A pair	6.7/1

The last piece of advice is "Never try to fill an inside straight." If you were playing draw, say, and have 4, 5, 6, 8 and a king, you might be tempted to exchange that king in the hope of a seven – to make 4, 5, 6, 7, 8, a high hand. There are forty-seven cards you have not seen and only four of them are sevens. 47/4 is almost 12/1. Making a straight at either end is twice as likely, however.

It really is important to realize that poker is a difficult game. The golden rule is "If you can't spot the sucker at the table – it's you."

FOREIGN PHRASES EVERY BOY SHOULD KNOW

CANADA IS HOME to people from many different cultural backgrounds. Our two official languages are English and French, but as a result of immigration, many other languages are spoken across the country today. In the chart below, you'll find phrases from some of the top ten languages spoken in Canada. If you want to impress – and surprise – your friends, neighbours or teachers, try learning some key words and phrases in a language you know they speak. Often, the first words you learn in a new language are the ones that will get you into the most trouble – swear words – but it's really a good idea to know how to say some friendly things too!

Phrases	French	German
Hello	Bonjour *Boñ-zhoor*	Guten Tag *Gooten tahk*
Goodbye	Au revoir *Oh-ruh-vwar*	Auf Wiedersehen *Owf vee-der-zayn*
Thank you	Merci *Mehr-see*	Danke *Dung-keh*
How are you?	Comment allez-vous? *Ko-mah talay voo?*	Wie geht es Ihnen? *Vee gayt es ee-nen?*
Fine, thanks. And you?	Très bien, merci. Et vous? *Tray byañ, mehr-see. Ay voo?*	Danke, gut. Und Ihnen? *Dung-keh goot. Oont ee-nen?*
Yes/No/Okay/Please	Oui/Non/D'accord/S'il vous plait *Wee/No/Da-cor/Seel voo play*	Ja/Nein/Okay/Bitte *Ya/Nine/O-kay/Bi-te*
Do you speak English?	Est-ce que vous parlez anglais? *Ess kuh voo par-lay ahn-glay?*	Sprechen Sie Englisch? *Shpre-khen zee eng-lish?*
Happy birthday!	Bon anniversaire! *Bon a-nee-vair-sehr!*	Alles Gute zum Geburtstag! *A-lez goo-teh tsoom geh-boorts-tahg!*
Happy new year!	Bonne année! *Bon a-nay!*	Ein gutes neues Jahr! *Ine goo-tess noy-ess yahr!*
I love you	Je t'aime *Juh tem*	Ich liebe Dich *Ikh lee-beh dikh*
No way! That's stupid.	Mon oeil! C'est stupide. *Mo-noy! Sey stoo-peed.*	Keineswegs! Das ist dumm. *Kye-ness-vaygs! Duss ist doom.*
My name is . . .	Je m'appelle . . . *Juh ma-pel . . .*	Mein Name ist . . . Mine nah-me ist . . .

Phrases	Italian	Portuguese
Hello	Buongiorno *Bwon jorno*	Olá *O-la*
Goodbye	Arrivederci *Ar-ree-vay-der-chee*	Adeus *A-day-oosh*
Thank you	Grazie *Grats-yay*	Obrigado(a) *Oh-bree-gah-doo(-duh)*
How are you?	Come sta? *Ko-may sta?*	Como está? *Koh-moo shta?*
Fine, thanks. And you?	Bene, grazie. E Lei? *Benay, grats-yay. Ay lay?*	Bem, obrigado(a). E você? *Baym, oh-bree-gah-doo. Ay vo-say?*
Yes/No/OK/Please	Sì/No/Va bene/Per favore *See/No/Va ben-ay/Payr fa-vor-ay*	Sim/Não/Está bem/Por favor *Seem/Now/shta Naym/Poor fa-vor*
Do you speak English?	Parla inglese? *Par-la een-glay-say?*	Fala inglês? *Fah-luh een-glesh?*
Happy birthday!	Buon compleanno! *Bwon kom-play-an-no!*	Feliz aniversário! *Fuh-leesh a-nee-ver-sar-yoo!*
Happy new year!	Buon anno! *Bwon an-no!*	Feliz ano novo! *Fuh-leesh ah-noo noh-voo!*
I love you	Ti amo *Tee a-mo*	Te-amo *Tay a-mo*
No way! That's stupid.	Neanche per sogno! Ciò è stupido. *Nay-an-kay pair sog-no . Chi-o ay stoo-pee-do.*	Nenhuma maneira! É estúpido. *Nay-u-ma ma-nay-ra. Ay es-shtu-pee-do.*
My name is . . .	Mi chiamo . . . *Mee kee-amo . . .*	Me chamo . . . *Muh shah-moo . . .*

Spanish	Polish
Hola *o-la*	Dzień dobry *Dzhehn do-bri*
Adiós *Ad-yos*	Do widzenia *Do vee-dzeh-nya*
Gracias *Gras-yas*	Dziękuję *Djen-koo-yeh*
¿Cómo está? *¿Co-mo es-ta?*	Jak się masz? *Yahk syeh mahsh?*
Muy bien, gracias. ¿Y usted? *Mwee byen, gras-yas. ¿Y oo-sted?*	Dobrze, dziękuię. A ty? *Dob-zheh dzehn-koo-yeh. Ah ti?*
Si/No/Está bien/Por favor *See/No/Esta byen/Por fav-or*	Tak/Nie/Dobrze/Proszę *Tahk/Nyeh/Dob-zheh/Pro-sheh*
¿Habla usted inglés? *¿A-bla oosted een-gles?*	Czy mówisz po angielsku? *Chi moo-veesh po ahn-gyehl-skoo?*
¡Feliz cumpleaños! *¡Fe-leez koom-ple-anyos!*	Wszystkiego najlepszego! *Fshist-kyeh-go nigh-lehp-shay-go!*
¡Feliz año nuevo! *¡Fe-leez an-yo nway-bo!*	Szczęśliwego Nowego Roku! *Shchen-shlee-veh-go no-veh-go ro-koo!*
Te amo *Tay a-mo*	Kocham Cię *Ko-hahm tsyeh*
¡No lo hago! Es tonto. *¡No lo ah-go! Es ton-to.*	Daj spokój! Nie wygłupiaj sie. *Da spo-kooy! Nyeh vi-gwoop-yigh syeh.*
Me llamo . . . *Me ya-mo . . .*	Nazywam się . . . *Nahs zi-vahm syeh . . .*

EXTRAORDINARY STORIES – PART FIVE: FRANCIS PEGAHMAGABOW

ONE OF THE GREAT but largely unsung Canadian heroes of the First World War was sniper and scout Francis Pegahmagabow. Pegahmagabow, an Ojibwa Indian, was the most highly decorated First Nations soldier in Canadian history and reputedly World War I's best sniper. The road to Pegahmagabow's wartime glory was not easy – yet some of his early hardships may have been just the thing that made him such an extraordinary soldier.

Francis Pegahmagabow was born in March 1888, on what is now the Shawanaga First Nations Reserve, just north of Parry Sound, Ontario, on Lake Huron's Georgian Bay. When Francis was about three years old, his father died and his mother returned farther north to her family.

Not much is known about Francis' childhood, but it's very likely that his early days were difficult and lonely. He lived in a variety of homes, with different families, sometimes working to earn his keep. In the years that followed, he would always describe himself as an orphan, and when he joined the military, he told officials that he had no family. Perhaps from necessity, Francis developed an intense independence and self-reliance at an early age. Even as a young man, he impressed many with his passion and his drive, including a local Crown attorney who helped him in his bid to return to school for five months at the age of twenty-four to complete his education. As Pegahmagabow's son would later say, "He seemed to thrive on his own determination."

This determination led him to a job as a seaman and marine fireman on a ship that travelled through the Great Lakes, delivering supplies to lighthouse keepers. During one of these voyages, he met an old Ojibwa man along the shores of Lake Superior who gave him a small bag made of hide, tied with a leather thong. About the mysterious contents of the bag, Pegahmagabow said, "Sometimes it seemed to be hard as a rock, at other times it appeared to contain nothing. What was really inside it I do not know." The Ojibwa elder told Pegahmagabow that he would soon be in great danger, and the tiny medicine bag would keep him safe. It would prove to be an uncanny prediction.

In the summer of 1914, tensions in Europe erupted, with Austria and Germany declaring war on Serbia and then Russia, France and Italy. Britain and her colonies then declared war on Germany on August 4, 1914. Pegahmagabow didn't hesitate. On August 13, he enlisted in the Northern Pioneers Battalion in Parry Sound. Perhaps the young man was looking for adventure. Perhaps he wanted to stake his own claim on family glory – his grandfather had been a warrior and a chief and had fought for the British in the War of 1812. Pegahmagabow might have hoped to prove himself a fearless soldier like his grandfather. Or perhaps he was still thinking of a childhood dream he had had. The Ojibwa believed that the dreams children had at night carried great meaning and could impart warnings. When Pegahmagabow was about seven, his foster parents had him swallow a little gunpowder in the hopes that this would make his soul more open to visiting spirits. It seemed to work. Sometime later, he had a dream in which a spirit assured him that he would be a great man and would save his tribes from slavery.

Whatever his motives, Pegahmagabow, or "Peggy" as his fellow soldiers called him, didn't have long to wait until he could prove himself on the battlefield. After landing in Europe in February 1915, Pegahmagabow's unit immediately joined the dangerous and horrific struggle on the front lines. Fighting on the Western Front in Europe (which stretched from the North Sea all the way to Switzerland) took place mostly in trenches dug into the soft mud. The tops of the trenches were lined with sandbags, the bottoms filled with water over which boards were placed so the men could walk from trench to trench. The air was filled with the stench of foul water, rotting corpses, human waste and explosives. Sniper fire, shells and the screams of men tore through the air. In order to gain territory, the opposing armies had to leave the trenches and expose themselves to bullets and shells on the bomb-blasted fields. Typically, hundreds of lives were lost for every few metres of territory an army was able to advance. After only a few months of living and fighting in these nightmarish conditions, Pegahmagabow and his unit joined the entire Canadian Division as it marched to Ypres in Belgium. In the ensuing battle, the German enemy unleashed a new and deadly weapon – chlorine gas. The gas poisoned the soldiers, burning their eyes and lungs. Many died in agony and others were maimed for life by the chemical. Pegahmagabow, however, survived this initial battle.

He and the 1st and 4th Canadian battalions were then ordered to join the French in a counterattack on the German army a short distance away. The French

army did not arrive in time, and the Canadians were brutally attacked by German fire. At least 400 Canadian soldiers – almost half of the entire battalion – were killed or wounded, but Pegahmagabow, the small medicine bag securely hanging from his neck, once again escaped with his life. By August of 1812, having survived many more battles, Pegahmagabow earned his first stripe and was promoted to lance corporal.

During these early battles, Pegahmagabow had exhibited exceptional fearlessness. While primitive wireless communications and field telephones had been used in the First World War, communication between units was nevertheless largely dependent on "scouts," soldiers who could make their way through the tunnels and trenches (often close to or through enemy lines) to deliver information to a neighbouring unit. The citation for Pegahmagabow's first medal acknowledged his work as a scout: "He carried messages with great bravery and success during the whole of the actions at Ypres, Festubert and Givenchy. In all his work he has consistently shown a disregard for danger and his faithfulness to duty is highly commendable." A later commendation for his accomplishments during the battle at Passchendaele provided more details: "This NCO [non-commissioned officer] did excellent work. Before and after the attack, he kept in touch with the flanks, advising the units he had seen, this information proving the success of the attack. . . . He also guided the relief to its proper place after it had become mixed up." And in recommending Pegahmagabow for his third medal, his commanding officer wrote, "During the operations . . . at Orix Trench . . . when his company were almost out of ammunition and in danger of being surrounded, this NCO went over the top under heavy MG (machine gun) and rifle fire and brought back sufficient ammunition to enable the post to carry on and assist in repulsing heavy enemy counterattacks."

But in these first months as a soldier, Pegahmagabow also proved that he had the skills to be more than just an excellent scout – his independence, stealth and marksmanship made him a very effective sniper. The role of a sniper or sharpshooter was very different from that of the regular infantry. The sniper, often with another soldier who would act as a spotter, advanced, usually under cover of darkness, until he was as close to the enemy line as possible. After crawling his way through the mud, he would have to find a good place to hide – a bomb crater or an abandoned trench, for example. The most important thing for a sniper's success was that his exact location could not be discovered by the enemy – a sniper and his spotter had to be masters of camouflage. From their hidden position, the sniper and spotter would watch the enemy's movements. They would try to collect information about what the enemy was doing and planning. They also looked for possible targets. They were particularly interested in wounding or killing officers and other high-ranking soldiers. Removing officers from the ranks would weaken the enemy's efforts to develop battle strategies and lead their units. But anyone who had the misfortune to make himself visible to the sniper, by raising his head above the trench walls, for example, could become a target. It was nerve-wracking for the soldiers to know that at any moment, even at night or when the battlefields were quiet, they could be gunned down by an unseen enemy.

While the sniper was able to wage psychological warfare against the enemy, in part because his foe did not know where he was, his job was extremely risky. If his location was spotted, he was close enough that all the enemy had to do was launch a shell in his direction and he would likely be killed. He could also be killed by enemy snipers. What's more, given that he was hunkered down between the two enemy lines – in "no man's land" – he could easily be trapped there as the armies advanced and the fighting engulfed his position. Shells and artillery fire from his own side could rain down on him. But this wasn't all that challenged a sniper. Sharpshooters and scouts spent days on end by themselves, marooned in no man's land. The isolation and boredom were intense. And snipers like Pegahmagabow were truly on their own. Cut off from any communication with their battalions, snipers were responsible for making their own way back to the rest of the troops for food or rest. If they were out of touch for too long, they could even be left behind if their battalions got orders to move on.

There are few soldiers who are cut out to be snipers. But Pegahmagabow took to the challenges of the job with enthusiasm. Perhaps because he had hunted game since he was a small boy, his marksmanship was deadly accurate. Over the course of his years of fighting, Pegahmagabow killed 378 enemy soldiers, making him one of the twentieth century's greatest snipers. And his years of independence and reliance on his own resourcefulness seemed to have prepared him for his solitary journeys through no man's lines, and even behind enemy lines. In fact, he seemed to delight in his abilities to move about like a ghost. Years after he had returned from the war, he would tell listeners of the thrill he got from sneaking into the enemy trenches and rubbing shoulders with Germans while they remained oblivious to his presence. At the Battle of Mount Sorrel in June 1916, he captured many soldiers. By war's end, he was responsible for capturing over 300 German soldiers.

Not only was Pegahmagabow an extraordinary sniper and scout, he also proved to be a tough, resilient combatant. After being wounded badly in the leg during the Battle of the Somme in July 1916, he was sent to England to recover. Despite the severe wound, which very nearly resulted in his leg being amputated, he petitioned to be sent back to the battlefield. He also returned to fighting after a bad bout of pneumonia. As a result of his dedication, Pegahmagabow became one of the few Canadian soldiers who fought more or less consistently for the entire length of the First World War.

By the time Pegahmagabow returned home to Canada, he had survived some of the First World War's most spectacular battles and had distinguished himself as a scout and sniper, as well as a soldier whom his fellow infantrymen liked and depended on. About the battle at Passchendaele, he wrote, "I had no relatives at home. I was only fighting for my comrades."

❀

On a warm August day in 1919, Ojibwa Francis Pegahmagabow stood along with 200 soldiers on the parade grounds of the Canadian National Exhibition grounds. The Prince of Wales (future King Edward VIII) was making his way down the ranks, congratulating the men and giving out commendations for excellence on the battlefields of Europe. When Prince Edward approached Francis, he pinned on him a Military Medal (the third-highest commendation awarded) and two bars, making Pegahmagabow the most decorated Native soldier in Canadian history. Sadly, this war-hero glory did not last long. When Pegahmagabow returned to the Parry Island area, he was treated like any ordinary "Indian" would have been at the time, which is to say not well at all. He was repeatedly refused loans under the Soldier Settlement Act of 1919, which he had sought to establish his own farm. (The agent in charge of loans thought that Pegahmagabow wouldn't make a good farmer, even though he had already cleared 10 acres by hand and put up a stable.) Pegahmagabow was, therefore, forced to live in poverty on the reserve. From 1921 to 1925, he was Chief of the Parry Island band, and he served as a band councillor as well some years later. But his post-war experiences made him increasingly bitter about how Native Canadians were treated. He spent most of the years after returning to Canada struggling with the government over the treatment of Native Canadians and speaking out on Native rights. He died on August 5, 1952, on the Parry Island Reserve.

Despite the poor treatment Pegahmagabow received in his later years, his exceptional war record is indisputable, and his legacy continues to be one of bravery, dedication and truly remarkable skill.

MARBLES

THE ROMANS played marbles. They were made from stone, clay or marble (aha!), though marble marbles were the most accurate. These days, glass and china marbles are still available in most toy shops. Do not be deceived: the version of marbles called Ring Taw can be frustrating and demanding – but it is the best. All you need is a flat surface, a bit of chalk, a bag of marbles – and a competitive streak.

We thought about trying to make a couple of marbles, but the temperatures involved would have meant you reading something called *The Suicidal Book for Boys*. Molten glass has different-coloured glass injected into it before being cut into cylinders and dropped into a rolling tray where the marble rolls itself to perfection.

Marble Names

Any marble you use to take a shot is called a **Shooter**, or a **Taw**. For the rest, there are as many names as kinds of marble. Some of the better-known examples are: Ordinaries, Oilies, Chinas and Dobbers.

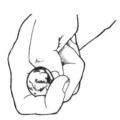

Fulking

Fulking is the name of the classic schoolboy technique for shooting.

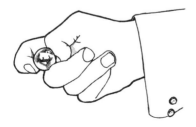

The professionals, however, (and they do exist) use "**knuckling down**." Greater accuracy is possible with that steering finger, though we liked the one we remembered from school. With fulking, there's a danger of letting it fall out and roll across the circles, which can be embarrassing. This can also lose you the game.

The Three Games You Need to Know
Ring Taw

1. Draw two circles in chalk, as you see below. The small one is 30 centimetres across, or a ruler's length. The larger one is 1.83 metres (6 ft) across. Remember that the distance from your elbow to your wrist is roughly 30 centimetres (unless you are tiny, obviously). Otherwise, find someone who is 183 centimetres (6 ft) tall and ask them to mark out the circle using the distance between their outstretched arms, which will also be 183 centimetres.

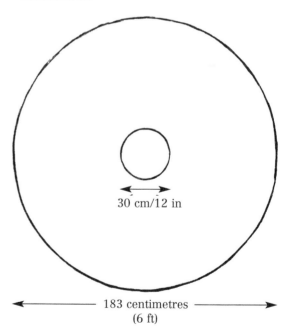

30 cm/12 in

←——————— 183 centimetres ———————→
(6 ft)

2. Choose which marbles will be risked from each bag – equal numbers from each player.

This is a skill game – it doesn't matter which ones you lose or win, just how many. Put them in the inner circle. We found tactical placing of one at a time worked well, taking it in turns.

3. The Taw can never be lost. It can be a personal favourite, a rare one, metal, marble, china, glass or even wood. Practise with your Taw and never allow it to be a stake in the game.
4. Decide who is going first.
5. First shot. The aim is to shoot the Taw from any point on the outer ring at the ones in the centre. Any marbles knocked out of the inner circle are pocketed by the shooter, who then takes a second turn, unless the Taw has vanished inexplicably. If you *can* find it, shoot from where it lies.
6. If you miss, or fail to knock one out of the inner circle, play passes to the next player. If your Taw stops in the outer circle, it stays where it is for Rule 7. If it stops in the *inner* circle, it must be bought out with a replacement marble from the offending player.
7. When a Taw is stuck in the outer circle, it becomes a target. The next player can choose to go for the centre or the Taw. If he hits the Taw, he has to be given a marble by the owner. He may not strike it twice. If *his* Taw gets stuck, play moves on again.
8. The game continues until the inner circle is clear.

Bounce About

This game is a throwing rather than shooting game – the marbles are in the air during the shot. Bigger marbles are better for this game.

1. The first player throws his marble forward about 150 centimetres (5 ft).
2. The second player does the same, trying to hit the first marble. (Other players can hit either and so on. This can be played by quite a few.)

3 All shots are underhand and from where the Shooter lands.
4 If a marble is hit, the owner either loses it or pays a marble forfeit from the bag. It's better to pay the forfeit so as not to lose your Taw.

That's it. All the tactics come from the play.

Hundreds

This is a surprisingly addictive accuracy game for two players.

1. Draw a small chalk circle – diameter 30 centimetres (12 in).
2. Both players shoot a marble at the circle from an agreed distance.
3. Both in or both out gets nothing.
4. One in the circle earns ten points and another turn.
5. First to a hundred wins.

Fouls

1. In Ring Taw, the shooter's knuckle must touch the outer circle. Lifting is a foul.
2. "Fudging" is pushing the hand forward – and a foul. The marble must be shot with the thumb alone.
3. After the game has begun, no contact with marbles in the inner circle is allowed, except by the Taw.

The world championship is played every year in Tinsley Green, West Sussex, England. In essence, it is Ring Taw, with forty-nine marbles in the inner ring, worth a point each. The winner is the first to knock out twenty-five with the Taw.

Playing marbles is not about how many marbles you can buy. It's about the ones you win and lose – it's about skill and your Taw.

A BRIEF HISTORY OF ARTILLERY

The ability to strike an enemy from far away has always appealed to soldiers and generals alike. Bows have been found from as early as 7,400 BC, preserved in a bog at Holmegaard, Denmark. They may go back as far as 20,000 BC. Though such weapons were powerful and accurate, there has always been a search for more destruction and greater range. A city cannot be battered into submission by archers, after all.

The Meare Heath yew bow from Somerset, England – dated to circa 2500 BC.

Archimedes is one of the most famous early inventors of artillery weapons. In the defence of Syracuse in 214 to 212 BC, he used bronze mirrors to focus the sun and burn enemy ships.

The truth of this story was doubted for a long time. In the early 1970s, a Greek scientist, Dr. Ioannis Sakkas, employed sixty Greek sailors in an experiment to see whether it was possible. All the men carried large oblong mirrors and used them to focus the sun onto a wooden ship about fifty metres away. The ship caught fire almost immediately.

Archimedes was an extraordinary thinker, the Leonardo da Vinci of an earlier age. He invented a number of other artillery weapons to sink Roman galleys, or hammer them from the city walls. He was not alone, however. The Greeks developed knowledge of pulleys, water pumps, cranes, even a small steam engine. It was a period of extraordinary scientific advancement – all of which was useful in creating weapons of long-distance destruction.

Early weapons were based on the spring power of a bow arm, pulled back by muscle or by a ratchet, as in this picture. Understanding pulleys in particular means that a man can repeat an easy action over and over to move large forces very slowly. In other words, heavy weapons can be wound back with the use of a few simple principles.

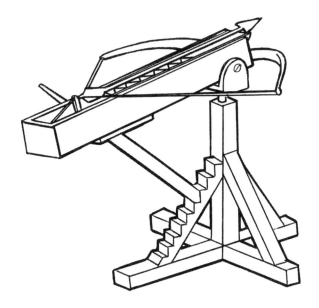

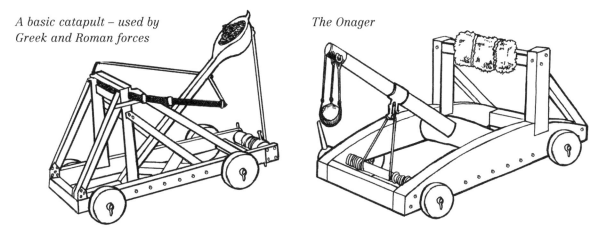

A basic catapult – used by Greek and Roman forces

The Onager

Torsion is the force gained by twisting. The Romans improved on Greek inventions, perfecting the use of ropes of woven horsehair and sinew as their spring. The heavy Roman **Onager** was capable of sending a 45-kilogram (100-lb) rock up to 365 metres (400 yd). An "Onager" is Latin for a wild ass or donkey – with a fearsome kick. It is similar in principle to the catapult, with a sling-like cup and a single torsion bar.

The **Ballista** was a Roman bolt or stone shooter. It used two torsion springs and had a range of up to 411 metres (450 yd). The Romans also perfected a *repeating* ballista, invented by Dionysios of Alexandria. By simply winding a handle, the ratchet came back, an arrow dropped into place and was fired as soon as the winch reached its maximum point. This was the first machine gun – long before gunpowder.

Every Roman legion carried heavy onagers and thirty **Scorpion** bows – a smaller form of the weapon that could be carried on a single cart. Roman success in war depended on much more than discipline and a good gladius!

The last type of this sort of engine is a **Trebuchet**, powered by counterweights. This form of artillery was able to launch heavier weights than any other kind. However, the enormous counterweight needed meant that they were practically immobile once set up and worked well only

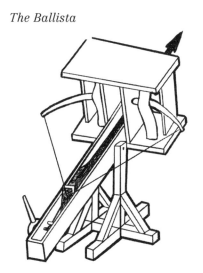

The Ballista

The Trebuchet

when battering city walls. They were in use throughout medieval times until the invention of cannon. Pulleys and ratchets were used to pull down the arm and load it. When released, the arm snapped forward and the second section whipped over at high speed.

Later, gunpowder and iron-foundry techniques combined to create smooth-bore cannons. Compared with early engines of war, these had a much longer range and were faster to load. Although China had gunpowder in the eleventh century, it was European countries that really exploited its use as a propellant in the thirteenth century. Roger Bacon, the English Archimedes, wrote down a formula for gunpowder in code in the thirteenth century. The combination of sulphur, charcoal and potassium nitrate, or saltpetre, would change the Western world.

The picture above is of "Mons Meg," a Flanders cannon cast before 1489 and currently kept in Edinburgh castle. It fired a stone ball of 150 kilograms (330 lb) more than 2.4 kilometres (1.5 miles).

For the next 600 years, cannons would remain essentially the same – smooth-bore muzzle loaders, lit by a taper or a flint-lock. Iron balls would be used instead of stone as they were easier to mass-produce and make uniform. Cast-iron barrels took the place of softer wrought iron. Cannons at sea could fire chain, or bar shot to destroy enemy rigging and clear the decks of boarding parties. In the basic principles, though, Nelson's cannons fired in the same way as those from the thirteenth century. As with most long-lasting technologies, if they weren't replaced, they were perfected.

Mortars and **Howitzers** were also perfected during the nineteenth century. A mortar fires at very high angles compared with a cannon, a howitzer between the two. Progress was fast and furious as a single clear advantage could mean the difference between winning a war and being invaded.

Types of Royal Navy Bar and Chain Shot

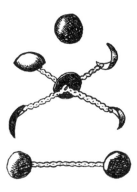

World War I British field piece, firing twenty-seven-kilogram explosive shells.

Rifling a barrel involves casting spiralling lines inside that make the ball or shell spin as it leaves, giving gyroscopic stability. Although it had long been in use for hand weapons, the practice was first applied to artillery around 1860. The new breed of artillery would be breech-loading, have reinforced barrels and be able to fire shells with astonishing accuracy.

The heaviest versions of these shell-firing weapons could be miles behind the lines, firing huge shells in a parabola (arc) at the enemy positions.

The twenty-first century – British Challenger 2 tank.

No chapter on artillery could be complete without a mention of **tanks**. From World War I onward, these awesome machines have changed the face of warfare by allowing powerful artillery to be extremely mobile and well armoured.

In modern times, artillery can take the form of inter-continental missiles, striking from hundreds or even thousands of miles away and with a greater force than anything else in this chapter. In a sense, artillery has reached its ultimate stage, where cities can be flattened without a single soldier entering the combat zone.

Shells can now be armoured in "depleted uranium" – uranium with most of the radioactive isotopes removed. This is a heavy metal and hard enough to be ferociously efficient as an armour-piercing round. Though it is actually less radioactive than naturally occurring uranium, it is chemically toxic and should not be ingested. Dust and fragments from DU shells remain dangerous for a very long time.

We have come a long way from bow-based spring weapons. Until the invention of the machine gun, it was still possible to march into cannon fire and expect at least some of your army to reach the enemy. World War I changed that, the obsolete tactic going the way of the cavalry charge. It is difficult to predict the course of the future, with such immensely powerful weapons now available. Wars nowadays tend to be fought on a small scale, with major players being very careful to limit the destruction. In theory, Britain could have dropped nuclear weapons on Argentina during the Falklands War, or the U.S. on Iraq in the first or second Gulf War. Neither country took that step. Let us hope it does not happen in our lifetimes.

THE ORIGIN OF WORDS

ENGLISH IS AWASH with interesting words and phrases; there are books the size of dictionaries chock-full of them. Here are twenty of our favourites – words and phrases with origins so interesting they should be part of general knowledge.

1. **Boycott**. Captain Charles Cunningham Boycott was a rent-collecting agent for an English landlord in Ireland in the nineteenth century. He was considered particularly harsh and locals refused to have anything to do with him. His name became a word meaning "to ostracize." It is used as a verb – "to boycott," and as a noun – "the boycott went well."

2. **Hallowe'en**. "Hallow" is an old pronunciation of "holy," still sometimes found in the alternative version, "All Hallows Eve." The "-e'en" part is a common contraction of the word "evening." Hallowe'en means "Holy evening" – also known as "All Saints Eve."

3. **Canuck**. An informal nickname for a Canadian, as in, "That boy is a proud Canuck, and he sure loves hockey!" There are several theories about the origins of the term. Some say it dates back to 1835 and was used by Americans to describe French-Canadian loggers in U.S. lumber camps. Others connect the word to the Iroquoian *kanuchsa*, meaning "hut," or to Connaught, the surname of many early Irish immigrants to Canada. Johnny Canuck, a cartoon character developed in 1902 who rebelled against Uncle Sam (an American cartoon character), has come to personify all things Canadian.

4. **Hooligan**. Almost certainly derived from the surname of an Irish family, "Houlihan," whose name became synonymous with bad behaviour in the late nineteenth century.

5. **Thug**. One of many Hindi words adopted into English (like "pyjamas" and "bungalow"). The "thugs" were a sect of robbers and murderers in India.

6. **Toque** A toque, sometimes spelled "tuque," is a winter hat in Canada, but not in many other places. When the word first appeared in the sixteenth century, it meant small cap. But most of the world doesn't recognize the term, so it's a good way to spot fellow Canucks

7. **Assassin**. The Arabic word *hashshashin*, meaning "hashish eaters," was the name given to a violent Syrian sect in the Middle Ages. To create a murderous frenzy, they took hashish (cannabis) amid chanting and dancing. The English word "assassin" ultimately derives from this.

8. **Whisky**. From the Gaelic *uisge beatha* (Ishka Ba-ha), meaning "water of life." Other languages use very similar phrases – *aquavit* for strong spirit in Scandinavia, *eau-de-vie* for brandy in France, *aqua vitae* in Latin. *Vodka* is Russian for "little water."

9. **Tawdry**. Means cheap and flashy. This word comes from the phrase "Saint Audrey's lace." St. Audrey was a seventh-century princess of East Anglia who took religious orders. As a girl, she had been very fond of necklaces, and when she succumbed to a throat disease, she felt it was punishment for her vanity. "St. Audrey's lace" or "Tawdry lace" was tainted, or flawed, and came to mean flashy and poor quality.

10. **Hat trick**. Possibly a term that was imported from the game of cricket, a hat trick is when a hockey player scores three goals in the same game. In the 1940s, haberdashers in Toronto and Montreal would give players brand new hats for scoring three goals. Fans soon followed suit and threw their hats on the ice. The fastest hat trick in NHL history? Chicago Blackhawk Bill Mosienko scored three goals in twenty-one seconds in 1952.

11. **Exchequer**. In Norman England, money-counting tables were often covered in a checkered cloth. The practice was common enough for the table to become known as an *eschequier*, meaning "chessboard," and the word transferred to English as "exchequer," a word for the treasury.

12. **Auspicious/augury**. In English, the words have to do with telling the future. "It seemed an auspicious moment to apply for his job, when Jenkins fell down the well." Both have their roots in the Roman practice of using the flight of birds to tell the future. An expert in this field was known as an *auspex*, derived from a combination of *avis*, meaning "bird," and *specere*, "to look." These charlatans were literally "lookers at birds," and the word survives 2,000 years on.

13. **Chivalry**. The moral code of knights, who tended to ride horses. The name is derived from the French word for horse, *cheval*, which in turn comes from the Latin *caballus*. "Cavalier," meaning off-hand or "too casual" (a cavalier attitude), also comes from the same root.

14. **Chortle**. A word invented by Lewis Carroll (writer of *Alice in Wonderland*) as a combination of "chuckle" and "snort." This type of combination is known as a "portmanteau" word. He also invented the word "portmanteau" to describe words of this type, like "brunch," which is a combination of "breakfast" and "lunch." Clever man.

15. **Conspire/Expire/Respire**. All these words have their origin in the Latin, *spirare*, to breathe. Conspirators breathe their plots together. A man who "expires" has the breath go out of him. Respiration is breath.

16. **Denim**. This is one of many products linked to its place of origin. The hard-wearing cloth was created in Nîmes, a southern French industrial town. It was known first as *serge de Nîmes* and then as *de Nîmes*.

17. **Laconic**. The region inhabited by the Spartans of ancient Greece was named Laconia. Philip of Macedonia (the father of Alexander the Great) sent this warning to the famous warriors of the city, to frighten them into obedience: "If I enter Laconia with my army, I shall raze Sparta to the ground." The Spartans replied with a single word : "If." "Laconic" means terse, or to the point, in recognition of the Spartan style. The word "Spartan," meaning bare and without ornamentation, also comes from that warrior culture.

18. **Shambles**. Although it is now used to mean a chaotic scene, this word originally meant a slaughterhouse. In fact, reference to the fact that shambles were relocated after the great fire of London in 1666 can be found on Christopher Wren's Monument (next to Monument subway station in London). The word origin goes even further back to Old English for a table, *scamul*, which is connected with the Latin for "bench," *scamnum*. Rows of these would form a meat market.

19. **Mob**. This word is simply a contraction of the Latin phrase *mobile vulgus* (MOB-e-lay, VULG-ous). *Mobile* means fickle and *vulgus* means crowd.

20. **Quick**. In Old English, *cwic* meant "alive," a meaning we still see in "quicksilver," another name for mercury, as the liquid metal seems almost to be a living silver. You may also have heard the phrase, "the quick and the dead," meaning "the living and the dead," or "cut to the quick," meaning "cut to the living flesh." "Quick-tempered" also retains some sense of the original meaning, though the modern meaning has mainly to do with speed alone.

THE SOLAR SYSTEM
(A QUICK REFERENCE GUIDE)

THE SUN. THE CENTRE OF THE SYSTEM

- 149 million kilometres from Earth (93 million miles).

- The sun alone makes up 98 percent of all the mass of the solar system. If it were hollow, it would take 1.3 million Earths to fill it. The temperature on the surface is a mere 6,000 °C/ (11,000 °F), while the internal temperature is 15 million °C (27 million °F).

- Age: Best current guess is 4.6 billion years. We expect it to survive for another 5 billion years before becoming a red giant, then a white dwarf, before finally burning out. Do not worry about this – Earth and everything else in the solar system will be destroyed during the red giant stage.

MERCURY

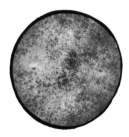

- Mercury is the closest planet to the sun, at only 57 million kilometres (36 million miles). It is the second smallest in the system. The surface is cratered in a similar way to Earth's moon. There *is* a thin atmosphere, containing sodium and potassium from the crust of the planet. Most of Mercury seems to be an iron core.

- Temperature: Hot. 430 °C (810 °F) by day, −180 °C (−290 °F) by night.

- Rotation around sun (Mercury's year): 87.97 days. This is the fastest in the solar system and as a result, Mercury was named after the Roman messenger to the gods, who had wings on his feet.

- Moons: None.

VENUS

- The second planet from the sun, at an average 108 million kilometres (67 million miles). Venus has been called the morning or evening star, also Hesperus and Lucifer. Venus is the brightest object in Earth's sky apart from the sun and our moon.

- Venus can be seen crossing the sun in 2012. If you miss that one, you'll have to wait until 2117, which is quite a long time. Remember that pinhole or reverse projection from a telescope is a good idea when looking at the sun – **never** look at it directly, especially with a telescope. The sun would be the last thing you ever see.

- Rotation around sun (Venus year): 224.7 days.

- Moons: None.

- Atmosphere: Complete cloud cover resulting from 97 percent carbon dioxide, the rest nitrogen. Hostile to life as we know it. Surface pressure 96 times that of Earth, so before you could even begin to choke, you'd be squashed flat. The average surface temperature is 482 °C (900 °F). Uncomfortable, to say the least.

- Venus was named after the Roman goddess of love because lonely men sitting in observatories can be quite susceptible to shiny, pretty things in the sky. Its movement across the heavens has nothing to do with actual love, however.

EARTH

- The third planet from the sun, at 149 million kilometres (93 million miles).

- Like baby bear's porridge, Earth is neither too hot nor too cold. It is *just right* to harbour life. Its atmosphere is made of nitrogen, oxygen, 0.03 percent carbon dioxide and trace gases, such as argon.

- Earth is the fifth-largest planet in the system. It has a magnetic field and a liquid nickel-iron core.

- Rotation around the sun (Earth year): 365.25 days.

- It has an elliptical orbit that means the sun to Earth distance varies from 146 to 152 million kilometres (91 to 95 million miles) at different times. Earth rotates on the same plane as nearly all of the other planets in the system, as if they are embedded in the surface of an invisible plate. Very neat. We call it home.

- Moons: One, which rotates around Earth in 27.3 days. With an astonishing lack of imagination, we call it "the moon."

MARS

- Fourth planet from the sun, at an average of 226 million kilometres (141 million miles).

- Gravity: One third that of Earth's.

- No significant magnetic field, which suggests the core is now solid, though it may have been liquid in the past.

- Rotation around sun: 686.98 days.

- Average temperature: –55 °C (–67 °F).

- Mars has ice caps at both north and south poles, made up of water ice and frozen carbon dioxide. It has an atmosphere of 95 percent carbon dioxide, 3 percent nitrogen and 2 percent argon and trace gases. Like Earth, it is tilted on its polar axis and experiences seasons, which can involve ferocious dust storms. Despite various probes and landings, we have yet to set foot on the red planet.

- Moons: Two, named Phobos (Fear) and Deimos (Panic). Mars was named after the Roman god of war. The Greek version of Mars was the god, Ares, who had two sons. The moons are named after them.

JUPITER

- The fifth planet from the sun, at an average: 778 million kilometres (484 million miles).

- Jupiter is by far the largest planet in the solar system and the fourth brightest thing in our sky, after the sun, the moon and Venus. It takes twelve years to orbit the sun. It is sometimes called the amateur's planet, because it can be found easily with a basic telescope, or even binoculars.

- We haven't been to Jupiter and we probably never will – so our knowledge is based on observation and the occasional orbiter and probe. Science means we are not blind, however. For example, an effect of gravity is that it causes a passing object to accelerate, which is why you will occasionally see film sequences of spaceships using a "slingshot around the sun" effect. The increase in speed can be measured and compared to other figures we already know. Piece by piece, we build up a picture of a planet – even one where the pressure and gravity is so crushing that we are unlikely ever to ever get a probe down to the surface.

- Jupiter's mass can be predicted from its effect on its moons – 318 times that of Earth. However, if Jupiter were hollow, more than a thousand Earths could fit inside, which means it must be composed of much lighter gaseous elements. This was confirmed by the *Galileo* probe in 1995, which dropped into the outer reaches of the atmosphere and found them composed of helium, hydrogen, ammonia and methane. In many ways, Jupiter is a failed sun – 80 times too small to ignite.

- Beneath the gas layers, pressure increases to more than three million Earth atmospheres. At that level, even hydrogen has properties of a metal and Jupiter has a solid core that must be one of the most hostile places imaginable. Winds there will range up to 644 kph (400 mph) and at those pressures, the chemistry of the universe that we think we understand will be completely alien. At temperatures of between –121 and –163 °C (–186 to –261 °F), ammonia will fall as white snow.

- Moons: Around sixty-one, with a faint ring of debris. There are hundreds, perhaps thousands, of rocks orbiting Jupiter. Whether they are referred to as moons or not is a matter of opinion. Galileo discovered the four largest in 1610. They are: Io, Europa, Ganymede and Callisto. Given their size, they deserve a special mention. They are named after lovers of the chief god of the Greeks, Zeus, whom the Romans called Jupiter.

  1. **Io**. The closest to Jupiter, pronounced "eye-oh." It has a diameter of 3,125 kilometres (1,942 miles), a little less than the Earth's moon. It is intensely volcanic and its closeness to Jupiter's magnetic field generates three million electrical amps that flow into Jupiter's ionos-phere. It orbits Jupiter in 1.77 days, at a distance of 354,000 kilometres (220,000 miles).

2. **Europa**. The smoothest object in the solar system. It takes 3.55 days to orbit Jupiter. Its surface is ice, but a weak magnetic field of its own may indicate that there is liquid salt water below the surface. It has a diameter of just over 3,155 kilometres (1,961 miles). Europa orbits Jupiter at a mean distance of 670,000 kilometres (420,000 miles).

3. **Ganymede**. The largest moon of Jupiter and the largest moon in the solar system, with a diameter of 5,471 kilometres (3,400 miles). It orbits Jupiter at a mean distance of 1,068,000 kilometres (664,000 miles), taking 7.15 Earth days. Ganymede is larger than Mercury.

4. **Callisto**. The last of the Galilean moons. It has a diameter of 4,828 kilometres (3,000 miles) and orbits at 1,880,000 kilometres (1,170,000 miles) from Jupiter. It is similar in size to Mercury and orbits in 16.7 Earth days.

SATURN

- The sixth planet out from the Sun, at 1,377 billion kilometres (856 million miles).

- Like Jupiter, it is a gas planet, with atmospheric pressure condensing hydrogen into liquid and even metal toward the core. Still, we think the overall density would be low enough for Saturn to float on water. It takes 29.5 years to orbit the sun.

- The atmosphere is composed of 88 percent hydrogen, 11 percent helium and traces of methane, ammonia and other gases. Wind speeds on the surface are more than 1,600 kph (1,000 mph).

- The rings stretch out more than 135,000 kilometres (84,000 miles) from Saturn's centre. They were first seen by Galileo in 1610, though he described them as handles, as he saw them end on. The Dutch astronomer, Christiaan Huygens was the first to recognize them as rings, separate from the planetary surface.

- Temperature: –130 °C (–202 °F) to –191 °C (–312 °F). (Very cold!)

- Moons: Quite a large number if you count very small pieces of rock, but there are fifteen reasonably sized moons, ranging from Titan, the largest (second only to Ganymede in the solar system and even possessing a thin atmosphere), down to Pan, which is about 20 kilometres (12.5 miles) across. The NASA probe *Huygens* landed on Titan in 2005.

- Saturn is the Roman name for the Greek god Cronus, who was father to Zeus.

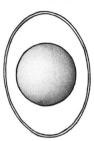

- The seventh planet from the sun, at an average distance of 2.86 *billion* kilometres (1.78 billion miles).

- It has 11 rings and more than 20 confirmed moons, though as with Saturn and Jupiter, there are probably many more we haven't spotted yet. It is 67 times bigger than Earth, but has a mass only 14.5 times that of Earth, qualifying it for gas giant status, though on a smaller scale to Saturn and Jupiter.

- The space probe *Voyager 2* reached Uranus in 1986, our only source of knowledge at the time of writing, apart from Earth observation.

- Rotation around sun: Eighty-four Earth years, though it spins on its own axis even faster than Earth – 17.25 hours.

- Uranus has an atmosphere of 83 percent hydrogen, 15 percent helium and 2 percent methane. The planet core is nothing more than rock and ice. It has a huge tilt on its polar axis, so that one pole then the other points at the sun. This means each pole receives sunlight for forty-two Earth years. Average temperature: –197 °C (–323 °F) to –220 °C (–364 °F).

- Moons: Twenty-seven. All named after Shakespeare characters, with names like Cordelia (closest), Ophelia, Bianca, Puck, Rosalind, Desdemona, and so on.

- In mythology, Uranus was the father of Saturn, grandfather to Zeus/Jupiter.

NEPTUNE

- The eighth planet from the sun at 4.5 billion kilometres (2.8 billion miles).

- Neptune is the fourth largest in the system. It has 4 rings and 11 known moons. It is the last of the gas giant or Jovian planets – 72 times Earth's volume, 17 times its mass.

- It is believed to be composed of ice around a rock core, under an atmosphere of hydrogen, helium and methane.

- Every 248 years, Pluto's erratic orbit brings it inside the shell of Neptune's orbit, making it the farthest planet from the Sun for a twenty-year period. The last time this happened was from 1979 to 1999, when Pluto moved back out. Neptune is the last of those planets that orbit on the same flat plane as Earth.

- The existence of Neptune was predicted before it was seen, like Halley's comet. The orbital track of Uranus seemed to be affected by the gravity of a large mass. The path and location of that mass were mathematically plotted, then searched for – and Neptune was found. It was first observed in 1846.

- The only vehicle from Earth to reach Neptune was *Voyager 2*, in 1989.

- Rotation around the sun: 164.79 Earth years. It has an axial tilt of 29.6° compared to Earth's 23.5°, suggesting it has a similar movement of seasons, though to be honest, it's so cold, you'd hardly notice, or care.

PLUTO

- The ninth planet from the Sun at 5.87 billion kilometres (3.65 billion miles).

- Pluto is what happens when a stray lump is slowly drawn into a neat solar system. However, Pluto is grown up enough to have a moon and has a tiny effect on the orbits of Neptune and Uranus. It is so small and distant that, even knowing it was there, it still took the telescopes of the world twenty-five years to find it for the first time in 1930. It took until 1978 for anyone to spot the single moon, Charon.

- We haven't managed to get a probe out that far, but the Hubble telescope has mapped 85 percent of Pluto's surface. It has polar caps and seems to be a ball of rock and dirty ice. It does have a thin atmosphere of nitrogen, carbon dioxide and methane.

- Being a dark and miserable place, Pluto was named after the Roman god of the Underworld (Hades to the Greeks). Charon was the boatman who ferried the souls across the River Styx.

- In 2004, Dr. Mike Brown of the California Institute of Technology announced the discovery of a tenth planet – one about three-quarters the size of Pluto, more than 134 billion kilometres (84 billion miles) away from the sun. Sedna is reddish coloured, has no moon and its classification as a planet is somewhat dubious. There are, after all, more than a few scientists who think that Pluto should be declassified, never mind this tiny lump of ice. At least Pluto has a moon.

Aɴᴅ Fɪɴᴀʟʟʏ, Cᴏᴍᴇᴛs, Asᴛᴇʀᴏɪᴅs ᴀɴᴅ ᴏᴛʜᴇʀ ᴅᴇʙʀɪs . . .

- The sun is such a massive object that its gravity affects a vast volume of space, trapping objects such as **Halley's Comet**. These tend to be dirty balls of ice, sometimes just a few miles across. Halley's was large enough to have an effect on the orbital paths of the system and Edmund Halley's achievement is that he predicted this mathematically without seeing the comet. In fact, he never saw it. It wasn't until sixteen years after his death, in 1758, that sky watchers on Earth saw the comet once more. It is visible from Earth every seventy-five to seventy-nine years and has been recorded since 240 BC. The next appearance is in 2061. It is extremely unlikely that the authors of this book will see it, but there is a chance you will . . .

- The **inner asteroid belt** lies between the orbits of Mars and Jupiter. It is composed of hundreds of thousands of rocks varying in size from grains to large ones hundreds of miles across. It may be debris from a planet-sized collision, or just the building blocks of the system, left over after everything started cooling.

- **Meteors** reach the system as it travels in space on the end of the milky way galaxy. They are usually made of stone silica, more rarely iron or nickel or a mixture of all three. They can make a bright trail as they reach Earth's atmosphere and hit friction. If they don't burn up, they can hit the planet below with more force than an atomic bomb – but that almost never happens. (See Dinosaurs.) The best time to look for them is August 9 to 16 and December 12 to 16. Meteors in the summer shower are known as the Perseids, as they appear in the constellation of Perseus. At its height, one a minute can be seen. Meteors in the winter meteor shower are known as the Geminids, as they appear in Gemini, near Orion. Both showers should be visible even from urban locations. They won't last forever – the Geminids only came into existence in 1862.

- That's it. The rest is space and cosmic radiation.

THE TEN COMMANDMENTS

———✦———

WHAT COMPILERS of modern versions of the Bible sometimes fail to appreciate is that the language of the King James Version has a grandeur, even a power, that their versions simply lack. It is no hardship to "walk through a dark valley." On the other hand, "the valley of the shadow of death" is a different matter. Frankly, the rhythm and poetry are part of the effect and not to be lightly cast aside. We can find no better example of this than the Ten Commandments themselves. Book of Exodus, Chapter 20, Verses 1–17:

And God spake all these words, saying, I am the Lord thy God, which have brought thee out of the land of Egypt, out of the house of bondage.

1. Thou shalt have no other gods before me.

2. Thou shalt not make unto thee any graven image, or any likeness of any thing that is in heaven above, or that is in the earth beneath, or that is in the water under the earth: thou shalt not bow down thyself to them, nor serve them: for I the Lord thy God am a jealous God, visiting the iniquity of the fathers upon the children unto the third and fourth generation of them that hate me; and shewing mercy unto thousands of them that love me, and keep my commandments.

3. Thou shalt not take the name of the Lord thy God in vain; for the Lord will not hold him guiltless that taketh his name in vain.

4. Remember the sabbath day, to keep it holy. Six days shalt thou labour, and do all thy work: but the seventh day is the sabbath of the Lord thy God: in it thou shalt not do any work, thou, nor thy son, nor thy daughter, thy manservant, nor thy maidservant, nor thy cattle, nor thy stranger that is within thy gates: for in six days the Lord made heaven and earth, the sea, and all that in them is, and rested the seventh day: wherefore the Lord blessed the sabbath day, and hallowed it.

5. Honour thy father and thy mother: that thy days may be long upon the land which the Lord thy God giveth thee.

6. Thou shalt not kill.

7. Thou shalt not commit adultery.

8. Thou shalt not steal.

9. Thou shalt not bear false witness against thy neighbour.

10. Thou shalt not covet thy neighbour's house, thou shalt not covet thy neighbour's wife, nor his manservant, nor his maidservant, nor his ox, nor his ass, nor any thing that is thy neighbour's.

Verses 18 and 19:

And all the people saw the thunderings, and the lightnings, and the noise of the trumpet, and the mountain smoking: and when the people saw it, they removed, and stood afar off. And they said unto Moses, Speak thou with us, and we will hear: but let not God speak with us, lest we die.

COMMON CANADIAN TREES

If you have ever hiked through a vast Canadian forest, you won't be surprised by the fact that close to half of Canada's landscape is covered by forest and some of those trees have been around for a very long time—the douglas fir and red cedar monsters in Cathedral Grove, British Columbia, date back 800 years, and one fir near Whistler is thought to be 1,300 years old.

The natural environment in temperate regions does favour trees, but human activity does not. To our ancestors, forests were an essential part of the rural economy, providing timber for houses, animals to trap, fuel for fires, wild mushrooms and herbs. A system evolved called "coppicing," where an area of undergrowth and small trees was grown for periodic cutting, managed like any other crop. The forestry industry in Canada replants trees for every one that gets cut, but we can't take our trees for granted. We must all work to preserve our national forests and parks.

There are hundreds of different varieties of trees all over Canada, too many to list here. It is a good idea to know the common trees and how to identify them, since it is as important to understand the earth around you as it is the heavens above. Such knowledge might even be useful when it comes to making things from wood. Leaves, bark and size are all clues to identifying trees. Buds are a good clue to identifying trees in the winter.

Balsam Fir (*Abies balsamea*)

The balsam fir is native to most of Canada, from Newfoundland to Alberta, and it is popular as a Christmas tree. The wood is also commonly used for paper, and the tree is a favourite food source for moose and other animals.

- **Bark:** Smooth and grey when young. As the tree ages, the bark grows scaly and dark brown.
- **Leaves:** Flat, blunt needles 1.5 to 2 centimetres (0.6 to 0.8 in) long that are dark green.
- **Buds:** Winter buds are globe shaped, half a centimeter in diameter and have orange-green scales.
- **Buds:** medium, can grow up to 25 metres (82 ft).

Jack Pine (*Pinus banksiana*)

The jack pine is the most widely distributed pine in Canada, covering the area from the Northwest Territories all the way to the Atlantic Ocean. Compared to some of its fellow pines, it is a relatively small tree. The jack pine is an important food source for porcupines, which eat its bark.

- **Bark:** Thin, smooth, and pale grey when young. As the tree ages, the bark becomes furrowed and dark brown.
- **Leaves:** yellowish-green needles shoot off in pairs that are 2 to 4 centimetres (0.8 to 1.6 in) long.
- **Buds:** pale reddish-brown, often cylindrical, 3 to 5 millimetres (0.1 to 0.2 in).
- **Size:** small, can grow up to 20 metres (66 ft).

Red Oak (*Quercus rubrum*)

Oak trees have been considered sacred by people throughout the ages, from the Greeks and Romans to Christians in the Christian Church. These trees are especially prone to being hit by lightning, even when they are surrounded by other trees. An oak, if not felled by human beings or nature, can live for two to three hundred years.

- **Bark**: When young, grey and smooth. As the trees age, the bark develops flat ridges that are separated by fissures.
- **Leaves**: Longer in length than width with a curve between lobes.

- **Buds**: Shiny, reddish-brown and pointy.
- **Size**: medium to large, can grow up to 35 metres (115 ft).

Red Pine (*Pinusa resinosa*)

The red pine is an evergreen known for growing tall and straight, and is a very old species. A fossil of a tree resembling a red pine was found in Minnesota and dates back to the Cretaceous period. White-tailed deer like young red pines, but they're considered poor habitat for birds and animals.

- **Bark:** Orange, brown, and grey, the bark grows rough, tough and scaly as the tree ages.
- **Leaves:** Needles are 10 to 16 centimetres (4 to 6.25 in) long in bundles of two and dark green. The needles are quite brittle and snap when you bend them in half.
- **Buds:** Small, oval-shaped and reddish-brown in colour.
- **Size:** medium, can grow up to 25 metres (82 ft).

Sugar Maple (*Acer saccharum*)

The sugar maple is a hardwood tree that grows in Eastern Canada, but it was favoured by the ancient Romans too, who used shafts of the wood to make their spears. Each spring a sugar maple produces sap that is boiled down to make maple sugar and syrup. It can take 40 litres (10.5 gal) of sap to make 1 litre (0.2 gal) of syrup.

- **Bark:** Grey and dark with long, flat vertical ridges that curl out in one direction.
- **Leaves:** Wide with a u-shaped space between three lobes.
- **Buds:** 6 to 12 millimetres (0.2 to 0.5 in) long.
- **Size:** medium to large, can grow up to 35 metres (115 ft).

Tamarack (*Larix laricina*)

The tamarack is found in every province and territory, is able to survive extremely cold temperatures and is thus often seen at the Arctic tree line. The tamarack does well in many different soil types and is even found in swamps. The name tamarack comes from the Abenaki word *akemantak*, meaning "wood for snowshoes" or "showshoe boughs."

- **Bark:** Smooth and grey when young, becomes brown and flaky, sometimes appearing reddish or dark grey as it ages.

- **Leaves:** Very needle-like, tamarack leaves are 2 to 5 centimetres (0.8 to 2 in) long in tufts of 15 to 20.
- **Buds:** Very small, numerous and reddish in colour.
- **Size:** medium, can grow up to 15 metres (50 ft).

Trembling Aspen
(*Populus tremuloides*)

The aspen is a type of poplar tree that is found in all provinces and territories of Canada. Its name comes from the shimmering appearance of the tree's leaves when they are moved by wind. By area covered, it is the fifth most common tree in the country.

- **Bark**: Smooth and whitish-grey, growing furrowed and browner with age.
- **Leaves**: Broad oval leaves 3 to 7 centimetres (1.2 to 2.8 in) long with fine teeth on edges.
- **Buds**: Oval shaped and pointed, brown, shiny and 6 to 7 millimetres (0.2 to 0.3 in) long.
- **Size**: medium, can grow up to 25 metres (82 ft).

White Spruce (*Picea glauca*)

The white spruce is as also known as the skunk spruce since its needles can be smelly when you crush them. The provincial tree of Manitoba, the white spruce is an evergreen tree found across Canada. Grouse, squirrels, porcupines and even black bears eat parts of the white spruce.

- **Bark**: Thin, light grey and smooth, the bark becomes scaly as the tree ages.
- **Leaves**: Spruce needles are 1.5 to 2.2 centimetres (0.6 to 0.9 in), relatively short with square shafts, four sided, whitish-green in colour and sharp.
- **Buds**: Narrow and cylindrical, 3 to 6 centimetres (1.1 to 2.4 in) long, orange-brown in colour.
- **Size**: medium, can grow up to 25 metres (82 ft).

COMMON CANADIAN TREES

EXTRAORDINARY STORIES – PART SIX: THE FRANKLIN EXPEDITION

COMMANDER JOHN FRANKLIN'S 1845 expedition to find the Northwest Passage to the Pacific Ocean through the Arctic began as a grand and optimistic quest to extend the British Empire's reach around the globe. In the end, however, the voyage became one of the Victorian era's most baffling mysteries. Franklin's two huge ships and all of his 129 men disappeared, shocking the world and leading to over forty search expeditions. In fact, more men died looking for the missing expedition than had perished on the initial voyage. And while the searchers uncovered some clues about the tragic fate of Franklin and his men, it took almost 140 years and the work of Canadian scientists to uncover the truth about the harrowing final days of Franklin's team.

When fifty-nine-year-old John Franklin set off on his fourth expedition to the Arctic in May 1845, he could have been forgiven for his unbridled optimism. After all, he was a seasoned explorer, having made many treks through the stormy Atlantic and Pacific Oceans. And he was a survivor: he had fought in the Napoleonic Wars, had overcome a shipwreck in the South Pacific and had returned home after nearly starving to death on a previous Arctic expedition. And beyond his own wealth of experience, he was to be accompanied by a strong and dedicated crew. With Franklin were Commander James Fitzjames, Captain Francis Crozier and 126 other elite Royal Navy and British Merchant Navy crew members under his command. Two vessels had been provided by the British Navy for the expeditions, HMS *Terror* and HMS *Erebus*, warships that had been reinforced with sheets of iron to help them withstand travel through Arctic sea ice. The two ships were equipped with all of the very newest technology: each had a steam locomotive engine attached to a propeller that could power

the boat if necessary. The ships had also been outfitted with a boiler and hot water pipes to heat the men's sleeping quarters and all other parts of the vessel. The galley stoves had special devices that would take the salt out of ocean water so that it could be used for cooking and drinking. And the crew had an ample supply of food. A newly invented process allowed provisioners to preserve fresh food in tin cans. These cans could be stored for years, meaning that sea-faring men could enjoy meat and vegetables throughout their journey—instead of having to rely solely on wormy sea biscuits and salted meat. The Franklin expedition had in its ships' holds enough canned goods to last for at least three years.

They had also brought barrels of lemon juice to prevent scurvy (a disease caused by a lack of vitamin C), a decent assortment of modern medicines, a doctor, thousands of books, mahogany desks, the finest china and silverware and, of course, plenty of guns and ammunition. No previous Arctic expedition had been so lavishly supplied. Everything boded well for this to be the voyage that would finally chart the Northwest Passage and in doing so garner honour, fame and even riches for its commanders and crew.

There was a good reason the British government had provided so well for this new expedition. The European economy was dependent on trade with China and East India, yet to get there, vessels from Europe had to sail all the way to the southernmost tip of Africa and around the Cape of Good Hope to reach the Pacific. The voyage was not only extremely lengthy and costly but also dangerous. For over 300 hundred years, European explorers had been looking for a shortcut: a way to cross the top of the globe through the Arctic sea that navigators assumed joined the Atlantic and Pacific Oceans. Anyone who could find the passage would go down in history as the discoverer of one of the world's most important trade routes. And any country that could claim sovereignty over the waters of that route would become enormously wealthy and powerful.

There had been over fifty documented expeditions into Arctic waters before Franklin and his men set out. But it hadn't been easy. The waters north of Canada contain a confusing maze of islands, bays and inlets. The shifting ice is also a serious problem. In the warmest months, the sea is littered with huge icebergs. As the weather cools, great chunks of ice, or pack ice, choke the water and can trap

The *Erebus* and the *Terror* left England on May 10. They travelled to Greenland, where an accompanying supply ship transferred coal and other goods to Franklin's boats before heading back to England. The sailors on that supply ship were the last British souls to set eyes on Franklin and his men. A year passed with no word from the expedition. And then another. When three years had gone by, people began to ask questions. Why hadn't the ships returned? Why had there been no word of the ships and their crew from other seafarers? Every previous Arctic expedition had eventually returned — all fifty of them, in fact. How could it be that the best-

The Erebus *and the* Terror *were considered mighty, invincible ships able to sail the most treacherous of seas.*

and even crush ships between the massive frozen boulders. While there was some hope that this expedition might be able to push through the passage in one year, Commander Franklin and his men knew there was a chance the ships would spend the winter in the Arctic.

equipped, best-trained, most modern of British marine enterprises had simply vanished?

The British government posted huge rewards for the rescue of Franklin and his men. In 1848, the first search parties set out. Dozens of ships and hundreds of men braved the treacherous Arctic waters searching for survivors or for clues about the fate of the lost expedition. For two years, no one could find any sign of it. Finally, in 1850, the first traces were unearthed. North of Baffin Island, on the shores of Beechey Island, rescuers discovered the graves of three of Franklin's crew members. Wooden grave markers identified them as John Torrington, John Hartnell and William Braine. The search party also found evidence that Franklin's men had camped on the island for a time – there were stone circles that would have surrounded tents, the remains of a garden, a carpenter's shop, a shooting gallery, several look-out platforms and over 700 empty tin cans. The rescuers investigated the refuse and at least one of the coffins. They were looking for a note that would have told them where the ships or the crew might have been headed, but there was nothing. The grave markers suggested that the three men had died during the first winter. So where were the other 126 men? Could they still be on their ships or be living somewhere on the frozen tundra?

The search team trapped and collared foxes in the area, leaving messages on their collars in hopes that Franklin's men might shoot one and discover that rescuers were looking for them. They floated hydrogen balloons with messages. They painted huge signs on cliff faces, and they left caches of food for Franklin's men to find. Finally, in 1854, an explorer named Dr. John Rae met some Inuit who had some of the silverware from Franklin's ships. These Inuit had not seen Franklin or his men, but they had heard tales of them. Apparently, their ships had been crushed in the ice and the surviving sailors had made their way over land, dragging with them their lifeboats on sledges. The crew had been hoping to hit a waterway that would take them south, but the Inuit reported the men had died of starvation on their journey.

When Rae reported this news back in England, it was met with skepticism. In 1857, Lady Jane Franklin, Commander Franklin's wife, hired Captain Francis Leopold M'Clintock to investigate the Inuit's stories. When the Captain

arrived on King William's Island, where the Inuit had said Franklin's men were seen, he discovered other natives who had some of the crew's possessions. He also found a skeleton dressed in a British naval uniform, lying face down as if the man had fallen dead in his tracks, and a small cairn containing two notes that described some of what had happened to the expedition.

In the notes, Captain Crozier explained that the expedition had been forced to spend its first winter (1845–1846) on Beechey Island. When the warmer weather arrived the next spring, the crew members continued on their way until they were trapped again by freezing ice off the northwest coast of King William Island. (Their route suggests they were very close to completing the trek through the Northwest Passage— only 90 kilometres (56 miles) were left uncharted.) The men spent another winter on board the frozen vessels, and then on April 22, 1948, after having been trapped in ice for over nineteen months, the remaining 105 men abandoned ship. Twenty-four men, including Commander John Franklin, had perished on board the boats. Captain Crozier finished his message by saying that the survivors were heading for Back's Fish River.

Sure enough, M'Clintock and his search party found a lifeboat not far from the cairn. It was packed with supplies and the haunting figures of two clothed skeletons. But the boat was pointed back toward the spot where the ships had been abandoned. These sailors seemed to have either lost faith in the overland trek or had hoped to return to the ship for some reason. In the years following M'Clintock's initial discoveries, other searchers found skeletal remains on the west and south coast of King William's Island and heard more stories from the Inuit about starvation along the crew's final march. In 1879, an American searcher named Frederick Schwatka met an Inuk woman whose son had seen an abandoned boat surrounded by many human skulls and other bones along the mainland shore of Starvation Cove (south of King William's Island). It seemed apparent that the last of Franklin's men had perished there.

Despite the discoveries of so many searchers, questions remained about what really had killed Franklin's men. People understood that scurvy would have plagued the sailors after the lemon juice and fresh vegetables had been depleted, but this didn't explain why so many men died so soon aboard the ships. And despite the onset of scurvy, the men had plenty of food to last for three years – and they could have hunted to supplement their food stores. What's more, the men who had left the ships had clearly perished – but why? The Inuit of the area had survived and travelled in the same harsh conditions for thousands of years.

As time passed and more became known about the Arctic and Arctic life, it became clear that many factors contributed to the tragic fate of the expedition. As far as the ships' voyage was concerned, navigators discovered that the route around King William's Island was a doomed one. The ice mass in that area does not always clear in the summer – meaning that Franklin's ships had sailed into a deadly trap. But more important, though the ships had been outfitted with the latest technology, none of that cutting-edge innovation had gone into the sailors' clothing or gear. The British Navy of Franklin's day was convinced that its uniforms and clothing were superior to anything else available. The men, therefore, wore cotton gloves, unlined leather boots, light canvas pants and thin wool sweaters. No matter how many layers the crew members donned, they simply were not protected from the extreme cold of the Arctic, and frostbite and hypothermia would have taken their toll once they left the boats, if not before.

In 1984, Dr. Owen Beattie, an anthropologist from the University of Alberta, journeyed to Beechey Island to discover more about what had befallen the expedition. On an earlier trip to the island, one of Beattie's assistants had found a partial skull. Tests on it showed evidence of scurvy but also a very high lead content – enough to suggest that the man had been suffering from lead poisoning before his death. On his return visit to the island, Dr. Beatttie and his team dug up the three corpses that were lying in shallow graves. The bodies were frozen solid and were therefore perfectly preserved. Autopsies showed that all of the men had been suffering from tuberculosis and had died from pneumonia. And all were showing clear signs of severe lead poisoning.

Beattie collected tin cans found at Beechey

The mummified remains of seaman John Hartnell, found on Beechey Island.

Island. These, he discovered, had been improperly sealed. The food inside them had probably spoiled. Sailors who had died on the boat and some of those who had started the march might have died from food poisoning. And the spoiled food would have meant that the sailors likely faced starvation long before anyone had anticipated.

But the tins showed something else as well. In the early days of canning, the solder used to seal cans contained lead. In fact, the solder on the cans from Beechey Island was 90-percent lead and ran along the inside of the cans where the food could absorb it. The lead may have weakened the sailors enough that they succumbed to other diseases, like pneumonia. The men of the Franklin Expedition had likely been slowly killed by the very food that was meant to keep them healthy and alive during the most trying of voyages.

And this is when the most harrowing picture of the expedition's final days begins to take shape. Symptoms of lead poisoning include fatigue, loss of appetite, stomach ailment and severe mental deterioration, including confusion, paranoia and violence. For years, researchers had been puzzled by the contents of the boat found on King William's Island. There had been all sorts of useful items from the ship littering the area around the stone cairns, including a medicine chest, camp stoves, clothing, axes and rope – in M'Clintock's words, "every article . . . which could possibly be dispensed with." Yet the boat that the sailors were dragging along the tundra in their last desperate efforts at survival was crammed with the oddest assortment of goods –

silk handkerchiefs, toothbrushes, button polish, scented soap, curtain rods and silverware. Button polish? Curtain rods? Now, Beattie thought he had discovered why. In the final throes of lead poisoning, the sailors may very well have been going mad. Who knows what illogical decisions, wild behaviour and violence contributed to their horrific final months? And Dr. Beattie made one more grisly discovery.

At Booth's Point, on the east coast of King William's Island, Beattie and his team found a pile of human bones. There was no doubt that these belonged to the members of the Franklin expedition. Looking carefully at the bones, Dr. Beattie noticed long, straight grooves in many of them. He knew these were knife marks, which could mean only one thing: rumours that had circulated for over a century, confirmed by Inuit reports, were true. In their final days, the few remaining men from the Franklin Expedition had turned to cannibalism in a desperate effort to survive.

In 1914, the problem of getting back and forth between the Atlantic and Pacific Oceans was finally solved with the building of the Panama Canal through Central America. To this day, travel through the Northwest Passage is too slow and dangerous for commercial travel and shipping. The true tragedy of the Franklin expedition and all of the failed rescue attempts may be that so many men lost their lives on a quest that was doomed from the start. Polar navigation would have its value in the years to come, but it never was the path to fortune that Franklin and his followers had hoped.

HUNTING AND COOKING A RABBIT

EVERY PROVINCE has its own gun and hunting laws and regulations. You should check with your local police station as to whether air guns are permitted, the age requirements and use restrictions. Many provinces offer gun and hunting safety classes, and we highly recommend that you take a course before handing any type of firearm. Most importantly, do not handle or use any type of firearm without adult supervision. There are two main types of air rifles: those you cock by pulling the barrel back on itself and those that work from compressed air held in a canister under the barrel. The type that cocks is cheaper and doesn't need recharging every 100 shots. It should last practically forever. Target shooting can be a highly enjoyable pursuit, but a powerful air rifle can also be used to hunt game—rabbits, pheasants and pigeons.

To hunt is not a game, nor is it a sport. We believe the experience is valuable as it gives an insight into the origin of those neat meat packages you see in supermarkets. The aim, however, should be to get lunch – if you kill something, you have to eat it.

It is possible to hunt rabbits with a bow and arrow, but the movement involved in pulling the string back tends to spook them and we cannot recommend this unless you are capable of holding a drawn bow motionless for ten or twenty minutes. Believe us when we say it is extremely hard to hunt rabbits with a bow. You tend to lose the arrows as well.

Before you go anywhere near a live shoot, spend time with a target set up at 18 or 27 metres (20 or 30 yd). You can make a simple bull's-eye by drawing circles around two cups on a bit of paper. Bring drawing pins with you to fix it to a tree.

One metre (1.09 yd) is a normal walking pace, so it's easy to set up the range. You need to be certain that when you have something in your crosshairs, the pellet will hit where you point it. The method here is to find a steady aiming spot, a tree stump, for example, and fire five shots at the bull, taking note of where they hit. If you are steady, they should be close together. If all of your shots at bull are hitting low and to the left, say, you'll need to adjust your sights to fire

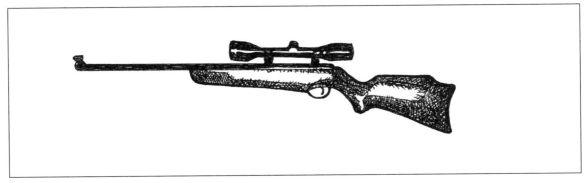

up and right. Practise until you can hit the bull regularly. You should not stint when buying the pellets – you want ones that are checked for quality and heavier than usual. Don't bother with the pointed-head pellets. Weight is far more important. It does cut the range a little but is more likely to result in a clean kill.

Finding the Rabbit

Get out into the countryside, for a start. In many provinces, it is not illegal to fire an air rifle within the confines of your own land, unless the pellets pass outside the boundary, in which case you are likely to have an armed police team turn up. Be sensible—look for rabbits where there are fields. Note that it is also illegal in most provinces to walk around with an uncovered weapon, but if the weapon is in a carrying sleeve, you can walk on public land with one. That said, the laws are different across Canada and may change from time to time. You should check with your local police station and never hunt on your neighbours' land without getting permission.

Rabbits never move far from their warrens. If you have ever seen one in a field, their burrow will be very, very close by. The best thing to do will be to note where they are seen over a period of time, to have an idea of where to find them. It is possible to come upon them on a walk, but it's a little hit and miss.

This is one place where exercising a little common sense wouldn't hurt. Go and ask the owner of the land if you can shoot rabbits. If it's a field, or a farm, there's a very good chance the owner will say yes. Rabbits breed like maniacs and are not much loved by farmers. You may even be given directions to the best spots. However, shooting a pheasant may provoke a very angry reaction.

Once in the area, find the warren. You might see rabbits in the distance, but as you come closer, they will all vanish. After you locate the complex of burrows, you should get between 18 and 28 metres (60 and 90 ft) away – the effective range. Much farther and you are likely to miss a kill. Much closer and they will remain nervous in your presence.

Have a pellet ready in the rifle, settle down flat on your stomach and wait. You will appreciate a warm coat and possibly even a Thermos of hot chocolate at this point. Your arrival will have startled the rabbit population and you'll have to wait ten minutes or so for them to return.

Don't have a rush of blood to the head and fire at the first rabbit you see. There will be a number of chances to shoot, but some rabbits will be too far away, or the rabbits might be too young. When you are ready, take the shot, aiming at the head behind the eye if you can. There is a great satisfaction in pulling off a difficult shot over distance. If you are with someone else, never point the gun at them, even if you believe it to be unloaded. An accident at that point could last a lifetime.

In the event that you merely wound the rabbit, you should reload, approach and fire point-blank at the spot behind the eye. Try to avoid causing unnecessary suffering. If you have missed, either move to another position, or read a book for half an hour. It will take that long for the rabbits to come out again.

Rabbits bleed, so have a plastic bag ready for transport. All you have to do now is skin it and eat it.

Skinning the Rabbit

This is not a difficult process, though it is a little daunting the first time. If you have a heavy-bladed cleaver, simply chop off the four paws. If you are stuck with only a penknife, break the forearm bones with a quick jerk, then cut the skin around the break in a ring. Remove the head in the same way. A serrated edge will cut through the bones, but a standard kitchen knife is likely

to be damaged if used as a chopper.

Cut a line down the middle of the chest, from head to anus. This can be fiddly if you're on your own, and a serrated edge is very useful. Be careful not to cut into the abdominal cavity – if you do, the stomach and intestines will spoil the meat.

With fingers, you can now pull back the skin to the hip and shoulders, yanking the fur off the legs like sleeves. When the legs are free, take hold of the fur at the neck and pull downward. The pelt will come off in one piece, leaving you with the carcass. The belly is quite obvious and bulges with intestines.

Holding the carcass upside down, take a pinch of loose skin near the rear legs and cut a line across it. As you turn the rabbit the right way up, most of the intestines will slide right out immediately and anything that doesn't can be scooped out with ease.

There is a partition between the stomach area and the upper chest that can be broken with a little pressure. Behind it, you will find the heart, lungs and a few other bits and bobs. Pull it all out. The heart, liver and kidneys in particular can be very tasty, but the intestines and stomach should be left well alone.

It is worth taking a moment to have a look at the various inner organs. Male rabbits will have testicles that should also be cut away. This is not for the squeamish, but that is the point of the chapter. If you buy a pork chop, we think you should realize what has gone into providing that meat for you. In a sense, killing for food is a link with ancestors going back to the caves.

PREPARING A MEAL

This isn't the place for a formal recipe, but it is worth covering the next stage. You could spit-roast the rabbit, but it is easier and more common to joint it – that is, remove the legs by cutting through the joints. Fillets can also be taken from pads of flesh near the spine. You can take a fair amount of meat off a single rabbit – enough, with vegetables, to feed two men and provide hot broth against a winter chill.

Place the meat in a pot with water and bring it to the boil, adding zucchini, a little garlic, carrots, leeks and celery until the pot is half full. Let it simmer for half an hour to forty-five minutes. Wild game is often pretty chewy because the muscles are used much more often than tame animals'. Nevertheless, rabbit cooked in this way is delicious, and the broth is very good indeed.

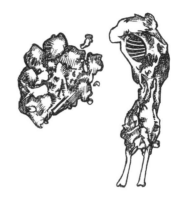

THE GAME OF CHESS

CHESS IS AN ANCIENT board game that came to Europe along the silk route from China and India. It is a game of war and tactical advantage, played by generals and princes down through the ages. Its exact origins are unknown, though the pieces may be based on the ancient formations of Indian armies.

It is a game for two people, played on a board of sixty-four alternately black and white squares. As with most of the best games, it is easy to play badly and hard to play well.

THE PIECES

Both sides have 16 pieces: 8 pawns, 2 knights, 2 bishops, 2 castles, (also known as rooks), 1 queen and 1 king.

The object of the game is to capture (checkmate) the opponent's king. White has the first move and then both players take it in turns until one triumphs.

SETTING UP THE BOARD

There should be a white square in the right-hand corner when placing the board. The pieces are arranged in two lines, facing each other. The pawns protect the rear line, which is arranged in the following sequence: 1. Rook; 2. Knight; 3. Bishop; 4. Queen; 5. King; 6. Bishop; 7. Knight; 8. Rook.

The queen always goes on her own colour – the black queen on the black square in the middle. The white queen will go on the corresponding white square.

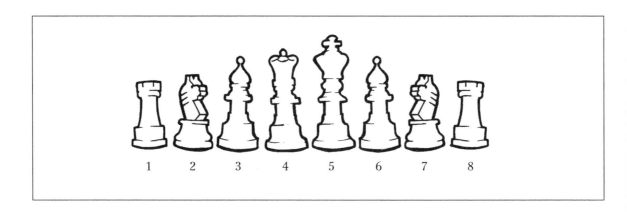

1   2   3   4   5   6   7   8

MOVEMENT AND VALUES

Each type of piece moves in a different way.

1. **Pawns** are the infantry and move forward, one square at a time – except on the first move, where they are allowed to lurch two squares forward in a fit of martial enthusiasm. They capture diagonally, to the left or right. They are the least valuable pieces but the only ones that can be promoted. (Value: 1 point.)

Knight

2. The **Knights** are the cavalry: mobile and difficult to stop. They move in an "L" shape of "two squares and one" in any direction. In the diagram, all the black pawns around the knight can be attacked. Crucially, the knight is the only piece that can jump over others in their path. Even if a rook blocked the way to one of the pawns above, the knight could still take the pawn. (Value: 3 points.)

Bishop

3. **Bishops** are the elephants. They move along the diagonals, though they are limited to white or black squares only. They work well together, covering both colour squares. They also do well in distance attacks, like machine guns or searchlights. (Value: 3 points.)

Rook/Castle

4. **Castles** (Rooks). These are the chariot forces. They control the straight lines on the board and are particularly useful in the endgame and for castling. (Value: 5 points.)

5. The **Queen**. This is the most powerful piece on the board and can move in any direction, without limit. (Value: 8 points.)

Queen

6. The **King** is the most important piece on the board. It can only move one square at a time, but in any direction. It can move two squares while castling. It cannot move into check. (Value: Game.)

King

Having the first move is an advantage, and most games tend to be won by white. Classically, black plays defensively, countering white's aggressive moves and taking advantage of mistakes.

Capturing. One player removes an enemy piece from the board by landing on the same square. With the exception of a king, any piece can take any other. A king is restricted by the fact that it cannot move into check, so a king can never take another king. Pawns can only capture diagonally, moving forward.

Check/Checkmate. If a piece threatens the king, so that in theory it could take the king, it is called "check." The king *must* either move out of check, block the check, or the attacking piece must be taken. If none of these are possible, the king has been caught – a checkmate, which is a corruption of the Arabic for "The king is dead."

Castling. After the knight and bishop have moved, the king can shift two squares either left or right, with the rook taking the inside square.

Castling Kingside　　　　　　　*Castling Queenside*

En Passant. This is an unusual form of pawn capture that is now common practice. When a pawn has moved down the board, it looks possible to avoid it by moving the opposing pawn two squares up. "En passant" allows pawn capture as if only one square had been moved.

En Passant

In theory, the game can be split into thirds – the opening, the middle game and the endgame.

OPENING

The idea here is to get out all your main pieces, known as "developing," before castling your king to safety. The centre of the board (the four central squares) is important to control. For example, a knight in the centre has up to eight possible moves. In a corner, he may have only two.

Some openings have names and long histories, such as "The King's Indian Defence" and "The Sicilian." There are many books on openings, but you should find one you like and stick to it, playing it often to understand it better. As an example, we'll show the moves of the King's Indian.

Remember, pawns cannot go backward, so move them carefully as you develop. Link them into pawn chains, one protecting the next. Try to avoid leaving a piece "en prise," or undefended.

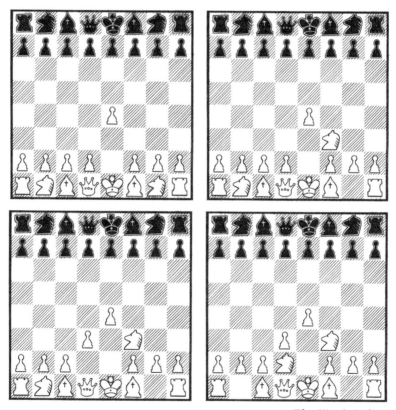

The King's Indian

THE MIDDLE GAME

Your pieces should be developed and your king safe. This is where you start to attack.

Advance your pieces to positions that help control the board and capture the enemy units. Even at this stage, you should be looking for opportunities to capture the enemy king, but don't overextend your pieces. If you want to move to a square with one piece, make sure it is protected by another.

A "pin" is a piece held in place by the danger of losing a more important piece behind it. Pins work particularly well against the enemy king. Your opponent is unable to move his blocking pieces as he *cannot* move into check.

A "fork" is when a piece threatens two pieces at the same time. The knight is particularly good at this and can be deadly when putting the king in check and at the same time threatening a valuable piece.

A "skewer" is the opposite of a pin, when a valuable piece is forced to move, thereby exposing a lesser piece to capture. A rook that threatens a queen may not get the queen, but may take the bishop behind her when she moves.

Remember to keep your king protected in your "castle," stay level on points and try to get ahead. Even a pawn advantage will show itself in the endgame.

THE ENDGAME

It is possible to win in the middle game, while the board is still full of pieces, but most wins occur in the endgame. The board will be stripped of the main pieces and pawns. Strangely, the safest position for the king is now the centre of the board, where its power can be used to attack and shepherd pawns toward promotion.

Promotion. If a pawn reaches the back rank of the opposing side, it can be exchanged for a queen, rook, bishop or knight. (You can have two queens! Just turn a rook upside down to represent the second one.) In the endgame, the threat of promotion can have a serious effect on tactics.

The endgame will involve combinations of pieces, as bishops and rooks, for example, attempt to limit the enemy king's movement, check him and then bring about a checkmate. Rooks are particularly strong in the endgame and should not be sacrificed early.

The aim is obviously to checkmate your opponent's king. This is the hardest part of the game and the last thing the novice learns to do *well*.

This is one of the only games where you get to match your brain directly against someone else's. It's a level playing field – except for experience, preparation and intelligence. Do not underestimate preparation. Many a clever boy has been beaten by a better chess player.

The game is played all over the world, with magnetic sets on trains or ornate bone carved sets in Indonesia. It's a language we all know, and every boy should be able to play chess.

TANNING A SKIN

MAKING LEATHER from skins must be one of the oldest human skills. That said, it isn't at all easy to get right, and it's worth knowing that small skins (like those of rabbits) can be air-dried after the fat has been cut away. The result will have the stiffness of a bit of cardboard, but there is a very good chance it will feel no better *after* the tanning process. Larger skins have to be tanned, or they simply rot.

First of all, cut away any obvious pouches of flesh on the inner side of the skin. The best way to do this is to stretch the skin onto a board, held in place with tacks at the edges. Use a sharp knife and a lot of care to remove the marbled pink fat without puncturing the skin beneath it. Stone-Age peoples used flints and bones to scrape hides. They also chewed them to make them soft. You might want to try this, though we thought it was going a little too far.

You don't have to get every tiny scrap of fat, but be as thorough as you can. A rabbit skin can be left in a cool room for about ten days and it will dry. Covering it in a heavy layer of salt speeds the process and also helps to prevent any smell of rotting meat. You may want to change the salt after two or three days if it becomes damp or obviously contaminated. When the skin has dried it will be quite rigid. At this point, you could trim off the rough edges with a pair of scissors.

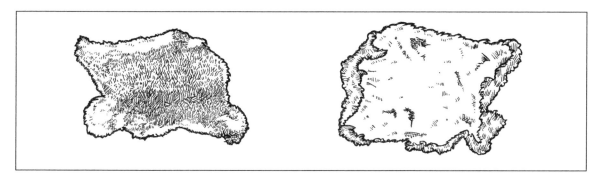

Tanning is the chemical process that makes skin into leather – a waterproof, hard-wearing and extremely versatile material. Almost all the leather we use is from cows, as it is produced as a natural by-product of eating beef. Various chemicals are useful in the process, including traditional ones from boiled brains or excrement. However, we used aluminum potassium sulphate. As well as growing crystals, alum solution can tan skin.

Once the skin is completely dry, it can be dipped in warm water with a little soap to cut the grease. There is a membrane inside all animal skins that must be removed before tanning. One way is to rub the skin back and forth on an edged object, like a wooden board or a large stone. We found steel wool useful, as well as the back of a kitchen knife. It took a long time. It smelled. Peeling off sticky wads of fatty membrane was not an enjoyable experience. Still, no one said it would be easy.

When the skin was about as clean as we could make it, we trimmed one or two of the rougher edges and prepared a solution of 453 grams (1 lb) alum, 124 grams (4 oz) calcium carbonate and 4.55 litres (8 pints) of water. It fizzes as you mix it up, but don't worry.

A rabbit skin should be left in the solution for two days, though larger skins can take up to five. Be careful how you dispose of the liquid, as it's a pretty potent weedkiller and will destroy grass.

When you take the skin out, it will be sopping wet and the skin side will have gone white. You now need to oil it thoroughly and leave it overnight. Ideally, you would use an animal oil, but those aren't easy to get hold of. We chose linseed oil, which is usually used for church pews. It smells quite pleasant, as well. We placed a plastic bag over it to seal in the oil and left it for another two days.

The next stage is to let the oiled skin dry, fur side out, but only until it is damp. This stage is crucial to create a soft final skin. While damp, you must "work" it. This means gently stretching it and running it back and forth over a smooth wooden edge, like the back of a chair or a broomstick held in a vice.

How soft the final version is will depend on how well it was tanned, how much flesh still adhered to the skin membrane and how conscientiously you work it. If it does dry out and is too stiff, it is all right to dampen it again and repeat the process. It will get softer, but it could take a few sessions.

Finally, a quick dip in unleaded gas is worth doing, just to clean it and cut through excess oiliness. It will make the skin smell of gas, obviously, but this fades in a day or two. You really should get an adult to help with this.

Once you have allowed it to dry completely, imperfections can be removed with a sanding block. The skin will resemble waxed paper, but it should be strong *and flexible* – and it shouldn't smell like a dead animal. Calfskin has been used as paper and rabbit skin could also be written on, though it would serve better as an outer sleeve for a small book, a drawstring pouch or, with a few more skins, perhaps a pair of gloves.

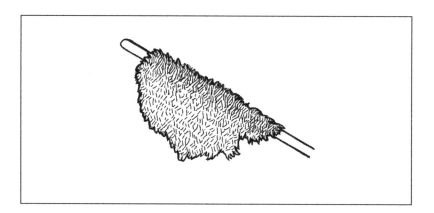

THE BRITISH EMPIRE (1497–1997):
"The empire on which the sun never sets"

FIVE CENTURIES of energy, triumph and disaster, heroism and invention are too full to be explored here in the detail they deserve. What follows is a summary of the rise and fall of the largest empire the world has ever known. The influence of language, custom, law and tradition continues, but the British Empire came to an end on June 30, 1997, when Hong Kong passed back into Chinese ownership. It is astonishing to think that almost exactly 100 years before, on June 20, 1897, Queen Victoria celebrated her Diamond Jubilee of sixty years ruling 375 million subjects. The idea that the Empire would vanish only a century later would have been laughed at, though Rudyard Kipling saw that the world turns on, regardless of human achievement. His poem "Recessional"

was read to Victoria. These four lines are particularly poignant.

> *Far-called, our navies melt away –*
> *On dune and headland sinks the fire –*
> *Lo, all our pomp of yesterday*
> *Is one with Nineveh, and Tyre!*

It has struck some that if an empire had to be broken against an enemy, Nazi Germany was a worthy cause. All the countries in the Empire sent men back for that conflict. They came from America, India, Canada, Nepal, New Zealand, Australia, South Africa – everywhere, in fact, where the people could claim a bond with Britain – to give their lives against a dark and terrible enemy. Perhaps that was the purpose of the British Empire – to be there at that time, when the future could have gone another way. As a legacy, perhaps that will do.

On May 20, 1497, John Cabot set sail from Bristol with a royal warrant to claim land for Henry VII. This was the first document of what would one day become the Empire. He made landfall in Newfoundland, on the north-eastern edge of Canada. His son Sebastian established the Company of Merchant Adventurers in London and secured a trade treaty with Ivan the Terrible in Russia. English trade interests were beginning to grow, and by the time of Elizabeth I they would come into conflict with the ambitions of Spain. There were several reasons for the rivalry. The Spanish royals had sponsored Christopher Columbus, they were Catholic where Elizabeth was Protestant, and most importantly of all, the two growing trade fleets competed against each other. English pirates would capture Spanish ships laden with gold, silver and slaves from their colonies in South America. In turn, English crews would be arrested and tortured whenever the opportunity presented itself. It was a brutal period, with fortunes for the taking, which helped to establish the English as a naval nation. Elizabeth I even leased ships to privateers in exchange for a tithe of the profits. It was simple: it rewarded daring and it brought vast wealth to Britain. As Sir Walter Raleigh said,

> Whosoever commands the sea commands the trade; whosoever commands the trade of the world commands the riches of the world and consequently the world itself.

Sir Francis Drake had first sailed with the privateer John Hawkins, a scourge of merchant shipping. In his turn, Drake became the most notorious of privateer captains, taking great pleasure in attacks on Spanish vessels. He saw the "Papist" Catholic Spanish as enemies to a Protestant England and was happy to ambush their ships and even a mule-train carrying silver from Peru to Panama. He became a popular hero in England and was a dashing favourite of the Queen. He was the second man

Sir Francis Drake

to circumnavigate the globe (after Magellan) – though he missed finding the legendary southern continent (Australia) – and reached California, naming it New Albion. He brought his queen £160,000 of profit from just one voyage – in a day when a man could live comfortably on £20 a year. He was knighted on the quarterdeck of his ship, the *Golden Hind*.

When he heard the Spanish were preparing a great armada in Cadiz, Drake took fifty ships out to attack them with fire-ships before they could sail out of the harbour. His fleet did so much damage that the Spanish took a year to rebuild. Drake said that he had "merely singed the King of Spain's beard," but Elizabeth would not agree to further attacks.

In 1588, the Spanish Armada sailed into the English Channel. Many of the Spanish ships were lost to strong winds and high seas, leading King Philip to comment later that "God is an Englishman." In addition to natural forces, the Spanish fleet was beaten by faster gunnery, nimbler ships and better captains, ending the likelihood that the future would be Spanish-led.

※

This was to be the hallmark of the early British Empire. Trade would drive its expansion, then war, almost always with European nations seeking their own wealth. Over the next four centuries, Britain would go to war with almost every European country. Perhaps because of Europe being a cauldron of conflict for the previous 3,000 years, the nations of the continent were superior to the rest of the world in terms of arms, tactics, ships, technology and materials such as steel. Holland, France, Spain, Germany and Britain all exploded outward, using their advantages to win territories and profit. One by one, all of the others were beaten home again. The French were finally stopped at Waterloo and the Germans in 1945. The Empire would eventually become the Commonwealth, in a peaceful transition, as the world headed toward the third millennium.

When James VI of Scotland combined the thrones to become King of England, Scotland and Ireland in 1603, the new century would provide fresh challenges for the nascent Empire.

In 1613, the East India Trading Company established its first settlement at Surat in India. Their aim was to grow spices in competition with Dutch traders. Exploration and adventure led the way, with men such as Captain John Smith, who named New England, and Sir George Somers, who discovered Bermuda when he was blown off course.

King James was a Presbyterian (of the Church of Scotland) and Puritans in England were deeply unhappy with his rule. In 1620, a disaffected group of them set sail from Southampton in two ships – the *Speedwell* and the *Mayflower*. The *Speedwell* was unseaworthy and they both turned back to Plymouth. The *Mayflower* then went out alone, carrying Puritans, crew and colonists recruited by the

Virginia Trading Company. They made landfall first in Cape Cod, but could find no decent shelter in the depths of a hostile winter. The second landing was at Plymouth in Massachusetts, named so previously by Captain John Smith. Many more would follow and over time Maine, New Hampshire and Connecticut were settled. The New World was opening up and by 1630, Boston and ten other settlements were established. By 1643, New Haven, Plymouth, Connecticut and Massachusetts formed a confederation as the United Colonies of New England.

In England, Charles I had taken the throne and actually lost it in the English Civil War with Oliver Cromwell. The American colonies began to taste their own freedom from the mother country. In 1688, William of Orange was asked by the English parliament to take the throne from James II, who was once again insisting England should become Catholic. William had a claim to the throne through being a grandson of Charles I and he landed with an honour guard, after James II had gone into exile in France. The Crown's grip on the American colonies became oppressive during his reign.

In 1707, the kingdoms of England and Scotland were legally and politically joined by the Act of Union, an important part of British history. Gibraltar (at the southern tip of Spain) became a British port in perpetuity by the Treaty of Utrecht in 1713. Minorca was also turned over to Britain but, more importantly, France was forced to drop her claim to vast territories in Canada. However, it would take military action to enforce British sovereignty over Canada. Even while a new capital was being built in 1748, French attacks on British settlements continued. Eventually, the French colonists were given the choice of swearing allegiance to the British Crown or being deported. Most chose to be deported.

In America, the struggle between France and Britain continued. A French expedition took control of the Ohio Valley and a messenger named George Washington was sent to tell them to withdraw. His small unit was made to surrender by the French. A much larger army that included 1,200 regular soldiers from Britain would be almost annihilated by a combined French and Iroquois Indian force. The rebellion spread, though this particular force was eventually routed and driven back. In 1756, the Seven Years' War with France began, and in America, Canada and India, as well as closer to home, French and British forces fought bitter battles.

❈

Robert Clive of India might have remained an East India Company clerk if not for the war. Famously he had tried to commit suicide twice, failing both times with a jamming gun. He was made an ensign in the Company army and became almost the archetype of that strange breed Britain could produce – men with an absolute disregard for personal safety and an

Robert Clive.

unshakeable belief in the rightness of their cause. The Mahrattas of India called Clive "Sabat Jung" – "Daring in War."

Calcutta was begun as a settlement by the British East India Company. The Company officials fortified their base in Calcutta against local insurrection. The Nabob of Bengal decided this was an act of defiance and sent a great host against the fort, overwhelming it. The 146 company employees surrendered on the condition that their lives be spared. They were held without water in a stifling room 7 metres by 5. In the morning, only twenty-three had survived what became known as "the black hole of Calcutta."

It could all have been lost in 1756. The French were growing in strength in India, while the East India Company had lost Calcutta and Madras. British colonies in America seemed vulnerable to French attack. In addition, Britain lost Minorca and Spain entered the war on the side of France in 1762.

In England, the prime minister, William Pitt (Pitt the Elder), came up with the idea of funding the Prussian army to wage war against the French-led alliance of Austria, Russia, Saxony, Sweden and Spain, allowing Britain to concentrate her troops in far-flung places such as India and Canada. He was particularly lucky in having Frederick the Great as his ally, as the man was a tactical genius. The Seven Years' War can be considered the first world war, given the scale of it. It is still the most successful war ever fought by Britain as it brought India and Canada into the fold and practically began an empire overnight. Pitt did not lack confidence: "I know that I can save this country and no one else can," he said.

Clive recaptured Calcutta in 1757 and after extraordinary subterfuge and negotiation, fought the Battle of Plassey against a French and Indian army of 50,000 with fifty-three guns. Clive had 1,100 British troops, 2,100 natives and ten guns. The French gunners continued fighting right to the end, but Clive's force routed the enemy and secured Bengal for British rule. It has been said that Plassey was the turning point, but in fact

The Death of Wolfe *by Benjamin West.*

there were hundreds of times and places where the British Empire could have failed. Only when we look back with an Olympian perspective does it seem inevitable. For those involved in its creation, every year survived was a gift and only luck, fortitude, bravery and cunning could hold it for the year after that.

In Canada, Pitt was fortunate to have another gifted soldier – James Wolfe. The fleet took an expeditionary force of 9,000 British regulars and 500 colonials from Halifax to take Louisburg and then Quebec from the French. In 1758, Wolfe led the attack on Louisburg carrying only a cane. The guns of the great fort were taken and turned on French ships in harbour. The first step had been taken to pushing the French out of Canada. However, the fighting was ferocious as fort after fort was captured throughout 1759.

Wolfe was made major general and took command for the assault on Quebec, an almost impregnable fortress above the St. Lawrence river. (James Cook was the surveyor of the river, the man who later went on to claim Australia and map New Zealand.) The night before, Wolfe gave a locket to John Jervis, a naval captain, to be sent to his fiancée if he died. As an admiral, Jervis would later play a crucial role in Nelson's career and lived until 1823.

Wolfe's army fought the French on September 13, 1759 on the Plains of Abraham in front of the city. Both commanders were mortally wounded. Wolfe died during the battle and the French commander died later that night. Quebec surrendered and the British garrisoned the city.

There were other battles, but on September 8, 1760, the French surrendered their interest in Canada. They had lost fleets to British ships and Britain was free from the threat of invasion. Bells rang in London to celebrate a year of victories.

※

The American War of Independence could also have been the beginning of the end. In a very real sense, this was a civil war between British forces who wanted to remain loyal to Britain and others who wanted to forge their own identity as a separate country rather than one ruled from abroad. The causes are complex, though part of the reason for the war was the level of taxes imposed by Britain on such products as sugar and, most famously, tea. "No taxation without representation" was the cry raised against King George III. The cry, needless to say, was ignored and further taxes were imposed on glass, lead, paper and just about anything else the British government could think of. Riots followed in America and bloodshed was inevitable. A change of government in Britain meant that all taxes were repealed except for the one on tea, but it was too late, and in 1773 in Boston 342 boxes of tea worth £10,000 were tipped into the harbour – the event became known ever after as "the Boston tea party."

Britain had reduced the size of the army after the Seven Years' War. Clive had at last managed to shoot himself, Wolfe was dead and Pitt was too elderly and frail to help the situation. George III suffered from porphyria, a disease that rendered him completely insane for temporary periods. From 1773 to 1783, Britain needed a great negotiator, a visionary. For once, there wasn't one, and the war was a shambles. Interestingly, the French played a crucial part, still smarting from their defeat in the Seven Years' War. Apart from providing supplies, France formed a league of "armed neutrality" with Spain, Russia, Prussia, Holland and Sweden to protect American shipping from the Royal Navy. A French fleet brought 5,000 men and 106 heavy guns from Toulon to support their General Lafayette in America. After landing the army, the French fleet attacked British ships waiting for a retreating British force under Cornwallis. With his back to the sea, Cornwallis was forced to surrender at Yorktown. Famously, his military band played "The World Turned Upside Down." In September 1783, Britain recognized the independence of the thirteen American states. George Washington became the first president six years later on April 30, 1789 – the year of the French Revolution. Napoleon Bonaparte had arrived on the world scene.

Canada remained a British possession, though limited autonomy was given soon after the American war and perhaps because of it. India was thriving to the point where the British government wanted more influence, and Pitt the Younger passed a law that gave the government oversight control of the East India Company in 1784. India had become the jewel in the Crown, though the Company was a force in the country for another hundred years. Trade continued to grow, though Britain abolished slavery in 1807 and then used the navy to enforce the abolition on the shipping of all other countries.

Napoleon was eventually beaten by an alliance led by Wellington on land, and Nelson's Royal Navy at sea. The Treaty of Vienna in 1815 effectively ended the threat of France to British interests. Parts of North Africa and a number of small islands remain under French control to this day, but the possibility of the world speaking French had passed. Even time would be measured through Greenwich rather than Paris, though the one place in the world that does not recognize Greenwich Mean Time is the part of France directly south of Greenwich. Perhaps unsurprisingly, they keep continental time – one hour ahead.

※

As the Victorian era began in 1837, the Empire continued to expand. Dutch Boers had established settlements in southern Africa by the beginning of the nineteenth century and Britain developed its

Queen Victoria.

own outposts in that rich land, though the Boer Wars didn't come till later. Hong Kong was gained by treaty with China in 1839 after trade wars over opium, tea and silver. In 1840, Britain claimed New Zealand and fought the warrior Maoris over the land for the next thirty years. In 1848, Britain made Canada largely self-governing and, when that was successful, used the same formula in Australia and New Zealand. This was the seed of the Commonwealth. In 1867, Britain united all the Canadian provinces into one dominion – one country. Afghanistan was occupied and then lost. India had railways, schools and hospitals built across it as part of a complex infrastructure. The Punjab was annexed after wars with the Sikhs, who earned the respect of the British with their courage and tenacity. Tea was introduced as a crop in India and Ceylon (Sri Lanka) by the British, intent on breaking the Chinese tea monopoly.

The Indian Mutiny of 1857 occurred when Sepoy soldiers rebelled against the imposition of British culture. For example, female infanticide had been outlawed and "suttee," the practice of burning a live widow with her dead husband, was also banned. Attempts to

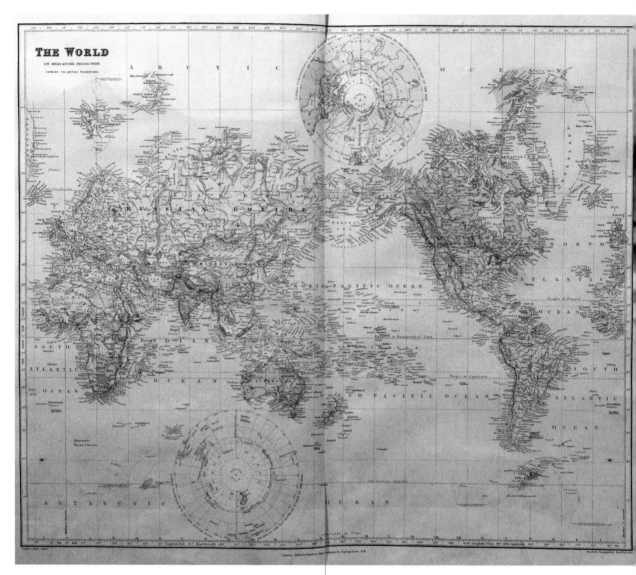

THE WORLD
ON MERCATOR'S PROJECTION

emancipate women did not go down well, and the spread of Christianity in India was seen as a threat to Islam and Hinduism.

Famously, the mutiny was set off by a rumour that the British rifle cartridges had been greased with pig and cow fat and were therefore untouchable to Hindus and Muslims. Indian regiments refused the cartridges and mutinied, murdering the white officers and rioting in a great release of horror and violence. British forces were heavily outnumbered by native troops they had trained and were besieged and massacred. The Gurkhas of Nepal and the Sikhs of the Punjab remained loyal. The Siege of Cawnpore was particularly brutal. Safe passage had been promised to a thousand men, women and children. They had barricaded themselves into the small fort for twenty days against an army of 10,000. When they came out, they were massacred. Five hundred and six children were hacked to pieces and thrown into a well. The British who came too late to relieve them were filled with rage at what they saw. Other atrocities followed, such as the British strapping Sepoys to the mouths of cannons as they were fired. The battles were fierce and brutal, with 182 Victoria Crosses being awarded for courage. Only the First World War would produce more examples of extraordinary heroism (181 were awarded in World War II, 626 in World War I).

Sir Colin Campbell, Sir Hugh Rose and Sir James Outram eventually broke the rebellion and India slipped back into an uneasy peace. The country would not become independent until 1947, after the Second World War.

Victoria's reign ended in 1901, with the Empire still growing. Germany and Austria would be the chief enemy in the new century, though France was always willing to take on new colonies if an opportunity presented itself. South Africa was the first battleground of the century, with Britain clashing with the Dutch over rights to the continent.

Some acquisitions, like the Transvaal in South Africa, were claimed in part to disrupt the power base of other countries before they became a threat. Nonetheless, political decisions had to be carried out by the army and navy, fighting the Dutch Boers.

World War I (1914–18) was fought at sea and on every continent, with Britain leading a block of allies against another block led by Germany. It does not need to be said that millions of lives were lost in the most brutal of conditions. The Germans under Kaiser Wilhelm were beaten after four years of war and the guns in France fell silent at 11:00 in the morning, on the eleventh day of the eleventh month, 1918. Remembrance Day is still marked every year with memorial services and the sale of poppies.

Former German colonies in Africa became British possessions, such as Cameroon, Togoland and East Africa. In addition, Iraq and Palestine became British Mandates, which meant Britain assumed responsibility for them, as well as adding Egypt, Cyprus, Kuwait, the Sudan and a host of other small states. With France on the winning side, Syria and Lebanon became French colonies. In all, over three million square kilometres were added to the Empire and when Britain laid claim to Antarctica in 1919, the Empire was the largest it had ever been.

❋

The Victorian era had produced many who saw the Empire as theirs by divine right. The drive to spread civilization produced missionaries and reformers like Florence Nightingale and William Wilberforce, who campaigned against slavery. Gentlemen adventurers were the archetypal example of young Christians who were prepared to risk their lives for more than the simple fortunes of Drake and Ralegh's time. The dream had altered to one that brought the light of British rule to those less fortunate, making the world a better place as a result. The British assumed a moral superiority as well as a financial and military one. The result was a spread of culture that altered the world forever.

Characters like Cecil Rhodes, who ruled what is now known as Zimbabwe, calling it Rhodesia, were from the same mould as Richard Francis Burton, T. E. Lawrence, James Brooke, Kitchener, Napier and a thousand other examples of the breed. Their achievements are astonishing in scale and breathtaking self-confidence. At the same time, Britain produced a stream of reformers and more liberal thinkers who stood against the brutal treatment of native populations and deplored acts of violence. Both types created an Empire capable of merciless ferocity in places such as Ireland and India – and a humanitarian philosophy that led to improved health and education for its subjects. As Mahatma Gandhi said in 1915,

> I discovered that the British Empire had certain ideals with which I had fallen in love. One of those ideals is that every subject of the British Empire has the freest scope possible for his energies and efforts and whatever he thinks is due to his conscience . . . I have said that government is best which governs least, and I have found it possible for me to be governed least under the British Empire. Hence my loyalty to the British Empire.

The idea of a "Nightwatchman" state, that is one that does not interfere in every aspect of people's lives, was a peculiarly British idea, quite different from the governments of the continent. It came about because the vast Empire simply could not be governed on the sort of scale that is possible today.

The years between the wars are generally regarded as a golden period by those who lived through them. The *Boy's Own Paper* gives an idea of the attitudes of the day, valuing attributes of manliness, fair play, decency, honour and an ability to play cricket. The idea that the century would see the end of British rule over almost all of it would have been preposterous. Yet, the Second World War was fought to resist the military rise of Germany – carrying with it a quite different and darker philosophy.

As Niall Ferguson said in his book *Empire: How Britain Made the Modern World*:

> When the British governed a country – even when they only influenced its government by flexing their military and financial muscles – there were certain distinctive features of their own society that they tended to disseminate. A list of the more important of these would run:
>
> 1 The English language
> 2. English forms of land tenure
> 3. Scottish and English banking
> 4. The Common Law
> 5. Protestantism
> 6. Team sports
> 7. The limited or "Nightwatchman" state
> 8. Representative assemblies
> 9. The idea of liberty.
>
> The last of these is perhaps the most important because it remains the most distinctive feature of the Empire, the thing that sets it apart from its continental European rivals. I do not mean to claim that all British Imperialists were liberals: some were very far from it. But what is striking about the histoy of the Empire is that whenever the British were behaving despotically, there was almost always a liberal critique of that behaviour from within British society.

Lord Mountbatten.

GROWING SUNFLOWERS

THIS IS SUCH A SIMPLE THING, but it can be fulfilling, and if we don't mention it here, a chance could be missed. These plants (*Helianthus*) are called sunflowers because they turn toward the sun, and when mature, their large, round heads resemble the sun. In French, they are called *tournesol* and in Italian *girasole*. You can find sunflower seeds in hamster food or at a health-food shop. Growing any plants and flowers can be rewarding, but sunflower seeds are particularly good as sowing to blooming takes only sixty days of a good summer. They grow at an unusually high speed with impressive results.

Plant the seeds in fertile soil in late spring. All you have to do is get hold of some of the black-and-white-striped seeds, put them in a little earth in a plastic cup, add water and wait a few days. They need sunlight, so make sure the cup is on a well-lit window ledge.

The growth shown below is after only one week. The seeds split open and rise on the stalks like hats. Remove the seeds when you can see the leaves.

Eventually, you may have to use thin wooden stakes to support the stems. They will produce one of the largest flowers you can grow anywhere, with a head full of edible seeds. The final height can reach 2.4 metres (8 ft)!

The second picture is after a month, almost 60 centimetres (2 ft) high. They have been repotted, which just means a little extra earth or compost and a good watering. If you have a spot that

receives regular sunshine, sunflowers will thrive in open ground – but check them for slugs and snails at regular intervals. To sustain this sort of growth speed, they do need water – so don't forget to give them a daily splash.

When the flowers finally fade in late summer, break apart the heads with your thumbs and you will find hundreds of the striped seeds ready to begin again next year. The shells contain a pleasant-tasting inner seed that can be eaten raw. You might also try roasting the seeds until they brown, then serving them with salt and butter. They are a good source of potassium and phosphorus, iron and calcium.

QUESTIONS ABOUT THE WORLD – PART THREE

---✶---

1. **How do ships sail against the wind?**
2. **Where does cork come from?**
3. **What causes the wind?**
4. **What is chalk?**

I. HOW DO SHIPS SAIL AGAINST THE WIND?

When the wind is coming straight at a boat or ship, it would seem impossible to sail into it. It can be done, however, by clever use of the sails and rudder.

Figure 1 is a plan view of a small boat with the main sail and rudder visible. The wind comes from the direction of the arrow marked "a" and would tend to turn the boat in the direction of the arrow "b." To counteract this, the rudder is put over as at "c" and the weight of the water against the rudder pushes the boat in the direction marked "d." Between these two forces, like a seed being squeezed, the boat slides ahead in the direction "e."

In order to get to a point windward (upwind), the boat must make this manoeuvre first to starboard (right) and then to port (left), as in Figure 2. The boat sails to starboard, "a," then after a time, the rudder is put over, "b," and the sail is set over on the other hand – and the boat heels over and progresses on the port "tack." By this changing or "tacking" from port to starboard and vice versa, the boat can, by a zigzag course, reach a point from which the wind is blowing – and it has sailed against the wind.

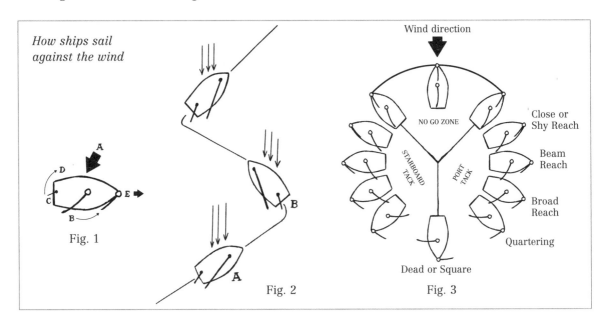

How ships sail against the wind

Fig. 1

Fig. 2

Wind direction

NO GO ZONE

STARBOARD TACK

PORT TACK

Close or Shy Reach

Beam Reach

Broad Reach

Quartering

Dead or Square

Fig. 3

2. Where does cork come from?

When a plant is damaged and its internal tissues are exposed, it is open to fungal and bacterial attack. In a similar way to the human body producing pus, many plant defence mechanisms release a fluid as part of the healing process. From a tissue within the plant, called "callus," new cells are formed to close the wounded parts. These cells quickly become brown, and assume the nature of true cork.

As human beings need cork in rather large quantities, we have found a tree that produces it in large supply, the Cork Oak (*Quercus suber*). The outer bark of this tree largely consists of cork, which can be peeled off in large strips during the summer season. This process injures the tree just enough to encourage it to produce more cork to replace what has been lost. That said, many wine producers are moving over to either plastic corks or screw-top bottles.

3. What causes the wind?

Winds are air currents, and their prime cause is temperature differences created by the uneven heating of the earth's surface and atmosphere by the sun.

Polar regions can be 71 °C (160 °F) colder than equatorial regions. Also relevant is the fact that in the tropics day and night temperatures differ by more than 10 °C (50 °F). In addition, every 1,600 metres (5,249 ft) we rise above sea level will drop the temperature by an average of eight degrees.

The earth's rotation also complicates matters, forming regular winds that were a boon to trade in the days of sailing ships. Currents of cold air from the arctic regions cannot keep pace as the planet spins and are deflected westward. North winds become north-west winds; the same happens in the southern hemisphere, south winds become south-east winds.

4. What is chalk?

Chalk is a soft kind of limestone (a carbonate of calcium). It consists of the shells of tiny animals called "foraminifera," which live in all parts of the ocean. When the foraminifera die, the insoluble shells form a sludgy deposit which hardens under pressure, and we get chalk. It is often found with flint, another stone composed of fossilized organic remains. Despite its relative softness, chalk can be found in huge cliff formations.

ROLE-PLAYING GAMES

THIS IS NOT a page telling you *how* to do something – you'll see why as you read. It's a short essay on role-playing games: what they are and how to get started. There are few inventions of the twentieth century that can combine entertainment with imagination so well.

Dungeons and Dragons was put together in 1972. It is still available from online bookshops or gaming stores. To get started you'll need the player's handbook, the dungeon master's handbook, some dice and, eventually, an adventure to play. It isn't that cheap to start, but after the initial outlay, costs are minimal – it's all imagination and the occasional pencil.

In essence, you buy the books, read them and choose a character for yourself. There are basic classes like Fighter, Thief and Magic-user. The character will start out with certain qualities, such as dexterity and strength, decided by the roll of a die. With experience, the character grows in power, endurance and knowledge. The game also grows more and more complex. Fighters win more powerful weapons, while Wizards gain access to greater spells. When we were children, we progressed from Basic to Advanced to Expert to Immortal levels, before moving on to battling at a national level and building an empire. You never forget the first time you are exiled from a country you raised from nothing.

You do need a few people for this – it is a social game, which is a recommendation. In a very real sense, it is a training ground for the imagination and, in particular, a school for plot and character. It may even be a training ground for tactics. If you want to be a writer, try D&D. For that matter, if you want to be a mathematician, try D&D.

The Dungeon Master (or DM) is the one who runs the game. He will either collect or write adventures – literally set in dungeons or just about anywhere. The characters battle the monsters he chooses and either solve his traps or fall prey to them, suffering horrible deaths. The players will develop characters with extraordinarily detailed histories, equipment and skills.

For us, D&D meant hundreds of hours at school and at home playing with pencils, charts, dice and laughter. If elves don't grab you, there are many other forms of role-playing – from Judge Dredd, to superheroes, to Warhammer, to a hundred more . . . but Dungeons and Dragons is still the original and the best.

UNDERSTANDING GRAMMAR – PART THREE

———— ✦ ————

Transitive and Intransitive Verbs

How often will you need to know the difference? Hardly ever, or not at all, but the odd thing is that those who do know these fiddly bits of grammar take *enormous* satisfaction from that knowledge.

Transitive verbs are verbs that must have an object (something the verb acts upon). For example, *to bury*, *to distract*, *to deny*, and many more. You simply cannot write them without an object – "John denied," "Susan buried." John has to deny *something* and Susan has to bury *something* for it to make sense.

Intransitive verbs are verbs that can be complete without an object: *to arrive*, *to digress*, *to exist*. For example, "The plane arrived."

Some verbs can be transitive or intransitive, depending on how they are used in a sentence (just to make things harder): "The fire burns" (intransitive). "The fire has burned my finger" (transitive – "my finger" is the object). "He has broken the glass" (transitive). "Glass breaks easily" (intransitive).

Again, though, this is not calculating parabolic orbits – recognizing whether a verb is used transitively or intransitively is a matter of care, common sense and memory.

The Tenses

It will come as no surprise to hear that verbs need forms expressing the past, present and future. There are important differences between someone saying "They have closed the gate" and "They will close the gate." The three *principal* forms of verbs, therefore, express these differences. They are known as present tense, past tense and future tense.

The Present Tense

There are five forms for a verb in the present tense:

1. Present Simple – *I write.*
2. Present Emphatic – *I do write.*
3. Present Continuous – *I am writing.*
4. Present Perfect Continuous – *I have been writing.*
5. Present Perfect – *I have written.*

The present emphatic form, "I do write," may look a bit odd. It is mostly used in negative statements ("You don't care, do you?") and in questions ("Do you care?") and strong, emphatic statements ("I do care!").

Sometimes, the present can be used to talk about the future – "I go to London next week" or "When he arrives, he will hear the news" – but the meaning is clear from the context, as it is here: "Tomorrow, I'm going to the store."

The present perfect "I have written" form may also look out of place at first glance. It is used in sentences such as the following: "*When I have written this*, I will come and speak to you." This is clearly an action that is going on in the present, coming from the past.

Similarly, present perfect continuous: "*I have been writing* all my life" – again, it suggests an action which is going on in the general present, if not at that exact moment.

The Past Tense

The past tense is usually formed by adding "d" or "ed" to the verb (love, *loved*; alter, *altered*); changing the vowel sound (swim, *swam*; throw, *threw)*; or remaining the same as the present tense (put, *put*; cast, *cast*).

When the verb ends in a single consonant after a short vowel with the stress on the last syllable, the final consonant is doubled before the "ed" ending (refer, *referred*; fan, *fanned*).

If the letter "y" ends the word after a consonant, it becomes "i" before the "ed" ending (try, *tried*; cry, *cried*).

You'll probably be able to find exceptions to these rules. English has taken so many words from other languages that no rules apply to all of them. However, these work well on most occasions.

There are four standard forms for the past tense:

1. Simple Past – *I wrote.*
2. Past Continuous – *I was writing.*
3. Past Perfect (Pluperfect) – *I had written.*
4. Past Perfect Continuous – *I had been writing.*

There are also a couple of specific constructions, such as "used to," that work in sentences about the past. "*I used to* write about relationships, but now . . ." Clearly, the writing took place in the past.

Similarly, adding "going to" is a common construction: "I was going to call you, but I forgot." The intention of calling took place in the past.

The Future Tense

First a note on "shall," a peculiar little word. It is often used interchangeably with "will." It survives in commandments as "Thou shalt not kill." Its main use is in expressing a future wish. The fairy godmother says "You *shall* go to the ball!" to Cinderella.

One distinction between "will" and "shall" is that "shall" implies some choice. When I was a boy, I was taught that only God could say "I will go to the store" as only he could be certain. The rest of us should say "I shall go to the store" because we could be hit by a bus, and not actually make it there. Admittedly, that example rather misses the point that being killed is a little more important than errors of grammar, but it was memorable at least.

The four forms for future time are:

1. Simple Future – *I will write*.
2. Future Continuous – *I will be writing*.
3. Future Perfect – *I will have written*.
4. Future Perfect Continuous: *I will have been writing*.

There is also a construction using "am going to," as in "I am going to kill you," and various other minor constructions using adverbs of time: "I am going home *tomorrow*," or adverbial phrases such as "The bus leaves *in ten minutes*."

. . . and that is about it for tenses.

If you've come this far, we know you'll be disappointed if we stop it there. "What about modal verbs? What about the subjunctive?" you will say to yourself. Prepare to be thrilled at the final two sections. This is the gold standard. Take it slowly.

Modal Auxiliary Verbs

Modal auxiliary verbs are irregular auxiliary verbs – the sort of verbs that give English a reputation for complexity. The language has many auxiliary combinations, mostly using "to be" and "to have" in combination with another verb: "I *am* going," "I *have been* watching" and so on.

Modal auxiliary verbs are often used to express the speaker's attitude "You shouldn't do that," or as a conditional tense: "Don't go any closer. *He could be dangerous*."

You use them all the time, however, so do not be too worried. Here is a list of them:

will, would, shall, should, may, might, can, could, must, dare, need, ought, won't, wouldn't, shan't, shouldn't, mayn't, mightn't, can't, couldn't, mustn't, daren't, needn't, oughtn't

Note that the use of "need" as a modal verb, as in "Need we do this?" is not that common.

Modal verbs have no infinitive or "-ing" form – "to should" or "maying" do not exist. There is no "s" form of the third person – "he can" not "he cans." They do not stand on their own and are always used in conjunction with other verbs – "May I go to the cinema?'

The Subjunctive

The **Indicative** mood is the standard factual style of modern English: "I walked into the park." The **Subjunctive** mood tends to appear in more formal English, when we wish to express the importance of something. This leads on from the modal verbs, as it too often expresses a wish, an uncertainty or a possibility. It is frequently formed using modal auxiliaries: "If only they would come!" This is a complex form, and scholarly works have been written on the subjunctive alone. With the limitations of space, we can merely dip a toe.

Present Subjunctive
In the present subjunctive, all verbs look like the infinitive but without the "to" – "do" not "to do" – and they don't take an extra "s," even in the third person: "We demand that *he do* the job properly."

The verb "to be" provides the most commonly used examples of the subjunctive form. In the present subjunctive, following the rule in the previous paragraph, "be" is used: "Even if that *be* the official view, I must act." In the simple past subjunctive, we use "were" throughout. Example: "If he *were* sorry, he'd have apologized by now."

Here are some examples of classic subjunctive expressions: "Be that as it may," "If I were a rich man," "Suffice it to say," "Come what may," "If I were the only girl in the world."

The subjunctive is also used in sentences beginning "If . . . ," as long as the subject is expressing a wish, an uncertainty or a possibility: "If I were twenty years younger, I would ask you to dance."

Lady Nancy Astor once said to Winston Churchill, "Winston, if I were your wife, I'd put poison in your coffee." He replied, "Nancy, if I were your husband, I'd drink it."

The subjunctive should *not* be used when the "If . . ." construction is a simple conditional: "*If you are ill*, the doctor will make you better." "If" is used here to indicate that one event is conditional on another. There is no sense of a wish or possibility. "If my doctor treats you, he will cure you" is another example of a simple indicative conditional. The speaker is expressing a fact conditional on the arrival of the doctor, rather than a speculative possibility.

The subjunctive is also used in certain types of sentence containing "that":

1. They demanded *that he take* every precaution.
2. It is essential *that they be* brought back for punishment.
3. I must recommend *that this law be* struck from the books.

Past Subjunctive

In the past subjunctive, all verbs take the common form of the simple past tense. "Have" becomes "had," "know" becomes "knew" and so on. As mentioned above, "to be" is a little different as it becomes "were" (and not "was"), but all the others are regular. Here are some examples:

1. He wept as if *he were being squeezed.*
2. I wish *you were* here!
3. If only *I had worked* in school.

Note that these can be indistinguishable from the standard past perfect "had worked," as in the table below. The "If only . . ." and "I wish . . ." beginnings suggest subjunctive.

The following table is almost the end of the grammar section. It covers the subjunctive in all the major tenses, using examples from the verb "to work" throughout. The important thing to remember is that it might look complicated, but *there is only one form of subjunctive for each verb tense.* If the example is "I work," then, all six persons of the verb use that form.

Mind you, don't expect to "get it" immediately – this is one of the really tricky forms of English. The answer, however, is not to stop teaching it and watch it wither away as generations come through school with little knowledge of their own language. The answer to difficulty is always to get your hands around its throat and hold on until you have reached an understanding.

Tense	Indicative	Subjunctive
Simple present	*He works*	*He work*
Present continuous	*She is working*	*She be working*
Present perfect	*He has worked*	*He have worked*
Present perfect continuous	*It has been working*	*It have been working*
Simple past	*We worked*	*We worked*
Past continuous	*I was working*	*I were working*
Past perfect	*They had worked*	*They had worked*
Past perfect continuous	*We had been working*	*We had been working*

In addition, here are eight simple sentences in the subjunctive. It is perhaps more common than you realize. Read each one and see how the subjunctive form of the verb is used.

1. He acts as if *he knew* you.
2. I would rather *you had given* a different answer.
3. If only *we had* a home to go to!
4. I wish *I could run* as fast as my older brother.
5. Would that *you were* my friend.
6. I suggest that *he leave.*
7. Thy Kingdom *come,* thy will *be* done.
8. If one green bottle *should* accidentally *fall* . . .

Now go back to the beginning of Grammar Part One and read it all again.

SEVEN MODERN WONDERS OF THE WORLD

THE SEVEN ANCIENT WONDERS are set in stone, but any modern seven must in some sense be a personal choice. Humanity has created many, *many* wondrous things. A Picasso painting is a wonder, as is a computer, a jewelled Fabergé egg, an aria by Mozart, the motor car, a cloned sheep. The list could be endless.

However, examples such as those don't seem to match the original style and intention of the original ancient wonders. Surely, a modern seven should have some echoes in the old ones. Otherwise, why have seven, say, and not nine? Our list comes from two rules. 1. It must be made by humans, so no waterfalls or mountains. 2. It must take your breath away. Here are seven modern wonders. You cannot look at any of them without this thought: How on *earth* did we build that?

1. THE CHANNEL TUNNEL

An engineering project to bore a tunnel between Folkestone in Kent and Calais in France – a distance of 50 killometres (31 miles), with an average depth of 45 metres (150 ft) under the seabed. France and Britain used huge boring machines, cutting through chalk to meet in the middle for the first time since the last ice age. When they did meet, there was less than 2 centimetres (²/₃ in) error, an astonishing feat of accuracy.

It took 15,000 workers seven years and cost £10 billion ($20 billion). Part of the structure is a set of huge pistons that can be opened and closed to release the

pressure built up by trains rushing along at 160 kilometres per hour (100 mph). There is also some 482 kilometres (300 miles) of cold-water piping running in the tunnel to ease the heat caused by air friction.

On the British side, the chalk that was dug out was left at Shakespeare Cliff near Folkestone. As a result, more than 360,000 square metres (90 acres) were reclaimed from the sea.

2. THE GREAT WALL OF CHINA

At 6,400 kilometres (4,000 miles), it is staggering for its sheer size and the effort required to build it. The Great Wall still stands today, though it is obviously not a modern creation. It was begun more than 2,000 years ago during the Qin Dynasty. Qin Shi Huang was not a man of small imagination. When he died, he was buried with more than 6,000 life-size terracotta warriors and horses.

The Great Wall was designed to keep Mongol invaders out of China, though it failed to stop Genghis Khan. It has a system of watchtowers and forts to protect inner China. Sadly, some sections have collapsed or been destroyed.

It is a myth that the Great Wall of China can be seen from the Moon. Many objects made by humans can be seen from space at low orbit, such as cities, rail lines, even airport runways. From the moon, however, the earth looks as if we've never existed.

3. The CN tower in Toronto, Canada

The CN Tower, located in Toronto, Ontario, is a great Canadian wonder. At a height of 553.33 metres (1,815 ft, 5 in), it remains the world's tallest free-standing structure, though a recent competing building in Dubai hopes to challenge its supremacy. The tower plays an important role as a television and radio mast, but it also offers a breathtaking view to approximately two million tourists every year. Built in 1976 by Canadian National (CN), the tower is still considered an engineering feat and can withstand winds of more than 300 kilometres (186 miles) per hour. A helicopter named Olga was used to fly up the thirty-six pieces of the tower's antenna, and when it was finally complete, it captured a new height record, topping Moscow's Ostankino Tower.

4. The Itaipú Dam

This colossal dam stands on the Paraná river on the border of Brazil and Paraguay. To build it, workers removed 45 million metric tons of earth and stone. The dam itself is as high as a sixty-five-storey building. It used enough concrete for fifteen channel tunnels and enough iron and steel to build 380 Eiffel Towers. By anyone's standards, that is extraordinary.

The hydroelectric power station run by the dam is itself over 800 metres (2,625 ft) long. It contains eighteen electric generators, with 145 metric tons of water a second passing through each one. Seventy-two percent of Paraguay's total energy consumption comes from this one dam.

5. THE PANAMA CANAL

One of the reasons the Panama Canal makes it to this list is because it joins two vast oceans and splits two continents. It is 80 kilometres (50 miles) long. Before it was built, a ship travelling from New York to San Francisco would have been forced to go all the way around South America. The canal took almost 12,800 kilometres (8,000 miles) off that journey.

It was originally a French project under Ferdinand de Lesseps. Although he was well respected in France, it took all of his charisma and energy to raise the vast capital needed to begin the enterprise. When work did begin, his men had to contend with parasites, spiders, snakes, torrential downpours and flash floods. Far worse was the threat of disease. Yellow fever, dysentery, typhoid, cholera, smallpox and malaria were all common. In those conditions, up to 20,000 workers died. In 1889, de Lesseps' company went bankrupt and the investors lost their money.

In 1902, the American government agreed to take on the Panama Canal and at the same time supported the independence of Panama from Colombia. The American president, Theodore Roosevelt, told his engineers to "make the dirt fly." The Americans rebuilt the site and set to work. By 1910, there were 40,000 workers on the canal and Roosevelt had brought in the army. It was completed in 1914.

The principles are similar to any British canal, but each lock gate of the Panama Canal weighs 680 metric tons. Fourteen thousand ships go through the canal each year.

6. The Akashi-Kaikyō Bridge in Japan, also known as the Pearl Bridge

The longest suspension bridge in the world. It is kilometres shorter than the longest actual bridge – the Lake Pontchartrain Causeway is over 38 kilometres (23 miles) long – but there is something particularly awe-inspiring about enormous suspension bridges. This one is 1,991 metres (6,532 ft) long. It took ten years to build and cost almost $4 billion. It is 710 metres (2,329 ft) longer than the Golden Gate Bridge in San Francisco.

After a tunnel, a wall, a tower, a dam, a canal and a bridge, most of the truly impressive human building projects have been covered. The last choice may not be physically enormous, but it represents the next stage and the future to come.

7. THE SPACE SHUTTLE

The Space Shuttle may be the most complicated machine ever built. It is the world's first proper spacecraft and though the current shuttles are approaching the end of their useful lives, they were the first step from single-use rockets to the dreams of science fiction. The first one was actually called *Enterprise* after the *Star Trek* ship, though it was only a test plane and never went into space. It is currently in the Smithsonian museum. Five others followed: *Columbia*, *Challenger*, *Discovery*, *Atlantis* and *Endeavor*. *Columbia* first went into space in 1981, beginning a new era of space flight. The program was temporarily suspended in 1986 when *Challenger* exploded shortly after liftoff, killing the seven-person crew.

On re-entry, shuttle skin temperature goes up to 1,650 °C (3,000 °F). It is the fastest vehicle humans have ever designed, travelling at speeds of up to 29,000 kph (18,000 mph).

It is used as an all-purpose craft, capable of launching and repairing satellites and docking with the International Space Station in orbit.

Onward and Upward

BOOKS EVERY BOY SHOULD READ

THE DANGER HERE is that you'll try to read books that are too hard for your age. The choices are from those books we enjoyed, but this is a list that all *men* should have read when they were boys. The first ones are the easiest – though not the best. Every title has been loved by millions. Like a reference to Jack and the Beanstalk, you should know Huckleberry Finn, Sherlock Holmes and all the other characters who make up the world of imagination. The list comes with suggested reading ages – but these are only rough minimums. Reading ability is more important than age.

1. Roald Dahl's books. From age five up, children will enjoy hearing these stories. *The Twits* is fantastic. *Charlie and the Chocolate Factory, George's Marvellous Medicine, The BFG* and *James and the Giant Peach* are all worth reading. For older readers, his short stories are nothing short of brilliant.

2. Kenneth Oppel's books. One of Canada's greatest children's authors, Oppel always takes readers to exciting new empires of adventure. His Airborn books chart a time when giant airships, rather than airplanes, ruled the skies. The Silverwing Saga brings the thrilling world of bats vividly to life. Ages ten and up.

3. The Winnie-the-Pooh books by A. A. Milne. Beautifully written, amusing stories.

4. Willard Price – a series of adventure books, with titles such as *Underwater Adventure, Arctic Adventure* and so on. The two main characters, Hal and Roger, are role models for all boys growing up today. Suitable for ages eight and above.

5. *Never Cry Wolf* by Farley Mowat. A classic Canadian book that tells the true, extraordinary story of Farley Mowat's mission to live among wolves in the frozen tundra of the Arctic. Twelve and above.

6. All the Famous Five books by Enid Blyton. Also, her Secret Seven series. These are classic adventure and crime stories for those aged eight and above.

7. *Fungus the Bogeyman* by Raymond Briggs. One of the strangest books in this list, but oddly compelling. For all ages, but probably ten and above.

8. *The Call of the Wild* by Jack London. In the frozen Arctic wilderness, Buck, half St. Bernard and half shepherd, learns how to be a great and loyal sled dog, but the call of his wolf ancestors is still in his blood. Ages eight to twelve.

9. *Grimm's Fairy Tales*, stories by Hans Christian Andersen; Greek and Roman legends. There are many collections out there, but these stories have survived because they are good.

10. If you love hockey, the Screech Owl series of books by Roy MacGregor is for you. Join this Canadian boys hockey team on their thrilling adventures as they play hockey at camps and tournaments around the world, solving intriguing mysteries along the way. Suitable for ages nine to thirteen.

11. *The Belgariad* by David Eddings. Fantasy series of five books, every one a gem. Eleven and above.

12. The trilogy of books called His Dark Materials by Philip Pullman. This epic series unlocks a fantasy realm where humans have lifelong animal companions called Daemons and heroic children fight to save the universe from evil powers. Confident readers ten and up.

13. *Rogue Male* by Geoffrey Household. An extraordinary story of survival against the odds. Suitable for eleven and over.

14. *The Lion, the Witch and the Wardrobe* by C. S. Lewis. The second book in the Narnia series. Lewis' books are superb fantasy stories for confident readers, twelve and above.

15. The works of S. E. Hinton (*The Outsiders*, *Tex* and *Rumble Fish*). These are classic stories about the misadventures and difficulties of growing up, for confident readers age twelve and up.

16. *Charlotte's Web*, by E. B. White. A powerful story of a pig and a spider! Eight years old and up.

17. *The Phantom Tollbooth* by Norton Juster. A classic adventure fantasy. It can be read by many readers from eight and up.

18. *Kim* by Rudyard Kipling – a classic adventure. Also, the *Just So Stories* and *The Jungle Book*. For confident readers, but well worth the time.

19. *The Thirty-Nine Steps* by John Buchan. This is almost the definition of a boy's adventure story, involving spies and wild dashes across the Scottish countryside. Also look for *Mr Standfast* by the same author.

20. The James Bond books by Ian Fleming. For early teen readers and above. These stories are quite dark in places – far grittier than the films.

21. The Harry Potter books by J. K. Rowling. Modern classics.

22. Mark Twain – *The Adventures of Tom Sawyer* and *The Adventures of Huckleberry Finn*. For confident readers of twelve and up.

23. Isaac Asimov – science fiction. He wrote hundreds of brilliant short stories, available in collections. Confident readers of twelve and above.

24. Terry Pratchett's Discworld books. They are all fantastic, funny and interesting. Start with *Sourcery*. Twelve and above.

25. *Ender's Game* by Orson Scott Card. A fantastic story of a young boy in a military academy. Confident readers of twelve and above.

26. *Midshipman's Hope* by David Feintuch. A space fantasy with a marvellous main character. There are seven in the full series.

27. *The Hitchhiker's Guide to the Galaxy* by Douglas Adams. Funny and clever – the old "five books to a trilogy" ploy. Twelve and up.

28. David Gemmell's books, such as *Waylander* – the master of heroic fantasy for fourteen and up. Read one and you'll read them all.

29. *Magician* by Raymond E. Feist. One of the best fantasy novels ever written – and a whole series of first-class sequels to follow.

30. The Lord of the Rings masterwork trilogy and *The Hobbit* by J.R.R. Tolkien. For confident teen readers.

31. Bernard Cornwell's Sharpe series. A terrific series of books, packed full of action and adventure. For confident readers, thirteen and above.

32. The Flashman books by George MacDonald Fraser. For confident readers, but a great dip into history and adventure. Fourteen and above.

33. *Animal Farm* and *1984* by George Orwell. Novels to wake the brain. For confident readers of fourteen and over.

34. *Brave New World* by Aldous Huxley. Like Orwell's *1984*, a famous story of a future we should fear.

35. *Lord of the Flies* by William Golding. Superb – but only for accomplished readers of fourteen and above.

36. H. G. Wells' *The Time Machine, The Island of Doctor Moreau, The Invisible Man* – books from one of the best literary minds of the nineteenth century. Fourteen and above.

37. The Sherlock Holmes adventures by Arthur Conan Doyle. The original classic detective mysteries. Loads of short crime stories and longer novels, like *The Hound of the Baskervilles*. Accomplished readers only. Fifteen and above.

38. *Gulliver's Travels* by Jonathan Swift. A novel that can be read on more than one level. It gave us the lands of Lilliput and Brobdingnag.

39. *Three Men in a Boat* by Jerome K. Jerome. The funniest book ever written, but only for accomplished readers of fourteen or fifteen and above.

40. Stephen King. *The Bachman Books* is a good starting point. His novels are quite adult in subject and can be very frightening. Accomplished readers only – fifteen and above.

THE DANGEROUS BOY CHALLENGE

———— ✦ ————

JOIN BOYS FROM ACROSS CANADA and take the challenge! Use this checklist to keep track of your Danger-defying accomplishments and move your way from level to level to earn the ultimate distinction of full-fledged Dangerous Boy.

Sportsman

❏ I have read the rules of soccer and lacrosse.
❏ I can play table football, and I know which team has won the Stanley Cup the most.
❏ I can name four kinds of fish common to Canadian waters.
❏ I can juggle and perform a coin trick on command.
❏ I made a bow and arrow or a slingshot.

Secret Agent

❏ I communicated with a friend using secret ink.
❏ I can give you tips on how to talk to girls.
❏ I can solve this cipher: IMDNEOSO!
                                AAAGRUBY
❏ I know how to use a tripwire to catch intruders who sneak into my room.
❏ I made a periscope, a timer, a tripwire or a magical crystal.

Voyageur

❏ I have built a snow fort, quinzhee or igloo.
❏ I have paddled a canoe and walked a portage.
❏ I can find north using a compass and know what NOT to do when a moose attacks.
❏ I can find the Big Dipper and the Great Bear (Ursa Major) in the night sky.
❏ I have built a flashlight or made a fireproof cloth.

Dangerous Boy of High Distinction

❏ I have read *The Dangerous Book for Boys* from cover to cover.
❏ I know why you should never try to fill an inside straight in Texas Hold-'em poker.
❏ I know what scat is and can spot the difference between bear prints and moose prints.
❏ I built a Dangerous workbench, treehouse or go-kart.
❏ I promise to share my Dangerous knowledge with other boys and to always keep true to my Dangerous spirit.

Take the challenge at **www.harpercollins.ca/dbfb**

ILLUSTRATION CREDITS

4–8. Seven Wonders of the Ancient World: Wills Cigarette Cards © Imperial Tobacco Limited

24. Ammonite fossils (© NHPA/Kevin Schafer)

25. Trilobite fossils (© NHPA/Kevin Schafer)

52. Bluegill (sun fish) © NCTC Image Library/U.S. Fish and Wildlife Service
Lake trout © Washington DC Library/U.S. Fish and Wildlife Service
Largemouth bass © NCTC Image Library/U.S. Fish and Wildlife Service

53. Muskellunge © Washington DC Library/U.S. Fish and Wildlife Service
Northern pike © Washington DC Library/U.S. Fish and Wildlife Service
Rainbow trout © NCTC Image Library/U.S. Fish and Wildlife Service

54. Smallmouth bass © NCTC Image Library/U.S. Fish and Wildlife Service
Walleye © Washington DC Library/U.S. Fish and Wildlife Service
Yellow perch © NCTC Image Library/U.S. Fish and Wildlife Service

59. Maurice "Rocket" Richard © Hulton Archive/Getty Images

61. Bobby Orr © Bruce Bennett/Getty Images

62. Team Canada Summit Series © Melchior DiGiacomo/Getty Images

64. Martin Brodeur, Olympics © Jamie Squire/Getty Images

70. Bob Gainey © Bruce Bennett/Getty Images

72. Wayne Gretzky © Bruce Bennett/Getty Images

74. Martin Brodeur © Andy Martin/Getty Images

83. Thermopylae map (*The Great Persian War* by G. B. Grundy, pub. John Murray, 1901)

84. Map of the Battle of Cannae © *The Times History of War*, 2000

85. Bust of Julius Caesar (Museo Nationale, Naples/ Scala, Florence)

87. Bayeux Tapestry, Bayeux, France (Roger-Viollet/Rex Features)

88. Map of Crécy © *The Age of Chivalry* by Arthur Bryant

90. Contemporary lacrosse (action shot) © CP/Lethbridge Herald/David Rossiter

91. Lacrosse stick © Canadian Museum of Civilization, artifact 111-1-553 (Image# S97-17382)

105. Robert Scott (© Popperfoto.com)

107. Captain L.E.G. Oates (Mary Evans Picture Library)

113–123. All images © Stephen A. Marshall

132. Northern lights © Roman Krochuk/stockphoto.com

138. Pileated woodpecker © Judy Ledbetter/istockphoto.com

142. Black bear © Paul Tessier/istockphoto

143. Grizzly bear © John Pitcher/istockphoto

144. Cougar © Westphalia/istockphoto

145. Coyote © Ben Renard-Wiart/istockphoto

146. Wolf © Eric Cola/istockphoto
Moose © Matt Keal/istockphoto

147. Skunk © Geoff Kuhera/istockphoto

159. Cirrus (© NHPA/Pete Atkinson)

160. Cumulus (© NHPA/John Shaw)
Stratus (© NHPA/Stephen Krasemann)

161. Map of Waterloo © John Mackenzie

165. Vimy battle scene/Library and Archives Canada/ PA-001020

168. Plains of Abraham © The Granger Collection, New York

170. Map of The Somme © John Mackenzie

171. Vimy recruitment poster/Library and Archives Canada/C-029484

181–183. Maps from 1667 to 1949 provided by the Atlas of Canada (atlas.gc.ca) © 2008. Data reproduced with the permission of Natural Resources Canada.

183. 1999 map © Collins Bartholomew

184. Voyageurs © North Wind Picture Archives

206–209. Naval flags © Collins UK

212. Josiah Henson stamp © Canada Post Corporation (1983). Reproduced with permission.

255. Francis Pegahmagabow © Mathers Museum of World Cultures, Indiana University/W-7679

263. World War I British field piece (© Popperfoto.com)
Soldier preparing shells (© Popperfoto.com)

264. British Challenger 2 tank © *Jane's Tanks and Combat Field Vehicles Recognition Guide* by Christopher F. Foss

277. Balsam fir © O. Diez/Peter Arnold Inc.
Balsam fir needles © Walter Muma/Wildwood Canada

278. Jack pine © Walter Muma/Wildwood Canada
Jack pine needles © Paul H. Wray, bugwood.org
Red oak © Biosphoto/MG de Saint Venant/Peter Arnold Inc.
Red oak leaves © Barbara Tokarska-Guzik, University of Silesia, bugwood.org

279. Red pine © Walter Muma/Wildwood Canada
Red pine needles © Keith Kanoti, Maine Forest Service, bugwood.org

280. Sugar maple © Walter Muma/Wildwood Canada
Sugar maple leaves © Paul H. Wray, bugwood.org
Tamarack © Steven Katovich, USDA Forest Service, bugwood.org
Tamarack needles © Walter Muma/Wildwood Canada

281. Trembling aspen © WILDLIFE/Peter Arnold Inc.
Trembling aspen leaves © WILDLIFE/Peter Arnold Inc.

282. White spruce © Bill Cook, Michigan State University, bugwood.org
White spruce needles © Joseph O'Brien, USDA Forest Service, bugwood.org

284. Franklin expedition/Library and Archives Canada/e002712085

286. Franklin – Josh Hartnell © Owen Beattie/University of Alberta

299. Colonial armies (Bibliotheque des Arts Décoratifs, Paris/Bridgeman Art Library)

300. Sir Francis Drake (Private Collection/Bridgeman Art Library)

302. Robert Clive by Thomas Gainsborough (Courtesy of the Council, National Army Museum, London/Bridgeman Art Library)

303. *The Death of General Wolfe* by Benjamin West (Private Collection/Bridgeman Art Library)

305. Queen Victoria (Private Collection/Bridgeman Art Library)

306. Map of the world: on Mercator's projection, showing the British Empire (© Guildhall Library/City of London/Bridgeman Art Library)

308. *Together* World War II poster (Private Collection/Bridgeman Art Library)
Lord Mountbatten (© Bert Hardy/Getty Images)

319. The Great Wall of China (© The Travel Library/Rex Features)

320. The CN Tower (© Paul Brown/Rex Features)
The Itaipú Dam (© AFP/Getty Images)

321. The Panama Canal (© Popperfoto.com)

322. The Akashi-Kaikyo Bridge (© Rex Features)

323. Space Shuttle (© Getty Images)

Illustrations throughout © Richard Horne, 2006 (http://homepage.mac.com/richard.horne/) except pages 19–22, 36, 76–81, 92, 94–95, 138–141, © Anastasia Danyliw

Acknowledgements:

"Sea Fever" by John Masefield reproduced by permission of The Society of Authors as the Literary Representative of the Estate of John Masefield.

"For the Fallen" (September 1914) by Laurence Binyon reproduced by permission of The Society of Authors as the Literary Representative of the Estate of Laurence Binyon.